THE CULTURAL PATTERN IN AMERICAN POLITICS

THE CULTURAL PATTERN IN AMERICAN POLITICS

THE FIRST CENTURY

Robert Kelley

Alfred A. Knopf/New York

To the memory of

RICHARD HOFSTADTER
1916–1970

Who taught historians of the American experience to think of its politics in cultural terms, and encouraged them, in the example of his own bold scholarship, to seek the meaning of that experience by exploring its largest themes and its most enduring issues.

THIS IS A BORZOI BOOK PUBLISHED BY ALFRED A. KNOPF, INC.

First Edition
987654321
Copyright © 1979 by Alfred A. Knopf, Inc.

Library of Congress Cataloging in Publication Data

Kelley, Robert Lloyd, 1925-
    The cultural pattern in American politics.
        1. Political parties—United States—History.   2. United States—Social conditions.   I. Title.
JK2260.K44 1979   329'.02   78-23823
ISBN 0-394-31954-0 *pbk*
ISBN 0-394-50279-5

Designed by Meryl Sussman Levavi

Manufactured in the United States of America

[The] historian has before him a discipline which, however industriously it accumulates knowledge, experiences again and again through the generations somewhat the same kind of arguments and disagreements about its matters of central concern. . . . [The] tradition of his profession is not so much to look for the perfection of microscopic units of research as it is to try to cope with certain insistent macroscopic questions. Eventually the historian must deal in such categories as the Reformation, the Renaissance, the Industrial Revolution, with wars and social upheavals, with the great turning points in human experience, still tantalizingly unexplained or half-explained, still controversial. . . . And yet the historian does not approach them with the expectation that he will "solve" them, that the cumulation of knowledge will put him in a position to do what the entire fraternity of historians has not yet been able to do, or even that there is any operational way to define the "solution" of such problems. . . . [He] must see in his own task—so big in its implications, so hopelessly complex, so triumphant over his professional forebears, and yet so formidably challenging that he must again take it on—nothing more nor less than a microcosmic representation of the human situation itself.

RICHARD HOFSTADTER

From "History and the Social Sciences," in Fritz Stern (ed.), *The Varieties of History: From Voltaire to the Present* (New York, 1956 and 1972), pp. 369–370.

Preface

In our own time, a revolution has taken place in the way historians look at American politics: they have discovered its cultural dimension. The result has been to give depth, richness, and realism to a scene that was formerly flat and one-dimensional. Now we read in the "new political history" not simply of the conflict of economic interests, based in quantifiable issues relating to income and profit, but of controversies among ethnic groups, styles of life, ideologies, moral values, and religious faiths. The history of cultural politics, with its sensitivity to the emotional as well as the rational side of human nature, reveals that American public life is not merely a struggle over currency policy and corporate privileges. It is far more complex—a kind of national folk theater in which ancient, almost tribal enemies contend.

Thus, in studying American politics, we no longer simply focus on farmers battling with bankers and laborers struggling with employers. Now we also see Scotch-Irishmen facing off against Englishmen, Catholics against Protestants, German Moravians against German Lutherans, pietists against freethinkers, blacks against whites, Chicanos against WASPs, teetotalers against drinkers, and Yankees against white Southerners. American politics is a dramatic scene filled with symbolic action. Its cast of characters is much more diverse than that in traditional historiography, and their dialogue is heavily charged with references to good and evil, corruption, inherited fears and hatreds, moral behavior, and national self-image.

The present time in scholarship is an especially felicitous one in which to examine American public life. Issue-oriented national politics were revived in the 1960s, after the relative quietude of the Eisenhower years, and scholars vigorously turned their attention back to that arena. The historical literature on American politics is now quite rich and voluminous. Hundreds of books and articles on different aspects and periods of the American political past have been published since 1965. As a result our traditional view of the nature and evolution of American political parties has been rendered obsolete in practically all of its aspects. While I was engaged some years ago in a comparative study of the Democrats in the United States and the Liberals in Britain and Canada during the nineteenth century, it seemed to me that a new synthesis was coming increasingly into reach. As I studied the rhetoric of the parties and sought to distill its inner pattern of ideology, two distinctive world views presented themselves, one forming the outlook of the Liberals and Democrats and the other that of the Conservatives and Republicans. At the same time, as one looked to see where the politicians in these countries got their votes, hitherto unsuspected linkages could be observed between the ideas of the party leadership and the cultural as well as economic interests of the voting groups being described by the "new political history." Put in different terms, the older intellectual history of politics, which concentrates upon working out the ideologies of the political elite, could make a fruitful juncture with the new studies, which focus upon mass voting behavior; that is, upon the political alignments of ethnic and other culture groups.

My purpose since then has been to test out over the two centuries from the Revolution to Watergate, in this and a succeeding volume, the patterns that this earlier study seemed to reveal. Writing a history with so extensive a field of examination is, of course, a risky enterprise. Narrating the course of events over a large span of time makes it impossible not to blur complexities, to flatten terrain that, if more closely studied, is clearly quite irregular. The writer must distill and compress and in so doing build a structure of interpretation that is orderly and coherent. However, no conceptual scheme, as William James long ago cautioned, is complete. Theories, he observed, leak at every joint. Life is pluralistic, and the most carefully devised formulas always leave something out, if for no other reason than that our language is an imperfect reflection, not an embodiment, of reality, and we must think in the words available to us. Furthermore, our own perspectives are always limited. Obviously, much will be omitted that to others demands inclusion.

These difficulties, however, are inescapable, and having allowed for them we must still attempt to search out larger patterns, to find the enclosing shape and nature of things. Taking long perspectives allows us, in fact, to see things otherwise hidden. The potential gain in understanding justifies the risks that lie in wait for those who would paint large canvases. In the present case, looking at the whole of the past two centuries of American politics does, I believe, reveal things we have not seen before.

What emerges is that there is in fact, in the nation's politics, a strongly marked cultural pattern that appeared as soon as the nation began and, in its larger outlines, has endured for two hundred years. This pattern involves both ideas and voter constituency. The Federalists looked at human nature, society, and the world at large in one way, and the Jeffersonian Republicans looked at them in another. To the present day, these same distinctive perspectives upon life identify, in broad terms, the Republican and Democratic persuasions. Also, as soon as national political parties took form, and thereby gave public expression to preexisting feelings, it became apparent that for ancient reasons certain kinds of peoples were already ranged bitterly against one another. Set apart by their ethnic and religious identities and their ways of living, they fixed their eyes unwaveringly upon traditional enemies. Thus, in a certain sense, it is what (and whom) people are *against* rather than what they are *for* that shapes their politics. Because cultural hostilities are so deeply engrained, so thoroughly bred into each of the nation's peoples that they seem a part of their bone and marrow, the party system, which in good part is based in these feelings, has been remarkably unchanging over the generations. Intensifying and interrelating with these cultural conflicts have been fundamental economic rivalries that also appeared at the beginning of national politics and have endured, if in modified forms, ever since.

For most Americans, politics presents itself in such a fragmented and convoluted form that it seems to lack order and coherence, beyond being an apparently cynical display of power seeking and profit hunting. Every human enterprise, however, has structure and purpose, obscured though they may be by our habit of looking at things in immediate terms and by the small span of the nation's politics we witness during our individual lives. Cultural political history is in this sense like pointillism in painting. Dots of different colors cover every part of the canvas's surface, and the person standing close to it sees no pattern. From a sufficient distance, however, it becomes apparent that the colors are massed in certain lines and shapes, and the underlying picture emerges. So it is in the case of American politics: it requires a sufficiently long and wide view to see its shape. It is important that we periodically attempt to do this, for as a democratic country it is in our common effort at self-government that we most reveal our nature. When we misunderstand our politics, we misunderstand ourselves. In larger terms, there is also an important human lesson to be learned from discovering that a major aspect of our lives, although confusing on the surface, makes sense. Thus, a truer understanding of what it is that we have been about in our politics, and to what purposes, can serve many good ends, personal and individual as well as public and social. My hope is that the present book will contribute to that better understanding.

Cultural political history is relatively new, and the story which follows has several novel aspects. For those who would like to read a discussion of the book's central concepts and learn about the meaning, origins, and philosophical implications of cultural political history, I have written an introductory essay. Those who prefer to plunge directly into the book's narrative and sort out its implications as they move along should begin with Part One, in which I explore the origins and initial stages of national politics in the Revolutionary and Constitutional period. Part Two narrates the birth and evolution of the two-party system during the Jeffersonian, or first, and Jacksonian, or second, party systems, from the 1790s into the 1850s. Part Three concentrates upon the era of the second American revolution (to borrow Charles Beard's still valid concept, although my treatment of it is different), that of the Civil War and Reconstruction. During these years, the Civil War, or third, party system took form. Part Four constitutes a retrospective look at the first century of national politics, to pull together and clarify what, in this complex story, we have seen.

Concluding the first volume of this study at the end of the nation's first century was not my original intention. However, this breakpoint eventually came to seem natural and unavoidable. In the early years of the nation's second century, after 1877, a new United States appeared and with it a new framework for politics. Profound reorientations occurred within both the national economy and the country's cultural structure, changes that created a politics considerably more complex and multipolar than in the past. Thus, though the Civil War party system endured to the great depression of the 1890s, the watershed of the Gilded Age cannot be passed over lightly. It requires a careful examination, for it must be understood as the beginning of a new order. (For those who would wish to see in general terms how my treatment of the first and second centuries will interrelate and to preview the main themes to be explored in the subsequent volume, see Robert Kelley, "Ideology and Political Culture from Jefferson to Nixon," *American Historical Review*, 82 [June 1977], 531–562.)

There are many to whom I owe thanks in connection with the writing of this book. Its dedication points to the scholar who provided a challenging model for a generation of American historians. Though not fortunate enough to sit in Richard Hofstadter's seminars, I was one of those who learned from him through his books, and thereby became his students. We are a numerous company now, and in this dedication I am trying to speak to his memory for those who share with me this status. While in graduate study many years ago, his writings sent me in the direction in which I have travelled ever since. Events brought us into a personal relationship in which he encouraged me in the undertaking of a book which appeared in 1969, and during its writing he gave me kind assistance. I know the present work would be a better book had I been able to have that experience again. Cut short in 1970 while still in full momentum, he left behind in his scholarship his own monuments. They reflect faithfully his charge to the historical profession, first uttered in 1956, which I have quoted following the dedication. This exhortation has always seemed to me to illuminate with great clarity, and with the wisdom which is the mark of humane scholarship, the spirit that should animate our enterprise.

At Alfred A. Knopf, Inc., Ashbel Green has offered his usual good editorial sense and encouragement, David Follmer has given the idea of the book important support, and Dorchen Leidholdt has supervised the manuscript's progress through the press with consideration and skill. The National Endowment for the Humanities accorded me a Fellowship in 1975–76, and the Humanities Institute of the University of California a Summer Fellowship in 1976. These grants gave me the freedom to conduct much of the research upon which this study is based, although in some of its more fundamental conceptions it builds upon perspectives gained in the writing of earlier books. Over many years, in my lecture courses and seminars in American intellectual and political history at the University of

California, Santa Barbara, I have had the benefit of searching interchanges with my students on the interpretive stance developed in this book and its predecessors. My debt to them is very great.

In 1976 Allan C. Bogue, University of Wisconsin, Madison, and Jacob M. Price, University of Michigan, Ann Arbor, in their capacity as program chairpersons for the 1976 (Washington, D.C.) Annual Meeting of the American Historical Association, invited me to present a Bicentennial address at that gathering on the general theme of this study, one in a series of such addresses entitled "The American Experience." This provided an opportunity to draw together in a distilled statement the leading points that were beginning to make themselves clear concerning the course of public life during the nation's first two centuries, a process that opened new perspectives and in major ways affected this book's conceptual structure. Upon that occasion, Geoffrey Blodgett (Oberlin College), Ronald P. Formisano (Clark University), and Willie Lee Rose (Johns Hopkins University) presented valuable Comments on the address, and Otto Pflanze (Indiana University), editor of *The American Historical Review,* kindly published the address and Comments, which has led to further useful interchanges with scholars.

At various times, I have sent drafts of chapters to colleagues, whose advice has been essential: John Higham, Johns Hopkins University; Paul Kleppner, Northern Illinois University; William G. Shade, Lehigh University; Richard Jensen, University of Illinois, Chicago Circle, and The Newberry Library; Stephen E. Patterson, University of New Brunswick; Gordon W. Wood, Brown University; Merrill D. Peterson, University of Virginia, who as chairman of the AHA session gave reactions to my Bicentennial essay; Owen S. Ireland, State University of New York, Brockport; Gary B. Nash, University of California, Los Angeles; Alfred F. Young, Northern Illinois University; Carl Anderson, University of Texas, El Paso, whose comments were in response to an address I gave at that institution; Joyce Appleby, San Diego State University; H. James Henderson, Oklahoma State University; James H. Hutson, Library of Congress; Eric Foner, City College of New York; Jackson Turner Main, State University of New York, Stony Brook; Carl N. Degler, Stanford University; James McPherson, Princeton University; and my colleagues at the University of California, Santa Barbara, Otis L. Graham, Jr., Morton Borden, Elvin Hatch, W. Elliot Brownlee, and Carl Harris. I hope they will believe that good use has been made of their advice. The community of scholarship is real and good spirited. Miss Shirley Bruce Henderson has provided valuable editorial skills in Part One on the Revolutionary and Constitutional period.

In a work of this nature, one is dependent most of all upon the historical researches of hundreds of colleagues. I wish my debt to them to be fully recorded. The vitality of the historical discipline is a remarkable phenomenon. So, too, is the close interconnection between its leading workers, so that the advance of historical knowledge is reasonably coherent and interactive.

To my wife Madge go my warmest thoughts in connection with this undertaking. In a conversation years long, I have benefited from her sympathetic hearing, her advice, and her feeling for style and lucid utterance. In time taken from her own studies and writing, she has read repeated drafts, listened and reacted to varying versions of the book's themes before many audiences, and encouraged me in every circumstance. The bibliography is her direct contribution, but her indirect influence is pervasive.

R.K.

University of California, Santa Barbara
February 1978

Contents

THE CULTURAL PATTERN
IN AMERICAN POLITICS

Introduction

A special problem faces historians of political parties. Many of their readers belong to parties now and have a settled sense of what it means to be a Democrat or a Republican, both in terms of ideology and party constituency. Even independent voters have firmly established views about the nature of the two parties. Existing loyalties, images, and stereotypes are strong, and everyone considers himself or herself an expert. As a result, when asked to view American politics from new perspectives, readers are resistant.

There is also a fundamental antipartyism within both the academic and public worlds, a sentiment that precludes many scholars and laymen from taking the parties seriously. A deep cynicism about the political process is widely shared, as is the feeling that independence from party politics is a good thing. Though millions of Americans declare a party affiliation for voting purposes, few actually devote themselves to working within the parties. Academics are thought to be intensely politicized, but in reality they avoid precinct meetings and the working party organizations. Though their votes may be predictably Democratic or even more radical in liberal arts departments (and often as predictably Republican in the professional schools), they are prickly, independent, firm in their own positions, and concerned more for principle than for organizational loyalty.

Consequently, academicians share the general public's abiding distrust of politicians, and politicians reciprocate the sentiment, rarely paying scholars the courtesy of reading their books or following their advice, perhaps with good reason.

Few historians, therefore, have ever written histories directly and specifically of one of the two major parties, although specialized accounts of political crisis periods exist in great numbers. Indeed, until the 1950s, the prevailing interpretation that dominated historical writing about politics made parties essentially irrelevant, in themselves, as forces in history. These interpretations assumed that parties were simply servants, often purchased ones, of particular economic interests. In general, the Republican party was seen as representing capital, the Democratic party as representing workers and farmers. Even in this division, however, which had a certain logic, there appeared an overlay of fraud and hypocrisy. Save for a few noble figures at the apex of national life, politicians were believed to be primarily interested in getting power, and ready to adopt whatever ideology at the moment seemed likely to gain votes. In the 1950s, another theme in political history surfaced: parties are little more than vehicles for releasing mass psychological frustrations, that is, for launching irrational and generally fruitless assaults upon presumed conspiracies among the profiteers or the disloyal.

All of these things are true of politicians and parties. In any understanding of human nature, selfishness, corruption, and unreasoning fears must be taken as real and continuing influences. However, use of the biographical method over many years has persuaded me that consistency and serious purpose throughout entire careers is more the norm among politicians than the erratic, self-serving shifts of direction that the conventional wisdom ascribes to them. Political rhetoric deserves close attention, for it reveals broad patterns of belief, patterns that animate entire parties and that individual politicians hold to with a dogged and often politically dangerous, even fatal, persistence.

Furthermore, if cultural political history has done nothing else, it has established the deep and enduring reality of the parties-in-the-electorate: the mass membership behind each party organization and leadership. Catholics have leaned strongly Democratic for two hundred years, and Quakers have persistently been in the other camp. The party organizations and the leaders in office are the tips of huge political icebergs that move through time with massive stability, changing slowly and surviving in their essential form for many generations. Even during the Civil War, when the Democrats in the

North were identified with the treason of their fellow Democrats in the South, most voters in that party held on doggedly. The Democratic portion of the Northern vote, even at its lowest point, hovered around 40 percent. Party history, in short, deals with two large clusters of different kinds of people (ignoring, for the moment, the minor parties) who hang together persistently in an association which, when closely examined, is historically and culturally understandable. There is little that is precise about this matter. Politics is not a function of engineering. The parties are not mutually exclusive in their membership, for there is much intermixing of social groups across the lines. What cultural historians usually discover is that specific groups of people lean but marginally in a particular direction. Yankees (i.e., New Englanders) over much of American history leaned Republican (and earlier, Federalist and Whig) in sufficient numbers to give that party a distinctive character, although many Yankees were strong Democrats. With relatively homogeneous groups like the Irish Catholics, who had a strong ethnic and religious identity, cultural explanations work well, for, historically, they have voted in bloc fashion. In other situations, where a culture group like the Germans is internally complex, less homogeneous, and subject to conflicting currents, the matter is more complicated. There is also a strong component of relativity in ethnic alignments, for local circumstances are often a governing factor. When German Lutherans were located near Yankees, whose moralism they disliked, they leaned Democratic, but when they were located near Irish Catholics, they tended to vote the other way. In addition, statistical risks are unavoidable when efforts are made to identify a voting precinct with a particular ethnic or religious group and to relate that fact to voting.[1] Thus the point to stress in party history is overall thrust, in character and mood. Nonetheless, we now have many historical studies of cultural voting, focusing upon widely varying settings and times, that confirm each other. The patterns, in short, are linking up. When cultural alignments in one period appear again in many others, it is difficult to believe that the method is unsound.

It is not, of course, as if we were studying something removed from direct human experience, as in scientific matters, which can be known only at second hand through sophisticated procedures involving mathematics and large instruments. In this society we all have some relatively direct experience of politics. The new political history gains much of its explanatory power because the view of politics that it provides resembles the situation we see around us in real life. Party politicians knew long ago that their memberships contained particular ethnic and other culture groups. American political history, however, has been written primarily by scholars of WASP cultural origins, and only in recent years have they begun to deal seriously—and not in denigrating terms—with the power of ethnicity in politics. In fact, it was a writer on contemporary public affairs, Samuel Lubell, who in his *The Future of American Politics* (1952) first directed scholarly attention to ethnicity in the political arena.

The origins of this new way of conceiving American political history merit some reflection. Such shifts in intellectual style and in modes of seeing things do not occur often, nor do they arrive unattended. Samuel Lubell's book would have had little influence if historians had not been ready to respond to it. What had occurred was the emergence of new assumptions about human nature and a new world view.

Historians had not thought formerly that their picture of the past was incomplete. For many years, they had been equipped with the spectacles of the Progressive historians and were satisfied by what they revealed. When they looked at political history, with Frederick Jackson Turner, Charles Beard, and Vernon Parrington they saw everything dominated and shaped by economic influences.[2] Locating points of conflict between economic classes and interests or exploring the geographic setting and its resources provided, so historians believed, a full explanation for everything, even for ideas. Political motivations were seen as based in rationally calculated decisions concerning profit and loss, land, and wages and income. The historical picture that resulted was in a sense nonhistorical, for economic motivations were immediate and contextual. Scholars could concentrate on studying existing class relationships, on eliciting vested interests, and pay little attention to the dimension of time.

However, in the 1930s and 1940s some historians began to shift in their sensitivities. The endlessly repeated formulas of economic political history had become arid, flat, and uninteresting. They had ceased, in fact, to explain. World War I had profoundly shaken the intellectual foundations of Western civilization, weakening the belief that humanity acted primarily in response to the promptings of reason and the logical calculation of economic interest. The Civil War now began to be seen as simply the product of hysteria and human bungling.[3] Then Adolf Hitler and fascism taught us—in a way far more powerful than the reflections of scholarship ever could—that feeling and passion have a life of their own in politics; that people will plunge the world into chaos for ideas, however mad and irrational they may seem to others; that tribal hatreds based on ancient memories and sharply diverging lifestyles can operate in public life with a power that earlier generations would have called demonic. A wide door was opened to the influence of Sigmund Freud and depth psychology, which focused upon irrational forces at work below the level of consciousness in personal lives and in society. The bleak existentialist ruminations of the theologian Reinhold Niebuhr introduced the themes of irony, paradox, and the reality of evil; that is, of selfish fears and the consequent hunger for power.

From these diverse sources, historians slowly acquired in the years following World War II a more complicated view of humanity than that which had satisfied those legatees of the long nineteenth-century peace, the Progressive historians. It became clear to us, in a way hidden to them, that the energies shaping public life are emotional as well as rational, cultural as well as economic. Furthermore, the immense concussion of two world wars in which millions had died and Western civilization itself had been deeply scarred produced a crisis of meaning. What, any longer, could people believe in? Could life be regarded only with cynicism and despair? Faced, also, with the challenge of fascism and during the Cold War with that of communism, American scholars shared with Western culture in general a need to find an intellectual grounding, a renewed sense of contact with the values and ideologies that had nourished humankind in the past. Within the population at large, this search for meaning led to the religious revival of the postwar years; for scholars, it meant a fascination with the history of ideas. In this circumstance, religion became once again a valid subject of study, no longer dismissed as an unprogressive, reactionary collection of superstitions. The life of the mind in its many precincts, whether in scientific, philosophical, theological, or social and political thought, absorbed the attentions of a growing number of historians.

Thus, although many historians of politics continued to write their narratives from the economic determinist point of view, by the 1950s a new way of looking at the past—intellectual history—was attaining enormous vogue. In a poll of historians taken in 1952, Merle Curti's *The Growth of American Thought* (1943; 2nd ed., 1951; 3rd ed., 1964) was selected as the book they "most preferred" among those works that had been published between 1936 and 1950.[4] In 1944 a young historian, Richard Hofstadter, had published a study of the American mind that had occasioned wide interest, *Social Darwinism in American Thought.* In 1948 his *The American Political Tradition and the Men Who Made It* appeared, a remarkable work that was to shape the ways in which most historians over the ensuing generation would understand the development of American politics.

Concentrating upon the common value system (consensus) that existed within the political elite, Hofstadter relied upon a growing tendency to turn to psychological explanations. In doing so, he broke through to a style of analysis, unlike that in existing scholarship, that possessed an almost startling power for younger scholars. Though, like Merle Curti, he still continued to ground ideas in economic interests and the social-economic environment, the internal dynamic of his way of thinking was leading in new directions. With his skeptical, sensitive, ambivalent vision, Hofstadter brought into the confident world of history writing, with its habit of placing people and motivations in economic categories, the subtle new modes of explanation that had been coming from Freud, Niebuhr, the sociologists Max Weber and Karl Mannheim, the literary critic Lionel Trilling, and the social psychologist T. W. Adorno.[5]

Then the full impact of the Cold War began to be felt by scholars. During that experience, which constituted an unusually long and intensive period of national tension induced by anxieties over threats from abroad, the power of ideologies within mass populations, and their tendency under the burden of fear to believe in conspiracies and to think in simplistic images, thrust itself with disquieting force —as in the McCarthy years—upon the academic community. It was during this period that Hofstadter's bold inclination toward social-psychological theorizing within history came to full expression in his book *The Age of Reform: From Bryan to F.D.R.* (1955). An astringent narrative alive to the irony in the human condition, *The Age of Reform* described politics as a scene of conflicting world views, often irrational in origin and nature, springing out of the particular cultural milieu in which they were generated and not simply out of broad economic interest. Those traditional heroes of historiography, the Populists, now appeared as conspiracy-obsessed victims of collective delusions. Their beliefs and mode of political behavior, which Hofstadter would later term "the paranoid style," arose from status anxieties, misinformation due to social isolation, and hatred of the city. The immigrant voters of the Progressive years were not noble sufferers with an automatic claim upon our sympathy; they were *ethnic* peoples bound by a cultural conservatism brought with them from the Old World. Unable to understand properly the concept of the citizen, they were natural enemies to moralistic, reforming Yankees.

What was occurring, although it was not fully realized at the time, was the absorption of intellectual history into a larger and more inclusive concept, that of cultural history.[6] In 1954 a lengthy discussion of theories current among cultural anthropologists that could be useful to historians appeared in a landmark pronouncement of the Social Science Research Council's Committee on Historiography.[7] In the same year, David Potter's *People of Plenty: Economic Abundance and American Character* stressed the importance of using cultural analysis to understand American values. In 1955 came John Higham's brilliant narrative of hostilities between native Americans and immigrants, *Strangers in the Land: Patterns of American Nativism*, which, like Hofstadter's and Potter's books, was soon being read in hundreds of classrooms. The American Studies movement, born in Henry Nash Smith's *Virgin Land: The American West as Symbol and Myth* (1950), was now in full momentum. Concentrating upon the motivating myths in American life as discovered in literary symbols, the new genre flowered in such works as John William Ward's *Andrew Jackson: Symbol for an Age* (1955) and William R. Taylor's *Cavalier and Yankee: The Old South and American National Character* (1961).

Then from quite a different line of country came Lee Benson's *The Concept of Jacksonian Democracy: New York as a Test Case* (1961). Concerned with being rigorously scientific in his procedures and with unearthing cultural patterns within the mass of the population rather than in the literature and political rhetoric of the elite, Benson drew heavily upon the computer revolution to analyze large bodies of statistical evidence concerning local voting performance and other social indices. He demonstrated with a formidable denseness of detail how prominently what he called "ethnocultural influences" displayed themselves in politics. Benson's kind of history was slow to build, for it required sophisticated quantitative skills and tedious programs of data collection and analysis. Through his direct influence, however, and that of Samuel P. Hays, who also urged historians to turn away from studies of the elite and focus instead on social history, the "new political history" with its emphasis upon "ethnocultural" factors was emerging with considerable strength by the beginning of the 1970s.[8]

The national situation had long been shifting in directions that encouraged the new historical consciousness. The rising tide of black militancy that had begun to surge in the 1950s was sending waves through all of America's minorities, setting off a new awakening of ethnic consciousness. In the long years of national crisis since the onset of the depression of the 1930s and the wars and threats of wars that followed, a sense of national unity had shaped the American temper. A mood of common Americanism and an atmosphere of team spirit had damped down ethnic separatism. Now, however, ethnic minorities came alive to a new consciousness of themselves, and "style of life" issues became ever more prominent. In the presence of this volcanic phenomenon, some of the historical discipline's leading figures arrived at a broader consciousness of where their work was trending. In 1962 Hofstadter observed that

> it now seems doubtful that the term "status politics" [which he had used in the 1950s] . . . is an adequate term for what I had in mind. . . . If we were to speak of "cultural politics" we might supply part of what is missing. In our political life there have always been certain types of cultural issues, questions of faith and morals, tone and style, freedom and coercion, which become fighting issues. To choose but one example, prohibition was an issue of this kind during the twenties and early thirties. In the struggle over prohibition, economic interests played only the most marginal role; the issue mobilized religious and moral convictions, ethnic habits and hostilities, attitudes toward health and sexuality, and other personal preoccupations.[9]

In 1964 the intellectual historian H. Stuart Hughes enthusiastically proclaimed the full development of the new way of looking at the past, observing that many historians were "at last ready to endorse the view that the widest and most fruitful definition of their trade [is] . . . as 'retrospective cultural anthropology.' "[10]

If Hughes is correct, and the flood of historical writing on cultural themes since his pronouncement indicates that many scholars agree, it is important to understand what the term "culture," as anthropologists have used it, means. Anthropologists themselves have argued almost continuously over its meaning since the Englishman E. B. Tylor first explicitly defined the concept a hundred years ago, for the phenomenon is exceedingly complex. In broad terms, however, there is wide (though perhaps not unanimous) agreement that "culture" refers to the realm of *consciousness,* as distinct from that of the material world and its demands. In this sense, as the anthropologists Franz Boas and Emile Durkheim both agreed despite their sharp divergences in other particulars, culture is *sui generis;* that is, it is a realm of human existence that is distinct to itself, with its own imperative and inclusive loyalties, its own dynamic power in shaping life independent of (though in interaction with) the material setting. Culture consists of values, beliefs, and world views, or what the anthropologist Clifford Geertz has recently called "socially established structures of meaning in terms of which people do . . . things." It is also generally agreed among anthropologists that "culture is governed by something other than man's rational faculties," as Elvin Hatch has written, "that the human animal is dominated more by emotion than reason, and that culture is grounded primarily in emotional processes."[11]

A. L. Kroeber, one of Boas's chief disciples, distinguished between what he called the basic and secondary features of human life: "those which are directed toward practical matters such as subsistence and survival on one hand" and the "value culture" on the other. Ruth Benedict, another Boas follower and one who wielded great influence in American thought with her book *Patterns of Culture* (1934), emphasized that each culture has a configuration, governed by its own internal premises, that is almost entirely free of the material exigencies of life. This configuration is inherited from the past and is so powerful in its hold upon human consciousness that it shapes the personalities of those who live within it. When Tylor first formulated the concept of culture, he held that people adopt certain ideas, values, religious practices and beliefs, customs, images of thought, and moral standards more or less consciously as tools for effectively meeting the particular group challenges they face. This position, however, has been consistently rejected by anthropologists in the twentieth century. As Hatch remarks, "This irrationality [of the culture] is an important principle to grasp [in the way Boas assessed] the meaning of human affairs. The Kwakiutl potlatch [a ceremony among northwest coast Indians], the religious wars in European history, and even the voting patterns of modern Western democracy illustrate the irrationality of tradition."[12]

Cultural anthropologists, with Emile Durkheim, are profoundly impressed with the power, indeed the primacy, of the collective life over that of individuals, and with the myths and symbols, the traditional beliefs and practices that, in symbolizing the collective life, claim mass loyalties. This consideration applies with particular force within relatively small societies and within those more or less fixed and homogeneous ones in which individuals have intense social relationships with others, formal rules of behavior are strong, social surveillance is continuous, and emotional loyalties to the traditional patterns and totems by which that people are identified are intense.

Individualism, in such societies, has little latitude of operation. In larger, more complex societies, the same conditions do not exist, and individuals have wider freedom to vary from general patterns and to choose their own way.[13]

The result of the absorption of the concept of culture into historians' thinking has been the appearance in their writings of a historical scene far more complex than that which preceded it.* Two dimensions of life, cultural and economic, share the stage formerly occupied by economics alone. This should occasion no surprise. As Geertz observes, "Scientific explanation does not consist, as we have been led to imagine, in the reduction of the complex to the simple. Rather, it consists . . . in a substitution of a complexity more intelligible for one which is less." The advance of thought "commonly consists in a progressive complication of what once seemed a beautifully simple set of notions but now seems an unbearably simplistic one. . . . Whitehead once offered to the natural sciences the maxim: 'Seek simplicity and distrust it': to the social sciences he might well have offered, 'Seek complexity and order it.' "[14]

The ambiguous situation of two dimensions in history, each independent of the other and yet in intimate interaction, should be familiar. It has long been held in Western thought that no explanation of human life that ignores its essential duality can in fact be valid. This traditional view had been forgotten by historians of American politics, so persuasive to them had seemed the power of economic influences alone, so settled and accustomed had they become to thinking in monistic terms. For Augustine and John Calvin, the dualism to focus upon was that of the flesh and the spirit; for medieval philoso-

---

*It is not my intention, in this brief discussion of the concept of culture, to ignore its very great and in a certain sense insurmountable resistance to a definition upon which all anthropologists can agree. Their debate goes on ceaselessly. Furthermore, as a tool of investigation, the concept of culture is filled with complexities. For his fellow historians, Robert F. Berkhofer, Jr., in *A Behavioral Approach to Historical Analysis* (New York, 1969), has explored with great sensitivity the gulf that lies between the mind of the observer, with his or her own cultural outlook and vocabulary, and the interior life of the mind experienced by those living within a past culture far distant in time and space. Cultural historians must be alive to the differences between the meanings they attach to words and the meanings of words used by the people being studied. As Berkhofer observes, "Just as anthropologists have only recently started to develop more sophisticated techniques to try to reconstruct the values and beliefs that lie behind the meaning of words when employed by a man in a given culture at a certain time, so historians must do more in this direction than they have previously . . . [by the use of] componential analysis, contrast-level study, programmed specifications, and other techniques of the linguistic anthropologists" (p. 148).

phers, the duality of life was to be found in the paradox of the particular and the universal, both present in the same phenomenon and pointing in different directions. The discovery of cultural politics, standing in an equally paradoxical and coexistent relationship with economic politics, provides historians with a mode of explanation that is true to life in its real nature.

In his recent McLellan Lecture (Miami University, Ohio) upon the American Revolution, Michael Kammen remarked that for the past decade

> we have had one school of thought, whose most prominent spokesman is Bernard Bailyn, which argues that a complex ideology (involving a profound mistrust of power) *alone* "explains why at a particular time the colonists rebelled, and establishes the point of departure for the constructive efforts that followed." . . . it seems reasonable to designate theirs an *ideological* interpretation. They have been challenged, especially in the past few years, by a group whose mentor has mainly been Merrill Jensen and whose counterthrust . . . the advocates . . . have themselves designated [as] the approach through *political economy.*[15]

While it is not clear that the protagonists are consciously and expressly advancing monistic (i.e., single factor) explanations, the controversy has that appearance. In the present work, it is specifically not my intention to advance a new monolithic interpretation based upon cultural considerations to replace another based upon economics. Rather, we must make room, it seems to me, for an avowed dualism of explanation in which neither the cultural nor the economic dimension is a product (i.e., an epiphenomenon) of the other, although the two dimensions are interactive.

I would think of the intellectualist/Bailyn position as described by Kammen (a description to which Bailyn might not agree) as subsumed within the larger framework of cultural history, and regard questions of political economy as distinct to themselves, necessarily just as operative in the Revolution and as valid to consider. The difficulty, a technical one, is to find a narrative strategy (and a personal competence in the subject matter) that allows for a blending that is judicious and true to life. I doubt that as an ideal it shall ever be achieved, since the mental universe of words and the external universe of life itself are so wholly different from each other and disproportionate, but it remains in my view our proper objective, while we acknowledge that it can be only partially realized. In the following narrative, I have tried to remain consistently alive to the economic dimension, though my tilt toward cultural explanations will display itself. In fact, since I have set out expressly to describe the distinctively cultural pattern in American politics from its beginnings to the near present, this is an almost unavoidable outcome. After so many years in which economics has loomed largest in our narratives, perhaps the situation requires an intensity of emphasis upon the other side in order to create in the readers' minds a reasonably balanced understanding of the American past.

The cultural approach to historical explanation has not in any event swept the field, nor will it. Books are still being written as if economic, class-based considerations explain everything we need to know to understand politics. Some of these books simply apply unquestioned traditional formulas; others, more sophisticated, express the rebirth in recent years of history with a Marxian temper. In these latter works, the role of capitalist influences in reform movements, in foreign policy, and in slave relations is freshly and often powerfully explained. Divergences in interpretive stance are inescapable, for historians will continue to approach their topic from the varying perspectives afforded them by their own life experiences and personal natures. For many, cultural influences will always be the float upon an economic wave. What matters, they believe, is still the timeless question: Who gets what, how?

In truth, economic controversies have absorbed the American people in some periods in their history much more than conflicts over values and ways of living. We shall observe a kind of tidal rhythm at work, an oscillation between periods in which cultural politics were at center stage and periods in which an economic crisis absorbed the nation's attentions. We will see, as well, that there was almost always a cultural dimension to economic controversies. When divergent groups argued over banking policy in the Jacksonian years, they were arguing over theories of economics that had profound implications for the moral order. Proponents of one point of view looked toward the emergence of a society entrepreneurial and economically modernizing in mood, while the other envisioned a country stable, traditional, and "natural." Thus in the history that follows, I shall be as concerned with working out the arguments over economic policy as I shall be with those over Catholicism and race relations.

Looking afresh at the political history of the United States from these vantage points, we discover rich and diverse ideologies at work, fashioning mutually contradictory modes of consciousness and belief. We see, too, powerful delusions and fears sweeping the citizenry toward critical moments of decision, and folk hostilities between ethnic and other culture groups so firmly established that they drive these peoples into fixed political alignments that endure for generations. Fed by images of a communal enemy that assign hateful qualities to traditional adversaries, these hostilities summon up ancestral memories, many of them reaching back to distant mother countries but others founded here in the New World. We are now sharply conscious of the confrontation between blacks and whites that began, for most Americans, in the North American colonies and runs through our national life from its origins. The history of cultural politics has also made us freshly aware of the power and complexity of the rivalry between those two home-grown ethnic groups, Yankees and white Southerners. Until they settled their account, American politics in its first century was essentially bipolar. The South and Yankeedom (the world of New Englanders whether at home or transplanted), two expansive and self-conscious cultures struggling for national supremacy, created the nation's central political conflict and the great crisis that culminated in the Civil War.

With regard to that conflict, the "new political historians" who deal in cultural interpretations have been asked to explain how these matters relate to such great national experiences. Said another way, what of the traditional question of causation? Cultural politics, as will be seen, spends much of its energies within local communities and the states, in connection with temperance, Sabbatarian, and other style-of-life issues. What were the connections that existed between the great constitutional arguments that proceeded in Washington and battles in Ohio and Illinois over prohibition and Sunday recreations? A sharp debate on this matter has occurred within the pages of the journal *Civil War History,* and Professor Willie Lee Rose, in her Comment upon my remarks at the 1976 Annual Meeting of the American Historical Association, took note of the emphasis upon cultural factors in American political history and remarked: "No general interpretation of our record will be convincing if it fails to account in a satisfactory way for the Civil War. . . . It hardly seems too much . . . to demand of any new sweeping interpretation of the nation's political history that it give a serviceable account of the causes of the Civil War and that, if that causation should turn out to be monolithic, the monolith be convincing indeed."[16] She went on to urge me, in preparing the present book, to address this issue. In a related criticism of the new approaches, Richard L. McCormick has insisted that "new political historians" have failed to make a connec-

tion between cultural political controversies and the whole range of
national policies, economic and diplomatic as well as constitutional.[17]

The causes of the Civil War have been debated since the event
itself began, and the controversy has filled libraries. Each effort at
explanation is in later reckonings seen to be incomplete and unsatis-
fying. Historians in the best of circumstances have their personal
world views that others may not share, and they are affected by the
mood of their times. Judgments shaped in periods of economic stress
tend to center upon material factors. In our own time, filled as it has
been with ethnic consciousness and conflict, a sensitivity to these
influences has emerged. Clearly, we shall approach that great national experience, the Civil War, afresh in each generation, looking
at it with new eyes and seeing its complexities in new ways.

My own position in these matters derives from the tradition of
philosophic skepticism. As the philosopher David Hume established
two centuries ago and more recently William Dray has freshly maintained, in human affairs it is not possible to say that any particular
thing or influence is the "cause" of a subsequent event. Human
experience cannot be seen as a single fact from any conceivable
vantage point available to us, and the processes of thought we are
given to use are too limited. We are able to place together certain
happenings in time but little more. What comes out of this process
is not a set of "causes" but rather a basis for understanding events as
reasonable and appropriate.[18]

Thus, the secession of the Southern states and the Civil War that
followed become more understandable when we learn that, before
the crucial decisions were made in South Carolina, in the Southern
states in general, in Washington, D.C., and in the North, certain
states of mind that sprang largely from cultural influences existed in
both sections. But so did a great deal else that at this point is hidden
to us, or in any event not described in this book. States of mind do
not necessarily produce specific actions. The world affords us many
examples of different outcomes that could have eventuated, given
the accidents of circumstance. The actual events that occurred make
sense when placed against the background of feelings, self-images,
inherited hostilities, racial fears, and conflicts in lifestyle and ideology
that are examined in this book. It has not been my intention to
achieve more than this. Cultural analysis offers us a deeper understanding, not a final explanation, of the Civil War, the Revolution, or
any other great national experience in the American past.

As to the question of what links may be seen between the local
cultural interests of each party's voters and the national policies of

their party leadership in economics and foreign policy, the narrative that follows will provide the most satisfactory reply. Suffice it to say here that even in foreign policy, a congruence exists between cultural constituency and party outlook. The Democrats, traditionally the party of the outgroups and advocates of the ideal of egalitarianism in internal domestic policy, understandably supported in Woodrow Wilson's time the equality of all nations, small as well as large, and the concept of self-determination by the smaller nationalities (ethnic groups) in Europe. In earlier times, the Federalist party hated the French because its core community, the Yankees, were ethnically English, conscious and proud of that fact, and they shared England's ancient hostility toward the Gallic people.

Throughout the century, as we shall see, great and continuing issues in American public life were Anglicization (adopting England's values and ways of living), political relations with the former mother country, and the flow of people, ideas, and economic influences that came from Great Britain for many generations after the Revolution. Through the first century and well into the 1900s, Americans lived and worked within a transatlantic Anglo-American culture of great vitality in which all things English had an unassailable authority for some, while for others they were hateful. The Americans had with England, in short, that classically ambivalent relationship that exists between colonial peoples and the metropolitan center, both before and after independence is achieved, or even between rich and powerful countries and those nations not former colonies but in important ways dependent upon them. This love-hate relationship entered constantly into political debate, fed the nation's imagery, and shaped the way Americans talked about and regarded peoples as diverse as the Catholic Irish, black slaves, and Adam Smith.

Cultural history possesses much of its persuasive power because, as in the case of the Anglo-American relationship, it brings with it the historian's unique commodity, the element of time. When the Irish think of the English, they think through a haze of memory reaching back for centuries. When anti-Semites think of Jews, the deposit of memory is millennia old. We shall observe that the Revolutionary crisis was perceived by colonials and the metropolitan English alike against the memory that each possessed about the nature of the English Civil War a century before, each interpreting that event differently and persisting in seeing the present conflict in its terms. It was commonly said by Loyalists and the English at home that the Presbyterians, who had helped prominently to lead the rebellion against the Crown, were seeking to reenact their role in that former conflict, only this time successfully. In the years before the Civil War, Southern whites delighted in calling themselves by that seventeenth-century appellation, cavaliers, and in calling Yankees by its opposite, roundheads, once more evoking images from the English Civil War, by that time two centuries old.

There is an additional reason why cultural history possesses a remarkably persuasive quality. Ethnic hostilities not only have deep roots in time but they still persist, as do conflicts over morals and styles of life. The lecturer talking of these matters senses in the audience's heightened interest the fact that almost every listener, whether black, WASP, pietist, Italian, or Jew, is thinking of similar experiences in their own lives or in those of their families. Following the course of particular ethnic communities through the flow of American history has the appeal of biography. It personalizes the narrative and in so doing makes use of another of the unique characteristics of the historical method. The stories of individual lives have often provided the most revealing window into past times and issues, for abstractions become concrete and understandable within them. Readers can identify with the feelings of particular persons because they have had such feelings too. Similarly, the Revolution comes alive when we are able to follow it through the experience of, for example, the Scotch-Irish, because the feelings they had toward the English are the feelings that, in different but nonetheless similar circumstances, we have had toward others in our individual lives. Modern persons have rarely been angry at a king, but anger at a group who assume an attitude of supercilious arrogance is a sensation known even to young people. They may not be stirred by economic conflicts, since as yet they may not have experienced them—in an affluent society such as our own, millions know little of the industrial warfare or farm protests of earlier times—but in cultural relations, antipathies coming out of the deep past still endure.

The historical study of politics has been strongly affected in recent years by influences flowing from political scientists. In one sense, these influences are purely quantitative; in another, they are closely related to concepts of cultural change. The emergence of quantitative history since the early 1960s has, in fact, reflected a shift among some historians toward closer relations with political scientists than has existed since the days of Charles Beard. If the new Cliometricians (historians who rely upon quantitative methods) are not publishing in the *American Behavioral Scientist,* their work is appearing in the *Political Science Quarterly* or in the *American Political Science Review.* The scholars whose work they draw upon, in their concern with bringing social science methods to bear upon political history, are such political scientists as V. O. Key, Jr., Walter Dean Burnham, and Samuel P. Huntington. From these men have come major concepts that have helped to shape the narrative of this book and bear some explanation here. They are: the notion of critical elections and the five party systems; and the concept of modernization, first studied in the developing nations of the world and then applied within American history.

V. O. Key, Jr., unusual among political scientists for his concern not simply with existing context of an event or events but with the dimension of time, elaborated his theory of critical elections in 1955. Key's theory holds that, at certain turning-point periods in American history, slowly building crises erupt dramatically to reshape the nature of the parties and inaugurate a new order of things.[19] Among scholars, this theory introduced a new chronology for American history and a new way of thinking about political parties. Up to this time, political science textbooks had depicted parties as extremely stable, concentrating upon the internal processes of bargaining and political balance. Now, however, parties were seen as experiencing periods of sharp disjuncture. According to this view, during these periods citizens are shaken out of their usual apathy (the condition in which earlier studies had placed them) by crises of unusual intensity. Conventions become turbulent, marked by great ideological polarization, and the two parties find themselves far apart on the issues. The emotional content of political life rapidly escalates, with voters and politicians both growing more rigid and dogmatic. Voters throng into the ballot booths in unusually high numbers, and major realignments occur in the balance of cultural and economic groupings behind each party. After this flash point, parties with a fresh mandate of national support enter office to undertake major changes in national policy. Then, the party system in a modified pattern becomes stable again, and a long period, usually about thirty to forty years, of relative stasis begins.[20]

Based on extensive quantitative analyses of voting cycles, it is accepted that there have been five "party systems" in American history. The first (the Jeffersonian party system) took form in the 1790s and ran into the mid-1820s. The second (the Jacksonian party system), emerging in and around the presidential election of 1828 between Andrew Jackson and John Quincy Adams, fell to pieces in the crisis year 1854, which was marked by the Kansas-Nebraska Act and sharp cultural rivalries. The third (the Civil War party system) was largely in place by 1856, when the modern Republican party ran its first presidential candidate, John Charles Frémont, and endured until the great depression that began in 1893. The fourth (the Progressive Era party system), its birth signalled in the off-year elections of 1894 and confirmed in the massive victory of William McKinley in 1896, persisted until the even more disastrous depression that began in the stock market crash of 1929. By Franklin Roosevelt's election in 1932, the fifth (the New Deal party system) was emerging, and in its larger outlines this system appears to have survived to the present day, though about this there is some uncertainty and continuing discussion.[21]

The concept of modernization, also absorbed from the political scientists, constitutes, along with the discovery of cultural influences, the other major new perspective from which historians are examining the American past.[22] The theory emerged primarily as an awareness of the profound social changes that occur in underdeveloped nations when they go through industrialization. In general, it is this process of economic change, urbanization, and bureaucratization—the increasing use of experts, operating by rational procedures in hierarchical organizations—that continues to attract the most attention among those concerned with modernization. However, there is also an awareness that the modernizing process has wide ramifications in the culture: the undermining of received bodies of traditional knowledge, disorientation in goals, loss of values in the presence of institutional and religious flux, and mounting levels of violence, delinquency, crime, family dissolution, and suicide. In C. E. Black's words, "Modernization must be thought of, then, as a process that is simultaneously creative and destructive, providing new opportunities and prospects at a high price in human dislocation and suffering."[23]

As an organizing theme, modernization has been widely used by historians in recent years, but primarily as an element in multifaceted explanations and not as an overall framework within which to see all of American history. We now have, however, in Richard D. Brown's *Modernization: The Transformation of American Life 1600–1865* (1976), the first full-length attempt by a historian to confront the process directly, develop a full theoretical stance as to what it consists of, and examine a long sweep of American history within that conceptual framework. Brown poses two ideal social types in conflict with each other, the traditional and the modern. The traditional society is stable, with little sense of differentiation between past and future, since both are assumed to be essentially the same. It is indifferent to time and innovation, characterized by face-to-face communication, organized in small villages and towns, localistic, and possessed only of human and animal power for transportation. Fixed hierarchies, toward which ordinary persons are deferential, govern the traditional society, and paternalism dominates both family and society. Social roles are not closely specialized, work and leisure flow into each other, and the religious and secular lives are intertwined. All of this expresses itself in a "traditional personality," a widely shared pattern of behavior and expectations.

Modern society, predictably, occupies the polar opposite of these attributes. It is characterized by dynamism, change, and the manipulation of the environment to achieve consciously developed goals by means of technologies. Time is measured, and the orientation is toward a future assumed to be different from the present. Vast sources of power multiply human strength and talents in modern society. The accumulation and dissemination of knowledge becomes an industry, regularly and rationally organized; literacy is widespread; and market forces and remote political influences govern human relations. Cosmopolitan, specialized in social roles, assigning prestige by function and not by inherited status, self-conscious, and bureaucratic, a modernized society has widespread citizen participation in the governing and decision-making processes. Hereditary authority is rejected, elitism criticized, and sovereignty assumed to lie in the people at large through the regular use of elections. Egalitarianism, freedom to live in diverse cultural styles, and liberty from restrictions—these mark the nontraditional pattern. In the "modern personality," passivity and fatalism give way to entrepreneurism, personal autonomy, and individual initiative.[24] Modern persons possess more generally a higher capacity for empathy, that is, for seeing themselves in another's situation and feeling a sense of responsibility for that person's welfare. Their ego systems are wider, more encompassing. Thus, modern reform movements are enabled to appear. Such movements rely, furthermore, upon the existence of a mass society, with mass political parties and mass means of information exchange, in order to create a sense of community over enormous continental areas. The concept of "citizen," carrying with it the assumption that individuals should be concerned about and active in public affairs, is essentially modern.

This schema is forbiddingly regular and architectonic. It is, in fact, so broad and unnaturally logical as to represent no particular society in history, as Brown himself observes. Yet it retains so close a resemblance to much that is familiar to historians as they study the course of nations through time that the concept of modernization has been an attractive one to use. Its weakness lies in its almost limitless flexibility. As Dean C. Tipps observes with scholarly whimsy, "The proliferation of alternative definitions [of modernization] has been such, in fact, that the ratio of those using the term to alternative definitions would appear to approach unity."[25] Despite the wide use of the concept since its emergence in the 1960s, no shared categories of analysis have appeared, and no internal controls or self-limiting factors have been found to make the notion a reasonably effective tool for close analysis. Where does modernization begin, and when does it end? What social changes does it encompass? How much more individualistic was the Gilded Age than colonial America? Does modernization apply simply to industrialization and economic development; does it relate to a broader phenomenon, humanity's increasing control over the natural and social environment? Or is it a total transformation of all aspects of human life, including changes in personality and reaching out to the world order? As yet, there are no shared conclusions about these questions. Modernization as a concept remains largely in the realm of value judgment and impressionism.

This is not to say, however, that the concept lacks all explanatory usefulness. Without question, a social order termed "modern" has evolved, one that is fundamentally different from what it left behind. I am primarily concerned with how various kinds of persons *felt* about the process, and therefore the term "modernization" will appear with some frequency in the following account. Among its complexities, as I shall point out, is that this concept, too, partakes of the dualism discussed earlier. There has been a strong tendency among historians to be alive to modernization as involved in economic change and industrialization. Allied to this is a tendency to identify the party that approved of this phenomenon and encouraged it (i.e., Whigs and the modern Republicans) as the modernizing political movement. There are also, however, cultural aspects to modernization, and in this regard the opposing party in American politics (i.e., the Democrats) has in important ways been the modernizing influence, with its emphasis upon egalitarianism and cultural as well as economic laissez faire. Freedom to live as one chooses, as regards dress, recreation, and sexual behavior, is certainly modern.

A word more must be said on the subject of ethnicity, a concept with its own complexities. I view ethnicity as a cultural phenomenon and not as something separate to itself. Thus, my practice has been to use the term "cultural politics" rather than "ethnocultural politics." Professor Ronald P. Formisano has objected to my usage, insisting that "cultural and ethnic politics are different phenomena. . . . Within any political arena, cultural politics can be understood to refer to clashes over broadly defined life-styles, symbolic groups, and beliefs, while ethnic politics has a relatively concrete reference to more durable and exclusive identity groups." He has also concluded that my conception of the Southern white community as ethnic in nature uses the term too broadly. "Southern identity," he remarks, "was not ethnic: from a territorial and economic base Southernness became a cultural difference and, among a significant minority, an aspiration to a national identity."[26] Criticism from so seasoned a scholar in this field is not easily dismissed. However, Professor Formisano's own terminology leans toward my usage. Ethnic "identity" is a matter of consciousness, and the realm of culture is precisely that of consciousness. As in the case of the Southern white community, historical memory, symbols and myths, shared values and a shared sense of the enemy are what give to ethnic groups their essential reality.[27]

It is in a certain sense surprising that books on the subject of ethnicity devote so little space to defining the term, often relegating this point to a passing footnote. Leonard Dinnerstein and David M. Reiners, in their book *Ethnic Americans: A History of Immigration and Assimilation* (1975), inserted in the preface the following brief note: "We use ethnic group to mean a group with a shared culture and sense of identity based on religion, race, or nationality" (p. xiii). Lawrence M. Fuchs remarks in the introduction to a volume he edited: "I use the word ethnic in its broadest sense to include nationality groups such as Italians, religious groups as broad as Protestants and as specific as Quakers, ethno-religious groups such as Irish Catholics or Jews, and racial groups such as Negroes." They may have important differences among themselves, he observes, "but the members of each group share a distinctive historical inheritance which has given them an identifiable and particular social and cultural tradition. That is my definition of ethnicity."[28] "In most of the world," writes Edgar Litt, "the bonds of Blood, Believer, and Brother as strongly define political interest and conflict as do the bonds of class or locale ... that is, those [ethnic] distinctions based on race, religion, or national origin."[29] In this sense, he continues,

> ethnic politics should not be viewed as a parochial phenomenon, some-
> thing peculiar to the likes of Tammany, for there are few places on
> earth where ethnicity is not presently of political import ... Afrikander
> v. Bantu, Kikuyu v. Luo, Yoruba v. Ibo, Bahutu v. Watusi, Kurd v.
> Iraqim, Muslim v. Hindu, Ukrainian v. Great Russian, Great Russian v.
> most Eurasian groups, Mongolian v. Chinese, the overseas Chinese v.
> most of Southeast Asia, the overseas Indians v. most of eastern and
> southern Africa, Turk v. Greek Cypriot, Arab v. Jew, Ladino v. white
> Spanish, Welsh v. English, Walloon v. Flemish, Czech v. Slovak, Chris-
> tian v. Jew, Protestant v. Catholic, Catholic v. Buddhist, black v. white,
> and on we could go; this list merely scratches the surface. One can
> even discern conflicting subgroups within the opposing groups (thus,
> orthodox v. reform Jews, Afrikaans-speaking v. English-speaking
> whites, Ulster v. Celtic Irish), particularly in Africa and the Middle and
> Far East.[30]

Ethnic communities display varying styles. Pluralists simply want to be tolerated by the dominant majority within their country; assimilationists wish to be absorbed into full participation in the larger national life; secessionists work toward political and cultural independence; and militants aim at domination over the other culture groups.[31] There are always those members of ethnic communities who do not rigidly identify with that minority, who do not feel it to be their ingroup. Their membership is sociological but not psychological. Indeed, a major phenomenon in ethnic politics, with which I shall be much concerned, is the internal exile. Internal exiles are people who identify with groups to which they do not belong. They are reluctant ethnics who wish to leave their communities and cross over to the other side, whether it be lower or upper in social status (the latter is most common). Restraints, however, may keep them in the group of their birth; they may be held back by the exclusiveness of the privileged majority or aspects of their own inescapable ethnic identity. Many within privileged ethnic communities turn inward, waving the Union Jack or parading Old Glory. Among the under-privileged, however, or those who are part of such communities, there are considerable numbers of people who are negatively oriented toward their own people and are pulled outward by the new values and aspirations they have taken on. It is in this shadow world between cultures that the "marginal man" lives. He or she occupies the peripheries of two cultures simultaneously, often being not wholly accepted by either. Indeed, entire groups of people may be characterized by this dualism, this divided identity.[32] We shall observe this dilemma within the world Carl N. Degler has termed the "Other South," as opposed to the "Majority South."[33] By contrast, there are cultures so homogeneous and intensely self-conscious, like the Irish Catholics through much of American history, that little of this ambivalence appears.

My own conception of ethnicity does not apply only to the excluded, to those who are "outsiders in their own land."[34] The English-descended were an ethnic group too, though we rarely think of them in this way. They simply happened, in the American situation, to be initially in the majority and so closely identified as the host culture that they were perceived as the archetypical Americans. For clarity, I at times refer to the "metropolitan English" to establish a reference to those living in England itself. In general, however, I use the term "Yankee" to refer in a generic way to the English ethnic community, even though there were thousands of English in the South, for example, to whom the term "Yankee" would certainly not apply. I do this because, in fact, New England with its Yankee symbol operated through much of the century as the locus classicus, the core homeland of a self-consciously English lifestyle and outlook. This lifestyle was of course prominent also within the Southern elite. Henry Clay will appear for us in this mode, as a symbol of Southern Whiggery and the "Other South" in general. The South, however, in its general culture, did not remain Anglicized for very long after independence. There was too extensive an admixture of Scotch-Irishmen and Germans, too pervasive an egalitarian, frontier, and Jeffersonian atmosphere. Yankees looked eastward to England for cultural as well as economic nourishment, keeping close ties with that country. Most Southern whites looked westward, knowing that they were condemned in England for their slaveholding, and fashioned for themselves a different, aggressively American, identity.

In the modes of ethnicity discussed above—pluralism, assimilation, secession, and militancy—both Yankees and white Southerners perceived each other as militants, attempting to dominate everyone else. In reality, militancy was much more prominent in the Yankees. Southern whites at first followed the route of pluralism, working essentially for equal standing and toleration, and eventually moved on to secession. This central confrontation in American history, through the time of Reconstruction, will provide the core of the history herein presented.

We will observe a party politics, therefore, fueled by two kinds of impulses, economic and cultural, that surge tidally, so that one is sometimes more dominant than the other. Such a politics operates in a deep dimension of time. It is responsive to the power of ancient animosities between kinds of peoples, and proceeds within a framework that is transatlantic. Party politics behaves as a system in the sense that all elements are interlinked. Profoundly ideological, it exists for long years in a stable condition and then erupts in upwellings of violent feelings that force the fashioning of a new party system.

The leadership of the parties deals in a rhetoric of images and dreams, in visions of what the nation should be and whence comes its ills. Individual persons seek political leadership for many motives, but among them an ideological perspective is usually an essential element. Henry Clay and Abraham Lincoln spent their lives in politics because they wished to *do* something with their country. From the Founding Fathers and from across the Atlantic came venerable ideologies, honored political world views, with the power to inspire and energize such men. Each generation of politicians, whatever its immediate objective, seeks in some sense to locate itself in relation to these larger world views and to work in its own time from within the legitimating moral authority they provide. As we shall see, for much of the nation's first century a common ideology of "republicanism" provided the justification for the very existence of the United States and the content of the political philosophy that all parties insisted was their own. However, each political party thought the other's definition of that ideology meretricious and corrupting. They could work together when in the common task of throwing off the British, but thereafter they would divide to follow their varying versions of republicanism.

We will also see that there are two communities within a political party, that of the leadership and that of their following. While the former, to oversimplify the matter, has ideas, the latter has interests. The two do not always stay in harmony. Historians have traditionally assumed that the rhetoric of political leaders and newspaper journalists reflected the ideas of their constituencies, a not illogical position. However, the new political history has shown how in particular circumstances this assumption can mislead. It has been standard historical fare that Lincoln was elected because he won over the German voters to his antislavery cause. But now we are aware that, although

German editors of strongly reformist sentiments were so inclined, the German masses continued determinedly to vote Democratic because they disliked black people and could not abide the Yankees who led the Republican party. Irish Catholics were unswervingly hostile to the civil service reforms pressed forward by the man they helped elect, Grover Cleveland, since by requiring skills and education such reforms would restrict the access of poor Irish Catholics to government jobs.

Cultural politics is not, in fact, a completely attractive phenomenon, and historians have reacted to it in troubled spirit. Tribalism does things that we know only too well and from which it is natural to recoil. The racism of both Southern and Northern whites and the temperance crusades of the Yankees are familiar subjects for disapproving comment. Richard Hofstadter found the antiurbanism of the Populists disturbing. With his commitment to the life of the mind, to the liberating power of reason and ideas, he lost his early faith in "the people." He deplored their paranoid hatreds of each other and their anti-intellectualism, and he regarded McCarthyism as a form of populist radicalism that drew strength from Ivy League–hating ethnics.[35] In this sense, what the new political history has uncovered for us is not necessarily a politics that we can uncritically admire and celebrate.

However, the essential fact is that democratic political ideals have their origins within minorities. Although afflicted with their own prejudices and bigotries, the outgroups are the ones among whom the basic ideals of the democratic order have been most energetically agitated, for in their parochial self-interest they have need of the protection of such ideals. It was the British outgroups in the eighteenth century—the Scots, the Irish, and the Dissenting religious sects among the English—who kept alive the republicanism and the ideals of political liberty and equality that the colonials appropriated and made their own. The critique of capitalist economic power and monopoly that the heirs of Jefferson made the core of their economic ideology came from the Scotsman Adam Smith. The very assertion that all men are created equal was written by an American who made a point of claiming Welsh descent and who smarted at what he felt were the superior airs and arrogance of the metropolitan English. Jefferson, we must keep in mind, was a member of what was then, within the larger context of the British empire, an outgroup looked down upon by the mother country, the colonials. The constitutional separation between church and state that characterized the new United States had been demanded for generations by Presbyterians and Baptists, angry at those who had previously held superior legal status, the Anglicans (Episcopalians), and those who in New England still had this superior status, the Congregationalists. It was the zealous pietists in the Northern states, a minority within the broader American society, who had the most to do with setting in motion the events that led eventually to the freeing of the slaves.

Cultural identity, like all things human, is paradoxical; it is a source of both fruitful and destructive potentialities. To deplore ethnicity and the self-concern and mutual distaste of culture groups is simply to deplore the human condition. This is neither my preference nor my intention in this book. We are all, in fact, members of particular subcultures in American life. Some are small enough to be easily identifiable, and they have attracted attention; others are so large that their members are unaware that there is anything special about their ways of living, and they do not carry an ethnic tag. Everyone, however, shares in whatever qualities the history of cultural politics reveals about the American people.

The tone of the narrative that follows, therefore, is not critical but analytical and descriptive. Lord Acton insisted in the late nineteenth century that the historian's task is to sit in stern judgment upon the past. His friend and adversary, Father Johan Dollinger, demurred, saying that it is instead to explain and to understand. Without following Dollinger in all things, for there is much in the past about which as human beings we cannot be neutral, it was primarily in his spirit that the following narrative has been written.

part one

REVOLUTIONARY ORIGINS

I

The First Revolution: Independence

For a century after their founding, the English colonies on the North American coast grew slowly, far removed from the centers of western European life and little attended. In New England, the Middle Colonies, and the South (the Chesapeake Bay country and South Carolina), a thin scattering of villages, isolated farms, and tobacco and sugar plantations close to tidewater were inhabited by people living the unchanging lives of isolated rural communities. From the 1720s onward, however, swiftly moving changes transformed colonial life. Population grew rapidly, quintupling to 2,250,000 by 1775. Towns flourished, doubling every quarter of a century as transatlantic trade mounted. Settlements pushed westward into the interior along a broad front, fed by heavy immigration pouring in from northern Ireland and Germany. Slavery expanded enormously in the Southern colonies; Virginia's slave population grew from 6,000 in 1700 to 170,000 by 1775. Communication across the Atlantic became easier and more rapid, rising affluence made the colonies an ever more profitable market for the home country, and people, books, and ideas moved back and forth in a swelling interchange. In the 1730s a Great Awakening of religious enthusiasm began sweeping the colonies from north to south. The Great Awakening brought the colonies together in a common cultural experi-

ence for the first time and left as its legacy an aroused, sensitized, and
combative public temper. Then a series of great international wars
broke out in the 1740s, set off by the ancient rivalry between England and France. These conflicts made heavy demands upon the
colonies, causing severe growth pains and sparking controversies in
every colonial city and region.

Now the distinct difference between the political setting in the
colonies and that in Britain was felt. Half, perhaps three-fourths, of
the adult male white population had the vote. Also, the colonists
were uncertain about which persons possessed superior social status
and hence who should rightfully hold office. Ambitious men on the
rise competed more readily with each other for popular favor and
elective position in the colonies than in Britain. Moreover, colonial
governors had governing powers denied to sovereigns in Britain
since the Glorious Revolution of 1688. The colonial assemblies battled constantly with them over their use of this authority and generally won wide respect and high standing among Americans. As a
result, a seat in the assemblies was a prized acquisition, competed for
eagerly. Furthermore, government in the colonies, unlike that in
London, had a great deal to do. Rising population, trade, and the
westward movement of settlement propelled a constant stream of
pressing issues into the public conversation. Towns had to be
founded, land apportioned, Indian relations negotiated, roads built,
civic buildings erected, schools funded and colleges chartered. To be
responsive to change, laws were continually being modified.[1]

In this setting, an awakening of democratic politics spread through
the colonial towns and cities, where the new transformations were
felt most dramatically and modern economic relationships with their
attendant ways of living emerged earliest. A recognizably modern
form of politics appeared in the colonies, a politics far more advanced
than that of Europe. Traditionally, government had been cloaked in
mystery; it was seen as an institution of which ordinary persons were
properly ignorant. The colonial masses had deferred to their betters,
even if less obsequiously than in England, and had left such matters
largely in their hands. In the classic phrase, the elite spoke and led,
the people were silent and followed. Now, however, the common
people were seized by the conviction that they had a rightful role in
government. Political clubs were created, issues publicly agitated,
caucuses held to choose candidates, and tickets formed to group
together nominees of similar persuasions.

With a wider audience to be reached, politicians relied heavily upon pamphleteering and newspapers to mobilize supporters and educate them about issues and personalities. The voters were encouraged by colonial dissidents to be critical of governments, a process which began breaking down venerable patterns of deference toward superiors. An antiauthoritarian mood emerged and threw open all established principles and institutions to question. This, in its turn, led to the conviction that leaders elected after public nomination and debate were no longer to behave as they pleased in office. Rather, they were to maintain continuing ties to their supporters and work for policies their voters advocated. Of course deference toward persons higher in the social scale persisted, especially in the countryside. Nonetheless, fundamental shifts were occurring, even if by small steps; to each generation the changes it observed seemed dramatic innovations. When forelocks were no longer pulled, caps lifted, and curtseys made, and when ordinary men began challenging aristocrats at the polls and marching in the streets, it seemed that the moral order was undergoing seismic upheaval. By the 1750s, the relative political calm that had characterized the internal government of the colonies was gone. Instead, a milling, boisterous, almost chaotic factionalism dominated the scene.[2]

When in 1765 the government in London decided to raise a revenue in the colonies by the Stamp Act, it walked directly if inadvertently into this turmoil. The explosion of outrage that the Act set off in the colonies erupted not simply because the issues were grave and substantial, but because the colonials had become a volatile, politically reactive, and mobilized community. For ten years, until 1775, they argued with London; for eight more, until 1783, they fought for and won their independence. The ensuing four years, until 1787, saw the people of the new United States of America struggling with the fatal weaknesses of the Articles of Confederation. Then they carried through the second revolution of this historic generation—the forming and ratification of the federal Constitution in 1787–1789. Under the new government, all the raw materials existed for the swift emergence of something equally new in the world: national political parties based in the common people. Before George Washington completed his presidency in 1797, a bipolar, two-party national rivalry had formed. Ever since, with relatively brief intermissions, the two-party system has provided the American people with their principal means for mobilizing and focusing their opinions, making common national decisions, and choosing those who are to govern them. In the heat of this continuous encounter, they have argued out their beliefs as to the nature of themselves as a people, the way the nation should be shaped, and the great purposes to which it should be dedicated.

Americans were driven into opposing political camps during the Revolutionary years by motives that were immediate and contemporary and at the same time centuries old. They had brought with them to the New World ancient ethnic identities that were almost tribal in nature. Each of the colonies' separate peoples had a firm conviction, rooted in bloody ancestral memories, that certain other peoples were their folk enemies to be battled at every opportunity. Within the British Isles, the English, Scots, Irish, and Welsh had been at each other's throats, literally and figuratively, for centuries. In this long struggle, the English had held the advantage, for they were by far the wealthiest, most powerful, and most numerous people in the Isles. Furthermore, as those closest to the Continent, they had for long periods been the most economically advanced. From this position of superior strength and more sophisticated development, the English had tried to dominate the other British peoples and to shape them in their own image—in the classic fashion of cultural majorities everywhere. The Welsh had been physically incorporated into the English nation in the sixteenth century but had retained their separate identity. In 1707 Scotland, though clinging to its individuality in ways of life and self-concept, had given up its independence to join with England and form the United Kingdom under one crown and Parliament.

The Irish had been long subjected to waves of conquest, massacre, and colonization by English and Scottish Protestants. The latter, settling primarily in Ulster in the north of Ireland during the 1600s, had by the eighteenth century become a distinctive, separate people, the Scotch-Irish.

The English millions regarded these much less numerous ethnic outgroups in Scotland, Wales, and Ireland as crude, hill country tribes—in one sense comic, in another contemptible. In their turn, the Scots, Welsh, and Irish thought the wealthy and self-important English arrogant and domineering. After the Union of 1707 between Scotland and England, the English complacently used the term "England" to refer to the whole. The Scots, however, preferred the more inclusive terms "Britain" and "the British," insisting that the nation be pluralistic in its self-concept as well as in its internal reality and not be forced into a single English mold. This cultural struggle would never subside. When in the nineteenth century British politics were made more democratic and the Scottish, Welsh, and Irish outgroups gained appropriate voting privileges and representation in United Kingdom politics, the underlying ethnocultural pattern immediately revealed itself. The ethnic minorities lined up behind the Whigs and their successors, the Liberals. The Tories and their successors, the Conservatives, were overwhelmingly the party of England and English preeminence in all things.

Each of these peoples had their own national religion. The Scots and Scotch-Irish were Presbyterians, that is, Church of Scotland adherents. Their theology was dour and Calvinist, and their form of church government dispensed completely with bishops. Instead, a federation of self-governing congregations in which lay elders had effective authority governed Presbyterianism. The mass of the Irish people were Roman Catholic, a faith hated by all Protestants. Within England, the church established by law and the religious home of most English people was the Church of England. Headed by the monarch and governed by royally appointed bishops, its worship was formal and liturgical. Its theology conceived each person to be in an individual relationship with a kindly, forgiving God, and its spirit, rooted in the hierarchical priestly system and effective parish control by local gentry, was aristocratic. The union between Anglican church and English state was complete at all levels. Bishops sat in the House of Lords; church courts had wide jurisdiction over secular matters, such as divorce and inheritance; and the Church's Book of Common Prayer was adopted by an act of Parliament.

Following the English Civil War of the 1640s, many Englishmen had refused to accept Anglican ritual or theology. They formed separate Protestant sects, to which the authorities reluctantly allowed freedom of worship after 1660. There were the stiff-necked English Puritans and their Congregationalist churches (termed "Independent" in England, but the American usage "Congregationalist" will be followed in this narrative), who, like the English Presbyterians, shared a Calvinist outlook with the Scots and Scotch-Irish. There were Baptists, Quakers, and other Dissenters, as they were collectively called, who formed a distinct people within the English nation. By the late eighteenth century, there was also the burgeoning Methodist movement as well. Dissenters were denied the vote in municipal corporations, were rarely elected to Parliament, could not hold royal office (so that the government was wholly Anglican), and could not attend Oxford or Cambridge universities, a fact that led them to create a separate, parallel educational system. The Anglican majority looked down on Dissenters as strange, excessively moralistic and religious persons who should give up their odd conceits, join the Church of England, and thereby rejoin the nation as fully patriotic subjects of the Crown. Until 1869 Dissenters were required to pay taxes to support the local Anglican church and priest, just as everyone in later generations was to be required to support the public schools whether or not they made use of them.[3]*

Religious identity, like ethnicity, also shaped the British political parties. The Church of England was traditionally allied to the Tory party. Both believed that England should properly be a homogeneous Anglican nation and that Dissenters, if they obstinately refused to be Anglicans, should rightly be an excluded caste. On their side, Dissenters were traditionally allied to the Whigs. Of course, in the eighteenth century both parties were more an orientation and a cultural identity than they were organized parties in the modern sense, and they held within their ranks a wide variety of views. However, Whig leaders, who were often religious skeptics and given to rationalism in the French and Scottish style, were impatient with the notion that people—in any event, Protestants—should be penalized for their religious beliefs. With John Locke, the seventeenth-century philosopher of Whiggery, they advocated religious tolerance and were wary of too much power lodged in the monarch's hands. Far more than the Tories, the Whigs were identified with the cause of representative government and the supremacy of Parliament in the constitution, for it was the sustaining Whig myth that their side had won the great victory for these principles in the Glorious Revolution of 1688. Edmund Burke, leader of the more liberal Whigs during the years of the American Revolution and a Protestant Irishman

---

*On the Dissenters in eighteenth-century English life, C. C. Bonwick observes that It is well known that English Dissenters enjoyed a profound sympathy for the American colonists and were strongly affected by the experience of the Revolution. Memories of a shared intellectual ancestry in seventeenth-century Puritanism sustained a rich bond of affection and were fortified by close ties of friendship and a warm sense of community which far outlasted the formal severance of the imperial connection. ("English Dissenters and the American Revolution," in H. C. Allen and Roger Thompson [eds.], *Contrast and Connection: Bicentennial Essays in Anglo-American History* [Athens, Ohio, 1976], p. 88.)

David Beers Quinn, in *The Elizabethans and the Irish* (Ithaca, N.Y., 1966), pp. 7–13, describes the deep prejudice of Englishmen toward the outlying minorities in the British Isles in the sixteenth and early seventeenth centuries, observing that the "core of Englishness [was fixed] firmly in the Southeast [of England]—where it has remained. . . ." A passionately argued book which complains of the persistence of this English condescension in the mid-twentieth century is Owen Dudley Edward, Gwynfor Evans, Ioan Rhys, and Hugh MacDiarmid, *Celtic Nationalism* (London, 1968).

himself, criticized the English majority for its arrogance, opposed its attempt to put down the colonials, and welcomed the end of the war. Coercion, said Burke, never succeeds.[4]

The colonials, as provincials in the British empire, were as much outsiders as the Scots themselves, as much looked down upon by the metropolitan English. Furthermore, most of them, except in the Southern colonies, were Dissenters. They disliked Anglicanism and resisted efforts to make it the established church in the colonies (as by the mid-eighteenth century it was in the South and in the four counties around the city of New York). In New England—with the exception of Rhode Island, home of separatist Baptists—the Puritans had their own world. Their Congregational church was established by law, and they intended to maintain their religious purity. They knew that their colonies formed a specially privileged enclave within the empire, in contrast with the position of their Dissenting coreligionists in England. After 1763 the Bishop of London led a campaign to elevate Anglicanism in power and standing within the colonies. Thus, religious issues hammered out harsh political lines within all of the colonies just as the revolutionary troubles were beginning. American politics in the late colonial period were, in the profoundest sense, transatlantic. Within the larger framework of the British political community, most colonists instinctively leaned Whig.[5]

In the eighteenth century, the colonies expanded rapidly in population and trade and assumed an ever more important role in Britain's wars against the French. Thus, as the century passed its midpoint, the mother country and its colonies intermingled more than ever before. Books, ideas, customs and values, men and women, trading vessels, newspapers, court decisions, troop ships, ways of governing and living—these and many other influences flowed back and forth across the Atlantic in mounting volume.

Many colonials, especially those who lived along the seaboard and were largely English and Anglican in origin and culture, warmly encouraged this heightened interchange. Almost universally they admired things English, and their influence produced an increasing Anglicization of colonial life, making it ever more like traditional England and less distinctively American. To them, the United Kingdom's institutions, especially its parliamentary system and the liberties won in the Glorious Revolution, were sacred. Anglophiles in the colonies gloried in being members of the powerful and resplendent British empire. They held in awe Britain's aristocracy, its brilliant

naval officers, and its pomp and ceremony. Southern planters modeled themselves after an idealized image of the English country
gentleman, and the colonial upper classes aped London fashions.
Colonial judges began wearing British scarlet robes; Anglican circles
of power and influence clustered around the royal governments; and
Church of England membership in the colonies surged dramatically.
A major feature of this wide movement toward Anglicization was the
tendency of leading American politicians to form close relationships
with prominent political leaders in London.[6]

On the other hand, powerful social changes in the colonies exerted
a strong push away from Anglicization. Some 250,000 Scotch-Irish
arrived in the colonies in the eighteenth century. They settled vast
regions of countryside from parts of northern New England through
the Hudson Valley in New York and from western Pennsylvania to
the back-country South. As Presbyterians and ancient enemies of the
English, the Scotch-Irish were leaders in the anti-Anglican cause,
especially in the Middle Colonies of New York and Pennsylvania and
in Virginia. An equally huge influx of immigrants came from Germany, and though for many years the Germans generally shunned
politics and kept to themselves, they eventually formed an important
element in the anti-English coalition. At the same time, a quickening
sense of being distinctively "American," as opposed to being English,
captured the colonial mind. Americanization even showed itself
among the Dutch of New York and New Jersey. In religious practice,
they split between an American faction that adopted the speech and
values dominant in the colonies and another faction that kept ties
with the Dutch Reformed church in Holland, held to the language
of the home country, and fiercely resisted all innovations in worship.
When the rebellion against British rule broke out, the Coetus (Americanized) Dutch clergy became leading rebels, and the Conferentie
(traditional) leaders became Loyalists.[7]

The Great Awakening, a vast religious revival that began in the
1740s and swept through the colonies, pervaded all controversies.
New Light clerics, younger than their Old Light antagonists, rejected the established Old Light ways of preaching and experiencing
religion, which had become calm and rationalistic. The faith in reason that stemmed from the scientific discoveries of the seventeenth
century had taken the fire and passion from religious observance. In
response, New Light preachers among the Congregationalists, Presbyterians, and Baptists—the Dissenters, in English terms—turned
sternly on their countrymen. They preached a jeremiad that frightened sinners and convinced multitudes that America had fallen into

sinfully corrupt, luxurious, and irreligious ways. Since the first Puritan settlements, it had been taught in New England that America was the special hope of God, that here the pure and undefiled community of the truly religious would appear. But now, said New Light preachers, that blessed community, in which all were bound as one family under God to live simple lives of self-denial and virtue, was in mortal danger. There was too much wealth and too much change, too much pride in humanity and too little humility before God.[8]

Thus, an increasingly taut confrontation emerged between everything that was local and rooted in tradition and everything that was transatlantic, Anglicizing, cosmopolitan, and unstable. The colonials were a provincial people, and they regarded their style of living as not only good but of God. Especially outside the commercial seacoast towns, colonials resisted the changes that seemed to flow from remote centers of power and sophistication. London symbolized wicked sloth and immorality, and many feared its mounting influence in colonial life. Quiet, culturally stable villages and towns in places like rural New England found themselves steadily invaded by the chancy and affluent world of the transatlantic trading community. Modernizing economic trends endangered traditional community cohesiveness by enticing farmers to look out for themselves and to raise crops for distant markets instead of simply for their own needs and those of their villages. Commercial, profit-oriented values fragmented accustomed relationships. Most colonials preferred stability and regarded all change as evil. As Kenneth A. Lockridge observes, people desired "nothing so much as to be left alone to run their own affairs." The new economy, however, closed in on them. Population mounted rapidly in response to better income and health; in important regions in the northern colonies, land became more costly, heavily settled, and difficult to buy; and the future looked less palatable than the past. Thus, "much of rural America was made ripe for a very special kind of political mobilization by the social changes of the eighteenth century."[9]

When the Stamp Act crisis initiated the Revolutionary argument in 1765, the love-hate relationship between the colonies and Britain shifted its balance. An extravagant loyalism had flourished in the flush of victory that followed the end of the French and Indian War in 1763. Now bitter rejection and rebelliousness began to grow. An undercurrent of resentment toward the arrogance of the metropolitan English had always existed, and in the new atmosphere, complaints arose at that "species of haughtiness" with which they governed. "It was equally as much from her manners," Tom Paine was later to say, "as from her injustice that [Britain] lost her colonies." The metropolitan English always treated Americans, said George Mason of Virginia, in "the authoritative style of a master to a school-boy." They were so convinced of their superiority that Benjamin Franklin, while serving as Pennsylvania's agent in London, finally despaired of reconciliation. It was common in England to speak of "the American colonists as little more than a Set of Slaves at work for us." As the Whig statesman Edmund Burke observed in 1777, in explanation of London's policy toward the colonies, "I know and have long felt . . . the unwieldy haughtiness of a great ruling nation, habituated to command, pampered by enormous wealth, and confi-dent from a long course of prosperity and victory."[10] On both sides, the conflict was triggered and driven onward as much by inflamed feelings, induced by a long relationship of inferiority and superiority, as by any other motivation.

The transatlantic situation was filled with potentialities for political paranoia. The colonists were classically ready to believe that they were endangered by hidden conspiracies among the wealthy and powerful in England. They were remote from the centers of effective decision making and ignorant in any immediate sense of what was happening in the royal ministries in London. Within the empire as a whole, the colonists were in a minority position—and conscious of that fact—subject to forces, largely beyond their control, that seemed to be freely manipulated by the London government. Their ways of living were being changed by influences flowing from England, and time seemed to be running out. Possessed of a deep religious sensibil-ity, the colonists had recently, by means of the Great Awakening, been made to be critical of all government and to think that an apocalypse impended. A conflict between absolute good and abso-lute evil appeared to be in the offing, one in which the enemy was sinister, powerful, and sensual.[11]

"Evidence" supporting colonial fears was numerous and over-whelming. The Bishop of London's concerted drive to establish an Anglican bishop in the colonies, a personage who would outrank all colonial governors by his membership in the House of Lords, stirred up Dissenters' memories of religious oppression. They would be forced to fall on their knees in the streets, it was said, to worship his passing carriage. He would use his political power to crush their religious freedom, and all would have to submit to "that yoke of episcopal bondage, which so miserably galled the necks of our

Forefathers." Dissenters had always suspected Anglicanism of being too close to Roman Catholicism to be truly Protestant, and now rumors rushed about that Roman masses were being celebrated publicly in London and that popery was sweeping Britain. Thus, it appeared ever more desperately necessary to fight off the suspected Anglican plot against Dissenters' liberties and preserve America as the last stronghold of true Protestant faith. The factual reality of the situation was that the British government had no intention of setting off the uproar that would certainly erupt if it tried to install a bishop in the colonies. The colonists, however, persisted in their delusions.[12]

In the British Isles there were many who also suspected that the royal government was seeking to destroy liberty. Calling themselves the "True Whigs," they comprised a small community of radical Whigs who had little support among Englishmen generally but were firmly believed by the colonials. Radical Whiggery, it must be noted, was culturally located; that is, the True Whigs were primarily members of the British outgroups. "It is immensely significant," writes Caroline Robbins, "that [the home of True Whiggery and] the most fertile ideas in politics and in economics are to be found in eighteenth-century Ireland and Scotland."[13]* Within England itself, the radical critique came from the Dissenting religious sects. They demanded that the government be responsive to public opinion—a radical idea in aristocratic, eighteenth-century England—that its election be by means of an equitable franchise, and that it respect natural rights, among which was religious equality. Dissenters condemned concentrated power, insisting that the branches of government should be separated and balanced against each other, and they

*The origins of the term "Whig" are significant. It appeared after 1680 in English politics to refer to members of Parliament who protested Charles II's use of his prerogative powers. It was a shortened version of "Whiggamores," a term for Presbyterian guerrilla fighters in southwestern Scotland who were in rebellion against Stuart policies in that country. Therefore the name "Whig" implied a sanctimonious, puritanical, fanatical traitor and rebel and would always be linked to English Dissenters. "Tory," conversely, was contemptuously applied by Whigs to their political enemies. A "tory" was a particular type of Irish robber and outlaw. Its Catholic connotations were applied freely by Whigs to late seventeenth-century Tories, devout and rather High Church Anglicans whom the Whigs accused of being covertly in league with the Pope. Tories were noted for their praise of the king's prerogative (that is, his ruling within his own presumed powers without reference to law or Parliament) and their intense loyalty to the Church of England. It is revealing that to find terms hateful enough to throw at each other, English politicians had to turn to Scotland and Ireland, countries which in English eyes were uncivilized and backward. (David Ogg, *England in the Reign of Charles II* [Oxford, 1955], II, 608–613.)

argued for complete separation between church and state. In particular, they called for a system of secular, rather than church-dominated (i.e., Church of England), public schools, a proposal for which Dissenters had immense respect because of its potential for allowing the poor and exploited to rise. To protect the rights of minorities, True Whigs called for a federal system in the British Isles and within the empire at large. Scottish and Scotch-Irish Presbyterians and English Baptists and Congregationalists took these egalitarian ideas with them to the colonies during the great migrations of the eighteenth century. Scotland was a hotbed of liberal and radical political ideas, and, like the English Dissenting sects, the Scots maintained close intellectual contact with the American colonists.[14]

Put in its broadest terms, radical British Whigs believed in *republicanism*. They drew this ideology from a European tradition of political thought centuries old, and one much condemned. Republicanism was as abhorrent to its eighteenth-century enemies as communism to its antagonists in the twentieth century. To be a republican, in the eyes of most Europeans, was to be guilty of mad designs upon law and order, true religion, and morality. Monarchy was sanctioned by the ages as the true guarantor of stability and justice. Republicanism, as in the examples of republican Rome, Machiavelli's Florence, and Cromwell's England, was the symbol of instability, violation of property, and the tyranny of rule by demagogues—the condition into which republicanism was believed inevitably to decay.

The contrast in world views ran across the entire spectrum of thought. Monarchists insisted that the common people were selfish, greedy, jealous of wealth, and turbulent. The masses needed to be ruled by a strong and titled aristocracy essentially independent of their control and supported by the rich and well-born among the untitled. Sovereignty must be lodged in a single person who would symbolize the state and rule effectively. Republican thinkers in Britain refrained from actually demanding that the Crown be abolished, but nonetheless they insisted that the people were the true possessors of sovereignty. The fountain of social virtue, they were therefore the only true guarantors of social justice. For this reason, ultimate authority should be rooted in the community at large, and anyone holding power should be elected by the people and subject to popular opinion. The source of debauchery and self-indulgent luxury, republicans claimed, was the ruling aristocracies. Monarchists praised social hierarchy as divine, believed government properly to be an elaborate and awesome mystery entrusted to those in higher station, and stressed the need for centralized power. Republicans advocated social equality (though not "leveling"); simple and austere government by virtuous persons drawn from society at large; and separated, rather than concentrated, constitutional authority. To the monarchists' insistence that the state was divine and that government should not only support the true faith but foster morality and piety, republicans answered that government was properly a secular institution and that church and state should be kept separate. Republicans insisted that no single religious body should be specially privileged.

The radical British Whigs were fascinated by power. It seemed to them an utterly ravenous force, growing outward in every direction (as was cultural Anglicization itself). Liberty seemed to be its natural prey. Robert Walpole, prime minister from 1721 to 1742, had argued that the executive power had to grow in order to meet effectively England's mounting needs, but for radical Whigs this was a monstrous doctrine, an excuse for tyranny. Among Whigs generally (most of whom rejected republicanism and had little to do with the radicals) it was a cardinal item of faith that English liberties would be safe only if the strong and preeminent Parliament they had established in the Glorious Revolution of 1688 were preserved. In this sense, Whiggery seemed to flow into the republicanism of its radical wing and was therefore constantly subject to the charge of disloyalty to the Crown—a charge that even the radical Whigs recoiled from in alarm. One king beheaded, a century before, was quite enough. They had no wish, in addition to their other problems, to be charged with regicide.

The True Whig persuasion looked upon Britain not as a separate entity, but as part of the broad arena of European civilization. In these wider precincts, running eastward to the Polish and Russian plains, radical Whigs saw tyranny triumphant everywhere. Britain, in their eyes, stood as a beacon of endangered liberty, as an enclave of political and religious freedom whose security needed constant protection from internal as well as external enemies. Every indication of enhanced royal power in Whitehall—the offices of the royal ministries—sent shock waves through the radical Whig consciousness. An alarming trend set in after 1760, with George III's accession to the throne. A monarch who wished actively to rule instead of simply to reign, he and his ministry built a "King's Party" in Parliament. In part, they accomplished this by using bribes—"golden pills" —to get favorable votes in Commons and by appointing members of Parliament to meaningless but lucrative royal offices. Here was proof to radical Whigs, and even to more moderate Whigs such as the followers of Edmund Burke, that a Tory plot to gain centralized power was destroying the balanced constitution. Corruption was the means by which would-be tyrants were eroding England's hard won liberties.

For years this argument in London, often shrill and sometimes hysterical, was waged in British pamphlets and newspapers for all the colonies to read. Sensation and scandal filled the transatlantic political world. Week after week, year after year, radical Whigs insisted that the sufferings of British society could be linked to a Tory network of wealthy landowners, the Crown, the Church, the Bank of England, and unscrupulous entrepreneurs who secured government favors in return for graft. Strong government, True Whigs said, was always and everywhere the tool of the wealthy and powerful. Its very existence helped unprincipled men exploit the community at large. The British government and upper classes were terrified that such criticisms might lead to social revolution, and they harassed critics, employed spies to search out enemies, and closed down newspapers. In the most spectacular case, they pressed prosecution of John Wilkes, a favorite of London's masses, who was repeatedly elected to the Commons—and as repeatedly expelled.[15]

Colonials widely believed the charges made against the British government by radical Whigs. Thousands of them were, in any event, predisposed by their outgroup status in the empire to believe the worst of the English and their government. Then, during the decade of mounting frictions from 1765 to 1775, they found alarming "proofs" springing up on their own side of the Atlantic that the conspiracy against liberty was spreading to America. The Stamp Act of 1765 had been interpreted as an inescapable signal of the ministry's intentions. Spawned in London, it was enforced by royal officials in the colonies, some of them native-born people who appeared to place England's needs before those of their own countrymen.

Then came a sudden increase in the number of royally appointed posts in the colonial governments, bringing in strangers from Britain to govern and to earn their salaries by strict enforcement of the navigation laws. The Crown ruled that the colonial judiciary could only hold their posts at royal pleasure, a decree with threatening implications. Vice-admiralty courts, under no colonial control, were assigned much wider jurisdiction over colonial trade. In October 1768 two regiments of royal infantry disembarked in Boston to strengthen the authority of royal officials struggling to enforce the new system. A standing army, bold, stark, and actual, evoking all the legendary fears that Whigs had long kept alive about such royal instruments of oppression, was now resident in one of the colonies' chief cities. The subsequent Boston "massacre" confirmed these fears.

In this setting, the republican ideology of the radical British Whigs was widely taken up and echoed in the American colonies. With Tom Paine leading the way, patriots began insisting that America was itself essentially republican. Samuel Adams of Massachusetts spoke from the heart of the puritanical Yankee tradition as well when he condemned the spreading evils of luxury, profanity, and impiety. America, he said, must separate from Britain or lose its soul. Once separated, traditional virtues could be regenerated, and a Christian Sparta built in the New World. New Light clergy were electrified by the controversy with Britain. Now they preached not only of debauchery but also of the similarity between America and Israel as the "covenant people of God." Americans, they said, would be betraying their divine destiny if they bowed to the preachings of Anglican priests who, especially in the Northern colonies, insisted that the colonists' duty was to obey constituted authority, to obey their king's orders. Congregational and Presbyterian ministers insisted that colonists must battle for their liberties.[16]

For Dissenters in the North and South, the Revolution was their political awakening. Presbyterians and Baptists who had flooded the Pennsylvanian and Southern back country now pushed forward to take major roles in the politics of their colonies. In New York, and even in New England where non-Congregationalist Dissenters were few, the same process occurred. No longer outgroups, for their cause of religious freedom and equality was now that of the colonies themselves, Dissenters entered the mainstream of national life. If the Revolution were won, the special legal status of the Anglican church and the political power of its members would be swept away. In many colonies, Baptists and Presbyterians, joined in the late eighteenth century by the rapidly growing Methodist community, became dominant once independence was secured.[17] This in turn meant that the internal government of the states was no longer an exclusive prerogative of the English ethnic community. The Scotch-Irish, the Germans, and the rural Dutch could now participate fully in a politics that was multiethnic and multifaith. So, too, could the politically awakening artisans, merchant seamen, and laborers of the seaport cities. During the Revolution, they dramatically emerged from passivity to take a prominent role in an American society that was becoming ever more democratic.[18]

The Revolution, then, was a continental awakening of national consciousness that drew on every human motivation. During its course, those who were rebels—as opposed to those who became Loyalists—came fully to a realization of themselves as a separate people in the world. They were uniquely blessed, they believed, by an inheritance of liberty that London was now seeking to take away. Their sacred mission was like that of the Puritan founders before them, whose dream was reborn among Americans during the Revolutionary crisis. They must demonstrate to the world a plan for human government and society that, by its example, could lead humanity toward freedom and dignity.

These feelings erupted in a new political context in which masses of ordinary people were ready for mobilization in a great cause. Traditional outgroups' ancient ethnic feelings of bitterness and resentment toward the dominant English were kept alive by the haughty, superior attitudes that Englishmen displayed toward those whom they thought inferior, be they Scotch-Irish, Germans, or simply colonial Americans of generalized British descent. Fed by deep historical memories, these hostilities were sharpened by religious animosities. Anglicans, Congregationalists, Presbyterians, Quakers, and Baptists confronted each other, as did the Conferentie and Coetus Dutch and the Lutheran and pietistic Germans, in a constant adversary relationship, each struggling to either absorb or hold off the others.

Profound social changes in the colonies led to a pervasive sense of alarm and a consequent readiness for fundamental reform. The transatlantic relationship had come to seem in many ways burdensome. It involved an ever tightening framework of economic constraints; it threatened traditional values of honesty and virtue; and it posed a standing danger to political liberties. An ideological conflict swelled, intensified by political paranoia on both sides. Within the colonies, a sharply ambivalent political culture, growing in divergent directions, contained ever higher levels of tension. Anglicization, urged by those who admired English life and wished to re-create its institutions in the colonies, warred with Americanization. Cosmopolitan, modernizing influences set off waves of social anxiety in regions seeking to hold onto lifestyles that were folkish, localized, and traditional. Stability and homogeneous life patterns were giving way to flux, instability, and novelty.

All of this was set within a transatlantic political culture with its common stock of categories, names, and world views. Within that universe of discourse, a group of radical British Whigs speaking from the perspective of the outgroups in the British Isles—the Scots, the Irish, and the English Dissenters—set the terms of ideological battle. They attacked what they conceived to be a Tory and Anglican conspiracy that thirsted for dictatorial power, and the colonials, listening to them, described their argument with London in similar language. The colonials came to think of themselves as the inheritors and protectors of a divinely inspired republican order. Austere and libertarian, born of that sainted Whig achievement, the Glorious Revolution of 1688, this order seemed to them in mortal danger. Its salvation became, in colonial eyes, a world mission. So inspired, in July 1776 the colonies' duly chosen representatives, assembled in congress, proclaimed their belief that all men were created equal and that life, liberty, and the pursuit of happiness were the proper objects of government. Declaring the United States of America independent of the British Crown, they mutually pledged in its cause "our Lives, our Fortunes and our sacred Honor."

II

Revolutionary Politics in the States

In the traditional historical narrative of the Revolution, a single entity, the American colonies, stands in unified protest against the British. We now have access to a new and more intriguing picture. Historical studies that have concentrated upon particular states—one of the most fruitful new approaches of recent years—reveal that each state experienced the Revolution differently, that there were, in fact, several revolutions going on simultaneously. Another fact, one long understood by practicing politicians but ignored by historians, is now, by this process, becoming clear: for most Americans politics is essentially a local experience. It is crucial to realize how much of American political activity, through most of the nation's history, has had its focus within the states. For many years in the early nineteenth century, Washington, D.C., practically disappeared from view, so tiny was it as a capital, so few were its powers, and so irrelevant was it to the daily lives of American citizens.

"Virginia," said Thomas Jefferson, "is my country." This primary sense of identification with one's state persisted well into the twentieth century. The original thirteen states had existed separately and largely independently for many generations before a national government was formed. After the Revolution, the American people looked to their state governments to oversee everything in which, as citizens, they were most immediately concerned, just as earlier they had looked to their colonial governments. State governments vigorously intervened in economic matters by regulating, guiding, and stimulating business, farming, industry, and transportation. They also conceived of themselves as responsible for the moral health of the community, as in colonial times. This meant a deep and continuing involvement in, and endless controversy over, cultural issues. Local and state governments controlled schooling, a social function with profound cultural implications and one constantly discussed and debated. In addition, they governed Sabbath activities, styles of dress, forms of recreation, sexual relations, and the use of alcohol. The Constitution prohibited only the federal government from having ties with a church. In several New England states, the Congregational church continued to be established by law; it was the official religious body supported and recognized by the state well into the nineteenth century.

The states provide us, therefore, scenes of great and intriguing interest. Their inner lives are complex; their public controversies are sharp and sustained; and the outcomes of their internal struggles frequently decide the course of national events. In studying states' histories, concrete details replace abstractions; general patterns become real and tangible because they can be observed in their actual settings. During crisis periods, national questions obsess the country, and Americans watch affairs in Washington closely. But when those periods subside, the public consciousness concentrates again on local horizons, local issues, and local control.

Narrowing our focus from the nation to the states allows the cultural dimension of politics to take its proper role in our understanding of American life. In Washington, for constitutional reasons, the questions at issue have been primarily economic and diplomatic, though for long periods essentially cultural questions such as race relations have also dominated affairs. However, cultural political warfare is battled out primarily at the local level, where the sense of community has been strongest and governments have traditionally struggled to maintain a moral consensus in ways of living. We learn, as well, the meaning of the truism that the different parts of the nation live in different ways. The speech, life-styles, and historical memories of different regions contrast sharply with one another, often exciting a mutual dislike and derision that survive even in the twentieth century. Much of American history must be understood as a conflict not only between groups whose ethnicity springs directly from abroad but between home-grown ethnic groups as well. Being a white Southerner in the United States has been as much an ethnic identity as being a Scot in the United Kingdom, though the Southerner's historical memory cannot run so far into the past. So, too, through most of American history New England Yankees have carried with them a cultural identity strongly marked, persistent, and polarizing in politics.

During the Revolutionary years, the shape of subsequent national politics emerged within the several states. Four states will concern us here: Massachusetts and Virginia, which led the way in the Revolution and became leaders of the Northern and Southern blocs that later appeared within the nation, and New York and Pennsylvania, the largest of the Middle States. Although they were internally confused and ambivalent because of their strikingly mixed ethnic and cultural nature, New York and Pennsylvania eventually came to provide the central core around which the new nation formed itself. Indeed, precisely because they were so culturally pluralistic—a confusion of tongues, religions, and peoples—within these two states we will see emerging, for the first time, essentially modern, mass-based two party systems.

Massachusetts was a special world. It was one of those political communities so intensely concentrated, homogeneous, and self-conscious in culture that its influence reaches far beyond its borders. The fighting between British troops and American patriots began, it must be emphasized, in Massachusetts and not elsewhere. London was right: Boston was the most "insolent" city, the seat of the most radical troublemakers. Republicanism flourished mightily there, for New England Congregationalists were in close touch with their coreligionists in England, among whom republicanism and radical political ideals were common currency. Around Congregationalist chapels in England, whose self-governing congregations hired and fired their own ministers, there had always clung an aura of popular democracy. That the Congregationalists in both Old and New England held respectful memories of Oliver Cromwell tied them, in Anglican eyes, to tendencies toward anarchism and irreverence for proper authority.

The republicanism of the New Englanders had a distinctive quality. Their task, they believed, was a divine one: the creation of a uniquely holy order, in covenant with God, that would provide a model for all of humankind. Thus, New England republicanism was moralistic and pious. The ethical health of the whole community was of supremely important concern. Radical New Englanders condemned not only the English system of government but impiety, luxury, profit-oriented individualism, and all the other corruptions that they felt were pouring in from profligate, monarchical, and Anglican England. For them, the Revolution was to be a moral purge, readying America for its world mission of serving as a shining example to all nations.[1]

Massachusetts' remarkably homogeneous culture was revealed in the membership of its legislature, the General Court. More than four out of five members were both English descended and Massachusetts born. One hundred and three Congregationalists sat in that body from 1784 to 1788; the next largest group consisted of seven Presbyterians. Anglicanism had a strong constitutional position, for Massachusetts was a royal colony, and Anglicans dominated the ruling circles around the royal governor. Nevertheless, they formed a small, almost foreign element that swiftly lost influence once the Revolution began.[2]

In the 1760s, when the Stamp Act controversy opened the quarrel with Britain, Massachusetts was still a relatively stable society, though there were signs of significant change. Traditionally, its ways of life had been centered in the village, a fact that distinguished New England from most colonies to the south. To the extent that the communally organized village with its anti-individualistic mood still survived, New England was less modern than other colonies. Closely gathered around their Congregational churches, the Yankee villagers were almost unchanged in their ways of daily living from their counterparts in the English Middle Ages. Their social ideal, widely observed, was that ordinary folk should be soberly deferential to those of higher social rank. When town leaders explained their actions before town meetings, the citizens listened thoughtfully and then "concurred unanimously." Such a historical picture should not be overemphasized, of course, for unanimity has existed in no human society, and New England's villages had their tensions. Nevertheless, New Englanders prized unanimity as their governing ideal, a reflection of their belief that all decisions are founded in God's wishes and that right is clearly distinct from wrong.

On the other hand, the common people in New England participated in politics far more than the people in New York and the colonies southward. Boston in particular was vigorously democratic. There was open debate on every topic, secret ballots, election of public officials by popular vote, and referendum voting on many issues. Furthermore, the prized consensual community was in fact breaking down in the Puritan world. Modernization had long been reshaping ways of living in Boston and other seaboard towns. Individualism in all things, involvement in the transatlantic trading community, and a secularization of daily life were the dominant trends. In the mid-eighteenth century, these influences reached into dozens of interior towns, which together formed a transitional zone, whipsawed between modernism and tradition. Attracted by the profits of growth and change, these towns yet looked back in dismay at the fading traditions of the past. Diversity and pluralism were creeping in, replacing stability and homogeneity of faith and behavior. Influences from abroad grew stronger than local autonomy. Farming was becoming commercialized, unemployment and poverty were now noticeable, and religious sectarianism divided churches and towns that previously were overwhelmingly Congregational.[3]

A crucial transformation from *Puritan* to *Yankee* was in fact underway. In the former cultural mode, which was dominant in New England until the middle decades of the eighteenth century, the stress was upon obedience to authority. Puritans distrusted democracy, and they viewed the public welfare and law and order as superior to individualism. All self-seeking passions, in particular avarice and greed, with their associated tastes for luxury and wealth, were subject to strenuous efforts at social control and discipline. By the mid-1700s, however, a growing passion for liberty, a mounting readiness to demand that rulers serve their subjects well or be replaced, and a far more unrestrained search for wealth and individual advancement were shifting the balance in New England's social order. The "Yankee" was appearing. The result was that public life became turbulent, partisan, and uncomfortable for those in authority. "Puritan resistance characteristically turned inward and produced guilt," observes Richard L. Bushman. "Yankee resistance more often turned outward and produced conflict. . . . The Yankee claimed more liberty for himself and allowed less power to authority, reacting violently and quickly to the least oppression." Where the avid pursuit of gain had formerly been condemned, it was now becoming acceptable. Self-interest was even being given an honorable place in social values. Nevertheless, Yankees remained God-centered people. They never lost their awareness of the larger society and its prior claims upon individuals. Those in other sections of the country could well recognize New Englanders as a special people. "Each of these traits —a defensive independence, cupidity tempered by regard for the public good, and yearning for the divine underlying hardheaded rationalism—was securely embedded in the cultural genes of the generation alive in 1765."[4]

It was in the interior towns, where this transition was being felt most sharply, that the Revolution was most passionately fostered. Here was the heartland of that group of legislators in the General Court of Massachusetts who were called the Country party. Their rivals, generally termed the Court party, were a body of legislators who came from the seaboard towns clustered around Boston (itself so large and varied that it supported both sides). The two groups did not comprise the leadership of organized mass parties in the electorate at large. This stage of political development was not to be reached in America for many years to come. Rather, they were parties or factions within the legislature that drew their names from Britain, where the Court faction in Parliament supported the royal government and the Country tradition opposed it. Around 1700 Country party members in Massachusetts began to call their antagonists "Tories," thus appropriating more of the political imagery used in England.

The Country party spoke for the farmers of the province, who had long insisted that they were being exploited by the merchants and bankers in Boston, with their Bank of England ties. Indeed, rural radicals cursed merchants for all the sufferings of the colony:

> [They] imported luxuries to seduce the people . . . [and] hoarded specie [gold coin], driving commodity prices down and interest rates up. And while the farmer made little headway in his own quest for abundance, the merchant waxed strong, his warehouses full, his coffers bulging, and his family enjoying all the fruits of plentiful prosperity.[5]

As spokesmen for the Crown, for the empire, and for the needs of transatlantic traders, the Court party represented to their enemies everything that was foreign and cosmopolitan—everything, in effect, that was pushing Massachusetts in modernizing directions. That they leaned toward the Anglican church and were Anglicized in their styles of life made them even more distrusted. Country party men, who attacked the British connection, were by contrast traditionalists. The people for whom they spoke were intensely localist, the more so the farther inland from the Atlantic. Samuel Adams, their leader, was convinced that the righteous and cohesive community of the Puritan past, as he idealized it, could be revived. In his rustic, patched clothes a symbol of simple republicanism, and with his voice constantly raised against British tyranny and corruption, Adams was a charismatic figure revered by multitudes and hated by Loyalists.

At first Adams worked with those Boston merchants, growing in number, who were being driven to distraction and bankruptcy by the recent British practice of dumping large quantities of goods directly on the colonial market rather than selling them through local mercantile houses. Such businessmen wanted to wrest control of the American economy from the British. By the early 1700s, however, Adams decided that these men could not be relied on to be true republicans. He turned, therefore, to the yeoman farmers of the small towns and villages scattered widely in the Massachusetts interior. In so doing, he awakened a force hitherto relatively dormant in the controversy. Rural democrats were more radically democratic, more violent, and more inclined to use vigilante methods than were their city counterparts. They often forced Loyalists and royal officials to flee to the coast. Thus aroused to a new sense of their importance, Massachusetts' rural people, who comprised most of the colony's population, threw themselves enthusiastically into the Revolutionary cause. Its ultimate objective, to them, was to seize power from the wealthy and the profligate and return it to the people.[6]

The "single most commonly used word" in the rhetoric that erupted from the countryside, Richard L. Bushman observes, was "slavery."[7] If British troops were to be "free to roam the countryside and dominate the cities, if every Parliamentary statute and tax could be enforced and American rights violated at will," then the yeomanry would be driven into bankruptcy, would lose their farms and their independence, and be forced, in effect, into involuntary servitude to the remote powers in London. The readiness of country folk to spring into immediate action in order to defend themselves from this fate was demonstrated with dramatic force in the fall of 1774. At this time a spreading rumor that an armed conflict had occurred with British soldiers in Charlestown propelled the country folk out of their long spell of passivity into a kind of mass furor. An eyewitness reported that he had never seen "such a Scene before—all along were armed Men rushing forward some on foot some on horseback, at every house Women and Children making Cartridges, running Bullets, making Wallets, baking Biscuit, crying and bemoaning and at the same time animating their Husbands and Sons to fight for their Liberties, tho' not knowing whether they should ever see them again."

This excited sensibility rested upon a vivid realization, kept alive by continuing troubles with London over many generations, that the people of New England lived in a special condition of economic as well as religious freedom from oppression, a condition exposing them to special dangers against which great vigilance had to be maintained. They had founded their colony explicitly to escape the power of lordship as exercised in England by manor lords and Anglican bishops. Again and again from Puritan pulpits and in the peculiarly democratic politics of New England the threatening image of a corrupt, power-hungry establishment in England was held out for execration. Not only did this establishment espouse the cause of false religion and crush Dissent wherever possible, it hungered as well to reassert over the free yeomanry of Yankeedom the same direct control and economic exploitation that great landowners exercised over English and Irish tenants. At the colony's very outset, the Massachusetts government had moved to exclude manor lordships by refusing to collect quit-rents and forbidding all feudal exactions.

Thus, New England villages were distinctive in the Anglo-American community not only for their Dissenting faith and local self-government, but for the complete absence of lordship and the universality of free-holding farmers who held title to the land they tilled. New Englanders well knew the precarious nature of their position; events rarely let them forget their special status in an empire governed by a powerful land-holding nobility in England. Three-quarters of the land in England was owned by landlords; two-thirds was so held in Ireland, where the sufferings of the tenant peasantry were notorious.

"It is true," said John Adams, "that the people of this country in general, and of this province in special, have a hereditary apprehension of and aversion to lordships, temporal and spiritual. . . . there are few of the present generation who have not been warned of the danger of them by their fathers or grandfathers." Furthermore, New Englanders were convinced that the extortion of tax revenues by London would soon bring into the colonies the superstructure of oppression and corruption that in England had been built upon the principle of lordship. Sam Adams described it pungently:

> standing armies and ships of war; episcopates and their numerous ecclesiastical retinue; pensioners, placemen, and other jobbers, for an abandon'd and shameless ministry; hirelings, pimps, parasites, panders, prostitutes and whores.

This "Engine of Oppression" meant impoverishment for the ordinary farmer; it meant turning the social order back to the cruel, oppressive, and degrading life that common Englishmen had lived in the past and in many cases still lived. Great lords would rule the countryside, and independent farmers would become tenants and

laborers paying "rack rents [to] ... haughty and relentless landlords
who will ride at ease, while we are trodden in the dirt."

Much is known of the mood within the villages of New England,
but considerably less about that in the Middle Colonies and the
South. It appears likely, however, that this intensely localistic temper, certain to be aroused to anger by London's efforts to reach
inland in order to extort taxes and impose a way of life conforming
to the English model, extended throughout the colonies in areas
similar to back country Massachusetts. Jackson Turner Main has
searched out the social background of some 1500 legislators who sat
in the state legislatures in the 1780s and has discovered broad unifor-
mities among them. Those whom he has identified, by their voting
records on key issues, as of predominantly localist views tended to
come from a wide band of territory generally lying twenty to thirty
miles inland from navigable waters. These were areas lacking ready
access to markets, relatively non-commercial in character, and recently settled. Sparsely populated, the home country of the localists
held few distinguished families. Instead, ordinary farmers who were
markedly democratic in their attitudes predominated. With few if
any slaves or servants and living far from urban centers, they had
little leisure or surplus wealth. Until the Revolution, they also had
little political influence upon the affairs of their colonies. In New
England the localist interior held Puritan villages; in the Middle
Colonies and southward into Virginia and the Carolinas, it held
Dutch Calvinist farmers, Germans of varying faiths, and Scotch-Irish
Presbyterians. Looking forward to the 1790s, Main has found that in
that decade, when the two national parties were forming, the localist
legislators of the 1780s flocked to the banner of Thomas Jefferson and
his Republican party, the precursors of the modern Democratic
party.

Against the localism of this broad region was poised the cosmopolitanism of a narrow strip along the Atlantic coastline and inland along the several major rivers (as far as ocean-going vessels
could navigate). The state legislators of the 1780s who came from this
region were generally urbane, well-educated and well-traveled men
who held wide perspectives upon public affairs. Their home districts
were well populated, Anglicized in culture, and predominantly English descended. Here were the colonial cities, the centers of the
political power, aristocratic supremacy, and an orientation to over-
seas trade. Here, too, were the colonies' capital resources and such
cultural life as existed in the forms of newspapers, colleges, and
journals. In the South, cosmopolitan legislators came from the Tide-

water, with its great plantations tied directly to English merchant houses and fashions. In the later national politics of the 1790s, those who had been state legislators of markedly cosmopolitan views and style of life in the 1780s (except for the Southerners among them) turned overwhelmingly to support Alexander Hamilton and the Federalist party. During the Revolution, as we shall see, there were few in the South, even among those of cosmopolitan outlook, who were not rebels. In the Middle Colonies and New England, however, reluctance to separate from England and outright Loyalism were strongest in the cosmopolitan band of territory. Anglicans lined up strongly on the cosmopolitan side, as did the Quakers of Pennsylvania, a people much battered by charges of Toryism because of their pacifism and neutrality during the war.[8]

In Massachusetts, Thomas Hutchinson was a classic example of the cosmopolitan, Anglicized politician. Native to the province and from an honored family, by 1763 he had become leader of the Court party. As lieutenant governor (appointed royal governor in 1771), chief justice, and president of the Council—all at the same time—he symbolized to his republican enemies the very concentration of authority that they believed was destroying the British and colonial constitutions. Hutchinson steadfastly resisted all proposals to inflate the currency, a plan called for by farmers to raise prices. In 1748 he had achieved a brilliant deflationary stroke by linking the province's paper money to coinage sent by London as repayment for Massachusetts' expenses in a war against French Canada. In his view, the economic health of the province depended on a close alliance between business and government.

Tory to the bone, Thomas Hutchinson was more loyal to the Crown and to England, both of which he idealized, than were the English themselves. At the same time, he loved Massachusetts and labored to serve the province well. He believed that only within English protection and inspired by the English example could Massachusetts find safety and achieve healthy growth. Cool in his religious affections, he remained formally a Congregationalist but was a close friend of the Anglicans, whose church he frequently attended. He found the zealous Puritans distasteful.

Hutchinson was appalled at the anti-British and republican ideology of his Country party antagonists. He threw himself into a long and unsuccessful effort to frustrate their activities and strengthen Britain's supremacy over the colonies. He was a nationalist, too, but his nationalism was *Anglo*-American: he identified with the larger political community, the encompassing British empire.

For his pains as Stamp Act commissioner, the common people of Boston broke into his mansion and utterly destroyed it.

Indeed, Hutchinson and his circle of wealthy entrepreneurs had long been hated by Boston's artisans and workmen. They insisted that Hutchinson's investor-oriented policies had caused the alarming rise in poverty and social privation that the city was experiencing. A strongly radical culture swiftly took form among the urban workers of Massachusetts. Though fewer in number than the farmers, this group became an ever more important element in the republican Revolutionary coalition. In 1774 Hutchinson's enemies became too much for him, and he fled the province, spending the rest of his years in England. At his death in 1780, he was still grieving that the people of New England had been corrupted and led to disloyalty by malignant demagogues.[9]

Virginia and Massachusetts differed profoundly. Virginia, the Old Dominion, was large, diffuse in settlement, and after Bacon's Rebellion of 1676 a relatively quiet colony free of the recurrent quarrels that kept Massachusetts' politics turbulent. New England had sought to embody a transcendent religious ideal, but few goals attended the founding and development of Virginia and the Southern colonies save the getting of money and individual advancement. In this secular and materialistic setting, the Church of England was by law established. Nonattendance at its services could result in fine and imprisonment as late as Revolutionary times. Furthermore, the gentry-dominated vestries, which governed the Church in a strange quasi-Congregationalist arrangement that largely ignored the distant Bishop of London, also dominated local government. However, the Church's priests had little social status, often being emigrant Scotsmen and Irishmen. Consequently, they had little influence on their parishioners. Beginning in 1730 Scotch-Irish Presbyterians and German Lutherans moved down into the Virginia back country from Pennsylvania, and the authorities allowed them to take over the vestries in that region and worship undisturbed.[10]

A proud and prickly individualism suffused the culture of white Virginia. Because they owned their own land, the yeoman farmers, small planters, and great plantation owners prided themselves on their sturdy self-sufficiency. That they were armed, and made regular use of their weapons, was central to their sense of independent manhood. A vast rural scatteredness lay over a colony that, since 1700, had seen a huge influx of black slaves and the rise of baronial mansions in the Tidewater. Out of this situation, as Edmund S. Morgan has observed, grew what has always seemed paradoxical in the slave-owning South: a deep commitment to ideals of equality, freedom, and republicanism. By the 1730s a white laboring class had practically disappeared. This, together with the fact that almost all planters, large and small, raised the same crop—tobacco—and had the same economic interests to protect, created a unity within the white community that continually surprised European visitors. Relations between large and small planters were open and relaxed. They were all white men, made conscious of this shared identity by the constant presence of black slaves, and they were all of the master, rather than the laboring, class. It must be observed that despite the relatively easy relations existing among white men, class consciousness was nonetheless strong in Virginia. The colony was an elitist community in which the proud aristocracy monopolized government. However, the aristocrats won office by direct appeal to the votes of the small planters, who seem to have acquiesced willingly to the leadership of men with whom they shared so much.

In mid-eighteenth-century Virginia, republican ideals were ardently held and widely popular among both the aristocracy and the small-planter class. They closely read and often quoted the writings of radical British Whigs. Thomas Jefferson was not alone in paying careful attention, as well, to French rationalism, anticlericalism, and libertarian philosophy. Republicanism praised farmers as the source of social virtue and political independence, venerating them as the chief protectors of society against tyrants. These concepts struck a deep chord within Virginians. Theirs was not a colony of cities, and they were proud of this fact. They were contemptuous of the ignorant working poor of Anglo-American cities, and they bitterly resented the power of city merchants and bankers in England over their fortunes as planters.[11]

In a bold conjecture, Professor Morgan has suggested that perhaps the existence of slavery itself was the strongest source of Virginia's republicanism.

> The presence of men and women who were, in law at least, almost totally subject to the will of other men gave to those in control of them an immediate experience of what it could mean to be at the mercy of a tyrant. Virginians may have had a special appreciation of the freedom dear to republicans, because they saw every day what life without it could be like.

Furthermore, in Virginia there was no white working class likely to be made rebellious and troublesome by the widespread advocacy of republican ideals. "There it was. Aristocrats could more safely preach equality in a slave society than in a free one. Slaves did not become leveling mobs." In a freemasonry of whites, none of whom had any *local* revolutions in mind, republicanism could be safely advocated.[12]

Virginia's royal government was seated in Williamsburg, with its Anglican College of William and Mary. The aristocracy was so extensively intermarried that when the House of Burgesses met with the governor it was like a family gathering. Another factor promoting unity of outlook was the overwhelmingly English descent of most Virginians. The Scotch-Irish Presbyterians and German Lutherans in the back country kept largely to themselves until the Revolutionary troubles began, so the homogeneous cultural atmosphere in Williamsburg's politics persisted.[13]

Virginia's planting world, however, was deeply troubled in the mid-eighteenth century. These proud men, in their wigs, carriages, and London fashions, living lavish and lordly lives seen elsewhere in the colonies only around Charleston, South Carolina, were in a grave economic predicament. As commercial farmers, their income came primarily from selling a single crop in a faraway market over which they had no control. The price of tobacco was dropping disastrously, and the planters' debts, intensified by their ways of living, were huge. Bankruptcies swept the colony. Even more than the Northern colonies, the South had no sovereignty over its economic system. The British controlled the currency, loan capital, and prices (primarily through Scottish agents for Glasgow trading firms who lived along the Tidewater's rivers). Planters considered themselves slaves of their creditors, an infuriating status for men who actually owned slaves. They nourished a deep anger toward distant traders and financiers whose grip they could not shake off.

In the Northern Neck, between the Potomac and Rappahannock rivers, was a region of especially large plantations, purchased out of the huge landholding of Lord Fairfax. Here progressive-minded planters such as the Washingtons tried to diversify their farming to reduce their reliance on tobacco, and to shake free from indebtedness by trading directly with England. There was even talk of creating a commercialized urban marketplace in the South, like Philadelphia in the Northern colonies, but little came of it. In the 1770s, when a severe slump in the English market dried up sources of credit, the situation seemed even more hopeless and protests grew more shrill. The great planters swung to the view that there must be a radical change in the imperial governing structure before they could control their economic welfare.[14]

Disturbing, too, was the rise of a second culture in Virginia that challenged the gentry's ways of living. The Great Awakening of the 1740s had reached deeply into Virginia, with profound results. Scotch-Irish Presbyterians were strongly affected. Their ministers began arriving in hitherto Anglican regions to preach a new style of religious observance: public readings of the Bible together, singing of hymns, and intense devotional exercises. Anglican priests and the vestry gentry protested strongly, for the idea that Virginians could forgo Anglican services and that an itinerant minister could preach to all and sundry ran directly counter both to the law and to the ideal of the unified community under gentry control. For a time in the 1750s it was even seriously proposed that the Toleration Act of 1689, which allowed English Dissenters to have separate chapels and freely exercise their own faith, did not apply in Virginia.

However, under the charismatic leadership of a remarkable man, the Presbyterian minister Samuel Davies, Dissent won its full legal rights in the colony and the respect of many within the gentry. Then, during the terrors of the French and Indian War (1756–1763), the courageous performance of the Scotch-Irish and their Presbyterian ministers on the frontier, where they were exposed to savage fighting, further enhanced their standing. "Let us," said Davies, "show ourselves worthy of protection and encouragement, by our conduct on this occasion." His powerful sermons attacking cowardice and calling upon Virginians to act the "honourable part, worthy of a man, a freeman, a Briton, and a Christian," were widely circulated in pamphlet form. After these events, Dissenters in Virginia were left quite alone by the authorities.[15]

The Baptists were in an important sense a more disturbing element in Virginia. Their style of belief and behavior was a standing reproof to the pride and the self-assertive violence of the gentry culture. In contrast with the planters, who placed great emphasis on lordly bearing and meeting others while mounted on lofty and elegant horses, and who flashed to arms and dueled to defend their honor, the Baptists preached plain dress, austere and gentle living, devout prayer, and humility. Whereas planters were stiff individualists, the Baptists were a communal people who called each other brother and sister and stressed good fellowship. The heart of Virginia's aristocratic culture could not have been more sharply called into question.[16]

The gentry responded partly with contempt and ridicule. The Baptists were not "manly," and manliness was prized above all else. Sometimes these feelings resulted in violent attacks on Baptist ministers. More common, however, was a tacit agreement with the austere new teaching, for there was a great fear among Virginians that the colony was falling ever more deeply into corruption. Many remarked on the growing violence and disorder of Virginia's daily scene. There was much harshness and brutality in everyday life induced by the presence of the slave system. Drunkenness was a common phenomenon, as were quarreling, slandering, wrestling, and savage fist fights. To many Virginians, there seemed to be a severe need for the orderliness and self-restraint called for by Baptist teaching.[17]

Worry over local conditions combined with a larger conviction that Virginia was being corrupted by its ties to England. Extravagance, so lavishly and ruinously displayed in the Tidewater mansions, was seen as destroying virtue and livelihood. The public and private literature of Virginia was filled with lamentations and outcries of self-criticism as biting and pervasive as that of New Englanders. To many, the colony seemed on the verge of ruin. None could forget the great scandal among the aristocracy that had erupted in 1766. In that year, it had been revealed that John Robinson, long the speaker and treasurer of the House of Burgesses, had over many years embezzled £100,000 from the Virginia treasury to assist 240 of his nearly bankrupt friends. This disclosure, which led to years of lawsuits and dishonor, shook the ruling class to its roots and lastingly injured its morale and prestige. The corruption of morals that all could read of in every newspaper coming from England seemed to have seeped fatally into Virginia as well.[18]

Then there was a growing hostility to the Church of England and its privileges. In the "Parson's Cause" affair of the 1750s, the Church of England had tried to force Virginians to provide tax funds for Anglican clergy stipends at traditional rates. (This followed an attempt by Virginians, which London had disallowed, to lower these stipends.) The affair occasioned a vituperative argument, extended litigation in which men like the Scotch-Irishman Patrick Henry became famous for anti-British utterances, and eventually an outburst from the Bishop of London, who called the Virginia legislature "treasonous." An anticlerical current, which had always existed in secularist Virginia, became strengthened after 1740 when many planters began to join Dissenting churches, and the "Parson's Cause" permanently estranged many from the Church. Such Virginians were ready, in the Revolutionary period, to give warm support to

New Englanders like John Adams who attacked Anglican pretensions and the threat of religious tyranny.[19]

The crisis with England, therefore, came at a time when Virginia
had sore doubts about itself and was already leaning toward some
fundamental changes in its relationship to the home country. When
the challenge to American rights came from London in 1765, it was
interpreted as an intolerable affront to Virginia's pride and manliness. Its leaders were "haughty and jealous of their liberties, impatient of restraints," wrote an observer in 1759. They were "scarcely
[able] ... to bear the thought of being controlled by any superior
power." If the metropolitan English had an inveterate habit of authority bred into them by generations of success and preeminence
as a ruling people, so too was authoritarianism bred into slave owners. For many years Virginians had governed their colony practically
without any direct interference, and they intended that this situation
continue. They believed that the House of Burgesses was a legislature equal in the empire to the British Parliament, under a common
king. In this stand, Virginia was distinguished by an almost universal
solidarity, leading to a remarkable harmony of purpose during the
Revolution. There were, indeed, few Loyalists or Tories in Virginia
during the Revolutionary crisis.[20]*

The Middle Colonies were a world apart from New England and
the South. Not only were they a mixture of peoples, tongues, and

---

*In his McLellan Lecture at Miami University, Ohio, Jack P. Greene confirmed the
picture of Virginia presented in the foregoing passages, summarizing its state of mind
just before the crisis in the following words:

In the early 1760s ... the Virginia political community ... faced the future with
an uncertain blend of anxiety and confidence. It was anxious over the unhealthy
state of the tobacco market, the pernicious effects of black slavery upon white
society, the disturbing crisis in moral behavior, and, more than at any time since
the very first decade of the century, the colony's constitutional security within an
empire whose leaders were showing disturbing signs of a growing disregard for the
political welfare of its peripheral members. But it was also confident in the basic
stability, responsiveness, effectiveness, and virtue of the Virginia political system
and in the colony's long-term future within an empire that enjoyed so great a
blessing, so great security to liberty and property, as the British constitution. Over
the next quarter of a century, this peculiar combination of anxiety and confidence
would in considerable measure shape the responses of the Virginia political community to a series of political challenges of a magnitude undreamed of in 1763.
("Society, Ideology, and Politics: An Analysis of the Political Culture of Mid-
Eighteenth-Century Virginia," in Jack P. Greene, Richard L. Bushman, and Michael Kammen, *Society, Freedom, and Conscience: The American Revolution in
Virginia, Massachusetts, and New York* [New York, 1976], pp. 75–76.)

faiths, but also, until the Stamp Act crisis, they had little to complain
of within the empire. As the wheat colonies whose grain was widely
sold in the West Indies and Europe, they prospered vigorously in the
mid-eighteenth century. Philadelphia was one of the largest cities in
the British empire, with some thirty thousand residents in the 1770s,
and New York City was swiftly expanding. The upper classes of the
two cities profited from their participation in the flourishing transatlantic trade. Pleasant estates dotted the Philadelphia countryside,
welcoming its merchants to weekend retreats, and, in New York, a
landholding English and Dutch aristocracy created a powerful patrician world. Many New Yorkers instinctively disliked the righteous,
preachy radicals of New England and blamed them for the whole
uproar. Indeed, those living south of New England found New Englanders aggressive and power hungry. It was widely said that if New
Englanders succeeded in wrenching the colonies loose from Britain,
they would then establish an imperialism of their own. Yankees
would sweep down to dominate the other colonies and impose Congregationalism and Puritan ways of living on the other colonies.

New York Colony's politics were tumultuous throughout its history, for within itself the province was divided between ethnic
groups, religious faiths, economic interests, and ways of life. The
Dutch were centered in the Albany region, but they also had a strong
foothold in New York City, where in the 1760s they constituted
one-third of the electorate. In the early years of the colony, the
Dutch voted massively against the English, their conquerors, but by
the Revolutionary period they were no longer unified. The culturally
conservative among them (Conferentie) sided with the Anglicans on
most issues, for both groups were loyal to the principle of hierarchy
and traditional authority across the Atlantic. The Americanized, localist Dutch (Coetus), however, remained anti-English. There were
also large settlements of New Englanders in the colony, who occupied most of Long Island and were prominent in the counties around
New York City. Together with the Scotch-Irish, who populated the
appropriately named Orange and Ulster counties on the west side of
the Hudson River, New Englanders made the Presbyterian church
the largest in the province. (Outside of New England, Congregationalists and Presbyterians were commonly lumped together under the
latter name.) New York City, meanwhile, contained a substantially
Anglican ruling circle intensely loyal to Britain. The headquarters of
the British army were located there, as were other official departments, and the steady coming and going of English merchants and
ships gave a strongly English cast to upper-class culture. The aristoc-

racy resisted all efforts at separation from England and swung over, almost in a body, to the Tory side during the Revolution.[21]

The Anglican church was established by law in the four counties in and around New York City, permanently polarizing the colony's politics in an Anglican-Dissenter rivalry. In the 1750s King's College (now Columbia University) was opened in New York City, controlled by the Anglicans but supported by general taxation. This set off a controversy that made Chief Justice James De Lancey the Church's political champion and a young Presbyterian, William Livingston, that of the opposition. In the province's Assembly (the lower house of the legislature), a campaign flared up to resist efforts at establishing an Anglican bishop in the colonies and to eliminate all links between church and state. William Livingston led this assault, forming a Society of Dissenters that linked Presbyterians, Baptists, and similar religious communities. Again and again their proposals were defeated by the Anglican-dominated Council, the legislature's upper house. By 1770 this attack against Anglicanism merged with the larger crusade against English colonial policies. When independence came, all reminders of Anglican establishment were swiftly eliminated. "The Episcopal Churches in New York," ran a report in 1776, "are all shut up, the prayer books burned, and the Ministers scattered abroad. . . . It is now the Puritan's high holiday season and they enjoy it with rapture."[22]

Religious differences, in short, were the main source of political friction in the New York Assembly and became, throughout the Revolutionary period, the crucial force in determining political loyalties.[23] "Presbyterianism is really at the Bottom of the whole conspiracy," wrote Admiral Lord Richard Howe's secretary, "and will never rest, till something is decided upon it." Those bigoted Calvinists, said John Hughes of Pennsylvania, were "ripe for open Rebellion, when they poisoned the Minds of the people enough." When Cadwallader Colden, New York Colony's lieutenant governor, looked at the enemies of British rule, he was convinced that he saw a Presbyterian plot. Besides William Livingston, his family, and their Scotch-Irish followers in the countryside, there were others like the brilliant lawyer John Morin Scott and the journalist Alexander McDougall. The latter was called the "American John Wilkes" because an Anglican-dominated Assembly had imprisoned him on the grounds of seditious libel for criticizing the Assembly in print, and because he led the New York Sons of Libery.[24]

An extraordinary closeness existed between Presbyterianism and the American nation now forming. It was the one intercolonially organized church: its synods (elected representative bodies) had formed a national union in 1758. Self-governing and federally organized, Presbyterianism was the form of Calvinism that was diffused most widely in American life. Congregationalism stayed in New England and in western sections settled by Yankees, but Presbyterianism spread from New York to South Carolina. Like the New England Puritans, Presbyterians rooted their theology in the stern beliefs of John Calvin, and they shared the Puritans' distaste for English-born corruptions. Culturally attuned to republicanism, Presbyterians insisted that sovereignty must come from the people. Their ethnic identity made Presbyterians anti-English, and their austere social values stressed self-reliance, hard-working individualism, and a strict legalism.

In the Presbyterian view, humankind had a contract (covenant) with God to live according to His law. Similarly, in worldly affairs, they stressed contractual rights and duties between rulers and the ruled, as did the Calvinist Puritans of New England. Led by Oliver Cromwell in the English Civil War of the previous century, English Presbyterians and Congregationalists had in fact overthrown and beheaded a king for religious and constitutional misrule. Thereafter, from 1649 to 1660, they had sought to govern England under a republican form of government, kingship having been dissolved in Cromwell's Commonwealth. In the Restoration of 1660, which had brought Charles II to the throne and reestablished Anglicanism, the Calvinists had seen the collapse of their hopes. Thereafter, they had become excluded Dissenters. Now, in the 1760s, it was commonly said that the Revolutionary crisis in the American colonies was, at bottom, a revived attempt by the Calvinists to win the victory that, ultimately, had eluded them before.

Not all Scottish people in the colonies were on the patriot side. Scottish merchants who controlled the tobacco trade and were hated by the planters became Tories in the Revolution. There were also pockets of Highland Scots (often Catholics or Anglicans) in North Carolina and New York's Hudson Valley. An oppressed minority in Scotland, where Lowlanders dominated the scene, and in the colonies as well, Highland Scots traditionally looked to the royal government for protection. These exceptions aside, however, there was a profoundly fertilizing relationship between Scottish intellectual life, which was inveterately Whig, and the thinking of the Revolutionary leadership. At Princeton, William and Mary, Yale, and Harvard, the books on public affairs and human nature most closely read and passed from hand to hand were those written by the internationally famous scholars of the eighteenth-century "Scottish renaissance": Adam Smith, Lord Kames, Adam Ferguson, David Hume, and many others. The work of these men made Scotland the world's leading center of social science. The ideas they sent out were rooted in concepts of philosophic rationalism, free thought, and a skeptical, critical evaluation of all reigning dogmas, especially those of Tory, aristocratic England. Liberalism flourished in Scotland, a country proud of its common schools, its rugged Presbyterian individualism, and the openness and easiness of manners among its social classes. The contrast was often made between the illiteracy of the English masses and the schooled literacy of the Scottish working classes, between the obedience to superiors preached by the Anglican clergy and the prickly democratic questioning encouraged by Church of Scotland ministers.

Adam Smith's brilliant critique of English mercantilism and links between businessmen and government became the economic bible of Thomas Jefferson and, in fact, of the political tradition he founded. David Hume's political works shaped the thought of James Madison, who left Virginia to study at the Presbyterian College of New Jersey (later Princeton University). This institution had been founded in 1746 to train ministers for the rapidly growing Presbyterian community in the colonies and to maintain direct links with Scottish intellectual and religious life. John Witherspoon, a Scottish intellectual of high standing, became Princeton's president in 1768. Thereafter, he was a leader in the Revolution and signed the Declaration of Independence. Under Witherspoon's influence, in July 1775, the New York-Philadelphia Synod issued a pastoral letter that called upon all Presbyterians to support the colonial cause and to be brave in battle if war became necessary.[25]

Politics in New York were agitated by much more than religious differences. A host of other rivalries existed: New York City merchants and professional men against the landed gentry; upriver against downriver; the "court" against the "popular" party in the Assembly; the tenantry against the great landowners of the Hudson Valley; and the democracy of New York City against its pro-English upper class. Here as elsewhere, the artisans, merchant seamen, and laborers were politically awakened by the Revolution. Furthermore, the war itself produced volcanic tensions, for due to the province's strategic centrality, much of it was fought within New York's boundaries. Misled by the strong Loyalism in and around New York City,

London believed that the colony as a whole would provide a friendly base. From New York, the British could strike out to the north and south, if they could only break through Washington's army to the legendary "land of the Tories" that they believed lay somewhere within.

This made for bloody, bitter memories. In no other state during the Revolution were so many Loyalists driven out by angry patriots: some 35,000, or 18 percent of the entire prewar population of New York Colony. Perhaps twice that many remained, the object of envenomed hatred. Toryphobia was intense. The vote was taken away from all suspected Loyalists; Whig debtors were aided against Tory creditors; and the state was filled with midnight vigilante outbreaks, barn burnings, and persecutions. The Scottish Highlanders of the Hudson Valley were cruelly harassed. Indeed, the British secured half of their 25,000 native recruits in New York. The patriots were correct in saying that enemies were everywhere among them.[26]

The existence of so many thousands of Loyalists makes it clear that they were not simply upper-class Anglicans, though in the Northern colonies Anglicanism and loyalty to the Crown were of course closely identified. Loyalists seem often to have been cultural minorities whom the Crown had protected against a hostile majority: Scottish Highlanders in New York and the Carolinas and Scottish merchants in the South; the Dutch and Germans who, like the Anglicans, clung to transatlantic ties; the Quakers of Pennsylvania; and even, for a time, the Baptists of Massachusetts, who were persecuted by the Congregationalist majority. Loyalism was primarily, however, a seaboard, urban phenomenon, with New York City as its hub. For many, being loyal to Britain was only an extension of their efforts over many years to build essentially English institutions in America. They did not so much choose Britain in the conflict as they inherited the cause. They were too weak and scattered ever to have created a genuine "Tory party" in the Revolutionary crisis, but their letters to British leaders constantly misled London about Tory strength, resulting in fatal overconfidence on the British side.[27]

The patriots were all Whigs and republicans, or so they called themselves. However, they, too, were a coalition of culture groups unified only because they faced a common enemy: the royal government. When victory removed the unifying factor, republicans divided from republicans and regarded each other with dislike and suspicion. The issue shifted, to use Carl Becker's classic formulation, from whether or not the Americans would have home rule to who would rule at home. This new question crystallized New York politics around a man much loved and hated: George Clinton. An Ulster County Scotch-Irishman, Clinton had been a prewar leader of the Livingston faction in the Assembly and a popular general during the fighting in the Hudson Valley. Beginning in 1777, he spent twenty-one years as governor of the state, holding six successive terms until 1795 and a seventh beginning in 1800. A plain man who lived in a simple farmhouse, had little formal education, and was a republican in grain and principle, Clinton was venerated by the common people. He was especially fierce toward the Loyalists. Profoundly a man of the rural countryside, Clinton, through his wife's family, was linked to the farming and middle-class, rather than the patrician, Dutch.

When he became governor, the New York aristocracy thought Clinton quite above his social station. College-educated men in the state legislature rarely supported him, nor did men of cosmopolitan lifestyle and outlook, townsmen in general, or more than a fraction of the state's commercial farmers. Anglicans (called Episcopalians after the Revolution, when they formed the Protestant Episcopal Church of America), Quakers, and former Loyalists also opposed Clinton, for he was inescapably identified with all that was hostile to England and English cultural and economic influences. Small farmers and frontiersmen were the core of his voting support. Former militiamen, who had become politically mobilized by their wartime experiences, were Clinton supporters, but former officers of the regular Continental Army, with its strong discipline and lines of authority on the British model, opposed him strongly. They had thought militiamen a flighty and irresponsible lot during the fighting; the militia, in turn, thought them arrogant and dictatorial. Clinton, in short, both during and after the Revolution, was the chosen leader of localist peoples of modest incomes, not of the wealthy and the cosmopolitan—and so, indeed, he saw himself.[28]

Thus, the lines of politics that had existed before the Revolution persisted into the postwar years, though with crucial modifications. The previous governing system had been aristocratic. Few common people had voted in colonial New York or held seats in the Assembly. This was all swept away in 1776, when a new, more democratic constitution was adopted. After the start of the Revolution, many simple, plain men from the humbler classes—and usually from the ethnic and religious outgroups—became prominent in the legislature. Elitists like Alexander Hamilton, who moved among circles of wealth, power, and standing, were appalled at the democratization of New York politics. They looked upon the new legislators as ignorant, unfit for leadership, and motivated primarily by jealousy of those more fortunate than themselves. Elite families were alarmed at the smaller roles they now played in public life. Clinton was the symbol of these changes, and he was hated for it.

Then in the late 1780s, a new issue emerged in New York: whether or not to support the movement to create and ratify a federal Constitution. In this controversy, familiar lines of battle were formed. George Clinton and his followers were determined Antifederalists. They were localists: their horizons were bounded by the county courthouses and town councils from which they had sprung, and they distrusted the nationalism of their aristocratic enemies, who were firmly Federalist. Commercial leaders turned away from the Clintonians in frustration and anger, for they found themselves and their Federalism treated with suspicion. The Bank of New York was solidly Federalist in the struggle over the new Constitution, as was the New York mercantile community in general.

Revealingly, some officials of the Bank of New York had been Tories during the war. Indeed, it was common for former Loyalists to find political protection among the anti-Clintonians, many of whom had never been as hostile to English institutions and ways of living as the more determined republicans. Through the efforts of the larger property owners, Episcopalians, cosmopolitans, and prominent old families who opposed Clinton, former Loyalists regained their vote in 1785, and in 1786 their citizenship. Now, in the struggle over the Constitution, Tories gave it their warm support. The Federalists of New York City actually ran two prominent Tories on their ticket for the ratifying convention, electing them both. While New York politics in the postwar years were changed in form by being more democratic than formerly, the cultural pattern of prewar years endured.[29]

Under the libertarian laws of the Quakers, by the mid-eighteenth century Pennsylvania had become the most ethnically mixed of the colonies and one of the most populous. Tens of thousands of oppressed people had settled the most prosperous and bountiful of the wheat colonies, bringing in a kaleidoscope of languages and faiths. From Germany, torn by religious wars, there came Lutherans, Calvinists (German Reformed), and pietists (Moravians, Dunkers, Mennonites, Schwenkfelders, and many others). So numerous were the Germans that by the Revolutionary period they constituted perhaps 40 percent of Pennsylvania's 250,000 people. The Germans were quiet and inward-turning, bound in a separate world by their language. Little used to democratic government, they avoided involvement in the world of English-speaking politics.[30]

From the north of Ireland came the people who, as long ago as 1573, Queen Elizabeth called the "Scotch-Irish." During her time, they were induced by the royal government to begin crossing the narrow channel between Scotland and Ireland and settle lands the English were then clearing of the Catholic population—the "mere Irish." Densely populating Ulster during the seventeenth century, the Scotch-Irish made that province in the north of Ireland an industrious seat of Presbyterianism. Eventually, they came under repressive English policies which suppressed their industries and forced them to support a church alien to them, the Church of England. Then a series of killing famines in the eighteenth century drove them in great recurring waves of migration to the American colonies.

At first the Scotch-Irish headed for Massachusetts and Connecticut, whose Calvinist Puritanism they shared, but in that overwhelmingly English environment they were quickly made to feel unwelcome. When their first Presbyterian minister arrived in 1723, the local town council of Stirling, Connecticut, enacted a Remonstrance condemning his presence "because he is a stranger; and we are informed that he came out of Ireland; and we do observe that since he has been in town that the [Scotch-Irish] . . . do flock into town; and we are informed that [they] . . . are not wholesome inhabitants." In response, the Scotch-Irish moved away to form a sizable population in New Hampshire and Maine, where they were more independent of the Congregational authorities. However, most of the Scotch-Irish migration thereafter headed toward libertarian Pennsylvania, where all faiths were free of legal restrictions. Perhaps a quarter of a million Scotch-Irish immigrated to and settled in the American colonies after 1720. From their enclave in northern New England down to the Carolinas, the Scotch-Irish were distributed over a wide terrain, but it was in Pennsylvania that they were to figure most dramatically in American history. By the 1760s, they were estimated to form one-fourth of that colony's population.[31]

The arrival of the Scotch-Irish in America produced a political earthquake that shifted the whole landscape of colonial public life. It has long been recognized that the much later arrival of the Catholic Irish after the famines of the 1840s injected into American politics a force so powerful that it shaped the party system for at least a century thereafter. What has not been hitherto understood is that for the better part of the preceding century the Protestant Irish played this same role. We have seen how prominent they were in New York's politics. In Pennsylvania, where they were much more numerous, everything in the colony's politics seemed to begin and end with this contentious people.

It was not simply that the Scotch-Irish were Presbyterians and therefore ancestral enemies of the Anglicans; that, being Scottish, they disliked Englishmen. Nor was it only that from both of their homelands, Scotland and Ireland, came a steady stream of radical Whig republican ideas, which predisposed them to be prickly toward the established authorities and reformist in their politics. (A New England Loyalist was later to call the Scotch-Irish "the most God-provoking democrats on this side of Hell.") The Scotch-Irish were distinctive also in that they had already been frontiersmen in Northern Ireland. For a century and more, they had fought the Catholic Irish in a fierce struggle for land and life. Unlike their ethnic kinsmen in Scotland, the Scottish populace in Ulster had to struggle against the power of the established Church of England and pay it tithes. This made them passionate Presbyterians, ferocious in their hatred of Anglicans. An Anglican priest in Delaware, observing them in that colony in 1723, remarked: "They call themselves Scotch-Irish . . . and [they are] the bitterest railers against the [Church of England] that ever trod upon American ground."

Their long years of almost constant struggle against surrounding enemies had made the Scotch-Irish a dour, hard-bitten, combative people. They lived with guns, and seemed to know little other than fighting as a means to settle quarrels. They considered themselves a holy people fighting evil and sacrilegious ones, and their Presbyterianism was the center of their lives. In Northern Ireland, the Scotch-Irish congregations stayed close together, took their communion sitting around a great table, and minutely controlled the moral behavior of cobelievers. American Presbyterianism, insofar as it derived from the Scotch-Irish (other influences would be felt during the nineteenth century), would be especially severe and stern in theology. In the hands of the Scotch-Irish in America, Presbyterianism was a grimmer and more biting faith than it was in Scotland itself, where an easier way of life had allowed a certain latitude of belief and a quieter tone to seep into the "Auld Kirk."[32]

The Quakers of Pennsylvania were appalled by the arrival of these hordes of Scotch-Irish, for the Quakers and the Calvinists were ancient enemies. The theological gulf between them was wide and impassable. Quakers were a New Testament people who worshiped a loving God little concerned with law. The Presbyterians were an Old Testament folk whose God was angry with humanity's transgressions against His sacred laws and willing to consign to hell all those whom, in His inscrutable and sovereign will, He chose to meet that fate. In Scotland, and in England under Oliver Cromwell, the Calvinists had jailed Quakers; in New England they had even put them to death. That Quakers were overwhelmingly of English ethnic stock intensified their rivalry with the Scotch-Irish, calling up ancestral hostilities.

The Scotch-Irish had reason to dislike the Quaker-dominated colonial government in Philadelphia. Migrating to the western frontier, they had immediately fallen to fighting the Indians, just as for generations they had fought the Catholic Irish in their homeland. Moved by Quaker pacifist principles, the colony's Assembly refused to provide arms and support. Furthermore, it allowed the frontiersmen relatively few elected representatives. If this were not enough, the Proprietor of Pennsylvania, Thomas Penn, demanded high prices for the land he sold the Scotch-Irish. When they simply squatted on his property, a common practice, Penn sent agents to burn their cabins.[33]

In 1764, just a year before the Stamp Act crisis, a vigilante force of several hundred Scotch-Irish in a towering rage marched on Philadelphia. Called the "Paxton Boys" after their township near Lancaster, they were determined to compel changes in the colony's policies. Alarmed Philadelphians formed a body of minutemen under the leadership of Benjamin Franklin, who thought the Scotch-Irish a barbaric people. With this show of force, the matter was peacefully handled, but in the course of the confrontation many harsh things were said. Quakers were scandalized when the Scotch-Irish called them an infatuated faction "that have got the political Reigns in their Hand and tamely tyrannize over the other good subjects of the Province!" As early as 1729, the Quakers had feared that the Presbyterians would "make themselves the Proprietors of the Province." Now, in an outburst of abuse, which was not leveled at just the rebellious Paxton Boys, Quakers accused all Presbyterians of seeking to establish a religious tyranny. They were the "blood-ran, blood-thirsty Presbyterians, who cut off King Charles his Head." Always and everywhere they were "Quarrelsome, Riotous, Rebellious, dissatisfied with the publick Establishment [and enemies to] Kingly Government." They were robbers, crude and unclean hill people,

makers and consumers of bad whisky, bigoted and violently intolerant of those with different ideas, mere "white savages."

The Presbyterians of the colony were deeply angered by these
traditional English insults. They, in turn, accused the Quakers, whose
pacifism and pietist faith seemed to them un-Christian, effeminate,
and self-indulgent, of being utter hypocrites. Had they not, though
professedly plain people, grown scandalously wealthy as merchants
in transatlantic trade? Had not two hundred of them, supposed pa-
cifists, taken up arms to protect Philadelphia against the Paxton
Boys? The Scotch-Irish even accused Quakers of being accomplices
of the Indians, stirring them up against Presbyterians so as vicariously
to massacre their enemies.[34]

These outbursts so polarized Pennsylvania that thereafter its politics were crystallized into two embittered parties. Whatever the
Quakers proposed, the Scotch-Irish loudly opposed and were so
treated in return. With the assistance of Benjamin Franklin, the
Quakers now urged the royal government to take over the gover-
nance of the colony. They did so partly because they despaired of
ever settling their long-standing dispute with the Proprietor,
Thomas Penn, over the colony's affairs. Most of all, however, the
Quakers hoped that the Crown would protect them against growing
Presbyterian power. To placate London, the Quakers damped down
all resistance to the Stamp Act in Philadelphia and later to the Town-
shend Duties, making Pennsylvania the scandal of the colonial world.

On the Quakers' side, they now had in the Assembly the Proprietor
and his predominantly Anglican party (the Penns by this time had
converted to the Church of England), who were also courting London by keeping down patriotic ardor. Joining them were large segments of the merchant and financial class of Philadelphia, who were
Anglicized and cosmopolitan in lifestyle. The pietist German sects,
so far as they were political, also supported the Quakers' struggle
against the Scotch-Irish, for the pietists' religious beliefs and ways of
living resembled those of the Quakers. The pietists worried, too, that
they would lose their religious freedom should the allegedly domineering Presbyterians gain control of the colony. Altogether, this
meant that the Presbyterians received precious little assistance from
the Pennsylvania Assembly. Because German and Scotch-Irish areas
were not allowed proper representation during the years from 1760
to 1776, the Quakers usually held two-thirds of the seats and the
Anglicans another quarter.[35]

In opposition to this Quaker and Anglican coalition, a Presbyterian
party took form in 1766. Someone, the Scotch-Irish believed, must
enter the patriotic vacuum. The plan for a royal government in

Pennsylvania had to be opposed; the general assault on colonial liberties then underway from London had to be stopped. Behind the Scotch-Irish now gathered the German Lutherans, who, fearing that a royal government would take away the liberties they enjoyed under the Penn proprietorship, began to stir out of their political quiescence. Another group in the Scotch-Irish camp was the German Reformed, whose Calvinist theology made them natural allies of the Presbyterians.[36]

In addition to the Germans, the artisans and working class of Philadelphia were stirring. Although formerly passive and deferential toward the mercantile and financial aristocracy, they were spurred by the Revolutionary crisis to enter vigorously into the colony's public life (to some extent because party rivalry was so intense that their support was eagerly solicited). Furthermore, artisans and mechanics were pleased with the nonimportation agreements that patriots had instituted against British goods, for the agreements enhanced the demand for their own products. Presbyterian leaders in the merchant community joined with artisans and lawyers from their faith to launch a strong anti-British movement—with the help of Benjamin Franklin, now finally converted to the patriot cause. In 1774, just as a young Englishman and radical Whig, Thomas Paine, arrived in the city, a committee of merchants and mechanics was formed to insure that nonimportation survived as a policy.

At the same time, a fiercely egalitarian and republican philosophy swept the working classes. This ideology carried a strong bias against the power exercised by the city merchants over Philadelphia's welfare. Again and again, workers demanded that the closed circles of privilege and power that ran the colony's politics be broken apart so that the common people could assume their rightful role. By 1776 a new force, the militia, composed of poorer working people, was also emerging as an actively radical influence in the city's affairs. Thus, the Revolution provided the occasion for the first outspoken expressions of resentment against the rich by the formerly deferential poor ever to be heard in Philadelphia. Courted and praised by the Scotch-Irish as the core of the new republican order in America, these masses of humble people, together with the independent yeomanry of the countryside, closed ranks on the patriot side.[37]

When the climactic crisis between the colonies and Great Britain erupted, the Intolerable Acts of 1774 having closed Boston's port and quashed the government of Massachusetts, the Quakers took alarm. They were frightened that in an independent Pennsylvania they might be left to the mercies of their Scotch-Irish enemies. Accordingly, in January 1775 the Quaker Meeting of Pennsylvania–New Jersey, the most authoritative body in the American branch of the faith, issued a strongly pro-British "Testimony." Condemning "all combinations, insurrections, conspiracies, and illegal assemblies," it declared that Quakers were restrained from participating in such rebellious activities "by the conscientious discharge of our duty to Almighty God, by whom kings *reign,* and princes decree justice."[38] Thus, they publicly washed their hands of the Revolutionary cause, remaining passive and neutral thereafter in the fighting and being generally considered Tories.

Led by a group of Presbyterian merchants in Philadelphia, the Scotch-Irish and Germans now took leadership of the province, powerfully aided by the rush of events. In January 1776 Thomas Paine published his electrifying pamphlet *Common Sense*. Printed and reprinted, tens of thousands of copies of the pamphlet spread throughout the colonies with astonishing speed, for it stated in the most lucid and compelling ways the very thoughts toward which the patriots' minds had been tending. How absurd, said Paine in words that became famous, that an island should perpetually rule a continent! The colonies should declare their independence. Paine took the word "republicanism," which even yet had sacrilegious, disreputable associations, and made it respectable. In slashing phrases, he depicted the hitherto holy idea of kingship as an oppressive holdover from ancient tyrannies. Thus, he severed kingship from its base of historical legitimacy. America must break free entirely from such corruptions of human government and establish truly republican institutions: a continental legislature; unicameral state assemblies giving direct voice to the people's wishes through broad voting rights; frequent elections; and written constitutions that would guarantee the rights of persons and property and freedom of religion. A strong American nation should be constructed, safe and powerful under the direction of a vigorous and democratic central government. Furthermore, Paine insisted, it should be made economically independent by an active development of trade, industry, and cities.

Thus, for Paine, republicanism embraced not only liberty and egalitarianism but nationalism, rather than a scattered localism, and rapid, centrally directed economic growth, rather than a quiet, rural agrarianism. Out of this fertile combination, Paine believed, a new order of things for the world would emerge: a truly viable democratic way of life, freed of feudalism and aristocratic monopolies of wealth and power. "We have it in our power," he said, "to begin the world over again ... the birthday of a new world is at hand." The world is overrun with tyranny; freedom is a hunted fugitive. A powerful and democratic America could inspire the struggling masses of the world, fulfilling its mission as "an asylum for mankind."[39]

In May 1776 the Continental Congress effectively declared independence by calling on all colonies to establish new, nonroyal governments for themselves, expelling entirely "the exercise of every kind of authority under the ... Crown." Pennsylvania's republicans swiftly terminated the Quaker and Anglican-dominated Assembly and royal courts. They then summoned a constitutional convention in July and drew up a boldly republican form of government. Seen by many as the most radical in the colonies, the Pennsylvania government was designed to set an example of the democratic possibilities inherent in the new independence from royal rule. Dispensing entirely with the ideal of a balanced government in which powers were divided among three branches controlled by the different social classes (king, aristocracy, and people), the new constitution established an all-powerful, single-house legislature deriving its authority wholly from the people. There was to be no governor but a plural executive elected by the community to carry out the functions of government. The Saxon government of ancient England, republicans said, had been a simple and direct expression of the people. So it should be in Pennsylvania, where all were freemen and social ranks did not (or should not) exist. As history abundantly demonstrated, complicated governments were failures; they were oppressive and corrupt. Henceforth, Pennsylvania was to have mandatory rotation in office, wide suffrage, no property-owning requirements for holding office, open legislative proceedings, and popular election of judges.

When new elections were held, not a single person who had held an executive or judicial office under the British regime in 1775 won a public position. Only 10 percent of the legislators had served in the old Assembly. Equal representation for all counties and for the city of Philadelphia gave the frontier an appropriate voice. Presbyterians now held more than half the legislative seats; German Reformed and Lutherans together held another quarter. Quakers and Anglicans shared the fourth that was left—to this minority had the English been reduced. A completely new order had taken over; there was almost no continuity with the preceding regime.[40]

So it was that in Pennsylvania, within weeks of the Declaration of Independence, the argument over who was to rule at home was concluded. The republicans, America's Whigs, had triumphed over the Loyalists, America's Tories. Furthermore, the government was no longer to be run by the English ethnic community but by the Scotch-Irish and the Germans. As in New York, however, it was not long before the republicans were splitting into factions. The two-party rivalry that emerged revealed the new order of battle that would characterize American politics thereafter. The Presbyterians were austere republicans with a clear notion of the kind of purified America that the Revolution should give birth to, and in their zeal they soon began driving away former allies. The constitution for Pennsylvania that the Presbyterians had written alarmed many; its powers were so concentrated and so directly rooted in the will of the people that far more than simply the old Loyalist order seemed endangered. Furthermore, the Presbyterians and their German Calvinist allies were soon in command in every part of the state, rural or urban, west or east, old or new. From this power base, they began enacting puritanical and egalitarian reforms.

The Anglicans were expelled from the administration of the University of Pennsylvania, and the institution was placed under Presbyterian domination, a change in cultural identity that linked the university to the scientific rationalism then flourishing in Scotland. In the righteous spirit of the new constitution, which required voters and office holders to profess faith in Christ and the Holy Scripture, the Bible was printed at public expense, and theatrical companies in Philadelphia were sternly outlawed. Throughout the state, Loyalists were mercilessly hounded. Test oaths were required to affirm patriotism, a tactic aimed obviously at the Quakers, who had always refused to take oaths on the ground that their loyalty was only to God. The Presbyterians' egalitarian republicanism led them also to support the humble classes in their struggles against exploitation by the wealthy. All government assistance to business interests (such as loans to iron manufacturers) was terminated. The charter of the Bank of North America, widely condemned as a means for Robert Morris and his financial and mercantile circles in Philadelphia to squeeze wealth from the community, was repealed. Paper currency, desired by farmers who believed it created rising prices, was issued, and a mild protective tariff to aid Philadelphia's artisans was enacted.[41]

"Presbyterian tyranny!" became the cry. All that had been predicted of the authoritarian tendencies of Presbyterians seemed borne out by their actions. In the long argument with London, republicans had insisted over and over that consolidated power was a danger to everyone's liberties. On this ground, they had joined radical Whigs in Britain in reacting with alarm to any suggestion that the

Crown was gaining supremacy over Parliament. A system of balanced power, they had said, was the key to freedom. Now the proof of this position, which mistrusted all unchecked power, was spread out for all to see in Pennsylvania itself. There was no more eloquent critic of the new constitution than Benjamin Rush, a young physician who had been one of the leading figures in the Presbyterian party. As a student, he had acquired his Whiggism at the University of Edinburgh and later had helped convince John Witherspoon to become president of Princeton University. Now Rush, like many others, reacted in outrage against an arrangement that assigned all power to one agency of government and one political faction. The constitution makers, he said, had "substituted a mob government to one of the happiest governments of the world." They were not true republicans.

In 1779 a "Republican" party came into being to fight for a new form of government. The defenders of the unicameral legislature took the name "Constitutionalists." For a decade the controversy raged, until a more traditionally balanced document was adopted in Pennsylvania in 1790 (after the adoption of the federal Constitution). During the long struggle, the alignment in the Assembly was a familiar one. The Constitutionalists, who opposed change, were heavily Scotch-Irish, supported by about half the Germans (primarily the Calvinist German Reformed). They were strongest among the farmers of the rural interior, but they also had substantial support from the Philadelphia working classes. Not only were the Constitutionalists outspokenly democratic and egalitarian, but they also were profoundly localist in their sentiments and outlook. Like their Clintonian counterparts in New York, the Constitutionalists distrusted, as an Anglicized, aristocratic project, the campaign to establish a strong national government over the states. When the federal Constitution was written and proposed in 1787, the Constitutionalists opposed it. Thereafter, in the 1790s, the party swung behind Thomas Jefferson.

Those who called themselves Republicans were a revealing mixture of old and new. The party contained the Quakers and Episcopalians, as might be expected. In fact, practically all the Englishmen in the Assembly were Republicans. They were joined by a majority of the Lutherans and all the Baptists, who were alarmed at the threat of a Calvinist tyranny. But the Republicans in the Assembly also drew in a large body of the Scotch-Irish Presbyterians, perhaps a third of them. Many, like Benjamin Rush, recoiled from what they saw as too radical a republicanism on the part of the Constitutionalists, too

extreme a faith in the common people and in their presumed ability
to exercise unchecked power.

Many of these Republican Scotch-Irish were Philadelphia businessmen. Their partisan alignment doubtless was stimulated by the Constitutionalists' economic program, which had assaulted the privileges
of the mercantile and financial community. The chief leader of Republican forces among businessmen, however, was the wealthy Anglican Robert Morris. Born in England and married to an Anglican
bishop's daughter, Morris had agreed only most reluctantly to a separation from Great Britain. In these feelings, he was a true representative of the Philadelphia business world, for within it there was
considerable sympathy for Loyalists. Traders and bankers admired
the English and their ways and approved of Anglicization. When the
Revolution had come, they had been moderate in their rebel attitudes.

Assembly members of cosmopolitan lifestyle and outlook were
overwhelmingly Republican. So, too, were those from the more
prominent families and from the officer corps of the Continental
Army (militia veterans endorsed the egalitarian Constitutionalists).
When in the 1790s Alexander Hamilton's Federalists confronted
Thomas Jefferson's Republicans, there was little doubt as to the loyalties of those who had called themselves Republicans in Pennsylvania
politics of the 1780s: they swung heavily behind the Hamiltonians.[42]

Within these four states may be seen the broad outlines of the
national politics to come. Each displayed an inner conflict between
two cultural coalitions. During the Revolutionary years, these patterns of alignment and hostility surfaced in another arena: in the
sessions of the Continental Congress (1774–1781) and the Congress
under the Articles of Confederation (1781–1789). It was at this level
that the nation felt its way toward constitutional unity. It is to this
progression of events, and to a summing up of what all these influences, state and national, revealed about American public life, that
we shall now turn.

III

The Second Revolution: The Federal Constitution

The Continental Congress convened in 1774 and until 1781 served as the colonies' national government. In that year, the Articles of Confederation were ratified, and the Confederation Congress created by that document began its sessions. By this act of ratification, the United States of America formally appeared in the world as a legal and constitutional entity, giving the states for the first time an established framework of common government and a common identity.

The Continental and Confederation Congresses provided the first arenas in which national political groupings could take form. The parties formed within them had no base in the American people at large, however, for the citizenry had no national political function to perform. As yet there were no common public officials to be elected and no national electoral campaigns to be fought. The Congresses themselves were the only agencies of common government; no executive or judicial branch existed. Their membership consisted simply of men chosen by the state governments to represent them, not to represent the people of those states.

However, party activity within the Congresses was well organized and vigorous in spirit. Furthermore, it extended into the politics that later emerged under the federal Constitution. Two-thirds of the sen-

ators and half the members of the House of Representatives in the
first federal Congress had been delegates in the Continental and
Confederation Congresses. It is not surprising, therefore, that national political parties appeared so quickly after 1789: they had been
germinating for years.[1]

The Continental and Confederation Congresses are usually depicted as having been weak and ineffective. Nonetheless, they unified the colonies as a nation and declared independence from a great
imperial power. Thereafter, they successfully fought an arduous war
and maintained an active alliance and fighting partnership with powerful France. At the Revolution's end, the Confederation Congress
negotiated a peace treaty in which an enormous continental domain
reaching to the Mississippi River was secured. The Congress then
turned successfully to the task of providing a land policy and a system
of government for that vast western possession. Without significant
change, this system has formed the matrix within which a nation of
fifty self-governing states has come into being.

All the delegates to the Congresses were, in eighteenth-century
Anglo-American terminology, of the Whig persuasion. In varying
degrees, they shared the republicanism of the radical British Whigs.
Within this framework, it is a fundamentally accurate observation
that American politicians of practically all points of view worked
within a broad consensus of outlook, one that set them off from those
who ran the governments of Europe. In this sense, the central fact
about Americans in politics is what was common to them in comparison with the situation in Europe, rather than what set them apart
from each other. Whatever their particular position on the wide
spectrum of republicanism, American Whigs agreed that sovereignty
must lie in the people at large and that individual liberties must be
preserved. Power must be decentralized, and there should be no
titled aristocracies possessing a monopoly of government. A hereditary landowning class was anathema; the principle of each (white)
man living on his own land and subject to no feudal dues or burdens
was essential. Government should exist for the welfare and the happiness of its citizens, rather than the reverse. Americans should not
adopt the pomp and ceremony of feudal government, and they
should exist, as did almost no other nation in Western civilization,
without a reigning monarch. To be a sturdy republican meant being
a proud individualist who made his own way and had the right to an
expanding and wealthier future. Religious faith was to be each individual's free choice, and all faiths (by which most Anglo-Americans

in these years meant all *Protestant* faiths) were to be in equal standing. Republican government should be rooted in frequent elections based in a wide (white male) suffrage, and that government should be small, simple, and limited.

Within this broad consensus, however, the delegates who came to the Continental and Confederate Congresses differed widely. Indeed, conflict and contention, rather than the harmony of action and viewpoint that the term "consensus" seems to indicate, was to be the nature of American politics. Divisions appeared almost instantly, and they were.to persist. There was ample latitude within republicanism for bitter and continuing controversy over the most fundamental issues. It is more accurate to think of the ideology of republicanism as forming a universe of discourse rather than a prescriptive faith. It created a framework for argument; certain agreed-upon fundamentals provided the boundaries, and particular goals and a kind of language were shared. However, the meaning of those goals and the devices for reaching them remained quite unsettled.

Among the delegates to the Congresses, we may observe four modes of republicanism: one identified generally with the South, another with New England, and two with the Middle States (although there were adherents to each position scattered widely and numerously outside these particular regions). The Congregational New Englanders were sharply distinctive in their *moralistic* republicanism. Fervently religious, they believed church and state—as in their Puritan colonies—must work closely together to keep the community pure and godly. Government must be constantly active, supervising the people's public and private virtue. Thus, the Yankee model for America was an idealized version of New England's orderly peasant democracy: communal, pious, hard working, austere, and soberly deferential.

This led to the conception of the new United States as a virtuous and God-fearing Christian Sparta, to use Sam Adams' terminology. Its citizens must learn to sacrifice their individual welfare to the needs of the whole community. In such a republic, the common people would choose and follow those godly leaders, generally of good family and suitable substance, who best exemplified God's elect. Despite the general aura of political radicalism that hung about them, Puritans had never been comfortable with democracy. They conceived obedience to those in authority to be a religious duty. The magistrate, for whom the proper model was the sovereignty of God Himself, should actively guide and lead.

The commercializing, entrepreneurial mood that had been emerging in eighteenth-century New England fostered a parallel notion. In economic as in moral matters, government must take an active role. The republicanism of the Yankees, therefore, was a curious blend of policies, one calling for the holy community, the other encouraging economic growth and development. However paradoxical this sort of republicanism might be, looking simultaneously backward to the organic moral consensus of the past and forward to the entrepreneurial capitalism of the future, it carried with it a firm conviction that authority was a force of divine origin and must be used, and used vigorously, to make the community strong and virtuous.

At the opposite pole was Southern *libertarian* republicanism. Its representatives in the Congresses were secular men, prickly about personal freedom and hostile to meddling clerics. Most were of the aristocracy. Their manners were baronial, and they cared little for the stiff-necked democrats who had taken over the Middle Colonies and New England. The great planters were men of cosmopolitan tastes and outlook acquired through their more direct ties to English and French high culture. Used to thinking within wider horizons, in the late 1780s they would follow the lead of men like George Washington and James Madison in their push for a new constitution and a stronger national government.

In its inner heart, however, Southern republicanism was rural and localist. These influences, and the democratic values given enduring expression by Thomas Jefferson, were to shape Southern politics over the long run. Enlightenment ideals, drawn from Scotland and France, exerted a strong influence in this direction. Most Southern aristocrats tended to talk of natural, rather than God-given, rights and privileges. They believed that government should be small and inactive, limiting itself to the simplest social functions. Each person should be left the widest exercise of his individual freedoms, which included moral behavior and the right to possess slaves.

The Middle States were confused and ambivalent in their representation. Within them were two different modes of republicanism. One mode was strongly *egalitarian.* Its leaders were hostile to Philadelphia and New York business interests, localistic, and predominantly Scotch-Irish. The other mode of republicanism was *nationalist* and elitist. The leadership of this strong group centered in the business community of the two large cities. These men played a major and continuing role in the Continental and Confederation

Congresses. Anglicized, cosmopolitan, and entrepreneurial, they were uncomfortable with egalitarian democrats and sympathetic toward Loyalists, for they had themselves often been reluctant rebels. Yet, they were neither monarchists nor Tories. They rejected ties between church and state, and in their own fashion believed that sovereignty must reside in the community at large, which, if properly virtuous and conscious of the need for authority, would choose members of the elite to govern it.

Nationalist republicans had a bold vision of what America should become. As Robert Morris said, the country should assume the status of an empire of "power, consequence, and grandeur." It should vigorously develop its resources under the centralized leadership that a cooperative partnership between business and government would provide. Nationalist republicans were impatient with localists, for the American nation could realize its great future only if it developed a strong central government. Then the country could marshal its potentially immense energies within a moral climate that fostered team spirit and joint endeavor. As nationalists understood Anglo-American history, this was how the British had reached such peaks of power and prosperity, and they considered the United Kingdom, in these and other respects, an admirable model. Young Alexander Hamilton of New York was the nationalist republican's strongest spokesman.

In the ranks of New Englanders, who found appealing the ideal of the whole American community unified behind common objectives, nationalists also found support. Even such radical republicans as Tom Paine shared the vision of a strong and organically united America, with a solid core provided by a centralized banking system. Paine had little interest in the backward-looking republicanism that idealized the agrarian past and sought to preserve it. He believed instead that America could best perform its world mission of establishing republican democracy if it moved eagerly into the future and became ever more a nation of towns, cities, and industry. With these ideals, nationalist republicans could form an alliance with the artisans and workers of Philadelphia and New York based on their common preference for developmental economics. For a considerable period in the 1780s and 1790s, urban artisans and workers gave strong support to the Federalist cause.[2]

In Philadelphia, where the Continental Congress convened, these different kinds of Americans were soon in conflict. Congressmen from the South and Middle States generally disliked the Yankees.

They thought them too righteous, too intrusive and aggressive in their zealous puritanism. As moralistic republicans, Yankee delegates fretted at the dancing, drinking, and theatergoing they observed in Philadelphia, and they wanted to cleanse the city of these impurities. No Americans had more thoroughly absorbed the radical British Whig distrust of standing armies than the Yankees. All such bodies, they insisted, were threats to freedom. Yankees were uneasy about the Continental Army, which Washington had induced Congress to establish. They tried to hold down army salaries and praised the democratic militia, which in New England had expelled the British army. Yankees, in short, saw no need for a professional service.

At the outset of the Revolution, the Yankees were so outspoken about equality and the rights of the common people that delegates from the other states thought them dangerous levelers. In this spirit, Yankees worried continually that the war would enrich people. The unprincipled would seize every opportunity to rise above others in wealth and power. To forestall this possibility, Yankee delegates became militant economizers who fought every expenditure, scrutinized accounts closely, and demanded that the whole populace practice self-denial and individual sacrifice in the great cause.

Southerners, on their side, held these moralistic preachments in contempt. They wanted to civilize Philadelphia, with its dour overlay of Quaker and Presbyterian piety. Balls, fine wines, salons: these would be the marks of a life suitable to gentlemen. Southerners took little part in the attacks on profiteering, and they shared not at all in quasireligious utopian dreams of a new America rising from the ashes of the old. Nevertheless, they had a fervent republicanism of their own and were committed rebels. When in July 1775 the royal governor of Virginia, Lord Dunmore, reacting to the rebelliousness of the Southern colonies, declared martial law, caused Norfolk to be burned, and offered freedom to all slaves who would join the royal cause, the South "suddenly leaped forward in its radicalism to join New England." Together the delegates from these two regions constituted, in effect, the "Party of the Revolution." They swept the colonies to independence and war.[3]

The dreams of moralistic republicans were doomed to disappointment. By the early 1780s it had become abundantly clear that a Christian Sparta was not to be realized in America. The turmoil of a great revolution had shown that human nature was too fallen for regeneration by even such a cause, that warfare encouraged luxury

seeking, money making, and power intrigues. A malignancy of affluence seemed to be destroying the country. Prices were sky-
rocketing, and speculation had become a way of life. The people's
war turned out to be a bonanza for the wealthy. Newspaper editors,
like the people in general, were fascinated by the state of public
virtue, for in this virtue, it was widely believed, lay the success or
failure of the experiment in republicanism. The decline in national
morality drained enthusiasm for the cause. In its place emerged a
readiness to accept the leadership of those who insisted that the
Revolution needed, not utopian dreams, but pragmatism, organization, and prudence.

The British, meanwhile, were winning great victories in the South
at the opening of the 1780s, and the national fiscal system was in
shambles. Now the nationalist republicans of the Middle States,
joined by Southerners who feared that their region would be forced
into a separate peace, assumed leadership. They wanted to build a
strong central government by strengthening the Confederation
Congress. Robert Morris, much admired and much feared, was made
Superintendent of Finance—a new office—with broad powers to
bring order out of financial chaos. An embryonic national bureauc-
racy was formed in Philadelphia to supervise foreign and maritime
affairs and to direct the fighting of the war. Mixing business and
government in classic mercantilist fashion, Morris established a pri-
vately directed Bank of North America through which the nation's
currency would be controlled by Middle States financiers. Around
these bold initiatives, the "Party of the Nation-State" appeared in the
Confederation Congress, elitist and entrepreneurial in leadership.

By now, the South and New England were alarmed. They feared
that these maneuvers were the initial steps in the construction of a
new London in Philadelphia. Many regarded Robert Morris as a
profit-hungry manipulator. In 1782 and 1783, Southern and Yankee
votes defeated Morris' proposals, which would have established national taxation, paid by the states, to undergird the currency system.
With this defeat, the effort to unite the country by strengthening the
government under the Articles of Confederation collapsed.

However, a powerful new nationalizing force was arriving on the
scene. The Treaty of Paris, signed in 1783, gave the new nation
immense western territories, stretching from the Appalachians to
the Mississippi. This priceless dividend of the peace aroused great
excitement in Virginia. That state had already thrust a deep salient
into the interior, in the colonization of what eventually became Kentucky. Furthermore, Virginia was centrally located with regard to

the West, which held great promise for the future. With Thomas Jefferson in the lead, Virginians looked to the western territories as their salvation. The suffocating curse of lowered tobacco prices and fatal overcropping would be ended by the demands of this huge new frontier. Its needs and its trade would provide a basis for the diversification of Virginia's economy, and perhaps an opportunity to end its hateful reliance on slavery. Pennsylvanians were similarly excited by dreams of western development. Their state, with its western gateway of Pittsburgh where the Ohio River began, could be the chief departure point for western migrants and supplier of their needs. With these forces behind the dream of the West, the great Ordinances of 1784 and 1785 opened up its lands to settlement by the common people. They also insured that the West's governing system would be democratic and established the principle that future states would be admitted to the union on a basis of complete equality with their predecessors. An "empire for liberty," as Jefferson called it, waited to be born.[4]

These events produced a new surge of national enthusiasm. The republican excitements that had carried the American people into the Revolution had ebbed sharply after 1776. The bright new world that patriots envisioned had not come into being. Now, however, a fresh dream revitalized the national mood. Looking westward beyond the Appalachians at an apparently limitless green land, Americans could see in their future a westward-moving frontier of free individuals farming their separate lands and working out their own advancements with little reliance on either community or common government. Agrarianism would expand continentally; an honest and virtuous social order, rooted in rural farm life, would spread deeply into the interior. Since the virtue of the common people was widely regarded as the essential element in a successful republic, and since many feared the corruptions of eastern cities and transatlantic influences, the salvation of the nation lay in this new vision of the American future. Liberty would have a permanent foundation, for country life was confidently held to be the source of sturdy patriotism, of a jealousy concerning personal liberties that would never abide tyranny.

In this sense, it was the vast West that for many Americans revived their dreams of an egalitarian and libertarian republican nation, a United States in which every common person would find open advancement and the realization of his freedoms. Thus, the economic self-interest of multitudes of Americans could be harmoniously blended with freedom. At the same time, the interests of powerful states, Pennsylvania and Virginia chief among them, were also enlisted in the dream of the West. Together, these influences produced a potent source of political energy that shaped much of American history thereafter. It is important to observe that New England could not share directly in this experience and its associated vision. Physically separated from the western territories by the broad expanse of New York State, married to the Atlantic Ocean, and relying heavily upon its cultural links with England, New England would watch the frontier's advance into the interior with deep concern.

To realize the western dream, a strong central government was needed. There were Spanish and British forces positioned beyond the Appalachians that had to be removed, and there were powerful Indian tribes from whom title to the land must be secured. At this point, a historic and short-lived alliance took form. The nationalist republicans of the Middle States, aristocratic gentlemen like Alexander Hamilton who had in their minds a great nation with immense resources, found partners in the upper South. In the Northern Neck of Virginia, wealthy gentry, living on large plantations, were especially numerous. Among them were men like James Madison and George Washington, who provided a leadership that not only was nationally conscious in a way uncommon among Southerners, but was alert as well to ways of enlarging Virginia's future. Together, these two groups mounted a drive to form a new national constitution and a vigorous common government for the states.

They were assisted in their plans by the eruption of wide disorders in the several states during the 1780s. The ejection of royal governments in 1776 had released explosive democratic forces. Men of humble backgrounds gained a sense of confidence in their new public role and came rushing in to assume positions of authority. Of the roughly two hundred fifty aristocrats who had staffed the royal governments in the former colonies, only a small fraction were not driven into private life or exile. Resentments against aristocratic rule, which had been held in check by the traditional attitude of deference toward those in authority, erupted in angry outbursts. Extralegal bodies of protestors and rioters appeared, claiming to speak for the whole population. The Revolutionary cause itself had been spectacularly advanced by what was called "mob" action. Thus legitimated, mass demonstrations became common events. Physical harassment of public authorities emerged as an established pattern of political action. Legislators, judges, and surveyors were terrorized, and courthouses were burned down. As in Massachusetts' Shays' Rebellion (1786–1787), entire judicial systems were forced temporarily to cease operations as vigilantes tried to prevent collection of debts.

In many of the new state governments, the lower houses of the legislatures monopolized power. In the long struggle with royal governors over colonial rights, a struggle that had begun in the 1740s, the lower houses had acquired an almost charismatic hold over mass loyalties. After 1776 governors and all other executive officers were greatly weakened in authority, subjected to frequent elections, or entirely eliminated. In some places, judges were made to stand for election, and if their decisions were disliked, legislatures overturned them. The payment of debts was halted in response to mass appeals; paper currency schemes with inadequate backing were launched; and contracts were nullified. It appeared that the legislatures could pass any kind of legislation and assume any kind of judicial or executive function. They seemed to operate with no restraints whatever.

This contrasted sharply with the constitutional setting before 1776. The British government, whatever its imperfections, had at least provided a veto power. Its courts had received appeals from colonial courts, and laws could be disallowed by Whitehall. This superstructure was now quite gone, and minorities were in danger. The wealthy complained that they could not collect debts owed them. More serious was the situation of smaller religious groups. The Baptists of New England, the Quakers of Pennsylvania, and the Anglicans of New York formerly had been able to rely on imperial protection against the hostile majorities among which they lived. This was no longer possible. Indeed, the legislatures themselves were occasionally besieged by protestors, for the idea of representation was questioned by radical democrats. Legislatures, they said, could not speak for the people but must listen, instead, to the massed crowds of citizenry who brought pressure by threats of physical assault. Government, in this view, existed only in the people at large, not within legislative halls.[5]

By the late 1780s, the American public exhibited a pervasive uneasiness. The experiment in republicanism appeared in danger of collapsing. The elite had always distrusted democracy; now this feeling was shared in much wider reaches of the national mind. George Washington spoke for many when he observed that Americans had held "too good an opinion of human nature in forming our Confederation."[6] Shays' Rebellion stunned Massachusetts' established leadership, for it showed that even in New England, citizens in a republican order would not necessarily defer to proper authority. Was this, many asked, what they had fought such a great war to achieve?

The Tories and British authority were gone, Whig ideas were supreme, and yet harmony and stability still eluded America. If power had been perverted by London, said alarmed observers, now it was being perverted by the common people. Reforms were proposed at the state level to strengthen the upper houses of legislatures and give more powers to state governors, but these were bitterly resisted by those already in power and were rarely successful. The Constitutionalists in Pennsylvania—determined egalitarian republicans—condemned all such proposals as attempts to establish a House of Lords. Unicameral legislatures, the Constitutionalists insisted, spoke directly from the people, and must be retained. In reply to such views, Thomas Jefferson observed that "an *elective despotism* was not the government we fought for."[7]

In these circumstances, a second revolution took place, led by the nationalist republicans of northern Virginia and the Middle States. It was as deep and fundamental as the one that had separated the colonies from Great Britain. Faced by national confusion and disarray, a search for national order began and soon developed an irresistible momentum, sweeping everything before it. An aristocratic body met in Philadelphia in 1787 and labored through the sweltering summer to produce a new federal Constitution. It called for a strong system of central government that would be insulated from the people's direct control and yet be firmly and essentially republican. The Constitution's most striking feature was that it reached down through the state governments directly to the people at large to secure its sovereignty. "We, the People" ratified the new Constitution in bodies especially elected for that purpose. In the process of producing and ratifying the new Constitution, the state governments were pushed aside and sharply limited in their powers. They could no longer conduct foreign affairs, coin money or issue paper currency, pass ex post facto laws or bills of attainder, erect tariffs, keep troops without consent of the federal Congress, or impair contracts. Furthermore, the new document incorporated an unassailable attribute: "this Constitution, and the laws which shall be made in pursuance thereof . . . shall be the supreme law of the land, and the judges in every State shall be bound thereby."

It was a form of government that imposed clear limitations on simple democracy. The President was a powerful executive officer who seemed to tower in solitary eminence, his authority resembling in many ways that of the eighteenth-century British king. He was to be elected by an Electoral College, presumably composed of aristocrats, to be chosen in such manner as the states decided. Judges were not subject to election but could retain their positions during "good behavior" (i.e., as long as they committed no crimes). James Madison had lectured the Constitutional Convention repeatedly on the crucial importance of having a balanced constitution in which no single branch or social class could gain dictatorial power. We have learned, he said, that we cannot depend on the inherent virtue of the common people, which they had formerly been thought to possess, to make a republican government safe for its citizens.[8]

In a certain sense, in composing the Constitution its formulators were motivated by a conviction that "the best people" had lost control of politics. The real problem in the nation, they believed, was not so much its form of government as it was the parochial and narrow-minded people who seemed drawn to leadership in a system fragmented and localized. By establishing a government that presided over an immense continental arena, which in the view of those who wrote the Constitution only persons of education, vision, and suitable wealth could properly understand and manage, a social change of central importance would be achieved in the governing class. Society's true leaders would be inspired to reenter government and provide the large-spirited guidance that the nation presently lacked. Thus, republicanism would be saved from the excesses to which, with its democratic base, it seemed subject.[9]

As we have earlier seen, localist and egalitarian republicans in states like New York and Pennsylvania fought ratification of the new constitution. To them, it was both unwise and a danger to personal liberties. It was antidemocratic, tyrannical, and an ill-disguised effort, they said, to reestablish the aristocratic order that had been overturned in 1776. However, they were little able to stem the current. Antifederalists were, in truth, overawed by the brilliant younger men of the Federalist movement. The latter were college educated, cosmopolitan, marvelously fluent, and possessed of an instinctive habit of command derived from their aristocratic role in plantation or community or from service as officers in the Revolution. Their sophisticated style contrasted sharply with that of the rough democrats and county politicians who served in the state legislatures and led the Antifederalist cause.

Nevertheless, the Bill of Rights was written and adopted largely in response to Antifederalist criticisms. In this achievement, the egalitarian and libertarian republican traditions permanently entered into the national governing system. It was the moralistic republicans who lost out entirely, for the Constitution was a rigorously secular document. Indeed, this formal separation of church and state at the national level was one of the landmark achievements of the Revolutionary years. All faiths, at least in the eyes of the federal government, now had equal status.

From the time of the Constitution's ratification, the American people were given an entirely new political task. They would now participate in an electoral process that would choose an individual person to preside over the entire nation. A void was to be filled; someone was to be placed in that ancient position of leadership that the king had formerly occupied. This was a powerfully charged moral function. Kingship had always had a mystic quality, a quasi-religious role to perform. The President not only would reign and rule, as King George III had sought to do and so many of his predecessors had done, but would, like such men, symbolize the nation itself. That the obvious person who would become the first President, George Washington, was himself an almost regal figure served immediately to invest the office with a special aura. Indeed, save for making the office elective for a certain term of years and providing it with a limited rather than an absolute veto, there was little in strictly constitutional terms that differentiated the American presidency from the British monarchy, except that Britain's king was head of the Church of England as well as of the British state.

Almost by itself, the election of a President forced the emergence of national political parties. Candidates had to be chosen, and voters had to be mobilized in their support. Any hope for victory required the formation of parties that crossed state lines and gathered all possible electoral votes behind one person. This, in turn, led to the emergence of a unified political community that encompassed the entire nation. With the gathering of the first federal Congresses in 1789, therefore, the stage was set for great events. Mass political parties would soon appear for the first time in world history. By this means, government would be linked to the community at large in a fashion as yet unprecedented. The hopes of republicans of all persuasions to build in North America a democratic nation that would endure and flourish as an example to all humankind were, within reasonable human limitations, soon to be realized. Succeeding generations would learn that a republican system of government did not by itself usher in the good and just society but rather a society in which public virtue would continue to prove an elusive ideal. In 1789, however, that lesson remained to be learned.*

Within these opening chapters, much that is novel and complex has been presented. It will be useful here, so as better to understand the book's larger argument, to undertake both a summing up and a preliminary look forward. We have seen that within each state examined there was a conflict between two cultures, between two opposing coalitions or clusters of peoples driven apart from each other by cultural distinctions and hostilities sometimes centuries old, sometimes born within the American setting. In Massachusetts, the bipolarity that shaped its politics expressed itself in the rivalry between the Country and Court traditions. Behind the Country party gathered a Puritan religious community that knew itself to be an outgroup in the national framework within which it then lived: the British empire. For more than a century, Puritans in England had been an excluded caste, living by a pious set of values held in ridicule and denied political and social equality by the Anglican establishment. In New England the Congregational church was by law established, but the Anglican circles around the royal governor had great power and authority. Furthermore, Anglicanism's rising strength

---

*In *The Progressive Historians: Turner, Beard, Parrington* (New York, 1968), pp. 270–284, Richard Hofstadter's reflections speak to the Constitution's political significance.

The image of the Fathers as having put over a *coup d'état* . . . is highly misleading . . . [What] seems truly remarkable about [the Constitution] . . . is not its failure (in itself undeniable) to conform to abstractly conceived ideal procedures for the making and adopting of new governments but its long stride forward toward popular legitimation. . . . [The] Constitution was in fact a phase of American democratic development, a step in the transit of democratic institutions from the local and state level to central government. [We cannot] . . . ignore the avant-garde character of the American political system in the political evolution of the Western world. The truly remarkable thing about the Americans—though we would do well to attribute it more to fortune and necessity than to virtue—was that at a time when the continent of Europe still lay restive under autocracy and when even English democracy was in a rudimentary and emergent stage, they were beginning, in the modern sense of the word, to have politics. That is, they were developing effective pluralities of interests, forums of opinion, a broad popular suffrage, debate and discussion, bargain and compromise. This, with everything it involved for the possible ultimate self-assertion of the common man, was revolutionary, and was rightly so regarded by European contemporaries, who would have been puzzled by the question whether the Constitution was a reactionary document. . . . The United States continued to be regarded as a revolutionary force for more than a generation afterward. (Pp. 271–272, 283.)

within the mercantile and financial world in Boston was a constant threat.

The Country tradition, as a current in Massachusetts' cultural life, centered in a folkish, rural, austere, and reverent way of living that found its life meaning in New England as traditionally conceived. Rooted in the face-to-face local settings of small, inward-turning homogeneous communities, members of the Country party idealized the cohesive Puritan village as a place for the cure of souls to the greater glory of God. A pious republicanism, which to the Country tradition meant the continued health of a holy community founded in free and virtuous local self-government, provided a satisfying creed. The chief danger to the Country party's social ideal was an aggressive and oppressive Anglican England, which was seen looming behind the Court party. For generations the Country party had regarded the mother country as immoral and profligate, given to false gods and an arrogant habit of authority. In the Revolutionary period, its Anglicizing influences appeared to be moving in with such seductive power that the holy community was in danger.

The Country tradition was offended, therefore, by what it saw in the newer trends in the colony's economic life: the individualizing, profit-motivated, and impersonal forces in what is now termed economic modernization. Farmers were acutely sensitive, as well, to Massachusetts' unusual status in the British world as a province composed of free-holding agriculturalists. Tenantry, the exploitive power of manor lords, the example in Ireland and England of huge tracts of countryside in the hands of landowners who exacted heavy rents: these were dangers constantly feared and closely watched. If London were free to send its officials into Massachusetts to raise taxes at will, then, Yankees believed, all would be thrust back into feudal subjection, into slavery. Not only was their holy experiment in danger from Anglicanism, but their condition of independent yeomanry was under grave threat. Town artisans, a class undergoing a historic political awakening in the Revolutionary years, shared the deep distrust that country folk felt toward the steadily growing power of bankers, merchants, and London authorities. From this amalgam, an explosive mixture was formed.

On its side, the Court tradition spoke for all that was transatlantic and cosmopolitan. Tied closely to Anglicanism and English cultural influences, adherents of the Court party were concerned primarily with the needs not only of the mother country but also of the oceanic trading empire that tied the British world together and its banking and mercantile elements in Boston. Urban and flexible, Court leaders

were open to the transforming movements of economic modernization. They were impatient with the puritanical provincials and their
odd fears and massive distrust of everything done by the Court party,
and they worried about what the elite everywhere called the "mob."
When Massachusetts people protested in legislative chambers or in
the streets against English policies, Court party members saw these
events as but the most disturbing aspects of a general breakdown in
social authority and deference. Above all, the Court party was nationalist, which in the British context meant being proud of membership in a great empire and eager to advance its power and wealth.
It was the larger community, in short, to which Court members gave
themselves and their fortunes and in which they felt Massachusetts
should find its true destiny. Relatively few in numbers, the Court
party quickly lost leverage in Massachusetts when the fighting
started. Many of them, as native-born Governor Thomas Hutchinson
had done earlier, found it advisable to leave the colony. During the
Revolution itself, Massachusetts was practically a one-party state,
though in time the patriots began dividing among themselves.

The white community in pre-Revolutionary Virginia was not so
clearly divided into two political groupings, for it was unified by the
presence of its slaves. Nevertheless, Virginia contained its own version of cultural bipolarity. The colony was without cities, but it was
so closely linked economically to England that, in effect, its urban
component lay in London and Glasgow. These cities and their great
powers over Virginia's life aroused deep resentments and nourished
persistent fears. Virginians felt exploited; they distrusted distant
bankers and merchants, and they worried about the corrupting influences of the luxuries that flooded in with rising trade. The Anglican
church was by law established, but by the middle of the eighteenth
century, growing numbers of Virginians were becoming hostile to its
privileges. Many, indeed, were leaving its pews to join the Dissenting
churches of Presbyterians and Baptists. Others expressed their distaste for everything identified with Tory, Anglican England by turning to the Whiggish intellectual life of Scotland and to the
philosophes of France. Virginians found in those centers of learning
a skeptical scientific rationalism that scoffed at established churches,
urged the virtue of free and untrammeled thought, and praised the
rights of man.

Virginia's libertarian republicanism dwelt on the inviolability of
local self-rule, the right to revolt against tyrants, and the absolute
freedom of each individual to direct his own life. That the black race
was not considered human, and was therefore not within the claims

of this philosophy, was the widely shared rationale for one of the most ironic of human paradoxes. Indeed, the very presence of slaves among white Virginians may have intensified their devotion to liberty, for they knew at first hand what its opposite entailed. The gentry were often cosmopolitan in their tastes and lifestyle, but as opposed to London they were inflexible localists. A homogeneous farming society, Virginia lauded the agrarian life as the source of all public virtue and the ground within which independent yeomanry was nourished.

Loyalists were few in numbers in the South, but the rise of Dissent, especially of the Baptists, led to the formation of a distinct counterculture. Against the violence and individual assertiveness of the gentry, Baptists offered gentleness, communal closeness, and order. Not a movement that surfaced politically, it held within it the abiding possibility of an alternative way of living. The earliest version of an "other South," Baptists demonstrated that the unified white community could divide. The continued presence of the black race, however, kept this challenge muted and vulnerable for generations.

Here lies the explanation for an apparent paradox: why the two colonies most English in ethnic origins led the Revolution. Within the British empire, Massachusetts and Virginia had always been or had become cultural outgroups. They were deeply angered at their common enemy: the metropolitan English, with their traditional arrogance toward those they regarded as beneath them and their increased constrictions on the colonies' economic sovereignty. For these states, the Revolution was a political event in which almost all citizens thought of themselves as republican Whigs pitted against royalist Tories. Only later would they discover that the quality of their republicanism was sharply divergent in content. In the pre-Revolutionary years, however, Anglican Virginia was as restive as Congregational Massachusetts and as determined to keep sovereignty over itself and its inner life.

Massachusetts' and Virginia's cultural homogeneity gave each a unity and power of action, then and in later generations, that would provide some of the strongest forces in American public life. When their common enemy, England, was removed, Yankees and Southerners would take each other as their principal antagonists. The Yankees, with their confident pride in the purity and rightness of their ways of living and their urge to make America a house of the Lord, would seek to shape the new nation in their image. In this undertaking, their distaste for the South and its values would be eloquently expressed in word and gesture. The Southerners, alarmed as always for their safety as slaveholders and determined that they should be dictated to by no one, would adopt a continuing strategy of defense and local autonomy. This bipolar conflict between two American ethnic communities, alive and full of tension, would determine much of later American history.

At the heart of this rivalry would lie the contrast of two divergent lifestyles and two differing national visions. The Yankees would choose as their ideal character type the pious and industrious gentleman. They would take as their social model the corporate, consensual community, which would require the active use of government, that divine magistracy, to guide society toward holy objectives and a productive economic order. By directing personal behavior within group moral standards, a righteous nation would be created, standing as an offering to God and a lesson to the fallen world. A true republican order would be founded in a sturdy, self-supporting, and self-governing democracy led by its elect (of God by the evidence of their social standing and of men by their ballots).

In its political culture, therefore, New England was in a certain sense pre-modern, for these attitudes comprised a very old conception of government and society. New Englanders sought to keep alive venerable, almost tribal notions of the gathered people bound together by an interpenetration of church and state. However, there was emerging in New England a Yankee prototype that presented a striking contrast with the older Puritan lifestyle. This new character type was distinguished by an assertive and acquisitive individualism that led toward modern society. There was, therefore, a paradox, inherent in the New England character, that would lead in diverging directions. Nonetheless, in New England more than elsewhere in America, there would be an ethic that demanded the sacrificing of individual advantage and appetite to the common good.

In its people and culture, Massachusetts was so deeply English—English, that is, within the Dissenting tradition in the home country —that it would continue after the Revolution to draw sustenance and self-enhancement from its persisting economic and intellectual ties to the mother country. This relationship would be strengthened as Americans turned to look and move inward to the continental interior, leaving New England behind (although its people, as they moved westward, would plant a broad band of Yankeedom through western New York, northern Pennsylvania, and the Middle West). For its larger adventures and its economic development, New England would continue, therefore, to look outward to the Atlantic.

The lifestyle most praised by Southerners and elevated as a common ideal was that of the aristocratic gentleman living according to the gentry model: free-thinking, prickly of restraints, leisured, worldly, solicitous of slaves and the lower orders in white society, and above all proud of his manhood and his skills in verbal and physical combat. Closely allied to this concept was that of the independent yeoman farmer, fully equal as a white man to the gentry, devoted to the same personal values, and as much to be regarded as providing an esteemed pattern for living. Southerners believed in a libertarian democracy, composed of free white persons concerned primarily with their material advancement and jealous of their freedom from encroaching authority. Drawing on Enlightenment ideals of human freedom, the South sought to establish a mode of living that would be free of the restraining power of higher authority. The South advocated the absolute autonomy of each (white) male and stressed the equal standing of all such persons in society. Its world would be strongly secular. In later generations the white South would show intense team spirit and a fervent religiosity, but in the Revolutionary years the broad tendency of its culture was anticlerical and almost anarchistic in its individualism.

Virginia's links with England were destined to wither. The back country of the colony contained growing populations of Scotch-Irish and Germans who hated the English. In addition, the South's commitment to slavery would increasingly isolate the region as, with the later cotton boom, the slave system was regenerated and made completely dominant in Southern life. As the Northern states abolished the institution, and the English did the same in their empire, the South would become a moral pariah in the Anglo-American world. By then the homogeneity of feeling and identity among Southern whites would derive from their shared white skins and relative freedom from labor, not from a relationship to the former mother country.

Already, in Thomas Jefferson's world, there was a reaching out to sources of cultural nourishment in Scotland and France. Moreover, that enthusiastic turning inward to the West was soon to begin, an enterprise in which the South would seek to find a wholly American identity. All these tendencies would move together to make the South, during the first seventy years of the nation's existence under the federal Constitution, far more successful than New England in retaining the country's leadership. The South's localism, distrust of bankers, and its democratic republicanism would be attractive to an ever more egalitarian and libertarian white Northern citizenry, whose fundamental racism approved the exclusion of blacks from the new order. Its commitment to the West would give the South leadership in what was to become a national obsession, and its turning away from England—indeed, its often outspoken hostility toward that country—would be directly in the predominant American grain. As the Scotch-Irish and Germans continued moving down into and spreading out upon the vast upland South and the cotton lands, the remnants of the Anglicized Tidewater community, with its Episcopalian churches, would be left far behind, and Anglophobia would mount. Andrew Jackson, a Scotch-Irishman of the Carolinas and Tennessee, was to become the hero of his age by his stunning victory over the British at New Orleans in 1815, his later hounding of British agents in Florida in 1818, and his attacks against the power of British capital in American life in the 1830s.

There would always be currents moving against the South's dominant patterns of life. In part, they would stem from the stern preachments of Baptist, Methodist, and Presbyterian clergymen, who urged self-denial and God-centeredness. These values would stand in sharp contrast to the moral order created by slavery and racial oppression, with their inducements to violence, sexual license, self-indulgence, and human callousness. From the beginning of American history, there would also be a push toward Yankee ways and political values within Southern life. Indeed, many in the South would admire the Northern states, deplore the disorder and the cultural backwardness of their setting, and work for the reform of Southern ways of living. From these circles would come Southern Federalists in Jefferson's time and Southern Whigs in the Jackson years. The South, moreover, would become ever more aware that slavery made it an endangered and detested minority in the Anglo-American world. In time the region would take on a fortress mentality. By the 1850s an emphasis on team spirit, conformity to shared values, and a practically tribal religious consciousness would make the Southern white community ready—if in many quarters reluctantly so—to rebel against the national government over which they appeared to have lost control.

In New England there would also be influences leading in directions contrary to the region's original nature. The allure of trade and great wealth would stand against its simple piety. Commerce, industrialization, and an aggressively profit-oriented life would inevitably mock the holy enterprise. Urbanization would necessarily lead to variety in life patterns. The established Congregational church in Massachusetts, Connecticut, and New Hampshire would eventually come under fire from its religious enemies, so that the union of church and state that even Sam Adams believed in would be terminated. There would be, in fact, a tendency within the Country party's tradition of republicanism, with its emphasis upon localism and its hatred of aristocratic and financial power, that would make the political ideals of Thomas Jefferson attractive to many New Englanders. As against the strong Federalism and Whiggism of Massachusetts, New Hampshire, with its Scotch-Irish and its Baptists, would become the most Democratic state in the Union. The influx of Catholic Irish that would begin in the 1840s would do even more to accelerate the dissipation of the cultural homogeneity that had meant so much to the Yankees of the Revolutionary era.

For all their inner contradictions, however, the cultural identities that New England and the South would present to the nation would be strong, definite, and unmistakable. Yankees and Southerners would dominate political parties wherever they congregated in significant numbers, imparting a tone and character to public life that all would recognize. Thus did American politics acquire those two cultural personages who for so long shaped the country's history: the Yankee and the Cavalier.

In the complex Middle States, with their confusing pluralism of faiths, ethnic groups, and economic interests, the enemy was not primarily transatlantic, as in Revolutionary Massachusetts and Virginia. Rather, the Middle States peoples had a plentiful supply of adversaries within their own borders. On one side were the ruling circles, which had had little argument with their status in the empire before the 1760s. Indeed, tens of thousands of common people in these states, as well as large segments of the elite, were Loyalists. On the opposite side stood the cultural outgroups, numerous and powerful. The collision of two strongly self-conscious groupings of peoples in the Middle States was, therefore, especially harsh, and the cultural conflict that resulted was primarily internal. Since the enemy was close at hand and could be thought of as a traitor within, politics were particularly embittered, forging a political culture that was feud-prone and unforgiving.

The Scotch-Irish made their entry into American public life primarily in Pennsylvania and New York. It was around this politically sensitized people, who served as the core ethnic community on the anti-English side, that all patriot groups in these states gathered. As a Hessian captain in the British army said in 1778, "Call this war by whatever name you may, only call it not an American rebellion; it is nothing more or less than a Scotch Irish Presbyterian rebellion."[10] In

New York Colony, the Scotch-Irish assaulted the Anglican and patrician Dutch establishment; in Pennsylvania they attacked one that
was Anglican and Quaker. Not only were these coalitions that the
Scotch-Irish opposed primarily English in ethnic origin and Anglicized in culture; they were also urban, cosmopolitan, transatlantic,
and imperial in their sense of identity, being deeply involved in trade
and banking. They dominated Philadelphia and especially New York
City, held most of the wealth in their colonies, and prided themselves
on their relatively cultivated mode of living.

The Scotch-Irish Presbyterians also had a sizable representation in
the landed and merchant gentry. In this sense, the conflict between
the Scotch-Irish and their English antagonists was one between gentlemen, each drawing on religious outlooks and intellectual backgrounds that were elegant and sophisticated. Within the larger
context of the British empire, however, there was little ambiguity
about what Scotch-Irishmen represented in English eyes. They were
inveterate rebels, troublesome and restive under English authority.
Regarded as crude and violent, they were also condemned as hard-
drinking religious bigots, for all their Calvinist austerity and their
insistence upon the need for separation of church and state and
religious toleration.

The Scotch-Irish were, in reality, a stern rural folk who liked
their Scotch whisky—Englishmen drank gin or French wine and
brandy—and who possessed violent and fighting tempers that appalled Quakers and law-abiding Anglicans. Dour democrats, the
Scotch-Irish prized the principle of elected, representative government, both in their churches and in secular life. They thrived on their
ancient hatred for Englishmen and the Anglican church. Historically
Whig, in the Revolutionary argument the Scotch-Irish were
egalitarian republicans. Social rank meant English privilege. Their
allies in New York were the plebeian, Americanized Dutch; New
Englanders who had settled on Long Island; the artisans and working
class of New York City; and the Germans. In Pennsylvania the
Scotch-Irish aligned with the Germans (primarily the Calvinist Reformed, but often the Lutherans as well) and the artisans and laborers of Philadelphia. These groups combined to wrest control of
government in the Middle Colonies from the Loyalists, establishing
that essential geographic core of patriot resistance to the British
government without which the colonial cause would have been
hopeless.

After independence was declared, the republicans of the Middle
States did not close ranks as they largely did in Virginia and Massa-

chusetts. The cultural duality of Pennsylvania and New York was far too deep for this to occur. In both states a political rivalry sprang up almost immediately between egalitarian republicans, led by the Scotch-Irish, and nationalist republicans, led by the mercantile and banking classes in New York City and Philadelphia. The aggressively democratic tradition within Scotch-Irish Presbyterianism, which stemmed from radical Scotland and Ireland, moved ahead vigorously once it was in the ascendancy in Pennsylvania. We have seen that its adherents democratized the state's constitution and attacked the mercantile and financial interests of Philadelphia. In so doing, they sharply polarized the state's politics and prompted the opposition of a large and varied coalition.

In important ways, this two-party rivalry mirrored the political divisions within Pennsylvania that had existed before 1776. The Quakers and Episcopalians were ranged against the Scotch-Irish, and so were former Loyalists and the banking and mercantile classes in general. Many of the latter had been, if not Loyalists, friendly to Britain and ready only in the final moments to rebel. The Scotch-Irish also drove away their former allies, the Lutherans and the Baptists. They recoiled from Presbyterian aggressiveness, remembering the warnings issued long before by Anglicans and Quakers that if the Presbyterian Calvinists achieved control, they would establish a religious tyranny like that of the Congregational Calvinists in New England, where minority sects were persecuted. A sizable group of Scotch-Irishmen, probably from among the merchants, even turned against their egalitarian countrymen. In New York State, meanwhile, similar political events occurred. Clusters of culture groups and associated ideologies resembling those in Pennsylvania evolved, and a two-party battle began that followed a similar course.

In the late 1780s the egalitarian republicans in both Pennsylvania and New York suffered defeat. They watched in alarm as a nationalizing federal Constitution was written by their enemies. Men like the Philadelphia financier Robert Morris and the New York City lawyer Alexander Hamilton dreamed of an American empire to replace the one that had been left behind. Many of Morris' and Hamilton's following had been strong nationalists under the British Crown, thinking of themselves not simply as Pennsylvanians or New Yorkers but as proud subjects of a great empire, centrally governed to the (commercial) benefit of all. In this they shared the sense of identity with the larger community that we have seen in the Court party of Massachusetts.

In the new circumstances of independence, these Middle States' people became nationalist republicans. They called for a vigorous central government that would unify the country, give wide latitude to its entrepreneurs, and make the United States a power in the world. With their roots deep in the Anglicized seaboard aristocracy, they had little faith in the virtue of the common people—especially when so many of them were Scotch-Irish or German and who, moreover, distrusted any project of more than local dimensions. Capitalizing on the confusion and disorder of the mid-1780s, nationalist republicans were able to construct and win popular approval for a federal government that was quite independent of the states and imperial both in the fullness and extent of its powers and in the great domain over which it held authority.

Soon this nationalist ascendancy was to fade. Within a dozen years egalitarian republicans would recapture political supremacy in the Middle States. The ethnic outgroups and the artisan and working classes were growing. As they became more fascinated by national politics and drawn in growing numbers to the polls, they would also become more politically powerful. The Scotch-Irish of Pennsylvania would need only to win back the Lutherans and Baptists to establish an unbeatable coalition in that state. With this coalition formed, Pennsylvania would swing so solidly into the egalitarian and libertarian republican column, behind Thomas Jefferson and the South, that it would be called the keystone state for Jeffersonian Republicans in the North. In time, New York would see a similar, if somewhat more broken, progression toward domination by non-English outgroups and loyalty to the Jeffersonian tradition. The close identification between New York State and the Democratic party would eventually become one of the cornerstones of American politics. So long as this situation endured, a coalition composed of most of the South and the two Middle States would dominate United States politics and the government in Washington.

In neither Pennsylvania nor New York would there ever exist nearly so monolithic a political culture as developed to the north and south. The social structure and economic interests of the Middle States were too complex. The two large cities of Philadelphia and New York, with their strong leadership of Anglicized, cosmopolitan businessmen, would keep rooted in these states a powerful tradition that admired English institutions and ways. A huge westward migration of New England Yankees would cross into upstate New York, introducing into the state's politics thousands of voters hostile to everything in the Scotch-Irish and Southern traditions and everything anti-English in tone and morally libertarian. As the working classes grew with the swelling cities, other groups opposed to them would likewise grow. Thus, political coalitions would be so closely matched within New York State that victories would be won by narrow margins.

New England and the South were so evenly matched on the national scene that small shifts at the polls in Middle States' elections or within their delegations to Congress would tip the scales and decide the course of national policy. This would make the internal political battles in the Middle States crucially important and induce the creation of strong, well-organized parties. The Middle States' central role in national life would not be accompanied, however, by their fashioning of a recognizable cultural image. Too heterogeneous for the development of a believable cultural stereotype or an unchanging political stance, the Middle States would never acquire that distinctive role in the nation's consciousness played by the South and New England. As the people of the states along the Atlantic seaboard streamed westward, it was the Yankees and Southerners—not the people from the Middle States—who would stand out, establishing the cultural tone wherever they predominated. This was the more ironic because so much of the institutional structure of the rest of the nation, outside of the slave South, was to be modeled on that of the Middle States. Their pluralism and their blending of traditions and peoples was symbolized in their local government, with its joining of Yankee town and Southern county, a pattern that would become characteristic of the Midwest and beyond. It appeared, too, in their rigorous separation of church and state, born of necessity in a setting where many divergent religious groups existed and all must be protected, each from the other.

Perhaps the most distinctive contribution of the Middle States to national life would be that, in this heterogeneous cultural setting, the two-party system would first appear in its modern form. The Middle States were urban, Atlantic, and English. At the same time, they were extensively rural, closely tied and strongly committed to the West, and heavily populated by non-English ethnic groups. They were commercial, industrial, modernizing, and cosmopolitan, yet they were also agricultural, traditionalist, and localist. Although the Middle States were secular in their public institutions, they included thousands of people who believed that government should insure moral purity (as their particular faith conceived of it) and demanded that government do so. Out of the conflict of these cultural forces would emerge that bipolar form and style of American public life that would eventually diffuse itself throughout the American nation.

In 1789 George Washington arrived in New York City to take up his duties as President of the United States, and the new enterprise was ready to begin. The national government met briefly in that city, sat in Philadelphia for the next ten years, and in the early summer of 1800 finally settled in the City of Washington, District of Columbia. In this first dozen years of the nation's existence under the federal Constitution, the lines along which the country's public life would proceed thereafter were marked out with striking clarity. By 1800, with the election of Thomas Jefferson, the first national two-party system would be fully formed, and the basic pattern in national politics would make itself clear.

part two

THE JEFFERSONIAN AND JACKSONIAN PARTY SYSTEMS: 1789=1824, 1828=1854

IV

The Jeffersonian
Party System,
1789=1824

For thirty years after the federal government came into being, one question above all others obsessed the country: Would the new government survive? "The Founding Fathers," Arthur Schlesinger, Jr., has observed, "had embarked on a singular adventure—the adventure of a *republic.*" They looked back anxiously through history to the example of the Roman republic, which had come to a dishonorable end, overwhelmed by its inner corruptions. Republics were transient creatures, ever in danger from human propensities for luxury and indiscipline; too weak to survive, because founded in the general will. Thus, the founders "had an intense conviction of the improbability of their undertaking." The American republic was a lonely experiment in a world of monarchies, and it had a plenitude of enemies, most of all the powerful nation from which it had freed itself. For a brief time in the 1790s, republicanism seemed to be sweeping Europe behind Napoleon's armies, and Americans could feel that their bold venture was the beginning of a new order in Western civilization. Soon, however, Napoleon's creations degenerated into autocracies, and the self-governing democratic republic on the coast of North America was again solitary and endangered.[1]

The past record of American performance was not encouraging. The Articles of Confederation had decayed into impotence. The

confusions and excesses of republican government in the several
states during the years of the Confederation had clouded the formerly confident belief that a government founded in the people
would necessarily be wise and virtuous. The federal Constitution had
been written in good part to compensate for the instabilities to which
an unchecked democracy seemed prone, but no one could say with
confidence that the new government would be any more workable
than the old. Most of the English had long scoffed at the republican
idea, and Americans were keenly aware of their contempt. Government, to all but the radical Whigs in England, remained a mystery
to be conducted by an established elite, working within the stable
framework of the hereditary monarchy and House of Lords. The
mood in the United States, therefore, was anxious and unsettled. For
a generation Americans had been passing through an epic. Heavy
dangers and risky adventures had come to seem life's normal pattern, and the feeling of being caught up in a perilous enterprise
persisted until after 1815, when a long peace finally allowed a sense
of security to emerge.

Because the survival of the nation was at issue, politics in the
national capital were peculiarly violent and envenomed during the
early years of the new government. Each side was convinced that the
other secretly planned to destroy the republic, either to establish a
monarchy or to carry the new republic to democracy's extreme, the
primal chaos of anarchism. In fact, it would be misleading to speak
of this generation's politics as comprising a "party system." Few
believed their opponents should even exist or that political parties
were legitimate. George Washington condemned parties in his Fare-
well Address, urging Americans to avoid party activity, and his words
were widely echoed. Indeed, the inescapable fact that parties were
forming was brought forward as proof that the nation was falling into
fatal corruption.

Americans in these years believed that there should be only one
party, for truth was unitary and opposition was therefore disloyal.
Thomas Jefferson and his followers fully expected the Federalists to
disappear after his election to the presidency in 1800, and by James
Monroe's presidency (1817–1825) this was in fact occurring. The idea
of party as a proper, indeed essential, instrument in a democratic
republic was not to take hold until after the 1820s. Federalists and
Jeffersonian Republicans, in short, did not think of themselves as
participating in a stable two-party system involving oscillations in
authority as first one party and then the other won elections. The
Jeffersonian Republicans conceived of their victory over the Federal-

ists in the election of 1800 as a revolution, and so did the Federalists themselves. Thereafter, Jefferson denied military commissions to Massachusetts Federalists because they were thought to be disloyal by definition, and when that state opposed the embargo of 1807, charges of treason were freely levied. In fact, until 1844 no political party that had lost the presidency was able to win it back. Not until that decade did parties develop enduring and essentially modern internal organizations reaching upward from precincts through state committees to national nominating conventions.[2]

Nonetheless, in the Jeffersonian years the nation went through its first experience with a national two-party system. It constituted, within its limitations, the transitional stage in the mobilizing process that had begun during the Revolution. The clustering of peoples and ideas, of differing modes of republicanism, behind Federalists or Jeffersonian Republicans displayed the same order of battle observed earlier. The nation's basic polarities swiftly drove people into familiar confrontations and posed the same issues, if in modified form. This was, in fact, the heroic age in party history, and American politicians ever since have seen an epic quality in the conflict between Jefferson and Hamilton. Throughout the nineteenth century, politicians looked back to the founding years as the time of giants when fundamental political creeds were fashioned and articles of political faith having a sacramental quality were established. To be a Jeffersonian was a vital and living identity to William Jennings Bryan generations later, and Andrew Mellon, in the days of Harding and Coolidge, pursued his work as secretary of the treasury the more confidently with Alexander Hamilton's portrait on his wall.[3]

When Congress began its sessions in 1789, most of its members had served in the Confederation Congresses and had witnessed at first hand that system's fatal weaknesses. Some members had helped to write the new Constitution, and practically all had worked actively to secure its ratification. In this sense, they had been termed Federalists, though the name did not as yet connote membership in a political party. In the tariff bill of 1789, they moved quickly to provide the new government with a firm and continuing source of revenue, the absence of which had destroyed the Articles of Confederation. However, an extended argument occurred over the plan brought forward by Secretary of the Treasury Alexander Hamilton to pay off the national debt inherited from the Confederation government. Hamilton insisted that payment was essential in order firmly to establish the new government's credit among financiers at home and abroad, despite the fact that much of the money would go to speculators. After a sharp controversy, the proposal was agreed to in a historic compromise by which, in return for Southern support, it was agreed that the nation's capital would be placed within the slave states on the Potomac River. Then, in 1791, Hamilton urged that Congress create a Bank of the United States. The Bank would not simply regulate the currency from a central location; it would also accelerate development of the nation's resources by pooling capital in the hands of the financiers of Philadelphia and New York. With this great lever, they could guide the course of economic growth.

Congress passed the banking proposal, but by a divided sectional vote that clearly forecast the future. New England legislators and most of those from the Middle States were solidly in its favor, but Southern congressmen, led by James Madison, who were thoroughly aroused at the thought that the new government was going to be dominated by Northern interests, united to oppose the proposal. On almost every major issue that Congress voted on in the 1790s, a Yankee bloc containing most of the New Englanders voted in opposition to a Southern bloc only slightly less monolithic. Thus, the way in which Middle States' legislators voted, though much divided among themselves, was usually the way issues were decided.[4]

The confrontation between New England and the South that was now, in familiar fashion, beginning to polarize the Congress flowed into every question. It arose from the most fundamental cultural hostilities. Reared in their profoundly differing settings, Southerners and Yankees in Congress frankly did not like each other. New Englanders could not understand the slave-based Southern way of life, for which they had a settled contempt. Nothing else, they believed, so clearly revealed Thomas Jefferson's hypocrisy as his ownership of slaves. To New Englanders, Jefferson's talk of equality and democracy was a brazen, lying show. Slavery made black persons brutalized human beings and their masters an indolent, lordly breed. Southern planters had developed the habit of living in debt, assuming that the future would rescue them from the results of their extravagant ways, and to New Englanders this seemed not merely unintelligent but immoral. How could the nation be placed in the hands of men who were improvident? Southerners' characteristic amusements—bear baiting, physical combat, and drinking—offended moralistic New Englanders. The practice of dueling common among the Southern aristocracy fixed in the Northern mind an image of the Southerner as addicted to violence—an image that would persist into the next century and beyond. A Yankee's proud refusal to go into the street for a duel when challenged by an angry Southerner proved his manhood in Northern eyes, but rendered him effeminate and cowardly in the view of Southerners.[5]

In 1794 western Pennsylvania farmers, generally Scotch-Irish in origin and devoted to the manufacture of their folk beverage, *uisge beatha*—the "water of life"—angrily resisted payment of an excise tax on whisky. President Washington reacted instantly, sending a militia force of fifteen thousand men led by Alexander Hamilton to sweep the Pittsburgh region. Its objective was to demonstrate with overwhelming force that the new federal government would not tolerate the turbulence and contempt for law that had so disordered the Articles of Confederation period. Washington and Hamilton also suspected foreign (French revolutionary) intrigue behind the Pennsylvania uprising. They were convinced that the democratic societies that had been springing up around the country in the previous year at the urging of the controversial Citizen Edmond Genêt, the French Republic's first minister to the United States, were linked to the Whisky Rebellion. The democratic societies praised the French Revolution and campaigned in almost every state against aristocratic rule, the presumed threat of a revived monarchy, and Hamiltonian finance.[6]

The politicians who were now gathering around Washington and Hamilton and claiming the honored name "Federalist" thought the democratic societies pure sedition. To these people, the French Revolution was a horror; its attacks upon established religion and the institutions and values of aristocracy and traditional order seemed the essence of evil. Federalists believed French ideas to have captured Thomas Jefferson and the group gathering around him that was now beginning to call itself the "republican interest." Jefferson's followers openly advocated the French Revolution's cry of "liberty, equality, and fraternity." Jefferson himself was an intellectual who maintained intimate ties with French philosophers. Their praise of reason and science and their hostility to established churches were echoed in his own writings. Hamilton capitalized upon the involvement of several local democratic societies in the Pittsburgh region in the Whisky Rebellion. As French sympathizers, they were in his eyes enemies of order, true religion, and honest finance. If their rebellion were not crushed, he said, it would be giving "a CARTE BLANCHE to ambition, licentiousness and foreign intrigue."[7]

In his report to Congress upon the militia's expedition—which apprehended, finally, only a few luckless protestors, most of whom were eventually released—President Washington blamed the Whisky Rebellion on the democratic societies. This immediately set off an uproar in Congress. German Lutherans, who had formed the first such society in Pennsylvania, were offended by Washington's charge, as were Scotch-Irish Presbyterians, journalists, physicians and intellectuals in Philadelphia, merchants trading with France, and eloquent patriots from the days of the Revolution like Dr. Benjamin Rush, all of whom had joined the societies to work for a more egalitarian nation. Federalists pointed to the fact that many in the societies were members of ethnic outgroups—Frenchmen, Jews, and Irishmen—as proof of their subversive tendencies. When Congress voted on whether or not to support Washington's condemnation of the societies, Southern opposition was almost unanimous; the Middle States split widely, with the Scotch-Irish and Germans voting heavily against the President; and all but four congressmen from New England gave him their support.[8]

Then that most divisive of all questions, relations with England, burst into national politics. Americans could not be neutral toward the English: they either hated them or retained strong feelings of respect, admiration, and brotherly affiliation. Until well into the twentieth century, England was to be the most prominent object on the American horizon, the fact of recent parentage and continuing intimate cultural and economic relations making deep claims on the American mind. The relationship was to be one of those inescapable, constantly intrusive elements in national life. American newspapers would report on affairs in Parliament almost as closely as on those at home. British books on politics and economics, philosophy and sociology, literature and religion would form the staple of intellectual nourishment to the American mind a century and more after the Revolution. Hundreds of thousands of Englishmen, Scots, Welsh, and Irishmen would continue to emigrate to the United States through the nineteenth century, in a persistent westering which kept the Anglo-American community vital and alive. Americans, too, would remain keenly conscious that Englishmen looked down upon them as rude democratic provincials. This made them either anxious to emulate the English and gain their respect or resentful and aggressively American. It also made every facet of diplomatic relations charged and sensitive.

In 1794 President Washington dispatched Chief Justice John Jay to England to negotiate a treaty settling a broad range of unresolved disputes. Jay returned with a document widely regarded as toadying to the English, and an outcry erupted that dwarfed the Whisky Rebellion controversy. Jeffersonian Republicans instantly condemned the document, and Federalists labored manfully to defend it. New England, with its strong trading and cultural links to the former mother country, was strongly in its favor. Federalists insisted that "trade and friendship with England, under whatever conditions, was the only path to the preservation of the national autonomy." Elsewhere, however, Republicans called mass meetings to protest the Jay Treaty. In New York City, on July 4, 1796, the democratic societies of that community "assembled in full force, each carrying its insignia, and marched into the Presbyterian church," which had echoed to anti-English oratory since Revolutionary days. There they listened to Edward Livingston, eminent Presbyterian, Republican congressman, and supporter of Governor George Clinton, read the Declaration of Independence. The treaty was eventually ratified. It cleared British troops out of the forts they still occupied within American borders and opened trade with British possessions, and these gains were too vital to turn down. However, by the time the furor had finally quieted, the process of dividing Americans into Federalists and Jeffersonian Republicans was largely complete, within both the Congress and the country at large.[9]

The presidential election of 1796 saw the two parties well formed as national institutions and ready to fight the first party battle for control of the executive branch. The nationalist republicans of the Middle States and the moralistic republicans of New England had joined forces to form the Federalist party and govern the country. Their essential interests and their visions of what the United States should become were sufficiently compatible for them to work in concert, although not entirely comfortably, as a bitter rivalry that sprang up between New York's Alexander Hamilton and Massachusetts' John Adams would demonstrate. With support from former Loyalists in the Middle States, the Federalists had set out during Washington's years to build a strong and vigorous nation modeled on English lines. It was to be Anglicized in political style, Atlantic and eastward looking in its orientation, commercial and developmental in its economics, and friendly with England. Abroad, its enemy was to be England's enemy: France, and that nation's radicalism, irreligion, and egalitarianism. At home, Federalists wanted the American economy to be given central direction by financial institutions patterned after the Bank of England. As a political outlook that flourished primarily among the ethnically English, Federalism's heartland lay in New England and among the Anglicized Middle States aristocracy. Elitist in its social values, moralistic and aggressively religious, Federalism regarded the ancient enemies of the English, the egalitarian Scotch-Irish and Germans of Lutheran and Calvinist persuasions, with traditional distaste.

Convinced that it was they who had founded the country and that it was out of the bosom of their English culture that the nation had drawn its essential characteristics and governing system, the Yankees thought of themselves as the only truly "American" people and conceived of the nation in their own image. They conceived of the other peoples living in the country as variants of the true norm, alternatively comic and potentially subversive. How could these alien peoples be loyal to a Yankee nation? In response, the ethnic outgroups gathered together with most white Southerners in the Jeffersonian Republican party.

No controversy could have been more successfully dramatized than by the remarkable personages of the key protagonists themselves, Alexander Hamilton and Thomas Jefferson. Hamilton, now in his mid-thirties, was the kind of spectacular man around whom legends gather. A rather small, elegantly dressed New York lawyer of soldierly bearing and an admirer of everything British, he struck many as vain and arrogant and others as charming, patriotic, brilliant, and eloquent. The great achievements of great men were for him the chief events in history. "He did not think," writes his biographer John C. Miller, "that the people had leadership, political wisdom and initiative in themselves—leadership came from the exceptional individuals, the 'natural aristocrats' and the rich and educated." Driven by a search for personal glory, he believed that the United States as a nation should do likewise in its foreign policy.[10]

Hamilton thought the individual states weak and distracted entities that should have been eliminated in the new Constitution. The nation as a whole should have been placed under one powerful central government in which the chief executive, an elective monarch, would be preeminently the center of leadership and authority. In this, Hamilton fully inherited the traditional Tory view of legislative bodies as irritating distractions composed of obstructionists who were irreverent and lacked team spirit. As for republicanism, Hamilton was not a monarchist, but he had, nonetheless, grave concerns. In its egalitarian and libertarian forms, republicanism seemed to distrust governments so blindly that it would leave them too weak and the prey of foreign enemies. Hamilton worked hard to compensate for what he conceived to be this central fault in the federal government. In 1802, in a mood of despair, he remarked that "the present Constitution ... [is a] frail and worthless fabric."[11]

Thomas Jefferson and his Virginia colleague, James Madison, formed an intimate partnership that, in the essential nature of the two men themselves, contrasted sharply with the Hamiltonian style:

> Hamilton relished conflict; Jefferson and Madison hated it. ... Hamilton was dashing and arrogant; Jefferson and Madison were calm and deferential. Hamilton was a dandy; Jefferson was careless of personal appearance, and Madison wore little but black. ... Jefferson and Madison were essentially private men; for them the purpose of government was not national glory, but the protection of individuals in the pursuit of legitimate private interests. [They believed] ... the United States should seek not wealth but simplicity, not power but liberty, not national glory but domestic tranquillity, not heroism but happiness.[12]

Jefferson was cynical about "great men," whom he viewed as inveterate rogues. He distrusted the close union between capitalists and the government that Hamilton had in mind, regarding it as inviting corruption. He also drew back from the idea of encouraging the growth of factories and cities. The people at large, being uncorrupted by power, should be the true source of leadership in the new nation. Republicanism, in Jefferson's view, did not create weak governments but the best and the most just and therefore ultimately the strongest. An Anglophobe, he bitterly distrusted the English. Anything that leaned toward emulating their institutions and adopting their values was anathema to Jefferson. He took pains to insist that his lineage was Welsh, and he battled long and eventually successfully to disestablish the Church of England in Virginia, creating religious equality and freedom for everyone. He always believed the Federalists to be monarchists. Watching Hamilton, in early 1792 Jefferson wrote that "a sect has shewn itself among us who declare they espoused our new constitution, not as a good and sufficient thing itself, but only as a step to an English constitution. ... Too many of these stock jobbers and king-jobbers have come into our legislature."[13]

Jefferson's world view was rooted in the soil and in a profound localism. He loved the farming life and returned to it whenever he could, as evidenced by his freckled, sunburned face and by his personal style, "being very much," wrote a British diplomat observing him in the White House in 1804, "like that of a tall, large-boned farmer." From his experience in Europe as America's minister to

France, Jefferson had formed a distaste for cities and thought the
British irretrievably corrupted by power, aristocratic arrogance, and
ignorance among the masses. All of humanity, he believed, was by
natural law divided into Whigs and Tories, this division springing
from fundamental differences in personality. Whigs, in Jefferson's
view, were rugged, self-sufficient people who were capable of governing themselves and willing to let others do the same, thus in little
need of institutions. Tories, on the other hand, were either arrogant
men hungry for power and the privilege of lording it over their
followers or people so weak in spirit that they needed and desired
the protection of powerful men and governments.[14]

Jefferson regarded bankers warily and thought paper money an
evil. He believed it drove out good money (i.e., gold and silver coin)
and made the economy fluctuate erratically at the behest of scheming businessmen who profited by buying when things were cheap
and selling when they were dear. His economics came from the
French Physiocrats and especially from the Scotsman Adam Smith,
who in his *Wealth of Nations* (1776) warned that businessmen must
always be watched carefully, for they monopolized and wheedled
special privileges from governments at every opportunity, and that
protective tariffs, bounties, and every other device aimed at stimulating the economy only resulted in higher prices, unfair profits for
producers, and social injustice. Far better, Smith thought, would be
a system of "natural liberty" by which no favors would be given to
anyone, and all producers would be subject to the competitive discipline of the marketplace. So persuaded, Jefferson warned Americans
that society was not naturally harmonious, as Federalists insisted,
with its upper classes providing kindly and principled leadership and
its common people following in their humble sphere. Rather, society
was divided against itself by an unending conflict between the
classes, induced by the greed of the wealthy for more profits and
power. Thus Jefferson condemned speculation, "the spirit of gam-
ing," "the rage of getting rich in a day," and regarded Hamilton's
banking schemes as opening the way to ruinous speculative ventures
in which the innocent would suffer and the wicked would profit.
They all corrupted the people, he believed, sapping the moral foundations of honest republicanism.[15]

When in 1796 the Republicans ran Jefferson for the presidency
against John Adams, Washington's vice president and heir apparent,
they were so well organized and fought so vigorous a battle that

Adams won by only three electoral votes. (Jefferson became, as the Constitution then provided, Adams' vice president.) Behind the outcome of this election lay an epochal mobilization of the common people. The general populace, awakened by the excitement of the campaign, headed in record numbers to the polls. This outpouring of voters mounted steadily in the late 1790s. Until about 1795, an average of 25 percent of the eligible male voters had turned out for national elections, with no indication of an upward trend. The two-party rivalry now emerging, however, sent voting statistics soaring. By the presidential election of James Madison in 1808, as many as 70 percent of the eligible voters were entering the polls in states like Pennsylvania and New Jersey. In elections to state offices, voter participation rose to unprecedented levels: up to 98 percent of adult males.[16]

John Adams' single term as President (1797–1801) saw an almost unceasing political battle. The Quasi-War with France, an undeclared naval conflict on the open seas that began in 1797, possessed the national mind. Hamilton's "High Federalists" were eager to smite the French, and they demanded that Adams secure a full declaration of war from Congress. When he refused, they made his life miserable with their intrigues, practically expelling him from the party. The Republicans were traditionally warm to the French, not only because of their egalitarian and republican revolution but because of their ancient animosity toward the English. When the Republicans protested that Adams was in fact leading the nation to war with France, he replied by labeling them the "French party" and calling them seditious and treacherous. In April 1798 the French demanded a huge bribe of American negotiators in the "XYZ" affair. The American people soon learned of this action, and a wave of anti-French revulsion swept the country, venting itself everywhere on Republicans.[17]

Open fighting broke out in the nation's streets. Those wearing Adams' chosen symbol for Federalism and patriotism, the black cockade, attacked those wearing Republicanism's emblem, a red cockade. Invasion jitters sprang up, with the rumors spreading that the French planned to send a black army from Santo Domingo to incite a slave uprising in the Southern states. Others said that recently arrived Frenchmen in Philadelphia were planning to destroy that city by fire and massacre its citizenry. In 1798 and 1799 Jeffersonian militia units formed and began drilling in preparation for a feared imminent conflict with Federalists. Vice President Thomas Jefferson was placed under surveillance by Federalist patriots, who were convinced that he had direct contact with the French and received regular instructions on the best means for overthrowing the American republic. The newspapers were filled with attacks upon political enemies—attacks unparalleled in their ferocity, perhaps, since that time. Each party was devoted to its own variety of republicanism and convinced that it constituted the nation's only hope; each regarded the other side as by definition treasonous:

> Rare was the issue of the public press which did not record instances of personal abuse, politically motivated duels, threats of nullification, armed rebellions among the populace, and brawls on the floor of Congress. . . . Federalists absorbed this extremist political style more fully than did their Republican adversaries. They were far more abusive in their partisan assaults . . . [and] delivered their crisis prophecies with a force of invective unmatched at the time and seldom since surpassed.[18]

In this storm of anger and patriotic hysteria, the Congregational clergy of New England, Federalist to the core, was seized by a fantastic theory, put forward by the Reverend Jedediah Morse, alleging that the French Revolution had been spawned by a secret international conspiracy. Morse traced this conspiracy to a society of antireligious freethinkers in central Europe called the Bavarian Illuminati and insisted that its agents were even then at work within the United States, subverting its morals and government. Proof of this fact was seen to lie in the nationwide upsurge of Republicanism around Thomas Jefferson, whom the Federalist clergy regarded as the devil's own agent. The Jeffersonians had, of course, their own church following. The Presbyterians were staunch Republicans, and so, too, were the Baptists. According to the Baptists, the supreme issue in American life was the need to keep a separation between church and state, a principle now enshrined in the Constitution. For generations they had been harassed and oppressed by established church authorities, not only in Europe but in Congregational New England and in those colonial areas where Anglicanism had been the official state church. The Congregational clergy, wedded to the idea of church-state union, now seized upon Morse's anti-Republican statements as a weapon against Jefferson and their Protestant rivals. The outcry that came from Congregational pulpits so filled the nation's press with sensational allegations that in the late 1790s the world "Illuminati" seemed to be on everyone's tongue.[19]

There was much going on in the country that alarmed the moralists of New England. Everything virtuous, honest, and religiously moral and divine seemed under attack by forces of internal subversion. Out of New England came a lamentation, filled with a revitalized Puritanism, that echoed throughout the country. Where was that "Christian Sparta" to which the patriots had dedicated their lives? Where was that specially chosen American community, bound together in peaceful order, laboring dutifully and in reverent obedience to God's ministers in order to maintain an austere, self-denying, and holy social order? Moralists were convinced that American civilization was disintegrating sexually, ethically, and politically. Discipline had apparently disappeared, for wealthy and influential persons found themselves no longer treated with gestures of respect from the common people. An antiaristocratic sentiment swept the country, bringing into question all of the elite's symbols. This was most obvious in changing clothing and hair styles, alarming to traditionalists in any time because such changes are readily apparent and usually constitute, in those who initiate them, a defiant cultural statement. "It was about this time," writes Alfred F. Young, "that dress, common speech, and everyday habits were subject to . . . alterations. Silk stockings, hair powder, pigtails, and shoe buckles began to give way to short hair or small queues and less aristocratic garb." Soon there was the spectacle of Thomas Jefferson in the White House, with his own hair displayed upon his head in place of a wig, pantaloons instead of buckled knee britches, and a general air of indifferent, disorderly attire.[20]

All restraints on individual impulses seemed to be loosening, a trend running directly counter to the venerable Puritan notion that human appetites must be disciplined and controlled by superior authority. Stability, tradition, dependence of inferiors upon their betters, an organic balance and interconnectedness between hierarchical classes and peoples—these were being endangered by the mobile, self-reliant, and individualistic order that Jeffersonianism seemed to foster. Of particular concern were the youth of the country, who seemed to be flocking behind Jefferson's liberating leadership and causing all the turmoils and disorders of the time. On this ground, said Noah Webster, the voting age should be raised to forty-five and no one should be allowed to enter public office until reaching the age of fifty.[21]

New England Federalists were alarmed by the westward movement of the American people and the territorial expansion of the nation in that direction. When Tennessee applied for statehood in 1796, Federalists strongly opposed it. In the 1790s New England's congressmen by a three-to-one margin voted against the provision of funds for defense of the frontiers against the Indians. The Louisiana Purchase in 1803, carried through by President Jefferson, confirmed their worst anxieties. Federalists looked eastward across the Atlantic, thinking of the United States as the westward-most member of a community of civilized North Atlantic nations, the leader of which was Great Britain. That is, they envisioned the United States as a maritime republic whose frontier was on the high seas and in its beckoning worldwide trade, not in the shaggy wilds of the western territories. They preferred that those territories separate off at the Appalachians.[22]

The concept of wilderness was distasteful to Federalists, for it connoted lack of control, immensity, primitiveness, and savagery. Thomas Jefferson's fascination with the vast western territories (as revealed in his *Notes on Virginia*, which became a national best seller when published in Philadelphia in 1788) was almost in itself enough to make Federalists detest the region. Linked to the West were the kinds of scientific studies that religious men thought dangerous. Geology, zoology, and botany, disciplines which fascinated Jefferson and freethinking scholars at the University of Pennsylvania, had a radical flavor to Federalists. "Whenever modern philosophers talk about mountains," warned Clement Clarke Moore, a young anti-Jeffersonian scholar in New York, "something impious is likely to be at hand."[23]

Geologists' talk of mountains slowly eroding into their present form removed the direct hand of God in their creation; their notions of the immense amount of time necessary for the process challenged the orthodox view, based upon biblical studies, that the earth was less than six thousand years old. Botanists and zoologists pored over old bones and strange wilderness plants and speculated about evolution, another concept regarded by the faithful as dangerous. To Federalists, literary men were acceptable intellectuals, for they relied upon patrons and treated literature as an elite concern. Nor were Federalists alarmed by mathematicians and physicists, for they concentrated upon traditional, static views of the universe derived from Newtonian astronomical science. Those, however, who worked in the newer biological and earth sciences were suspect. Being "philosophical," to Federalists, meant being visionary, impractical, and religiously as well as politically unreliable. There was, in fact,

something particularly objectionable to the Federalist mind about Jefferson the inventor, Jefferson the anthropologist, Jefferson the president of the American Philosophical Society [based in Philadelphia and widely regarded as strongly Republican].... Whereas sympathizers saw in ... [Jefferson's] limitless curiosity and inventiveness evidence of an imaginative and far-ranging mind, Federalists, using the same evidence, found a mind that was flighty and irresponsible.[24]

When Jeffersonians proposed changes in public education to make it more democratic and more encouraging of students' individual initiative, Federalists saw this as a fatal permissiveness that would destroy society, that would eliminate the concept of education as devoted to the training of an elite. They were angered when, at Jefferson's urging, the College of William and Mary dropped ancient languages and knowledge of the classics as entrance requirements. Federalists regarded this as a watering down of the curriculum that would make it slack and easily traversed.[25]

They were alarmed at another aspect of the new America: the influx of immigrants from non-English countries. Nativism was powerful in ethnically homogeneous New England. Federalists were easily convinced that the nation's troubles were caused by foreigners who spread revolutionary ideas, maintained conspiratorial relations with foreign governments desiring the downfall of the United States, encouraged the spread of democracy, and were alien in their speech, dress, and style of life. "If some means are not adopted," said the Federalist congressman Harrison Gray Otis, "to prevent the indiscriminate admission of wild Irishmen & others to the right of suffrage, there will soon be an end to liberty and property."[26]

It was in this hysterical atmosphere that the Federalists pushed through Congress, in the month of July 1798, the Alien and Sedition Acts. As Harrison Gray Otis insisted, "French apostles of sedition" were active within the United States, and the President must be given peremptory power to expel them from the country. The Alien Act greatly extended the period of residence required before citizenship could be granted, and the Sedition Act aimed at silencing all critics of the Adams administration. Fines and imprisonment were prescribed for anyone who participated in a conspiracy that sought to impede "the operation of any law of the United States" or intimidated federal officeholders by advocating riot, unlawful assembly, or group action. Similar punishment was authorized for anyone who "shall write, print, utter or publish ... any false, scandalous and malicious writing ... against the government of the United States, or ... Congress ... or the President ... with intent to defame ... or to bring them ... into contempt or disrepute ... or to excite against

them . . . the hatred of the good people of the United States." Editors
were hounded and thrown in jail. Congressman Mathew Lyon of
Vermont, an intemperate Irishman, was briefly incarcerated for one
of his published writings, and large numbers of Frenchmen report-
edly fled from the country. Much graver events that threatened a
constitutional crisis lay in the passage by the Virginia and Kentucky
legislatures of protesting resolutions. Written by James Madison and
Thomas Jefferson, these resolutions called the Alien and Sedition
Acts unconstitutional and warned that the states were sovereign and
could nullify national legislation they considered obnoxious. The
other states in the Union refused to endorse the resolutions, recoiling
from such extreme statements, but a note had been struck, the sound
of which continued to reverberate until the Civil War.[27]

Federalism was now at its peak of influence and power. In the
nationalist mood that seized the country during the Quasi-War with
France, Federalists won large votes and major victories even in the
Southern states. Some of this success sprang from transient fears, as
in South Carolina, where the rumors of an invasion by a French black
army electrified the white population. Federalism in the South, however, had its own natural base of support. Fundamentally, it was an
identity taken up by those who disapproved of the South's dominant
ways of living. The mountainous western counties of Virginia were
overwhelmingly Federalist (until that party finally disappeared in
the 1820s) because their people held few slaves, were repelled by the
world of slavery, and resented the predominance in Virginia's politics that slavery gave to the eastern and southern lowlands. (During
the Civil War, these western counties would secede from Virginia to
form West Virginia.) Many Southern professional and commercial
leaders were Federalist. They rather admired Northern, even Yankee, values of hard work by white men, an educated citizenry, and
orderly, disciplined habits.

When George Washington and James Madison had urged the creation of a strong federal constitution, they encouraged the sense of
nationalism that had always flourished in certain Southern circles. In
the aristocratic, cosmopolitan Northern Neck of Virginia and down
along the Tidewater coast with its great plantations, Federalism was
prominent. Many within the Southern elite took pride in being associated with Washington and were active Federalist partisans. This
was a culturally reasonable alignment, for their elitism echoed that
of Alexander Hamilton and the Northern Federalists. Their cos-

mopolitanism and their friendliness with the English upper classes also made them pro-English. Until the War of 1812 broke out, Southern Federalists regularly defended the English, even when they violated American neutral rights on the high seas. It was common for Episcopalian Tidewater aristocrats to send their sons to English colleges and to maintain a sense of membership in high, transatlantic culture.[28]

Virginia, however, was fundamentally anti-Federalist. The Southside—that huge region south of the James river and inland from the Episcopalian, Anglophile Tidewater—was growing rapidly in population. It was settled by small planters of libertarian and egalitarian sentiments, many of them German and Scotch-Irish, as well as Baptist, Lutheran, Methodist, and Presbyterian. For them, Federalism was too elitist, too pro-English, too obviously a Yankee creation. With Jefferson, they liked the French and disliked the Jay Treaty. They were inward turning and localist, and they hated the idea of centralized controls, especially in the hands of moralistic, preaching Yankees. The Republican South was also territorially expansionist. It dreamed of western adventures and urged the admission of western states, which Federalists, even those from the South, opposed. James Madison himself soon drew back from his centralizing nationalism and became anti-Federalist. He worked hard in the funding controversy of 1790 to get the national capital placed on the Potomac precisely because, like most Southerners, he had begun to fear Northern predominance in the new nation and wanted the federal government where Southern influence could balance Northern appetites.

After the election of 1800 put a Republican Southerner, Thomas Jefferson, in the White House, Federalism's voting strength in the South began to fall sharply. Its decline was accelerated when Northerners discovered that Jefferson's election to the presidency owed its margin of victory in the electoral college (though not in the popular vote) to the three-fifths rule in the Constitution, which counted slaves as that fraction of a person in apportioning representation in Congress and therefore electoral votes. Northern Federalists began a long, obsessive hammering at the wickedness of that provision, demanding year after year that it be repealed. Consequently, where close to half the congressmen from the South were Federalist in 1798, by 1808 that figure had dropped to 15 percent.[29]

In other parts of the nation, a surging Republican tide in the late 1790s was also overtopping Federalist voting strength. Both Federalists and Republicans assumed, in fact, that the American people were naturally Republican in their attitudes, and this assumption proved to be correct once the nationalism of the 1790s began to fade and with it the towering prestige of Washington and his associates. In the long run, the cultural foundations of Jeffersonianism were to grow more dynamically than those of Federalism. Jeffersonian ideology was that of the most flourishing and rapidly growing culture groups in national life: those peoples who were antiaristocratic and anti-Yankee and were ready to challenge the elites and the Anglophiles for national supremacy. The heaviest concentrations of Federalist voters were in areas that David Hackett Fischer has characterised as "mature, static, homogeneous, and ingrown"—the Yankee Connecticut Valley, the Quaker homeland of western New Jersey and southeastern Pennsylvania, and aristocratic Tidewater Maryland and Virginia. Jeffersonian areas displayed "dynamism, expansion, and mobility."[30]

The four largest commercial cities—New York, Boston, Philadelphia, and Baltimore—had swung strongly Republican by 1800 through the impact of immigration from abroad and a rising working-class consciousness. The General Society of Mechanics and Tradesmen in New York City was distrustful of Hamilton's financial schemes and his Federalist elitism. The society went Republican in the mid-1790s, and so did the coopers, sailmakers, tallow chandlers, soap boilers, and (most Republican of all) the associated teachers, irreverent, freethinking scholars. Federalists disliked the "new immigrants" who since the Revolution had been pouring into New York City from Scotland, Ireland, and France, but Republicans welcomed them with open arms.* The Catholic Irish, of course, "became the

---

*Federalist hostility to the immigrants of ethnic minority stock was notorious.

The newcomers who streamed into the city in the 1790's—the Scots, British, Irish, German, French—were for the most part poor, in dire need, and of course were "greenhorns" to American life.... The ... Federalists were cool or hostile [to them]; such people ran up the cost of charity at the city almshouse, hated Great Britain, and, it was claimed, even brought in yellow fever. By default the Scots, Irish, and French, and to a lesser extent the new English, drifted perceptibly toward the Republicans.... In their native land many Scots had read Thomas Paine and been members of the radical Friends of the People. [Alfred F. Young, *The Democratic Republicans of New York: The Origins, 1763–1797* (Chapel Hill, N.C., 1967), p. 401.]

In Massachusetts much of Federalist "appeal within the state and most of their partisan oratory moved to a nativist cadence. Party leaders carefully exploited the theme that the Republican Party 'gives foreigners our loaves and fishes' to the neglect of the native-born, and they organized election campaigns against the 'too indiscriminate naturalization of *foreigners* in the Southern states' ... [which they said was part of a Southern plot] to destroy the sovereignty and independence of New England." (James Banner, *To the Hartford Convention: The Federalists and the Origins of Party Politics in Massachusetts, 1789–1815* [New York, 1970], p. 99.)

poorest of the poor, draymen and common laborers who dwelt in the city's most wretched slums. More than any other immigrant group they were subject to the slings and barbs of conservative prejudice." But soon they and the other immigrants took over the Tammany Society, making it enthusiastically Jeffersonian and forming branches all over the Northern states. In fact, Jeffersonians were far more adept than Federalists at forming grass-roots political societies. They seemed to revel in the gritty, sweaty world of mass democratic politics, while Federalists, with their more reserved lifestyle and elitism, held back. Federalists particularly prized their personal independence from party discipline and daily party affairs.[31]

Statewide, the Republican party in New York gathered around the core of the old anti-Federalist, egalitarian, and Anglophobic Clintonian party of the 1780s, with its deep roots among the Dutch and the Scotch-Irish Presbyterians. George Clinton, the Livingstons, and Jefferson's vice-president-to-be Aaron Burr (who in 1804 would kill Alexander Hamilton in a duel) were all of the Presbyterian faith. Joining them in the Jeffersonian Republican party in New York State were the Americanized Dutch Reformed and German Lutherans. When the Jay Treaty controversy revealed that Federalism was synonymous with being pro-English, thousands of New Yorkers who retained bloody memories of the Revolutionary War, much of which had been fought in their state, began to vote Republican. Antiaristocratic attitudes flourished, and Hamilton's economic programs and the banking community associated with it came under wide attack.

Jeffersonianism was profoundly localist (as were the groups traditionally behind George Clinton); it was egalitarian, regarding common farmers and workingmen as persons of dignity and value; and it was secular and libertarian, calling for a complete separation between government and religion. It resisted the Yankee idea of controlling private morals. These qualities attracted those who were alarmed at New England's "political clergy," who preached their furious Federalist politics from their pulpits. There were still important Federalist voting precincts in and around New York City, for Hamilton's economic program had wide support in the mercantile and shipping circles, which carried on a heavy trade with England. The city remained English in its culture and traditions. Many of its citizens had been Loyalists and Tories. Another boost to Federalist voting strength resulted from the huge migration of New Englanders into western and upstate New York that began after 1790. This made the region Yankee and puritanical in its loyalties and culture and a Federalist stronghold as well. By 1800, however, it was clear that Republicanism was seizing New York.[32]

Pennsylvania was also swinging Republican by 1800, becoming thereafter the keystone of the Jeffersonian party in the Northern states. The state had been loyal in the late 1780s to the nationalist republicans led by financier Robert Morris, who had helped create the federal Constitution. In 1790 Pennsylvanians had even adopted a new state constitution that dispensed with the radically democratic document that the egalitarian republican coalition, led by the Scotch-Irish, had established in 1776. The fact that the national government was resident in Philadelphia through the 1790s, with the Bank of the United States right next-door, kept a proud nationalism alive. There also were thousands of pro-English Loyalists in Pennsylvania's heavily Quaker eastern counties and a strong nationalist core, in the Philadelphia mercantile and financial community, that favored Hamilton's policies.

However, the egalitarian republican coalition that had formerly dominated Pennsylvania only awaited appropriate events to revitalize it. In the Jay Treaty crisis, Jeffersonian Republicanism in Pennsylvania grew rapidly. The Republicans of Pennsylvania

> were to favor the French over the British and deplore the ever-increasing centralizing tendencies of the Federal government. In those tendencies and assumptions of power they saw manifestations of aristocracy that were considered incompatible with free government. They had a real and sincere dread of monarchy and feared its rise in the United States. Made up principally of the former Constitutionalist group and continually strengthened by disaffected Federalists and incoming immigrations, they were eventually to succeed in overthrowing the ... [Federalists] before the beginning of the nineteenth century.[33]

Pennsylvania's population swelled enormously in the 1790s (from 434,000 to 586,000) due to immigration, and Pennsylvanians spilled westward into Republican, Whisky Rebellion country. In 1798 the Germans in the eastern counties had their own uprising, the Fries Rebellion, in opposition to new federal taxes levied to support the Quasi-War with France, and they were brutally treated by the Federalist militia. This event triggered a massive German Lutheran desertion from the Federalist party to the Jeffersonian banner. With Scotch-Irishmen like William Maclay, Thomas McKean, and Alexander James Dallas at their leadership, the Republicans massacred the Federalists at the polls, charging that they were pro-British, pro-taxation, and pro-Alien and Sedition Acts. In the gubernatorial election of 1799, the Republican paper *Aurora* attacked the Federalist candidate in revealing terms:

> Do not [his] friends . . . associate with British emissaries, British pensioners, British merchants, old Tories, Refugees, Traitors, aristocrats, monarchists? Do [they] not . . . *vote* for standing armies, Loans at Eight per centum . . . High public salaries, Increase of Public Debt, Heavy taxes, Excises, Imposts, House tax, poll tax, window tax, hearth tax, Cattle and horse tax, land tax, Alien Bills and Sedition or Gag Bills to cram everything down your throats?[34]

In the ensuing balloting, the Republicans won seventy-one of the eighty-six seats in the state's lower house and all vacancies in the upper house, and took twenty-nine of thirty-five counties. The harshest Federalist rebuff of all was in Philadelphia, where for the first time the Republicans carried their entire ticket. Pennsylvania was utterly lost to the Federalists.[35]

Even in Massachusetts, Federalism's stronghold, a new order was appearing. No state had been more firmly behind Hamilton's programs or so self-consciously English. Although Massachusetts produced no crop for export, its many seaport towns sent abroad the largest maritime fleet in the nation. Deeply involved in the transatlantic carrying trade, its business had quadrupled after 1789. When the Jay Treaty was signed, regularizing relations with England and opening the ports of its empire to American vessels again, Massachusetts strongly supported the treaty. As elsewhere, however, a bitter fight occurred over the issue, and thereafter the Republican party offered strong opposition within the state to the Federalists. The governor of Massachusetts in the mid-1790s was the venerable patriot Samuel Adams. That former firebrand of anti-English localism, who had ranged himself against the merchants of Boston with their transatlantic economic links and had approved the centralizing federal Constitution only reluctantly, was an enthusiastic Republican. Generally speaking, wherever Massachusetts' population was most homogeneous, stable, and slowest growing (and in Boston as well), Federalism was most fervently supported; wherever there was growth and newness, Republicanism thrived. In many seacoast towns, a new economic interest had grown up, based on trade with the Far East and with France. For prominent Republican families like the Crowninshields of Salem who were heavily involved in the French trade, Federalism was the enemy. Indeed, Republicanism was appealing to "new money" throughout the state, for it was push-

ing against the supremacy of older Federalist wealth and power and
determined to break open privileged sanctuaries, like banking, to all
comers.

The Congregational Church was by law established in Massachusetts, and its powerful voice rang out across the nation in the Federalist cause, but at home in Massachusetts it was deeply embattled. Its
members were caught up in wasting theological disputes; many were
drifting away to Unitarianism, especially in and around Boston; and
its pews were emptying, a fact that helps to explain the passion and
desperation that marked the attacks levied by its ministers upon the
Jeffersonians. Meanwhile, the dissenting churches were flourishing in
Massachusetts. Baptists, Methodists, and other sects insisted that
church and state be completely separated. These groups fought spectacular court battles, with the assistance of noted Republican lawyers
like James Sullivan, to free themselves from paying taxes to support
the Congregational Church. The dissenting groups grew so rapidly
that by 1810 they comprised almost 30 percent of the voters in the
state. Baptists were strong in newly settled regions like the western
Berkshires, where life was freer and more individualistic and voters
were Republican. Part of Massachusetts until 1820, Maine had a
strong community of Scotch-Irishmen and Baptists and was another
Republican stronghold. It was dissenting in faith, rapidly growing,
angered by Boston's economic exploitation and control, and hence
firmly Jeffersonian.

The role of the Baptists in the Jeffersonian coalition requires some
elaboration. Harassed and persecuted by the Congregational majority in Massachusetts and Connecticut for generations, the Baptists
had been forced to pay taxes that supported the Congregational
Church. Although they had constantly argued for the separation of
church and state, even Sam Adams had resisted them on this point
in the Revolutionary years. After 1773 they had adopted a policy of
massive civil disobedience, agitating, pamphleteering, and appealing
to the Continental Congress. All direct ties between the state and
institutionalized religion, the Baptists insisted, must be dissolved.
However, their reasons differed from Jefferson's. They wanted complete freedom of religion so that America would become truly Christian; so that God's true and lively word would triumph by the people
turning to the proper faith, the Baptist one.

There was always, therefore, an inherent paradox in the Baptists'
position in the Jeffersonian party. The Baptists had no wish to see
America become the secular, godless society dreamed of by rational-
ists and free thinkers. New England Baptists in the 1780s had held

no objection to the people being required by public authority to attend some form of public worship regularly, but only to that authority prescribing a particular form of Protestantism. Furthermore, they had not objected to Puritan laws against profanity, blasphemy, gambling, theater-going, and violation of the Sabbath, believing these things were necessary for the maintenance of a Christian society. Whereas Jefferson stated specifically that America was not and ought not to be a Christian country, the New England Baptist leader Isaac Backus believed firmly in a Christian commonwealth and a "sweet harmony" between church and state. Nonetheless, despite their disagreement with certain Jeffersonian objectives, the Baptists remained a hard-core Jeffersonian Republican voting group, and they would later follow Andrew Jackson with equal conviction.

In Massachusetts the growing strength of Jeffersonian voting meant that after 1800 the Republicans began winning elections. In their heightened rivalry, the parties now developed elaborate internal organizations for getting out the vote. The results were dramatic. While in the 1790s perhaps 20 percent of the eligible males voted, the numbers grew to over 40 percent by 1804 and reached almost 70 percent in 1812, a figure unsurpassed until the Civil War. As elsewhere, surging turnouts of voters seemed to coincide with a rising democratic, antideferential mood, and the Jeffersonians profited. The result was that, while the Federalists controlled Massachusetts until 1804, in that year Thomas Jefferson carried the state in the presidential election. Soon after the Republicans won a majority in the General Court (the state's legislature) and placed James Sullivan in the governor's chair.[36]

By the late 1790s the cultural pattern in the politics of the new nation was strong and clear for all to see. The mold was set for the first party system, and the shape of the future was obvious. Thomas Jefferson labored ceaselessly to build his party, emerging as the nation's first party manager and leader. He sent out streams of letters, wrote and circulated pamphlets, distributed information, constantly encouraged and counseled party leaders, personally undertook such major maneuvers as the Kentucky and Virginia Resolutions, and looked steadily toward his election in 1800 as President of the United States.[37] He thought of this event, and thereafter always described it, as the "Revolution of 1800." Although historians have traditionally treated this as an understandable exaggeration, acceptable as a bit of frivolous hyperbole from a major political figure, Jefferson was serious in his wording. There was nowhere in the world or in history a precedent for what he intended to do: using no other weapon than the ballot box, force a strong and determined party in full command of a national government to give up its power peacefully and depart. The Federalists did not in fact think of themselves as a party but as a *government.* So it had always been in the history of nations. Opposition was necessarily disloyalty and subversive factionalism with no legitimate claim to sovereign power. The idea of government as an institution to be shared alternately between organized political parties was as yet beyond comprehension. The Federalists would obey the voters' decision, but they would consider their defeat an unnatural event, a rupture and illegitimate overthrow of the rightful order.[38]

The Federalists' defeat, therefore, was inevitably thought of as a revolution, the only concept available in 1800 to describe a change of government unwillingly made and not called for by a ruling monarch. Thus, all the apparatus traditional in such events was brought out by the Republicans to achieve their "rebellion": committees of correspondence, extralegal gatherings, and the careful marshalling of all resources. When it became clear that the Middle States were swinging Republican, the outcome of the election was in little doubt. As Jefferson wryly remarked, "With Pennsylvania, we can defy the universe." He and his party won a massive popular victory in 1800, and he set out immediately to realize the one party ideal: "If we can hit on the true line of conduct which may conciliate the honest part of those who were called Federalists, I shall hope to be able to obliterate, or rather to unite the names Federalists and Republicans." In his inaugural address, Jefferson spoke the famous words, "We are all republicans: we are all federalists." It was not, of course, to be. Federalists looked upon his election with fear and loathing. As a Delaware leaflet, signed by "A Christian Federalist," put the matter during the election:

> Can serious and reflecting men look about them and doubt that if Jefferson is elected, and the Jacobins get into authority, that those morals which protect our lives from the knife of the assassin—which guard the chastity of our wives and daughters from seduction and violence—defend our property from plunder and devastation, and shield our religion from contempt and profanation, will not be trampled upon and exploded?

Many believed that Jefferson was an agent of the French Revolution and that his purpose was to destroy the federal government and reduce the nation to anarchy. This, in turn, would induce the people in desperation to dispense with the republican form of government and hand over to Jefferson the same dictatorial powers as had been given to Napoleon.[39]

Although while in power Jefferson was never an uncompromising ideologue—he retained much of the Hamiltonian system and eventually accepted some of its economic assumptions about the need for factories and national development—his actions as President were decidedly Republican. He slashed federal expenditures and revenues; almost dispensed with the military system; repealed the national court system that the Federalists had created, reducing it largely to the Supreme Court; and urged the states to do such governing as was needed. New England Federalists concluded that the federal government had become an alien institution. While in Philadelphia and in Federalist hands, the government had been located in a city New Englanders could understand and had been controlled by patriots. Now, it was down in the Potomac wilderness within a slave society, and everything seemed wrong and unnatural. Virginia had gained control. The ancient Yankee Federalist fear had been realized: a Southern conspiracy was in charge, infidel, opposed to commerce, anti-Yankee, and cursed by slavery.[40]*

The Louisiana Purchase of 1803 swept Jefferson to reelection the following year. Then came renewed warfare between Britain and France, and for seven years Jefferson and Madison tried despairingly to find a peaceful way to force the combatants to leave American trading vessels alone, for the British and French took them in such great numbers that United States foreign trade plummeted disas-

*Jefferson continued, nonetheless, to have strong Southern opposition. Led by the caustic John Randolph and the ideologue John Taylor, the "Quid" and "Old Republican" opposition to Jefferson in Virginia had expected him to recommend amendments to the Constitution that would restrict the power to borrow money, give states approval over raising armies, limit Presidents to one-year terms, shorten senatorial terms, establish direct election for all officers, limit the President's appointive power, and end all stretching of the Federal government's authority by the doctrine of implied powers—by what was called "construction." They blamed James Madison for the fact that Jefferson did not do so and pushed—unsuccessfully—to have James Monroe rather than Madison become President in 1808. The embargo against all trade with Europe, which Jefferson adopted in 1807, was very unpopular in Virginia. The Old Republicans, in short, were much more simple and extreme in their localistic republicanism than Jefferson. They looked toward a near extinction of federal powers and many years later were to flow into the Calhounite Southern wing of the Jacksonians, with an aura about them of nullificationism and threatened secession. See Harry Ammon, "James Monroe and the Era of Good Feelings," *Virginia Magazine of History and Biography,"* 66 (1958), 387–398; Norman K. Risjord, *The Old Republicans: Southern Conservatism in the Age of Jefferson* (New York, 1965).

trously. Hostile to the use of Hamilton's favorite tool, military force, Jefferson and Madison relied upon their long-held belief that American trade was so important to Europe that economic reprisals alone would be successful. This led to the Embargo of 1807–1809, which kept all American vessels at home. Its complete failure sent Jefferson to Monticello a grieving and dispirited ex-President when Madison entered the White House in 1809.

Once again powerful forces worked upon the American mind: the contrasting emotions of hatred for and admiration of Great Britain and fears over the fate of republicanism. The Federalists, much revived by these troubles, found endless justifications for England's plunder of American trading vessels. They argued that England's struggle against France was so crucial to humanity that a bending of neutral rights on the high seas was America's contribution to the cause. The Republicans, however, traditional Anglophobes, viewed the collapse of American commerce with great alarm, and they warned that the country's continuing humiliation by the British navy was certain to sap fatally the people's faith in their republican institutions. To Republicans, the true objective of the Federalists' pro-British policies was to destroy the government and bring about a reinstitution of monarchy. The "federalist monarchists," wrote Jefferson bitterly in 1808, "disapprove of the republican principles & features of our constitution and would I believe welcome any public calamity (war with England excepted) which might lessen the confidence of our country in those principles & forms," including that of letting "our vessels go out & be taken." Joseph Varnum, Republican Speaker of the House in 1810, observed,

> I have for a long time been convinced that there was a party in our Country, fully determined to do every thing in their power, to Subvert the principles of our happy Government, and to establish a Monarchy on its ruins; and with a view of obtaining the aid of [Great Britain] in the accomplishment of their nefarious object, they have Inlisted into her service, and will go all lengths to Justify and support every measure which she may take against the Nation.[41]

America's export trade was almost destroyed by British seizure of American vessels and seamen. It had been $130 million in 1807, it fell to $45 million in 1811, and in 1814 reached $7 million. Caught in an implacable war with Napoleon, the British were convinced that they were struggling to save liberty for all of humankind, and American protests were futile. Furthermore, as in the years before the

Revolution, the British completely miscalculated American anger and discounted, in any event, American powers of military reprisal. The British believed that they could proceed as far as they wished in interfering with American commerce, and war would not occur.

However, the Republicans felt driven to this extremity. They were carrying out a lonely experiment in the world: demonstrating that the republican form of government could survive. The enterprise was precarious, and an unending humiliation could not be borne. Even Americans were beginning to wonder how republicanism could survive if it could not maintain its neutral rights. As year followed year, and American seamen were freely impressed into the British navy and American goods seized as contraband beyond the limits traditionally accepted, it appeared that a republic could be toyed with at will. Eventually, in 1812, President Madison and the Republican majority in Congress—the Federalists adamantly disagreed—became reluctantly convinced that a declaration of war alone would save the republic. The issue had become a test of the nation's survival. If the new American republic could not forcefully protect its rights, it would never survive once Napoleon was gone. The great monarchies would be convinced that America was spineless and would pick the nation apart as soon as they had finished their struggles in Europe.[42]

So began this violently partisan war. New England Federalists resisted it with heart and soul. Now that it had begun and lurched on from disaster to disaster, they began to take the road to the Hartford Convention, a journey they had tentatively started on at least twice since Jefferson's election, only to draw back. The Federalist clergy were enraged by "Mr. Madison's war," and they believed confidently that Christian America agreed with them. Nathan Beman consoled his congregation with the words, "Most of the religion in this country and Great Britain is *strongly* and *vitally* opposed to this war." Elijah Parish of Byfield called upon his parishioners to "proclaim an honourable neutrality; let the southern *Heroes* fight their own battles. . . . Protest did I say, protest? *Forbid this war to proceed in New-England.*" An Episcopal cleric in Boston urged New Englanders to either "cut the connexion" that bound them with the Southern states, "or so far alter the national constitution, as to ensure yourselves a due share in the government." In the General Court of Massachusetts in 1814, "radical speeches, loudly applauded by galleries out of sympathy with moderation, hailed Britain, excoriated the administration, and proposed . . . drastic measures."[43]

During the last days of December 1814 and the beginning of

January 1815, while a treaty of peace was being signed in Ghent,
Belgium, the Scotch-Irishman Andrew Jackson was winning his great
victory over the British army before New Orleans. At the same time,
representatives chosen by the governments of Massachusetts, Rhode
Island, and Connecticut gathered in Hartford, Connecticut, to delib-
erate the question of what New England must do in the face of this
unconstitutional, unwise, and disastrous war. Relatively moderate
men were in control, and the convention's adopted statement counseled against secession or violent resistance. Cataloging the sins that
had thrust the nation into its present agonies, the convention called
for a series of constitutional amendments designed to restore the
balance that had been destroyed by the long years of Republican
rule. These amendments would apportion representation according
to the numbers of free white persons in a state; require a two-thirds
vote for admission of new states, a provision aimed at preventing "an
overwhelming western influence"; limit embargoes to sixty days and
require a two-thirds vote for their establishment; allow a declaration
of war only upon two-thirds vote; declare naturalized citizens ineligi-
ble for any Federal office; and prohibit a President from succeeding
himself or the election of a President from the same state in successive terms.[44]

The Hartford Convention effectively destroyed the Federalist
party as a national force. Its demands, drawn up when the national
government seemed everywhere in grave trouble and then presented in Washington when the capital city was delirious with joy at
the news of Jackson's victory and the peace treaty, made the whole
enterprise appear to the rest of the nation as subversive and unpatri-
otic. The political effects upon Federalism were known, within
weeks, to be crushing. Ever thereafter, Republicans were to taunt
Federalists with the Hartford Convention. Many years later, Andrew
Jackson would even assert that he would have hanged the convention's leaders as traitors.[45]

Within New England, however, the Hartford Convention solidified the Federalist party in the people's affections. It became a kind
of "lost cause" like that of the South after the Civil War. Indeed, to
a people who had long thought of themselves as a special and exclusive culture, as a righteous fragment whose mission was to save the
nation from its sins, the idea of living apart in austere purity of
doctrine and life had a strong attraction. "Rule, New England! New
England rules and saves," ran a popular song. The Federalist party
endured into the 1820s in New England as the holy vessel charged
with the ultimate redemption of the American nation. The Jeffer-

sonian Republicans in Massachusetts had already suffered an ironic blow: by securing passage of the Religious Freedom Bill of 1811, which made it possible for dissenters to cease paying taxes to support the Congregational church, they lost their claim upon that group. Thereafter, the Republicans' irreligious and anticlerical nature, inherited from Jefferson himself, drove most of the sects over to the Federalists, save for the Baptists, who remained staunchly Republican.[46]

During James Monroe's presidency (1817–1825), the first party system disintegrated. The sense of national precariousness dissipated: the United States and republicanism seemed finally secure and established. The great and powerful enemy, England, also receded. Time and again, until 1815, violent controversies over relations with the former parent country had driven people into opposing parties. Now that impulse was gone.

The War of 1812 had also worked a crucial change within the Republican party. The nationalism induced by the war and the vital need, pointed up by the conflict, for a strong national government produced an ideological shifting. Jeffersonians added nationalist republicanism to their creed. In 1816 they re-created Hamilton's financial system in the form of the Second Bank of the United States, located like its predecessor in Philadelphia; enacted the first genuinely protective tariff; and began to talk about launching internal improvements (roads, bridges, and other such public works) that would tie the several states together and open their resources.

Until this point, the two parties had divided between them the four modes of republicanism that had emerged in the Revolutionary years. The Jeffersonians had been libertarian and egalitarian; the Federalists nationalist and moralistic. Now the Republicans, by their nationalism, preempted an overwhelming share of the nation's fundamental republican ideology, producing an imbalance that left Federalists little leverage upon the national mind. Whenever this has occurred, as a century later during Franklin Roosevelt's New Deal, the effects upon the opposition party have been severe. Because after 1815 the Federalist party had also borne the stigma of disloyalty, it was never able to recover.

The withering away of party during the 1820s was understandable on other grounds as well. The ethic of party politics and the legitimacy of an exclusively political career had still little hold, especially among the older political generation. The latter conceived of politics as a duty to be left behind for private pursuits whenever the situation allowed. It was difficult in the best of circumstances for party leaders to find men to stand for or serve in public office. Furthermore, the generation of the heroic years was growing old. James Monroe was the last important figure of the Revolution to sit in the White House. The passions, loyalties, and obsessions of that time were fading. As one veteran Federalist from Boston advised Monroe when he first became President, he should not appoint to administrative posts any of the older men, even Federalists, for they were still absorbed by the past and its dying questions. He should choose instead from among the younger men who were of the newer America.[47]

James Monroe was devoted to nonpartyism. He thought parties harmful in a republic and set out immediately to establish good relations with Federalists. At the outset of his first term, he took a grand tour of the nation, the first to be made by a sitting President since Washington had done the same. Everywhere Federalists reacted gratefully to Monroe's advances, even in Boston, the only place in the country where Federalists were so active that they could not work with Republicans in jointly providing Monroe hospitality and public welcome. Throughout his two terms, Federalists had so little to complain of in this nationalist, magisterial, and austere man that they gave him steady support in Congress.[48]

American public life lacked those elements that sustain a two-party rivalry: highly charged issues creating a relatively clear ideological gulf between the parties; a strong conviction, held by each of two broad voting coalitions, of having an enemy whose control of the government must be fought; charismatic national figures around whom the passions of a mass political party could gather, and from whom that party could take much of its meaning; and enduring party organizations. There had been practically no opposition to Monroe's election in 1816—Rufus King was put forward by the Federalists, but the opposition was only token and he got few electoral votes. In 1820 the opposition received none at all. Politicians are drawn together by fears of a powerful antagonist, not by mutual affection. Left to themselves they scatter, driven apart by clashing interests and ambitions. "Historically the Republican party had been bound together," writes Monroe's biographer, Harry Ammon, "by a shared fear of Federalism as by a common set of principles. . . . It was this sense of solidarity against a common enemy which had enabled Jefferson to sustain unpopular measures such as the Embargo. With the elimination of the Federalists, the internal divisions in the Republican party between rival leaders, factions, and sections now emerged." The Republican party in Washington fell apart, factions plotting against each other throughout the Monroe years, and by the election of 1824 things were so disorganized that several candidates presented themselves to the nation. When none could win a majority in the electoral college, the House of Representatives had to choose between them.[49]

The physical setting of Washington, D.C., contributed to this fragmentation. It was still a wilderness community, widely scattered over a swampy countryside, with few real governmental functions to perform. For a considerable period the membership of Congress was larger than that of the entire executive branch. Moreover, the federal government was so remote from all other centers of population that it was almost totally ignored by the American public at large. There was, therefore, no organized public opinion to drive legislators together and force them to cooperate. Each branch of government lived completely by itself. Legislators occupied boarding houses around the Congress building; members of the executive roomed near the White House, located a mile and a half away; and members of the judiciary lived in yet a third location and avoided the others. It was an inward-turning, pressure-cooker environment in which nothing but politics was heard, day and night, since every other amenity and distraction, such as Philadelphia had provided, was lacking. There were no buffers, nothing to absorb or deflect the differences among antagonists. Southerners and Yankees, mutually hostile, lived in separate boarding houses, where they huddled together almost as if in military barracks, and talked constantly at dinner of the deformities and corruptions of their sectional rivals. Indeed, even people from the same region broke up into smaller parties, occupying different homes and rarely meeting save on the floor of Congress. In this body, there were no rules governing debate and the proceedings were totally disorganized, individualistic, and contentious. Because there were no recognized party leaders, there also was no discipline.[50]

Since presidential nominations were made by congressional caucuses, small, intense factions organized around chosen candidates and nourished persistent mutual hatreds. Until national conventions were devised, there would not be a reaching out to larger circles in the nation, and the people in general would not take a direct interest in who was chosen. Therefore, the succession struggles that occurred in Congress during Monroe's terms kept tearing people apart from each other. Thomas Jefferson had been a master at skillful relations with Congress, and he had made the system work. His successors, however, had practically no talents along this line. Only in the Jacksonian years when a new system of mass political parties was established would there be enough organized pressure upon Washington from the people to moderate its internally divisive nature and politics.

The so-called era of good feelings under James Monroe was a time of almost total legislative failure in Washington, with, as James Young observes, "not one memorable policy controversy at Washington that aroused significant citizen interest outside the capital. . . . On domestic policy the record is barren of any evidence of presidential leadership, either with regard to the Missouri Compromise of 1820 or the tariff battle of 1824–25." After months of confusion and secret bargaining among the factions in Washington following the inconclusive presidential vote of 1824, and just a few weeks before the inauguration was to be held in March 1825, the House of Representatives elected John Quincy Adams from among the contending presidential candidates.[51]

New England had the presidency once more in its hands, but the prize was a sterile one. Unable to muster significant support in the Congress, Adams was all but a complete failure in the White House. He spent long vacations at his home in Quincy, Massachusetts, brooding upon the failure of Congress to follow his bold inaugural appeal to ignore public opinion, which was inclining once again toward localism and distrust of governments, and to launch a broad Hamiltonian program of national development. Save for Franklin Pierce, a Democratic President from New Hampshire (1853–1857), the White House would not again be occupied by a New Englander for the rest of the nineteenth century.

The United States, as New England feared, was going in directions that would leave the Yankee homeland behind. However, the westward movement of New England's own people would in time shift the balance. Already widely settled in western New York and northern Pennsylvania, tens of thousands of migrating New Englanders would occupy a broad band of territory in the upper Middle West in which the Yankee impulse would continue to thrive. By 1860 this expanded Yankee world would be ready again to challenge and finally to defeat its Southern enemy. For many decades thereafter, the Yankee North would have that opportunity to shape the nation in its own image, an opportunity which, until the war over slavery, had been so elusive. In the interim, however, the Jacksonian years would witness a generation of explosive national growth and development and the rise, flourishing, and breaking apart of the second party system.

V

The Jacksonian Party System, 1828=1854: The Economic Argument

The quiet way of life that Americans had known in their local communities during the Jeffersonian years began to disintegrate in the 1820s, a period of accelerating social change throughout the transatlantic community. The time of wars was over, and the British and the North Americans could return to the labors of peacetime. For the British, their victory over Napoleon in 1815 ushered in half a century of soaring imperial confidence. Their fleets ranged the world, their rapidly progressing industrial revolution fostered a global expansion of British trade, and a pax Britannica held sway. Not until 1868 would a British prime minister, William Gladstone, warn the Queen that Britain could no longer conceive the affairs of the entire world to be under its authority. The Canadians, whose new sense of nationhood was given its first solid base by their successful fight against American conquest in the War of 1812, gained effective self-government after the Rebellion of 1837, and in 1867 brought their scattered provinces together to form the Dominion of Canada.

For the United States, the evaporation of foreign threats after 1815 meant that the republic was finally secure. The Americans were now free to turn inward and occupy their huge continental domain beyond the Appalachians. A cotton boom in the South, stimulated by the growing British textile industry's need for more raw mater-

ial, sparked a westward surge out of the southern Atlantic seaboard states into the gulf plains of the Deep South. Around 1820, a
northward-moving tide of Southerners from Virginia and Kentucky
crossed the Ohio River to occupy the lower Middle West: the southern sections of Ohio, Indiana, and Illinois.

In 1825 the completion of the Erie Canal opened the interior to
easy access from the Middle States and New England. Yankees
spread out through the fertile plains around the Great Lakes, turning
the upper Middle West as far as Iowa into a region culturally at arms
against the South. Then these two American ethnic groups—Southerners and Yankees—were joined by swarms of immigrants from the
British Isles and the European continent. Germans and Scandinavians stamped their ways of living upon the northernmost band of
territory in the Middle West—in Wisconsin, Minnesota, and the Da-
kotas—and established a large colony in the St. Louis region as well.

From 1815 to 1850 a new western state entered the Union, on the
average, every two and a half years. In the 1840s a sense of manifest
destiny seized much of the American mind (although many, especially in New England, held back). Texas was annexed, and then
armies were sent into Mexico, slicing off the northern half of that
country and incorporating it into the United States. Simultaneously,
a treaty struck with Great Britain added the Pacific Northwest, as far
as the forty-ninth parallel, to the nation. By the mid-1850s there were
thirty-three states in the Union, packed solid through the first north-
south rank of states beyond the Mississippi, and reaching westward
to include Texas and, on the Pacific Coast, California and Oregon.

This western explosion was matched in the eastern states by rapid
economic development: canals, railroads, and swift urban growth. To
foreign observers in the 1830s, an idle Northerner seemed a rare
phenomenon. When the sculptor Horatio Greenough returned to
the United States in 1836 after a lengthy stay in Europe, he was
astonished at the transformation. "Go ahead! is the order of the day.
The whole continent presents a scene of *scrabbling* and roars with
greedy hurry." National productivity surged in the 1820s; prices
climbed to a peak in the 1830s but dropped for a time in the 1840s.
In the 1850s, both productivity and prices soared upward again to
new heights. A business cycle had appeared, producing periods of
boom and bust. By the 1850s the factory system was so well developed that a specifically industrial cycle was also in evidence. A willingness to take risks formerly thought wildly imprudent became a
national characteristic. Land values rose, and hundreds of new com-

munities appeared seemingly overnight in the booming Middle Western states.[1]

At the same time, property tests for voting were disappearing, white manhood suffrage became the rule, and the nation's politics were democratized. Most offices were made elective, and modern mass political parties appeared. A communications revolution centering on the inexpensive newspaper, which made information widely and swiftly available, and a national fascination with mass education (save in the South) sent literacy rates soaring. For many years, the Second Great Awakening spread an evangelical excitement around the country, and a ferment of social reform swept the Northern states. The slave system of the South spread westward as rapidly as the free-labor system of the North, and abolitionism sprang up to hammer at slavery's evils.

The volatile and expansive years from 1815 to 1850 were, in short, an age of boundlessness when the ancient limits that had suppressed human aspirations seemed magically to disappear.[2] Out of the swift changes and new ideas grew the national issues around which the second, or Jacksonian, party system took form. Of these issues, the most pressing was the question of what was to be done about the economic explosion and its transformations. For many Americans, the answer was a simple one: do little, except to encourage and stimulate it. The boom was seen as an exciting opportunity that the government should assist. Economic prosperity was the realization of the democratic ideal, for it gave common people limitless opportunities to improve their condition. Those holding this buoyant outlook lived in favored locations, belonged to privileged classes, or possessed essentially modern, as distinct from traditionalist, personalities. They enjoyed breaking free from the past, experiencing fresh adventures. For them, the age of boundlessness was an invigorating era that demanded full exertions of talent and energy but returned liberal rewards. The entrepreneurial temperament had little patience with those who held back in alarm from the turbulent new order.[3]

Thousands of Americans, however, remembered the quieter times before the War of 1812 and were disturbed by the seismic changes that were swiftly taking place: the invasion of local communities by economic forces generated far beyond their borders; the growth of cities; the raising of crops and the manufacturing of goods for distant markets; price instability; the replacement of face-to-face economic relations with impersonality and a reduction of all things to money relationships; greater discipline governing time and productivity; and the breakdown of craft autonomy as factory systems made their first appearances. As recent observers of the modernization process have observed, it brings with it new opportunities and prospects while exacting a high price in human dislocation and suffering.[4]

Thus, the Jacksonian years were filled with an anguished outcry at the loss of quietude, secure family lives and status, and social confidence. Across the Atlantic in England, Victorians constantly complained that life was moving at an ever faster pace, that there was more competition, more worry, more threat of failure. Like their American counterparts, Victorians were proud of the material changes of the time and delighted in the rising statistics: more people, longer railroads, more coal. But, bearing an immense pressure of work, they were also haunted by anxieties and rarely secure. In the United States, as the business cycle began its early oscillations, even so mild a depression as that following the Panic of 1837 could set off widespread alarm and send prophets into the streets crying that the end of the world was near. In a fundamentally optimistic time a constant riptide of anxiety and fear was moving backward against the current. There was a deep and profound sense of loss.[5]

Many Americans, finding the times neither admirable nor bearable, reacted by direct physical assault. Violent rioting, a phenomenon largely unseen since the 1790s, once again became commonplace in the 1830s. "The horrible fact is staring us in the face," observed the Philadelphia *National Gazette* in August 1835, "that, whenever the fury or the cupidity of the mob is excited, they can gratify their lawless appetites almost with impunity." By the year's end, almost a hundred people had been killed in riots, and hundreds more were to lose their lives in succeeding decades. Journalist Hezekiah Niles carefully observed the upwelling of social turbulence and recorded from newspapers around the country in one week—the first week of September 1835—over five hundred incidents. *"Society,"* he lamented in his newspaper, *Niles' Register, "seems everywhere unhinged,* and the demon of 'blood and slaughter' has been let loose upon us. . . . [The] character of our countrymen seems suddenly changed." The specific issues linked to each riot were of many kinds. They grew out of ethnic hostilities, religious passions, class animosities, race conflicts, economic grievances, fears that American culture was becoming morally corrupted, political rivalries, and hatred of slavery. All gave witness to a society that seemed to be flying apart.[6]

Conditions once again were ripe, therefore, for a polarizing process to divide Americans into two political camps, each convinced that the other was a danger to the republic. Andrew Jackson's overwhelming defeat of John Quincy Adams in the presidential election of 1828 brought another element—the influence of a powerful personage loved or hated by multitudes—into the scene. The electorate began to come alive, energized by the first fiery two-candidate election since Thomas Jefferson had defeated John Adams in 1800. In 1828 the nation divided in a fashion almost identical to the alignments displayed in the "revolution of 1800." New England was solidly for Adams. Since the sudden eruption of the slavery issue in the Missouri controversy of 1820, the South had been looking for a Southern man who could win the presidency; now it solidly supported Jackson.[7] The Middle Atlantic states were mixed. By the time of this election, there was also a new group of players in the national arena: the nine western states that had formed beyond the Appalachians. All nine were in Jackson's camp in 1828, although Yankee immigration would later destroy their unanimity.

Around Jackson and Adams gathered the same kind of imagery that had been attached to the candidates of 1800. John Quincy Adams symbolized New England and its corporate, puritan values; its seemingly aristocratic and Anglicized lifestyles; its hostility to non-English immigrants; its emphasis upon a close partnership between the business community and governments; and its vigorous appetite for building a strong national government that would provide cultural and economic leadership for the nation. Henry Clay of Kentucky, a nationalist republican, was Adams's great lieutenant, serving as his secretary of state from 1825 to 1829. For years Clay had called for an "American System," in which the federal government would create an internally self-sufficient economy walled off from foreign competition. Under the American System, the government would adopt protective tariffs, build internal improvements, and maintain a centralized banking system. All of these proposals had Adams's firm support, for he "took great joy and a great interest," observes his biographer, George A. Lipsky, "in the growth of manufacturing in the United States. . . . One of the great purposes of his program of internal improvements was the stimulation of domestic industry to the fullest extent." With the organic view of society as an interdependent community that he had inherited from his New England forebears, government "was not in Adams's opinion an unfriendly, inimical force to be kept at a minimum. There was much that was dramatic and good, and even magnificent, that government should do, in fact must do, if it was to fulfill its purpose."[8]

Indeed, something very like the American System was already in effect as reigning national policy in the 1820s: a protective tariff, a program of national road building, and the Second Bank of the United States, all having been created during the Republicans' nationalist phase following the War of 1812. It was appropriate, therefore, that Adams, a nationalist in every sense, should be the symbol of this established order and that those who backed him should rally under the party name "National Republicans."

Far more exciting as a personality than Adams, however, was General Andrew Jackson, the hero of New Orleans. He would tower over the nation's politics through the entire period from his first election in 1828 to the middle years of the 1840s, when his protégé James K. Polk, also of Tennessee, was in the White House. Andrew Jackson was "a man whom two thirds of his fellow-citizens deified and the other third vilified," wrote James Parton, who lived through the Jackson years and wrote the first, still valuable, biography of the President.[9] Jackson was the first Chief Executive to come from beyond the Appalachians, and he symbolized those western frontier qualities that many Americans wanted to believe characterized the American people as a whole: manly courage, a readiness to fight in defense of cherished values, a reliance upon natural energies, intuitive rather than schooled wisdom, and an iron-willed strength of character. Though a wealthy plantation owner and leading member of the Tennessee elite, he was lauded as farmer and democrat, the voice of the common people against the aristocracy.[10]

Andrew Jackson was also a Scotch-Irish Presbyterian, a fact to which his modern biographers have given only passing mention. Parton—Jackson's contemporary as well as an immigrant Englishman—understood the importance of Jackson's ethnicity, and began his biography with several chapters on the theme. "[No] . . . man will ever be able to comprehend Andrew Jackson," he wrote, "who has not personally known a Scotch-Irishman. More than anything else, he was a North-of-Irelander." Born in 1767 in the back country of the Carolinas only two years after his parents had arrived from Ulster, Jackson still spoke with a faint Scotch-Irish burr as an adult. It was in the nature of the Scotch-Irish, Parton observed, from their long struggle in Ulster with the English on one side and the Catholics on the other, "to *contend* for what they think is right with peculiar earnestness. . . . It appears to be more difficult for a North-of-Irelander than for other men to allow an honest difference of opinion in an opponent; so that he is apt to regard the terms *opponent* and *enemy* as synonymous." In truth, Jackson was a man who seemed always to be battling against detested enemies.[11]

From infancy, Jackson had absorbed his people's ancestral malevolence towards Englishmen. Though a teen-age boy during the Revolution, he fought in bloody actions against British forces. He lost his two brothers in the fighting and his mother to war-induced disease. In the War of 1812 he was again fighting the British, throwing himself with grim persistence into difficult campaigns in the Deep South. It was fitting that the hero of the second war with the English, the towering figure who defeated their invasion force in the Battle of New Orleans, should be a Scotch-Irishman. In national politics, Jackson could be nothing other than a Jeffersonian Republican. In 1828 the old Jeffersonian coalition of voters in the country at large gathered around Jackson. To contrast their coalition with Adams's National Republicans, they called themselves "Democratic-Republicans," or simply "Democrats."[12]

In Andrew Jackson, therefore, the nation received its first ethnic president.[13] Indeed, when his two terms were completed, he chose another ethnic outsider to succeed him, the New York Dutchman Martin Van Buren. Around the United States Jackson's campaign managers trumpeted that he was an old Irishman and proud of it. Great cheers attended a Charleston, South Carolina, toast by a Catholic prelate praising Jackson, "under the influence of whose atmosphere the *Shamrock* becomes a *Hickory!!!*" The Irish Catholic vote was becoming important in Northern urban centers as early as 1828, and it was enthusiastically Jacksonian. DeWitt Clinton of the venerable Presbyterian dynasty in New York, who had flirted for some years with former Federalists, was now an all-out Jackson man. So, too, were the Scotch-Irish voters in Pennsylvania, a state in which Jackson piled up a two-to-one majority over John Quincy Adams.[14]

Jackson received all the epithets that Englishmen had traditionally thrown at Scotch-Irishmen. He was called a murderer, a drunkard, and a libertine. He was also a slave owner, a Southerner, and a western frontiersman, all of which intensified Yankee hostilities. Newspapers screamed that he was crude and violent, a wild man with a history of duels and tavern brawls in Tennessee. The confused circumstances of his marriage in the 1790s to his wife, Rachel, were exhumed and paraded about the country as cause for calling him an immoral adulterer. Pennsylvania Quakers had long accused the Scotch-Irish of being mad with a blood-thirsty hatred of Indians, and Jackson was indeed an inveterate Indian fighter. His attacks upon the tribes of the Deep South while he was military commander in that region rendered them utterly defenseless. (Later, as President, Jackson would refuse to protect them against the state of Georgia, and he provided for their removal to what is now Oklahoma along the Trail of Tears.) Voters were reminded, too, of his summary execution of offenders against military law under his command and his headlong, imperious tactics while leading a punitive expedition into Spanish Florida in 1818. Those who met Jackson were surprised at the contrast between his crude public image, circulated by those who hated him, and his actual self, for he was well mannered and gentlemanly, possessed of a remarkable natural dignity. But multitudes, knowing him only in their newspapers, thought him literally a criminal.[15]

Jackson's feelings about the economy and the government's relation to it were relatively unformed when he became President. His war-induced nationalism had been real and heartfelt, and he had earlier supported protective tariffs and the building of internal improvements to make the country stronger. He believed firmly that the federal government was supreme within the Constitution. When in 1832–1833 South Carolina sought to nullify federal tariffs on the ground that it was a sovereign state, Jackson turned back that challenge to federal supremacy and secured the Union by skillful political maneuvers and the threat of force. However, it was inconceivable that Jackson could ever come down on the Yankees' side. It was clear who his enemies were; he well knew the origin of the abuse hurled at him. And from Thomas Jefferson himself came thunderous warnings about the reemergence of nationalist Hamiltonianism. In his last years of life, Jefferson was visited by Martin Van Buren, who arrived at Monticello in 1826 to learn from the master at first hand. States rights and limited government: this was the creed that Jefferson pressed upon the New Yorker. Let individuals meet equally and without favor in the economic arena.

There was a new breed of politicians abroad, said Jefferson in a later public statement, who, "having nothing in them of the feelings and principles of '76, now look back to a single and splendid government of an aristocracy, founded on banking institutions, moneyed incorporations under the guise and cloak of their favored branches of manufacture, commerce, and navigation, riding and ruling over the plundered plowman and beggared yeomanry." His posthumously published *Memoirs,* which appeared in the first year of Jackson's presidency, were filled with attacks upon all those who, following the precepts of Alexander Hamilton, favored strong central governments and aid to capitalists. The *Memoirs* quickly became the political bible for Jacksonian Democrats, a sensational document mined constantly for authoritative passages and phrases to hurl at political enemies.[16]

Thus for twelve years, eight of them with Jackson in the White House and four with Van Buren as President, the United States had an administration that shared Jefferson's conviction that the wealthy classes worked busily behind the scenes to exploit society at large. There was, said the Virginian, an inevitable social conflict among the classes, not the "natural" harmony that Federalists had insisted upon. The government's role in this uneven struggle must be to battle the powerful. When Jacksonian Democrats looked at the booms and busts of their years—"the primal experience of Jacksonian life," writes Marvin Meyers, that "fixed the content, tone, and terms of politics for as long as Jacksonianism counted in America"—they attributed them to destructive speculation set in motion by privileged men who had the power, as insiders, to profit from the economy's gyrations.[17]

It was within this general framework that Jacksonians took up the issue that polarized American politics: the "war" over the rechartering of the Second Bank of the United States. Established by congressional charter in 1816, the Bank was headquartered in Philadelphia and had branches in the several states. It received and held the tax moneys gathered by the federal government and could invest this large pool of capital in ways that the Bank's trustees (only a minority of whom were appointed by the federal government) decided would best guide the economy's growth. It also supervised the paper money issuances of state-chartered banks by requiring them regularly to prove adequate backing in gold for the currency they printed. The Second Bank of the United States was clearly a financial institution of great power and one entirely under the effective control of private financiers.

Those who favored and those who opposed the Bank understood poorly the system about which they were arguing. It was to be many generations before American governments would have a reasonably reliable flow of statistics concerning prices and currency movements upon which to base their judgments. The general public, including bankers themselves, was in a similar condition, although the level of ignorance varied. Thus the Bank War was to be one of those controversies in which people relied, for lack of better information, upon their predispositions about traditional social enemies. In a similar situation not long before, when yellow fever had struck Philadelphia in 1793, Federalists, with characteristic nationalist patriotism, had confidently insisted that it had arrived with French radicals on foreign ships and called for exclusionary measures, a kind of tariff against disease. Republicans, with their suspicion that social ills came from within, had with equal vehemence asserted that the sickness had been domestically caused, and called for internal reforms: the draining of swamps and the flushing-out of stagnant canals.

So, too, in Jackson's time, Democrats set out to slay, in the Second Bank of the United States, a monster that they were sure was there but that, in fact, did not exist as they conceived of it. The Bank was not a monopoly, directed so as to oppress the people, and its powers, while substantial, were limited. The Bible itself, however, authorized distrust of money lenders. Banking, furthermore, was primarily an English monopoly or in the hands of Anglicized elites in seaboard cities. The Bank of England had been feared as an oppressive force for more than a hundred years. Andrew Jackson had read of the South Sea Bubble, an inflationary boom and collapse that had shattered the British financial system in the early eighteenth century, and from this he derived an abhorrence of speculation and bankers. The Panic of 1819 had resulted in widespread foreclosures of western businesses and properties by the Second Bank of the United States, and this fixed permanently in Jacksonian minds the image of the "monster bank."[18]

However, the Bank War was not founded simply in folk prejudices. The Anglo-American intellectual community for many years had been actively debating the whole question of banking and currency. Scholars saw that the fluctuations of the business cycle seemed to be clearly related, in some intimate way, to the management of currency: its volume, its backing in precious metals, and its supervision and issuance by public and private banks. Reformers on both sides of the Atlantic believed that the uncontrolled printing of paper money was the fundamental cause of the wild fluctuations in the price level. When there was an apparent glut, such money would lose its value, prices would be driven high, and the laboring and urban consuming masses would suffer cruelly. Soon thereafter, so it seemed, there would be a collapse and a depression, which would cause unemployment.

In England the radical journalist William Cobbett attacked "rag money" as the bane of the poor. David Ricardo, the English economist whose currency theories were authoritative into the twentieth century, insisted that "sound money" (i.e., paper currency backed by appropriate supplies of gold) was essential to maintain price stability and social justice. Endlessly discussed in England through the following decades of rapid economic growth and coincident social distress, currency problems finally led Prime Minister Robert Peel, with strong backing from Richard Cobden and the Manchester Radicals, to reform the British banking system. In the 1844 Bank Charter Act, the issuance of currency by the Bank of England and private banks was placed under stringent controls in order to get at the "loose money" that seemed to cause speculative frenzies.[19]

The Jacksonian Democrats' economists—William Gouge, Condy Raguet, and Van Buren's young adviser Samuel Tilden—closely followed the currency debates in Britain and agreed with Ricardo. They insisted that inflation hurt the poor, who at this time had no means of keeping wages rising with prices, and called for a reliance upon an international gold standard and a "sound" paper currency based upon that metal.* As for the Second Bank of the United States, Jacksonian economists believed its influence was consistently on the side of speculators, leading to unrestrained issuances of paper money. Furthermore, as good Jeffersonians, they believed that any such concentration of power, together with the opportunities for

---

*The international gold standard idea was born in David Ricardo's "specie flow" theory, which remained the basis for much of economic thought on currency until well into the twentieth century. Ricardo's theory, still much relied upon, ran as follows: When prices in a particular country begin to rise (i.e., inflation occurs), gold flows out of that country because foreign creditors demand payment in that metal instead of in depreciated paper currency. Because banks that operate under "sound money" principles are required to keep a proper ratio between the amount of paper currency they have printed and issued and the gold in their vaults used as backing for that currency, a national drain of gold abroad would force bankers to call in their currency issues in proportion to how much gold they were losing. The volume of paper money in circulation would therefore shrink, and prices would fall again (i.e., there would be fewer dollars available to bid for the same quantity of goods). If a country suffers from a price decline dropping below the world level (i.e., deflation occurs; in severe cases, a depression), gold would be more valuable there than elsewhere in the world. Gold could buy more because prices would be low. It would therefore flow back into that country, banks would be able to issue more currency, and the price level would rebound to the world level, bringing renewed prosperity. The gold standard idea, therefore, with its necessary link to "sound money" principles, was essentially an internationalist conception; that is, it assumed one world market, and called upon each nation to open itself to that market's operations in order to maintain relative price stability. (The principle that prices fluctuate according to the fluctuations in the available supply of money is central to "monetarist" economic theory, and all parties relied upon it in the nineteenth century. It has had a great resurgence in acceptance among economists in the mid-twentieth century.)

self-enrichment created by the Bank's secrecy of operation, inevitably led to the exploitation of the masses. Adam Smith himself, in *The Wealth of Nations* (1776), had said that banking was so inherently powerful and self-aggrandizing that the government should intervene. It should insure the existence of many small banks rather than a single large one, so that the influence of competition would induce restraint and social justice.[20]

In July 1832 a bill rechartering the Bank for another twenty years was placed before President Jackson. He vetoed the measure. At the same time, he did something that no former President had conceived of (and few in later years would copy): he sent a spectacular veto message to the Congress that declared open political warfare upon the rich and powerful while appealing to the people at large for support in this cause. Jackson condemned "artificial distinctions" brought about by laws that "make the rich richer and the potent more powerful," injuring the "humble members of society—the farmers, mechanics, and laborers—who have neither the time nor the means of securing like favors to themselves." The Bank was unconstitutional, destructive in its operations, and far too great a concentration of power in private hands. The President attacked the "monopoly" control the Bank had over the nation's finances, a power that he said profited only Englishmen and the wealthiest Americans who owned its stock. The nation's true strength, he said, lay not in centralized institutions but in "leaving individuals and states as much as possible to themselves." He would take his stand, Jackson insisted, "against all new grants of monopolies and exclusive privileges, against any prostitution of our government to the advancement of the few at the expense of the many." "The bank," as he had told Martin Van Buren, "is trying to kill me, *but I will kill it!*"[21]

Jackson's message set off an uproar. The Whig party sprang almost immediately into being to fight Jackson's "executive tyranny." Henry Clay of Kentucky and Daniel Webster of Massachusetts were the party's central figures, bringing with them the former National Republicans. John C. Calhoun of South Carolina brought in bitter-end states' rights Southerners who hated Jackson for his quashing of South Carolina's nullification campaign. The very name "Whig," in fact, was first used in 1833 by anti-Jackson men in South Carolina and Georgia. Now, for the first time in national history, an evenly balanced two-party system emerged in the Southern states. Indeed, well-organized two-party systems appeared for the first time in practically every state in the Union, for in most states until the mid-1830s one party or the other had been overwhelmingly in control. Since the competition was so evenly matched, to mobilize every possible vote the parties (with the Democrats leading the way) swiftly built essentially modern party organizations that reached down into the precincts and wards. State and national conventions began meeting regularly to choose candidates and hammer out party positions on the issues. The "party in the electorate" had finally taken form, with its cadre of regular party officials and its links to the "party in office" in the state capitals and Washington.[22]

American politics now became the country's folk theater, a continuing dramatic encounter with a cast involving tens of thousands of ordinary citizens. Within the intricate networks of committees and party meetings, absolute loyalty and obedience to the cause was demanded. The ethic of being a "party man," formerly condemned, acquired legitimacy, especially among the Democrats. Whigs, like the Federalists before them, tended to be most heavily committed in their private lives to nonpolitical institutions: their churches and their businesses. The wealthy classes leaned Whig, and they were resistant to the idea of party discipline, stressing the superior virtue of being independent in views and behavior. But the Democrats were supreme party men, preaching endlessly *"everything for CAUSE, nothing for men."*[23]

Politicians organized their parties in army fashion, issuing pronouncements like battlefield communications and studding their speeches with terms of combat: recruitment, drill, discipline, campaign operations, esprit de corps, attacks, conquest, fierce struggle, foes, militia, rank and file, tactics, victory, and *obedience*. They no longer were apologetic about political parties but praised them as unifying, educational forces, as the essential means in a democratic country for arousing public imagination in the pursuit of ennobling goals. Parades, wagon trains, marches, rallies, mass singing, floats, transparencies, and flags—all of these mobilized the opposing Jacksonian armies. In a nation that had no national sport or common folk activity save evangelism, politics attracted the passions that in later generations would center around mass spectator athletic events. Men like Daniel Webster could attract a hundred thousand people to their open-air speeches, and their orations ran on for hours. On these mass occasions, insignificant lives took on expanded dimensions by being identified with great men and great causes. Party battles provided the most direct and available means by which people who suffered from social prejudice could strike back at their enemies or those in superior social positions who were determined to show their dominance could concretely display their power. Rivalries of every cultural sort, heavily charged with status feelings and bearing little relationship to concrete issues, could be fought as party battles.[24]

The economic argument held the stage until the mid-1840s, when manifest destiny directed national attention to new topics. When Whigs looked at the swift economic developments in the Jacksonian years, they were excited and enthusiastic. They deemed it a noble cause to stimulate the rapid development of the country's resources and create opportunity for the enterprising. As opposed to the localistic and individualistic Democrats, Whigs were moved by a strong sense of national team spirit. With Henry Clay, they believed that the national and state governments should actively promote economic development through protective tariffs, internal improvements, and other aids to entrepreneurs. Regarding such businessmen as public benefactors, they strongly supported the corporate form of business enterprise, which most Jacksonian Democrats attacked; worried little about monopoly; and insisted that all, whether employers or workers, were laborers. The classes were not natural enemies in constant conflict, as Democrats said, but natural partners. Social agitators were, in Whig eyes, antisocial persons who willfully destroyed the harmony that properly should exist among the social classes and thus undermined the sense of community so crucial to the Whig spirit.

Mob violence was deplored by Whigs, who saw themselves as the special guardians of law and order, believing as they did in the sanctity of property, as well as proper deference toward those in authority. Social leadership, in the Whigs' view, should come from the captains of commerce, finance, and industry. The government's role was to create the conditions in which investment could flourish, provide capitalists with the aids and encouragements that they requested, and leave matters thenceforth in their hands. Since rapid industrial and commercial development was the central economic task before society, there should be an abundance of fluid capital to underwrite investment. This required that banks be largely free of government restrictions and that there be a currency policy that would encourage a rate of growth in the supply of paper money to keep pace with the needs of the economy. While Whigs did not openly call for inflation, they favored a rising price level that would aid those who made their living by selling and also insure plentiful loan capital for entrepreneurs. Thus, Whigs consistently supported more liberal currency expansion policies than did Democrats.[25]

An extensive study of voting on key economic issues within the legislatures of six states—New York, Pennsylvania, Ohio, New Jersey, Virginia, and Missouri—during the years 1833–1843 has shown that these differences on economic policy penetrated deeply and with remarkable consistency into local politics. At the local level the two parties did not differ appreciably on the issue of whether or not to build internal improvements with public money, for both parties supported this bipartisan obsession. But eight out of ten Whigs voted in favor of the many charters of incorporation now being applied for by entrepreneurs, and of measures that would free them to be more imaginative and venturesome by granting them the privilege of limited liability (i.e., stockholders would be financially responsible only to the extent of their investment). Democrats, with the same near unanimity, took the opposite side. They even opposed the creation of nonprofit corporations. Democrats also insisted upon the right of states to audit the accounts of corporations, amend charters, and remove limited liability. Distrustful of banking in the best of circumstances, they were suspicious of the existing system in which individual bank charters were granted separately by the legislatures. The system opened the door, they said, to corruption and special privilege.

After the Panic of 1837, many Democrats joined the Whigs in calling for "free banking." This would give everyone who could meet uniform funding standards the right to incorporate and form a bank. Thus, equal access would be insured, and society could rely upon competition among bankers to discipline them and make corruption less likely. However, when free banking worked poorly in practice in the 1840s, Democrats in several states moved to the position that banks should be eliminated entirely. This would return the country to the "natural" and "constitutional" basis of hard silver and gold coin. Whigs in the state legislatures opposed this step by margins of four to one.[26]

In Washington, Jackson and Van Buren pushed ahead on a similar currency program. After the veto of the Second Bank of the United States, all federal moneys were withdrawn from its vaults and deposited in locally controlled, state-chartered banks. Then, to move toward a hard money (gold coin) system, the circulation of all bank notes below the denomination of five dollars, moving upward by stages to twenty dollars, was suppressed. After the Panic of 1837, President Van Buren pushed this policy to its logical conclusion: in response to the urgings of Jacksonian economists, he called for the establishment of an Independent Treasury system by which the government would keep its money in its own vaults rather than in those of private bankers. This would make it impossible for bankers to speculate with the public's funds—which, Van Buren insisted, had been the cause of the depression—and allow for a final and complete separation of *bank* and state like that between *church* and state, a parallel often cited by Jacksonian Democrats.[27]

Van Buren's proposal set off wildly contrasting reactions. It was "the boldest and highest stand ever taken by a Chief Magistrate in defence of the rights of the people," said Frank Blair of Missouri. "[It is] ... a second declaration of independence." "The message," said the New York *Gazette*, "is a heartless, cold-blooded attack upon our most valuable and most cherished classes of citizens." Radical working-class Democrats jammed Tammany Hall to cheer Van Buren and to listen to Samuel Tilden in a long oration hold that business and government must be totally separated. The wealthy, Tilden said, constituted

> an organized class which acts in phalanx and operates through all the ramifications in society; concentrating property in monopolies ... and binding to it political power—it has established an aristocracy more potent, more permanent, and more oppressive than any other which has ever existed ... practically the ruling power in nearly every civilized nation.[28]

Enacted, repealed, and reenacted, the Independent Treasury system eventually became lasting national policy. In the mid-1840s, after the Democrats' James K. Polk had taken the presidency, Democrats combined forces with Peelite Liberals in Britain to complete the edifice of economic policy that they had been driving hard for so many years to construct. In the background lay some important shifts in attitudes. The monolithic Anglophobia of Jefferson's heirs moderated as they observed the rise of a Liberal Britain beside the Tory Britain of their party imagery. Indeed, it was a Liberal Britain that had begun to take part of its instruction from the American model. "English radicals [of the Age of Reform] saw the America of the Age of Jackson as an incandescent example," the English historian Frank Thistlethwaite has written. The America that John Bright and Richard Cobden praised—the America of free schools, free churches, and free votes—was "the hope of the world, just as for the insiders of the establishment, it was a subversive influence deeply to be feared." American achievements, actual or idealized, were constantly referred to in radicals' attacks against the aristocratic order in Britain. Jeremy Bentham, the founder of Utilitarianism, whose ideas upon government inspired reformers worldwide, wrote to President Jackson that he was "more of a United States man than an Englishman."[29]

While the British Parliament pursued its tumultuous debate over the Reform Bill of 1832, by which the first major step toward political democracy in Britain was taken, Martin Van Buren watched in excited approval from the galleries. In later years, like all Jacksonian Democrats, he cheered on the Chartist reformers of the 1840s, who sought to sweep Britain to universal manhood suffrage, and he grieved at their failure. Turning to his party colleagues in America, Van Buren urged them to cast off their prejudice against England. They should realize their cousinship, he said, with men like Robert Peel, who had braved the hatred of the aristocracy to serve "the happiness and welfare of the masses." In Britain, Van Buren said, public opinion had gained as much and in some ways more control over the government than it possessed in the United States. It was now clear that America no longer stood alone in the world as a free country but had been joined in this eminence by Britain:

> A line of separation, as yet not fully disclosed, has thus been drawn between England and America, on the one hand, and the antagonistic systems of the old world, on the other, which promises to endure as long as anything that depends upon the will or the action of man, and thus interests of the greatest magnitude have become the subject of common and equal concern to the two former Nations. Every assault upon those interests, whether immediately directed against them in Great Britain or in the United States, must be regarded as an attack upon both and will, it is to be hoped, be met with equal spirit by both.[30]

Because they shared ideas with the British Liberals, Democrats in New York City even began to acquire the name of the "English party." During elections in the 1840s, they were attacked as "Free Trade men" who used "British Money in our Elections, [as] allies and hired instruments of British manufacturers."[31]

In 1846 the epochal moment for a common effort on the part of tariff reformers on both sides of the Atlantic seemed to arrive. Polk was in the White House, with Robert J. Walker as his secretary of the treasury, and they were urging Congress to lower the tariff. At the same time Robert Peel was mustering his historic effort to repeal the Corn Laws in Britain and thus opening the United Kingdom to free trade with the world. Visions of an interdependent Anglo-American economic community were excitedly discussed, a community in which English manufactured goods (much cheaper than those made in America) would flow to the United States in exchange for American wheat. When Peel won his great victory, news of the repeal of the Corn Laws was hurried to America, where it helped secure passage of the Walker Tariff, which reduced imposts dramatically.[32]

Now the Manchester Radicals in Britain and the American Democrats had the substance of their dream: a transatlantic trading community between a Liberal Britain and a Democratic United States. It was a community whose basic economic nature was shaped by the ideas of the Scotsman Adam Smith, who since publication of his *The Wealth of Nations* had been the presiding genius for Anglo-American economic reformers. It seemed, in fact, that Smith's conception of a free economy in which governments gave no aid to capitalists and everyone was subject to the discipline of the market place was to be realized more in America than in his home country. Theodore Sedgwick, a leading Jacksonian Democrat, had observed in 1838 that Adam Smith's "voice has been ringing in the world's ears for sixty years, but it is only now in the United States that he is listened to, reverenced, and followed."[33] By the 1850s, however, Smith seemed finally to have triumphed on both sides of the water. Mercantilism in its traditional form seemed to have met its demise. Tariffs were low in order to encourage international trade and subject all producers to competition; a reasonably complete separation between government and business had been achieved; and "sound money" principles to keep prices low and damp down boom and bust oscillations were being observed. The flow of investment would follow "natural" channels, and the economy would move upward now that it had been released from what Democrats and Liberals described as the clumsy interferences and harmful restrictions of mercantilism. Wealth, equitably shared because it was no longer artificially diverted by governments into the hands of selfish capitalists, would begin steadily to mount, and everyone's standard of living would rise—if Liberal-Democratic economic theories were valid.

Soon after 1846, gold and silver were discovered in California and Nevada. The American and British currency systems were enormously expanded with the inflow of these precious metals, and prosperous times that seemed to confirm the new system ensued. Out of these conditions came the economic euphoria of the mid-Victorian years. Until the transatlantic economic collapse of the mid-1870s, Adam Smith's predictions seemed abundantly borne out: that dynamic natural forces, once freed of the hampering interventions of governments and their attendant corruptions, would create ever more abundance, widely shared. William Gladstone, as British chancellor of the exchequer, annually lifted British spirits by detailing how, year after year, the average Briton's standard of living was rising. America in the 1850s experienced its most explosive economic boom to that date. The capital invested in industry doubled, cotton prices soared, and railroad construction pressed forward feverishly. After the hiatus of the Civil War, the great boom was to continue unabated until the mid-1870s, though, as will be seen, under profoundly different national policies. The economic argument, apparently brought to a conclusion in the 1840s by a sweeping Democratic victory, would break out again in the 1860s and fill the last third of the nineteenth century with a full revival of the Jacksonian debate.

VI

The Jacksonian Party System, 1828=1854: The Cultural Dimension

Much is familiar in these Jacksonian arguments over the economy. Since at least the middle of the eighteenth century, traditionalists had sought to hold back commercializing, modernizing trends while localists had recoiled from cosmopolitan, nationalizing influences. Patriots in the Revolutionary years had generally taken a localist stance, opposing Loyalists because they were part of the transatlantic, Anglicizing world of trade and economic development. In Jackson's years, the Democrats championed a quiet, stable, localized, face-to-face society, simple in form and manageable. Their transatlantic partnership with the British Liberals was like that earlier relationship between Revolutionary patriots and radical British Whigs: it aimed at overturning elitism, deplored the power of the wealthy, and attacked the corruption it believed sprang from close links between government and business. The American Whig party advocated economic development through a vigorous use of federal and state governments to open resources and stimulate enterprise. Inherited from their New England stronghold, the Whigs' cultural Anglophilia—their admiration of things English—conflicted with their protectionist nationalism, that is, their desire to foster American industry and ward off English competition. In the Jacksonian years, as in those of the Revolution, the Anglo-American relationship remained charged, ambivalent, and contradictory.

The economic argument between Whigs and Democrats had profoundly cultural implications. The two parties were trying, by their divergent economic policies, to build or to preserve sharply contrasting moral orders and ways of living. Each had a different national vision. For the Democrats, their war against the Second Bank of the United States was not simply an economic crusade but an effort to restore the Old Republic of austerity and virtue that, in their idealized memory, they associated with the Founding Fathers:

> [Their campaign] . . . to destroy the Monster Bank and its vicious brood —privileged corporations, paper money—enlisted moral passions in a drama of social justice and self-justification. . . . To the Bank's influence the Jacksonians traced constitutional impiety, consolidated national power, aristocratic privilege, and plutocratic corruption. Social inequality, impersonal and intangible business relations, economic instability, perpetual debt and taxes, all issued from the same source. . . . The bank system suspends the real world of solid goods, honestly exchanged, upon a mysterious, swaying web of speculative credit. The natural distributive mechanism, which proportions rewards to "industry, economy, and virtue," is fixed to pay off the insider and the gambler.[1]

The Democrats were caught, however, in a paradoxical situation. They were traditionalists, and yet they were not. Adam Smith, their mentor, called not for economic primitivism but for steadily rising productivity. He wanted to release natural productive energies that would create ever more "opulence," as he usually termed it, but in conditions that would foster social justice, discourage monopolies, and remove opportunities for corruption. Although they talked constantly of capitalist conspiracies, Democrats, too, believed in economic growth, provided it was the result of natural forces and not artificially induced by speculating insiders. Jacksonian Democrats often participated actively in investment and entrepreneurism. The wealthy Democrat, then as later, was a familiar figure in national politics. Van Buren's young economic adviser Samuel Tilden, when he ran for the presidency in 1876, was the richest man to seek the office since George Washington. Democrats owned state-chartered banks, and the historians Richard Hofstadter and Bray Hammond had understandable reasons for concluding that the Jacksonians' war against the Bank was not the noble effort of their rhetoric but a campaign by acquisitive small capitalists to throw off the Bank's restraints.[2]* Certainly, too, the Democrats' effort at unleashing naturally dynamic forces within the economy helped create a booming national economy strikingly un-Jeffersonian in its social results. The Democrats did not re-create the Old Republic, quiet, simple, and austere, but rather an industrial giant. They relied upon sound money and marketplace competition to discipline entrepreneurial appetites, insure social justice, and spread wealth, but productivity and entrepreneurial energies were not to be so simply restrained.

The paradox in Democratic ideology did not end with economic policy. In their egalitarianism, Democrats actively pursued an essentially modernizing goal. Thomas Jefferson's ideas and those of his heirs led toward conceptions of equality of status and social class that have become the distinguishing characteristics of modern societies. In the Democrats' libertarianism, their insistence upon a secular state in which governments were not to be linked to churches or to exercise moral oversight of private lives, there was also a breaking from ancient practices. That the community should rightfully control moral behavior and individual lifestyles was a conception as old as human society. The ideology of cultural laissez faire headed in directions that eventually would flower in the sexual and cultural libertarianism of the 1960s, though the sight would have profoundly offended Jacksonian Democrats.

The Whigs, too, were caught in their own contradictions. In their impulse toward economic development, they were creating a new world: nationalist, cosmopolitan, developmental, and entre-

---

*John McFaul has provided strong evidence against the view that state bank men wanted to see the quashing of the Second Bank of the United States so as to be free from its controls.

The safest conclusion about banking interests during the Jacksonian era is that state bankers were reluctant to inject themselves and their institutions into politics. Other conclusions, though less certain, seem supported by the evidence. In each phase of the administration's Bank War—recharter, removal, and the post-removal panic—state banks generally did not support the [Jackson] administration. Where there was evidence of state bank support it was on the side of *the* national Bank or *a* national bank. The reason was a very simple one, and readily realized by state bankers: it was merely that the advantages to state banking operations of a national bank outweighed whatever disadvantages might exist in the financial relationship between state and national institutions. Whether as a valuable source of credit and other financial conveniences that only a national bank could provide, or as a regulator of state banking activities, the national Bank was welcomed by state banking interests. The alternative—the absence of a national bank—meant the disintegration of interbank relationships that Biddle had implemented and the withdrawal of an important stabilizing economic force. (*The Politics of Jacksonian Finance* [Ithaca, N.Y., 1972], pp. 56–57.)

preneurial. They assumed, however, that development would proceed within traditional forms. They thought of their laboring men and women in familial terms, as participants in a common enterprise who duly and dutifully followed orders. They were offended as well as outraged when workers became disrespectful and disobedient, demanding higher wages and better hours. Whig entrepreneurs had no intention of building the immense corporations and the swollen industrialism, with its abyss between labor and capital, that the future would bring. They wanted simply to transfer the traditional elitist order from estate and counting house, from shipping office and mercantile establishment, to the mills and factories of their idealized industrial future, which dimly they perceived of as re-creating in America the solid base for a powerful, traditional order like that in Great Britain.

In their political and social attitudes, Whigs were profoundly traditional. Although they learned and used the techniques of Jacksonian politics, they were uneasy with them and still conceived government as a mystery properly in the hands of the elite.[3] Most Whigs believed, too, in the moral supervision of private lives. Church and state should work together. The nation was rightfully to be thought of as a single moral community to be welded together in holy living, to be fashioned in the image of New England's "citty on a hill."

For the Whigs were essentially the Yankee party, in the sense that their strongest cultural and economic leadership radiated from New England. Whig leaders in New York State were almost invariably of English or Yankee ancestry. The wealthy in that state were also predominantly English or Yankee and belonged to the English churches (Episcopalian, Quaker, and Presbyterian, which, as will be explained, often meant Congregationalist). Democratic leaders, on the other hand, were considerably *less* English in their ethnic origins and more Dutch and German. The wealthy were only partially Scotch-Irish or Dutch and rarely German, Irish Catholic, or French; only partially Dutch Reformed and rarely Catholic, Lutheran, Baptist, Jewish, or Methodist.[4] Economic interests, in short, aligned with cultural identities and values. Whether Democrats were attacking the wealthy or the moralists, they were attacking essentially the same people. Thus, it made sense on cultural as well as economic grounds for the ethnic outgroups to be Democrats. They were workers and consumers for whom Democratic economic ideology was desirable, and they were either strangers in the land or long-resident non-Yankee peoples like the Dutch who needed protection from Yankee cultural imperialism.

The Whig-Democrat conflict was not, of course, a simple confrontation between mutually exclusive blocs of New Englanders and non-English outgroups. The ethnic communities intermingled, and individuals were then, as always, moved by many different motivations. The Yankee impulse was not monolithic, nor were the attitudes of the other ethnic groups whom ethnocultural research now reveals to have lined up strongly behind one party or the other. Even within New England, Yankees were divided among themselves, as they had been in Jefferson's time.[5] Massachusetts, of course, was as firmly Whig as it had been Federalist. Maine and New Hampshire, however, were not only traditionally hostile to Boston; their Scotch-Irish communities and their religious dissenters (including Baptists, Methodists, and French Canadian Catholics) made these states as Jacksonian Democratic as earlier they had been Jeffersonian Republican.*

What we observe, therefore, is often only a marginal preponderance, the center of gravity within particular cultural communities lying more on the side of one party than on that of the other. However, what is the striking and ultimately operative fact is that the cultural archetype, the identifying image, seems not to have been equally shared. It was Whigs in New England who were most identified with the Yankee image, just as it was Democrats in the South who seemed most proud to wear the name "Southerner." In both cases, they were culturally dominant in their own regions, establishing the prevailing mood and self-concept. By the Jackson years, westward-moving New Englanders had settled New York State in such huge numbers that they made up 65 percent of its electorate, but they were only marginally Whig. Thousands of New Englanders disliked the state-church ideology of Congregationalist Massachusetts and Connecticut, and they had left these states precisely to find freer lives to the west. However, despite this fact, the Yankees of New York were consistently associated with the Whigs and especially with

*Donald B. Cole, in his *Jacksonian Democracy in New Hampshire, 1800–1851* (Cambridge, Mass., 1970), observes that New Hampshire was probably the most Democratic state in the Union. Old, traditionally Congregational towns along the Connecticut River were Whig, but Portsmouth, the state's principal seaport city, and much of the interior, held strong Jacksonian Democratic partisans. They attacked the Congregationalists and their state-church proclivities; welcomed the Baptists into their ranks; condemned financiers, banks, and paper money; appealed to the "plain people" against the wealthy; gloried in democracy; deplored anti-Catholicism and offered friendship to the Irish; and opposed the movement to abolish slavery, taking an open role as the outspokenly antiblack party of the state, a common Democratic pattern.

that Whig stronghold, the puritanical and pietist Burned-Over District (so called because it was criss-crossed repeatedly by revival campaigns) in the western part of the state. James Fenimore Cooper, Jacksonian Democrat, whose vantage point was Cooperstown, New York, filled his novels with stereotypically hateful Yankees: shrewd, hypocritical, prating teetotalers who constantly intruded into other people's lives to instruct them in proper moral behavior. Their commercialism and speculative temper, Cooper believed, had helped destroy the Old Republic he mourned.[6]*

Nowhere have these cultural roots of economic conflicts been more subtly worked out than in recent studies of the bank controversy in the states of the Old Northwest and especially in Illinois. The most violent opposition to banks and paper currency in that state came from "Egypt," the older, southern section settled by farmers from the slave-owning South and by pockets of immigrant German farmers. Both of these peoples were traditional in lifestyle and outlook. The strongest support for Whiggish banking and currency ideas came from northern Illinois, a region populated by New Englanders. A busy, inventive people, in their own day New England Whigs in Illinois were "often contrasted with the slow-moving inhabitants of the southern counties, whom ex-Governor Ford described as 'unambitious of wealth and great lovers of ease.'" A Democratic editor replied that the Whigs' preference for "rag money" (i.e., their more liberal attitude toward issuances of paper money) "might be entertained with some favor in New England—as the idea of enriching a people by issue of paper money is not much more absurd than the burning of indefensive old women on the charge of witchcraft." The Illinois Whigs, in short, were "future-oriented and appealed to those men, *regardless of* [economic] *class,* who put their faith in economic progress . . . [by which they meant] the commercialization of soci-

---

*"Generally in his books," Marvin Meyers observes in *The Jacksonian Persuasion: Politics and Belief* (New York, 1959), "Cooper relentlessly presses the old quarrel of Yorkers with Yankees" (p. 67). Lee Benson, in his *The Concept of Jacksonian Democracy: New York as a Test Case* (Princeton, N.J., 1961), describes western New York as a New England colony. The "overwhelmingly Yankee counties in western New York 'notoriously' formed the enthusiastic core of the anti–Van Buren–Jackson forces. . . ." (p. 303). The "Chautauqua Yankees as a group might be called both puritans and innovators; that is, they believed in self-improvement in all respects, in man's responsibility to make the world virtuous and moral, and in social progress" (p. 306). In "Chautauqua County, Southern slaveowners . . . served as a negative reference group. . . . They described themselves as the party of 'Northern Freemen' and their opponents as 'Northern Dough-Faces' who 'ignobly cowered under the vaporings and gasconade of Southern 'Chivalry' ' " (p. 316).

ety." Commerce, said Ohio's Whig senator Thomas Corwin, was "the most efficient civilizer of our Barbarous race."[7]

Wherever Yankee Whigs went in their westward migration, they carried with them a righteous and confident urge to use the secular government to create a morally unified society. The Second Great Awakening, which began to surge in the late 1790s and did not run its full course until the 1850s, created a national mood within which moralistic Whiggism flourished. Churchmen universally agreed that America had become a violent, disorderly, and godless nation cursed with alcohol and moral misbehavior. By the Jacksonian years, the Second Great Awakening, which they launched, had become a nationwide evangelical crusade. Its most intense concentration was among the Yankees of the Burned-Over District in the western part of New York State. Here and in the northern counties of Pennsylvania—the Northern Tier—also settled by Yankees, true believers in Christ were confident that they were agents of the Holy Spirit. Christ, it was believed, was coming soon to usher in the millennium. Thus, the world must be purified in preparation for that Coming. So great were the energies of evangelical "ultraism" that it could not be contained within the churches. It spilled out of the pews and into the secular world, setting off a wide array of reform movements, among which abolitionism, temperance, and Sabbatarianism claimed the most adherents.[8]

The Sabbatarian crusade came alive in the 1820s. Its advocates demanded laws halting all movements on Sunday, including the transport of mail, the operation of canals, and even the delivery of milk. In 1827 Reverend Ezra Stiles Ely called for a "Christian Party in Politics" to pursue the divine causes. Temperance became a national campaign, focusing largely upon the lifestyle of the immigrants—their whisky and beer drinking and their Continental Sunday—and it was joined by condemnations of dancing, stylish and revealing modes of dress, gambling, Mormon plural marriages, brothel keeping, and all manner of allegedly licentious behavior.[9] In the late 1820s evangelical politics was vastly strengthened by the sudden appearance of the Anti-Masonic party, first in New York and then in other states. A Mason had been abducted and murdered for threatening to reveal Masonic secrets. When attempts to prosecute were apparently frustrated by an interlocking network of Masons in places of authority, a longstanding hostility to the order came to life. The Masonic order had a freethinking and rationalist reputation, dating from its eighteenth-century origins during the Enlightenment, and the pious had traditionally regarded it with suspicion. Now charges erupted that the order was a privileged, irreligious, and immoral body that was working to subvert true religion in America. Crying out that America must be purged of all anti-Christian influences—which included Andrew Jackson and his followers—the Anti-Masons grew so swiftly that they ran a presidential candidate in 1832 and elected many of their members to local offices.[10]

When the Whigs appeared as an organized party in the mid-1830s, they absorbed the Anti-Masons and all the various currents of pious, evangelical political moralism into their party. "Whig political picnics resembled camp meetings," writes Ronald P. Formisano about Michigan politics, "Whig rhetoricians spoke a political idiom resembling that of the evangelist, and the party caught an enthusiasm in those years which can be compared only to that of an extended revival."[11] Among the strongest of the Whigs were the Quakers, despite the fact that, in accordance with their quietistic faith, they avoided the enthusiasm and turbulence of the revival crusades. They, too, however, were pietists in their politics and hoped to see America transformed into a truly moral society. Furthermore, they were English in ethnic origins and traditional enemies of Scotch-Irishmen, Jeffersonians, and Anglophobes. Quakers also approved of the distinctive Whig amalgam of political moralism and the values of hard work, self-denial, and getting ahead. In 1844 the Whigs chose as their vice-presidential nominee the former New Jersey senator Theodore Frelinghuysen, a passionate advocate of the Georgia Indians' cause, who had been the "Christian statesman" of the Congress and its most zealous Sabbatarian. Within state governments, Whigs constantly pushed the cause of moral purity and reform. When in 1843 a Democrat-controlled legislature in Michigan amended and loosened laws that punished adultery and fornication, Whigs rent the air with cries of outrage, and their state convention roundly condemned the sacrilege.[12]

Whigs insisted that they were the party of decency and respectability, the guardians of piety, sober living, proper manners, thrift, steady habits, and book learning. The hard-drinking and hard-living vote seems clearly to have been in the Democratic camp, and all Whigs knew it. Many of them thought Democrats by definition to be dissolute folk or sympathizers with such behavior. Moralistic Whigs felt themselves bound by heaven itself to save such persons from their evil ways. Senator Frelinghuysen could not resist looking solicitously into the personal religious lives of his Whig colleagues Daniel

Webster and Henry Clay, and certainly Democrats were also fair game. Distinctions in lifestyle even characterized entire communities. Vermontville, a town in Michigan, was Yankee, church going, restrained in behavior, and Whig. The mining towns on the Keewenaw Peninsula on Lake Superior were rough, raw, lawless, and almost unanimously Democratic.[13]

However, many thousands of devout Protestants were Democrats. The Baptists, now growing rapidly into a huge national denomination, continued to fight against the state-church concept. With the Methodists, they were hostile to the invasion of public affairs by church influences. They also resented the superior ways of the Presbyterians and Congregationalists, who in the Northern states were the principal proponents of the "Christian party in politics" idea. Many Protestant sects believed there was a conspiracy among Calvinist clergymen to create a new theocracy. Thus, a large antievangelical bloc poured into the Jacksonian party to fight off state-church clericals. There was a constant public ranting at the money that ministers in the Calvinist denominations seemed to live on and at the threats these clericals presented to civil liberties. Southerners were especially hostile to the evangelicals, who were trying to help the Indians in Georgia and opposing Andrew Jackson on the issue. "Southern sensitivity about slavery, even before Garrison's crusade," observes Bertram Wyatt-Brown, "appeared in resentment of New England Sabbatarianism."[14] Then there were such Northern religious minorities as the Roman Catholics and Mormons, who either favored complete separation between church and state by conviction or for their own protection against the threatened Yankee ascendancy. As a Presbyterian minister in Michigan said, looking at this populous massing of enemies, "The mobocracy of the age hates us." So, indeed, the priesthood of the Church of England in the colonies must have felt when confronting Dissenters.[15]

Within the large Presbyterian community, in fact, the core of the church-and-state argument was fought out in the Jacksonian years. Presbyterian ministers who were Whigs were actually New England Congregationalists moved west. By the Plan of Union that the two Calvinist churches adopted in 1801, Congregationalists moving into New York became members of the already existing (Scotch-Irish) Presbyterian church. The agreement, however, was inherently unstable. Not only did Yankees and Scotch-Irishmen differ widely in style and theology, but they actively disliked each other. Congregationalists, with their long tradition of parish autonomy, tended to be much freer and more open in their theology than the stern, federally organized, and more creedal Scotch-Irish Presbyterians. Yankee Presbyterians joined enthusiastically in the revivalism of the Second Great Awakening. Soon they were preaching that salvation was open to all who chose it—a profoundly non-Calvinist concept. God, they said, had given humanity free will so that fallen persons could make their choice for Christ. The Scotch-Irish Presbyterians of the Middle Atlantic States and southward held to a much more somber, predestinarian faith derived from the Shorter Catechism of the Westminster Confession (1643). They firmly disapproved of the Yankee's moral reformism: church and state, in their view, must remain sharply separate. Out of Princeton University in New Jersey, the intellectual heart and chief seminary of Scottish Presbyterianism, they launched an "Old School" offensive against the "New Schoolers" in the north. In 1837 the conflict tore the denomination apart, and the western New York synods were read out of the church.[16]*

Democratic Presbyterians now ranged in open political hostility to Whig Presbyterians. In Philadelphia, the cultural distinctions were sharp and clear. New School Presbyterians in that city were classic Whigs: upwardly mobile, well-to-do, capitalist entrepreneurs in high prestige occupations or in merchandising and industry. Albert Barnes, their leading minister, preached that God showed His approval of individual persons by granting them worldly success. Old School parishes, by contrast, were peopled by artisans and laborers who held little property and listened to ministers who insisted that humankind cannot possess free will, for God is wholly sovereign. The Old School believed further that this earth provides no comfort to the soul and that great prosperity is no sign whatever of divine favor.[17] Elsewhere in the Northern states, the pattern repeated itself: in communities where Presbyterians were predominantly New School and Yankee, as in Michigan—a state that stood in the path of the Yankees' western migration—Presbyterianism was practically synonymous with the Whig party. Where Presbyterians were predominantly Scotch-Irish who derived from the eighteenth-century migration from Ulster and looked to Princeton University for leader-

---

*As Lois Banner points out,

> Presbyterianism, except for some areas in New Jersey, was a dissenting church. Unlike Congregationalism, it did not have a tradition of establishment in America. Religious diversity had always characterized the situation in the middle states. Presbyterians had always lived in cooperation and competition with a variety of other churches, and in Virginia, where there was an Anglican establishment, the Presbyterians had vigorously fought for disestablishment. ("Religious Benevolence as Social Control," *Journal of American History,* 60 [1973], 27.)

ship as they did along the Hudson River, in Pennsylvania, and in the South, they leaned Democratic.[18]

The greatest enemy of moralists in politics was the Democratic party organization and its leadership. The Democrats' strong Jeffersonian roots and their determined secularism made their party the home not only of the many outgroups thus far described but of that tiny portion of the American people who were freethinkers, deists, and agnostics. Jacksonian Democratic politicians were known for their worldly ways, and the agnosticism of the workingmen's groups which increasingly shaped Jacksonian policies made holiness popular among the employing classes. Such labor radicals from England as the spectacular Frances Wright said that Sabbatarianism "betrayed the whole soul of priestcraft," and temperance crusades received heavy Democratic abuse.[19]*

Many colleges of Yankee and moralistic persuasions were strongholds of Whiggery. However, the Democratic party had a strong relationship to the urban intellectual community. Urban intellectuals who were of a secular, reforming, "advanced," and rationalistic cast of mind looked back in admiration to Thomas Jefferson and claimed Jackson as their own. In the 1820s William Cullen Bryant appeared in New York City from New England as a devoted young Federalist. Soon, however, he was swept up by the charisma of the Democratic hero, Andrew Jackson. For the many years that Bryant served as editor of the *Evening Post*, he was Jackson's devotee and fervent partisan. The brilliant recluse Samuel Tilden, reared in a New En-

---

*The Whigs, it must be observed, never willingly surrendered the Jefferson legacy to the Democrats. Throughout the age of Jackson, they contended that they were the true inheritors of the sainted Virginian, that their name, Whig, was an accurate revival of the very political name that Jefferson had chosen for himself, for the appropriate reason that Andrew Jackson was a tyrant in the Tory tradition. "The politics of the age," Merrill D. Peterson writes, "gave four clear faces to the Jefferson image: the intransigent Democrat of the Jacksonians, the ruthless demagogue of the conservatives, the liberal and practical statesman of the Whigs, the state rights constitutionalist of the Old Republicans. But all these visages tended to merge into the imposing figure of the Father or Apostle of Democracy." After 1840, however, Jeffersonian polemics faded. "Democracy had triumphed, it seemed, and so had its Apostle. Men might continue to talk Jefferson, but it was in the nature of anticlimax and it added nothing to the generalized democratic image. Soon . . . the burgeoning slavery controversy changed the whole pattern of politics, its forces, ideas, and issues," and in this new scene, Jefferson was seen again in a new light. (*The Jefferson Image in the American Mind* [New York, 1962], pp. 110–111.)

gland village in the Hudson valley and given Jefferson's *Memoirs* as a child to learn by heart, joined Martin Van Buren's entourage as resident intellectual and economist. William Gouge, writing his books on money and banking, poured a steady stream of anti-monopoly, antielitist, and anticlerical ideas into the Democratic hopper. William Leggett scribbled his passionate editorials in the *Post,* excoriating bankers and the wealthy.[20]

Central to the ideology of Anglo-American, freethinking intellectuals was a conviction that clerics must be kept out of politics, that their moral preachments were arrogance and their attempts to control the lives of others a continuing danger to freedom of thought and belief. This led many Democratic intellectuals to reject abolitionism, for it emerged out of the camp of the enemy: zealous, moralistic, church-and-state Yankeeism. Northern Democrats opposed the expansion of slavery, but they would not support any crusade to overturn the social institutions of their traditional political ally, the Southern states.[21]*

The cultural divisions that separated Democrat from Whig in the Northern states were sharply intensified in the Jacksonian years by an epochal event: the arrival in the United States of enormous numbers of Irish Catholics. American political conflict to this point had been almost entirely between Protestants, for Catholics had been few in numbers. Between 1820 and 1840, however, some 700,000 Irish Catholics entered the country. Then the potato famines of the 1840s turned this already heavy immigration into a flood. In the four

---

*I intend to explore the question of slavery, black America, and the Democrats in the following chapter. Here, it may be observed that black voters in New York State fully recognized their political friends and enemies and voted accordingly. In the balloting of 1844, they voted 95 percent Whig. The Van Buren Democrats in New York State had for decades been identified with antiblack feelings. When delegates were being elected to the New York State constitutional convention of 1846, a leading Radical Democratic newspaper, the *Morning News,* opposed equality for black people. "The principal object of the Whigs who have participated in the movement for a Convention to revise the Constitution of this State, has been to procure the right of suffrage for the Negroes to the same extent that it is enjoyed by white citizens." In reply, the Whig *New York Tribune* stated that the "question of Suffrage is in truth fundamental to all others. On the one side stand Equality, Reason, Justice, Democracy, Humanity; on the other are a base, slavery-engendered prejudice and a blackguard clamor against 'Niggers.'" The "great laws of nature," said the *Morning News,* "do not permit two distinct and uncongenial races of men to mingle together in harmony or in mutual self-government." "Wherever in our State," said the *Tribune,* "there is no pervading Anti-Slavery sentiment, there the Loco-Focos [radical Democrats] are red-mouthed and vociferous against Black Suffrage at all hazards. Hostility to 'Niggers' is their great card" (Benson, *Concept of Jacksonian Democracy,* pp. 317–320).

years from 1847 to 1851 perhaps a million Irishmen came to America.[22]

Few issues caused such continuing turbulence in the transatlantic Anglo-American community as the "Irish Question." In northwestern England and western Scotland, large groups of Catholic Irish had settled in the ports and industrial cities, arriving without education, money, and skills and taking the lowest-paid jobs. They were regarded with alarm by English and Scottish workingmen because of their competition and with hatred because of their differences. Indeed, for centuries the British had looked upon the Irish as practically a subhuman people. They thought them ignorant, immoral, drunken, violent, unable to delay sensual gratification for the achievement of future goals, given to crimes with sharp instruments, and blessed only with a certain dumb willingness to engage in physical labor, musical talents, and a comical temper—attributes commonly applied by white Americans to Afro-Americans. In the 1840s, political cartoonists in England and America began depicting people from Ireland as ape-like and continued the practice for many decades.*

The Irish, in short, were the people who played the role of "blacks" in British life, and in the United States, the same attitudes toward them persisted. The Irish problem in Britain, which involved controversies over civil equality, economic justice, and self-government, created a continuing uproar that endured past World War I. The British people universally believed that radical Catholic Irishmen might murder any public official or blow up any government building, for the Irish Fenians—militant nationalists—vowed war on every agency of the Queen. The hundreds of thousands of English, Scots, Scotch-Irish, and Welsh who continued to migrate to the United

---

*L. Perry Curtis, Jr., in *Apes and Angels: The Irishman in Victorian Caricature* (Washington, D.C., 1971), writes:

> During the 1840s the acutely prognathous face became more and more identified with Irish peasants [in cartoons], whether or not they happened to be ardent rebels. After the launching of *Punch, Or the London Charivari* in 1841, the equation between snub-nosed, big-mouthed, and prognathous faces and Irish Celts became as complete as caricature could hope to achieve. . . . [They became] 'a cross between a garrotter and a gorilla.' . . . However brutish the faces found in British cartoons and illustrations during the 1840s and 1850s, Paddy remained essentially human in outward form until [the Fenianism of] the 1860s, when the era of acute midfacial prognatish began to turn into the age of the simianized Celt. . . . [The American cartoonist Thomas Nast] invariably produced [in the 1870s and 1880s] a *lusus naturae* or cross between a professional boxer and an orangutan. The degree of midfacial prognathism and the size of the mouth have to be seen to be believed. (Pp. 31–37, 58.)

States through the nineteenth century brought with them the hatred they felt for Catholic Irishmen, from whom they were separated by centuries of bloody memories. The arrival of the Catholic Irish, therefore, immediately shifted all political equations in America.[23]

Irish Catholics rejected the passivity that had marked the small community of Catholics already in the United States (about thirty thousand, mainly of English descent, were recorded in the 1790 census, primarily in Maryland and Pennsylvania). Irish Catholics demanded equal treatment and status. Their centuries of struggle against the Protestant English and Scotch-Irish had made them a militant, tightly knit, and devoutly Catholic people who fought angrily against nativist prejudice and actively defended their faith in public debate. The Irish demanded public funds for their parochial schools, opposed the reading of the Protestant Bible in the public schools, and frequently demonstrated in the streets for their cause. Their priests and bishops, in America as in Ireland, were their political as well as religious superiors, the captains of the Irish army.[24]

Wherever the Catholic Irish came into close contact with the British, they produced an immediate and striking effect: the Scots, Welsh, and Scotch-Irish shifted over en masse (in New York City, to the level of 90 percent) to join their former political enemies, the English, in the Whig party, for all Britons regarded the Catholic Irish with distaste and alarm. In key Northern states the *English* monolith within the Whig party began to expand into one that was *British*. New York City newspapers in the 1840s claimed that practically every "Orangeman" (Scotch-Irishman) in that city now voted Whig. When nativist anti-Catholic movements erupted, the Scotch-Irish were in the lead. Commenting upon the anti-Catholic riots that broke out in Philadelphia in 1844, the *Freeman's Journal* argued that "the most active, although not the most prominent of the Native Americans in New York, and probably in Philadelphia also, have been Irish Orangemen. They alone have been capable of furnishing the anti-social views with which our young *Natives* have been inoculated." No one, indeed, but an Ulster Scotch-Irishman could hate the Catholic Irish with such intensity, for they had been fighting each other for centuries and would continue to do so.[25]

From the beginning of the Revolutionary troubles to the time of Andrew Jackson, the Scotch-Irish had set the tone and form of American politics because their ancient hatred of the English and of New England Yankees had produced a sharp polarization between the parties. Now it was the Catholic Irish who would give nineteenth-century American politics its fundamental structure. Catholic Irish

lined up behind the Democrats, with their Jeffersonian openness to
ethnic minorities and their cultural laissez faire, to the level of 95
percent in New York politics in the 1840s. A Whig paper in Albany
estimated in 1844 that, of the hundred Catholic Irish voters in the
city, all but two or three would be anti-Whig. Indeed, "Catholic Irish
voted Democratic in New York State, whether they lived in urban
or rural communities, whether they were day laborers or freehold
farmers—in short, their voting represented an ethnocultural or religious group, not a place or class, phenomenon."[26]

In the rapid rise in immigration that occurred during the Jacksonian years, Germans were as prominent as the Irish. They arrived
at the eastern ports in such numbers that, by the 1840s, they were
the second largest immigrant group in New York state. Whether
Catholic or Protestant, Germans voted strongly Democratic. They
were aliens, and they knew that the Whigs disliked them. They were
as gregarious as the Irish, living closely together and fighting to
protect their culture. Like the Germans in colonial days, they were
a localist people, made to live apart by their language, and they
disliked Yankees and their causes. Germans loved their beer and
their convivial Sundays and were offended by the aggressively Yankee tone of the public schools—which in truth were often established
for the sole purpose of Anglicizing their children. Germans wanted
self-sufficiency, close-knit family living in their rural communities,
and little interference from the outside. They were sensitive to the
issue of religious freedom and separation of church and state, for
many were fleeing from revived religious persecution in their homeland.[27]

The Germans were less politically monolithic, however, than the
Catholic Irish. Germany itself was a culturally pluralistic country,
and its internal divisions came with the immigrants to America. The
Catholic-Protestant division among Germans was centuries old, and
in time it would produce divergent voting patterns. Divisions had
also appeared among different kinds of Protestant Germans already
long settled in the United States. In Pennsylvania, Germans who
were Lutherans or members of the German Reformed (Calvinist)
church were stolid and orthodox churchgoers who in their homeland
had been used to thinking of themselves as the established national
church of a particular principality or kingdom. The Lutherans and
German Reformed were "church" people, as distinct from what the
English would call "chapel" and religious historians would term

"sect" people; that is, they were not evangelists. The task of their church was instead to care for its nationals, to gather them together as a people, distinct and separate to themselves. They were not engaged in converting others to true Christianity but in ministering to the religious needs of those who, having been born in a particular political jurisdiction, were of the faith. Thus, Lutherans and German Reformed saw their religion as a matter of belief about God and humankind, not about social action. In politics, they were overwhelmingly Democratic.[28]

Those Germans who were Moravians and River Brethren, however, were much like New England Congregationalists and considerably less ethnically nationalist. Their faith was pietistic, zealous, moralistic, and outward reaching. Their task, as they saw it, was to reform the world. Like Yankees of similar religious attitudes, they were strong Whigs. Whereas Democratic newspapers in Pennsylvania regularly cursed the English and the Yankees, Whig newspapers, supported by the Moravians and River Brethren, praised Yankee schools and inventiveness. Theirs, they said, was the "party of religion, morality, and decency."[29]

The Dutch of New York, ancient occupants of the land and closely settled in the Hudson Valley, were another localist, non-British Democratic voting group. Speaking their native language, worshipping in their Dutch Reformed church, and maintaining cohesive, intermarried, and homogeneous farming communities, they, too, wished to be left alone. The New York Dutch had been close allies of the Scotch-Irish in the Revolutionary period, had supported George Clinton loyally, and were firmly anti-Federalist. The "proposition to form a central government . . . was greeted by the residents of [Orange] County with vehement protest . . . the people of Orange felt that the proposed federation was only a name for another form of tyranny, and that under the simple title of President lurked the authority of King." In the following decades the Dutch in New York voted steadily Jeffersonian, resisting change and holding stubbornly to old ways of thought and action. They especially disliked the "restless Yankees," with their impulse to use the government to enforce their ways or achieve common social and economic goals. Furthermore, the Dutch, who had held black slaves and had not cared for having had them freed, were both antiblack and antiabolitionist. In 1846 a referendum in Rockland County, a Dutch district, produced a vote of 96.4 percent against equal suffrage for black Americans.[30]

In the Middle West, similar polarizations existed between non-British outgroups and the Whigs. The French in Michigan were strongly Democratic. They had lived in that region since the eighteenth century as fur traders and *coureurs de bois* (forest wanderers). Like the Dutch in New York State, the French resented the flooding of Yankees into Michigan after the opening of the Erie Canal. In that state's constitutional convention in 1835, the first issue that Democrats and Whigs struggled over was whether to allow aliens (immigrants not yet citizens) to vote. Democrats were eager to give aliens the franchise after a year or two of residence; Whigs insisted that it be granted only to citizens.

Evangelicals in Michigan and elsewhere in the Old Northwest were appalled at the idea of letting immigrants vote, especially since so many of them were Catholics. A Whig newspaper in Detroit attacked "party demagogues . . . [who] are holding out every encouragement to the vilest of the outcasts of Europe, to swarm upon our shores, take possession of our polls and control our elections." William Woodbridge, their spokesman, put the matter in the most revealing terms: voters must be "of this Anglo-American family." Not only must they be intelligent and possessed of a devotion to liberty, but their "*habits* must likewise have been formed upon our [Yankee] model." As in New York State, people of New England descent in Michigan were in fact almost evenly divided in their party loyalties, leaning Whig. But among Yankees who were part of the elite, more than eight out of ten were Whigs.[31]

The Southern states present a subtle reversal in their cultural alignments in politics. Their dominant pattern of living and political belief was not puritanical and Yankee but Jeffersonian and slave-owning, with a strong Scotch-Irish overlay. Therefore, the Democrats in the South were not composed of the outgroups but were themselves, in effect, the establishment. Thus, if a person were part of what in Southern terms was an outgroup, the Whig party would provide political refuge. The large French population in Louisiana was Whig instead of Democratic like their countrymen in Michigan, for in ethnic politics, as in the Einsteinian universe, the laws of motion and behavior are relative to the local system. For Irish Catholics, who were Democrats in all states, the entire nation was the political system within which they operated, for they were widely spread and they encountered Protestantism everywhere. For Louisiana Cajuns, however, their world was Louisiana itself. They were lastingly resentful at the Jeffersonian takeover in the Louisiana Purchase of 1803, a bold stroke carried through without any gesture to local opinion.

Fearing American intrusion and domination, the French made the state politics of Louisiana so exclusively a struggle between the two ethnic communities that party identities in themselves were secondary. The French retained harsh memories of Andrew Jackson's behavior during the Battle of New Orleans, and the Americans who later came pushing in were Jacksonian Democrats. The French, therefore, voted Whig. They had been able, in 1812, to shape the writing of the state's constitution in relation to voting districts so as to keep themselves dominant in the state legislature, a position rarely achieved by a non-British people in American public life. Because their concerns were concentrated upon affairs within Louisiana itself, the French were indifferent to national politics. They did not turn out in large numbers to vote in presidential elections; the Democrats usually won the state with modest majorities.[32]

It has traditionally been said that Republican votes in the South increase with altitude, and so it was in the days of Whiggery. Unlike the lowlands, the immense central upland of Appalachia—its parallel mountain ranges running southwestward from Maryland and western Virginia down into northern Alabama and Georgia—had little experience of slavery. In the days of Federalism, western Virginia had been a stronghold of that party, for its people regarded the slave world of the lowlands, which dominated Virginia's government, with distaste. In Andrew Jackson's Tennessee, the Whigs had a traditional bastion of strength in the eastern part of the state, mountainous and fairly free of slavery, for Whiggery was the vehicle of protest against the dominant Southern way of life. Tennessee supported Jackson in his presidential elections, but thereafter cast its electoral votes for the Whig candidate, even in 1844 when its ex-governor James K. Polk was the Democratic nominee.[33]

North of Tennessee, Kentucky was another Whig stronghold. For twenty years after Henry Clay ran against Andrew Jackson for the presidency in 1832, Whigs dominated the state's politics and usually by a wide margin. Slaves were relatively few in the state, and it raised little cotton. Clay himself was a classic symbol of the "Other South." He was born in Virginia, the son of a Baptist minister, in 1777, a time when that faith was laboring against the South's violence and almost anarchic individualism. As early as 1799, in Kentucky politics, Clay was battling for the cause that he advocated all his life: the gradual emancipation of the slaves. Like Jefferson, he accepted slavery in practical terms, eventually becoming one of Kentucky's largest slave owners, but he consistently condemned the institution as evil. In 1829 he said blacks "are rational beings, like ourselves, capable of feeling, of reflection, and of judging of what naturally belongs to them as a portion of the human race," and he called upon Congress in 1832 to begin appropriating $10 million annually to buy the slaves' freedom. Clay rejected categorically the assertions beginning to come from John C. Calhoun and the South Carolinians in the 1830s that slavery was in fact a blessing.[34]

An ardent Jeffersonian Republican in 1800 and a leading War Hawk in the War of 1812, Clay was an entrepreneur in Kentucky hemp and hence a strong advocate of protective tariffs. He also consistently supported corporations against their enemies in state politics. By 1815 he was veering strongly Yankee in his sympathies and alliances. Visiting Harvard in 1818 to see his son, Clay later confessed himself to have been "astonished at the unjust prejudices prevailing at the South against [Yankees] and I returned full of admiration and esteem for them and of gratitude too for their kind and hospitable treatment of me." Optimistic in all his affairs, he regarded economic development as an unmixed blessing. In his "American System" he called upon the government to build a strong and prosperous American republic by establishing protective tariffs, building roads and bridges to open resources and link the nation's scattered regions, and maintaining a strong central banking system.

The key to the success of Clay's hopes lay in his forming an alliance with the northeastern states, for the South in general was hostile to his American System. He swung his support to John Quincy Adams in 1825 when the House of Representatives was choosing between presidential candidates, and he served as Adams' secretary of state —and thus, according to existing custom, as Adams' designated successor in the presidency. This led to howling charges of "corrupt bargain," charges that dogged him the rest of his life. Ethnically English and sprung from a church that in the South was a rival to the Presbyterians, Clay was attacking Andrew Jackson as early as 1818. He considered Jackson a dangerous military tyrant and heartless oppressor of the Indians, another non-white minority whose cause Clay advocated all his career—as did Whigs generally. A man who rarely handled guns, save in his three quixotic duels, and who had no soldierly career, Clay condemned the idea of military heroes being chosen to run the country. He professed himself to tremble for the republic's survival when Jackson entered the White House in 1829.

In his personal style of life and in his associations, Clay carefully modeled himself upon the standard of the English gentleman. His beautiful estate in the Lexington bluegrass, Ashland, was commonly described as an English manor house. In his speeches and letters, he said little about the working people but a great deal about the needs of manufacturers and wealthy planters. Like many in the northeastern states, Clay opposed giving western lands free to settlers and insisted that the funds derived from their sale should be spent upon internal improvements. Contending that the Mexican War was founded upon a mad rage for expansion and palpable falsehood, he wrote to the New York City journalist Horace Greeley, asking to be represented to the Northern public "as a Western man (I protest against being considered a Southern man) with Northern principles."[35]

Who, then, were the Southern Whigs? Within the mass of the Southern population, the record is at present unclear. Appalachia provided a massive Whig voting base, but so did counties along the lower Mississippi and through central Georgia and Alabama, where the per capita wealth of whites was high and slaves comprised half or more of the population. Perhaps the planters' cultivation of a lifestyle patterned on that of the English aristocracy led them to lean toward the Anglophilic Whigs and their aura of gentility. The urban population that existed in the prewar South—in 1850 there were only twenty-three cities with more than 2,500 people in the Southern states—voted Whig by a two-to-one margin. There are hints that the small immigrant white population, especially the Germans, voted strongly Whig like the French in Louisiana and that Baptists also leaned in that direction.

Within the Southern elite, which provided the party leadership, we are better able to discern voting patterns. Whigs were merchants, bankers, large planters, ministers, and professional men. They recoiled from the crudity and extremism that they observed among Democrats, and moved against the grain of Southern culture: its violence, its persistent frontierlike conditions, its anti-Yankee combativeness. They shared with Northern Whig colleagues, especially mill-owning "cotton" Whigs of New England, a desire to develop the nation's resources, diversify the economy, and build prosperous cities and a more civilized style of life. Like the colonial Tories in Revolutionary days, Southern Whigs identified with the larger national community and were more cosmopolitan, modernizing, and aristocratic in values than their antagonists. The Whigs nationally had inherited that atmosphere of gentle manners and good family earlier identified with the Federalists and with the English gentleman. Their values emphasized sophisticated restraint and moderation in personal style. Jacksonian Democracy, by contrast, with its Mike Fink and Davy Crockett overtones, set up a different ambience that Southern Whigs deplored.[36]

In the Jacksonian years, the Virginian William A. Caruthers published a novel in which a prominent character was a Southern "Whig archetype" who spoke up for "nationalism, harmony between the sections and personal moderation and self-control." Reproving a friend who hated Yankees, the Whig observed that Southerners "can learn something from the Yankee, just as they can learn something from the industrious and prosperous yeoman of their own back country." Such men were eventually to lose out in the South. Their places of leadership were taken by the violent ones who clapped on arms and shouted for war with the North. Then the Southern Hamlet emerged, the "man who . . . is introspective, given to brooding—one in whom the springs of action have become somehow impaired . . . the consciousness and the conscience of the South and . . . paralyzed by [his] knowledge." Jostled aside in the heat and rush of secession and civil combat, many Southern Whigs spent their later years in this despairing mood, conscious of a dream for their country, not simply for their section, that had been lost.[37]

At the opening of the 1840s, however, and even through that bursting decade and into the 1850s, Southern Whigs were confident that a healthy two-party system would continue to flourish in their part of the nation. In the four presidential elections from 1836 through 1848, roughly 2,750,000 votes were cast in the slave states, with a slight majority on the Whig side.[38] In these years most men in Southern politics were not talking of secession or even worrying about the survival of the nation. They were too busy discussing the same issues that captured Northern attention: land policy, banks, currency, internal improvements, protective tariffs—in short, the whole complex of issues that revolved around the question of how the national economy could be developed with the greatest rapidity and the surest justice to all classes. Joel H. Silbey has correctly warned against interpreting the events of these years in light of the knowledge that a civil war was coming, for this approach makes everything seem to point that way. Historians have assumed that sectionally divisive issues took everyone's attention. This was actually not so. Year after year in Congress, the two parties battled on even terms and with strong discipline. Northern Whigs united with Southern Whigs; Northern Democrats joined with Southern Democrats. Congressmen from the North and South voted their presumed sectional loyalties only fleetingly, for they entered the 1840s devoted to national institutions to achieve national goals. Real and shared economic interests ran across sectional lines. By this time party identity itself had also acquired a life, a history, and a meaning of its own. Parties could claim men's loyalties strongly enough to hold them together through shocks over sectional issues, primarily having to do with slavery, that in earlier decades would have sent them flying apart.[39]

In 1843 sectional issues began strongly to invade national politics. A drive to annex the Republic of Texas, a slave-owning country in a condition of almost continuous war with the Republic of Mexico over the question of its independent existence, began stirring powerful emotions. Indeed, the whole issue of continental expansion to the Pacific Coast now dominated national attention. It immediately became clear that Democrats and Whigs differed in their attitudes toward westward expansion, just as had Jeffersonian Republicans and Federalists before them. Whigs, New England centered, were almost unanimously opposed to further acquisitions in the West; Democrats were strongly expansionist. The sentiment of "Manifest Destiny" was first given its name in two New York City newspapers owned by the Irish Catholic and passionately Democratic John L. O'Sullivan, the *Morning News* and *Democratic Review.*[40]

There were, however, sharp differences among Democrats on the expansionist issue. Northern Democrats talked constantly of the Oregon Country, then a vague term referring to the immense region stretching from California to Alaska, and of the importance of the Canadians joining the Union. Southerners had little interest in any territories except Texas and the little-populated Mexican provinces beyond it, New Mexico and California. They drew back, furthermore, from absorbing the whole of Mexico with its millions of non-white peoples. For Northern Democrats, Manifest Destiny was an idealistic, nonviolent, and noncoercive philosophy. It centered simply upon opening the door to all of the United States' continental neighbors, welcoming them to join the Union—and confidently expecting that they would leap to do so. In this mode, intellectuals like the philosopher Ralph Waldo Emerson, the journalist William Cullen Bryant, the poet Walt Whitman, and the historian George Bancroft were enthusiastic expansionists. The use of direct military aggression to seize western territories, a tactic congenial to Southern Democrats, seemed to Northerners in the party a violation of the very values that to them ennobled the American nation. The fact that Texas was slave country vastly complicated the issue. Almost without exception, Whigs opposed its annexation because they were hostile to the admission of more slave states, and Northern Democrats were much torn in their sentiments.[41]

The result was that when President Polk initiated the Mexican War in 1846, it was condemned by both Whigs and Democrats in the Northern states. The labored excuses, centering upon a disputed border skirmish between Mexican and American troops, that Polk used to justify war were debated bitterly within the Congress and in the nation at large throughout the war. Polk's success in persuading the British to divide the Oregon Country in 1846 might have won him Northern friends, but Westerners were disappointed that he had not acquired the whole of that huge region. The proviso to the army appropriation bill offered in the summer of 1846 by Congressman David R. Wilmot, Democrat of Pennsylvania—to exclude slavery from any territory won from Mexico—provided the symbolic proposal that could be voted on repeatedly, in each succeeding year, and around which Northern sentiments could gather in the presidential election campaign of 1848.[42]

The Democrats chose as their candidate Lewis Cass of Michigan, a firm expansionist and opponent of the Wilmot Proviso. What he proposed as a solution to the problem of whether or not to allow slavery into the new territories won from Mexico was the principle of popular sovereignty: allowing the people who settled those regions to decide the question for themselves. This convinced many Northern Democrats that a Southern slaveholding conspiracy had taken over their party, a belief they had firmly held ever since Martin Van Buren had been denied the Democratic nomination in 1844. The most outspoken were the "Barnburners" of New York, so called because they were said to be so eager to root Southern control out of the party that they were willing to burn down the barn to expel the rats. Barnburners, in turn, called Northern Democrats who favored Southern-leaning policies "Hunkers," for they allegedly hungered so for the patronage positions Polk could bestow that they supinely supported the expansion of slavery.

Whigs sought to reassure the South in 1848 by choosing as their nominee the popular Mexican War general Zachary Taylor. A Southerner and slave owner, Taylor was nonetheless a long-time resident of the Northern states and a man devoted more to the nation's survival than to slavery. Even so, young "Conscience" Whigs were furious. Henry H. Wilson of Massachusetts rose on the floor of the Whig nominating convention to call Taylor's nomination "another and a signal triumph of the Slave Power" and, vowing to do all he could to defeat him, "strode out of the hall in a scene of uproar and confusion."[43]

This set the stage for the almost spontaneous appearance, in a burst of righteous enthusiasm, of the Free Soil party. Conscience Whigs, Barnburner Democrats, and former supporters of the Liberty party, an abolitionist splinter group, gathered in Buffalo, New York, in August 1848 to organize the party and nominate Martin Van Buren. He was not an abolitionist—indeed, the Free Soil party had few abolitionists in its membership—but he had publicly proclaimed both his opposition to the extension of slavery into new territory and his belief that Congress had the constitutional power to prevent that extension. Free Soilers insisted that the Wilmot Proviso was really the "Jefferson Proviso," that it was an attempt to apply to the new territories the same ban on slavery that Jefferson had been responsible for placing in the Northwest Ordinance of 1787. The Free Soil convention called for every Northern town and ward to establish "Jefferson Leagues of free soil and free principle." In 1849 Free Soilers were to convene the first national commemoration of "the Jeffersonian Ordinance of 1787."[44]

The Free Soil party lost the election of 1848, but so did Lewis Cass and the Democrats. The Southern states were not ready to accept the solution of "popular sovereignty" in the territories, for that would have left their rights to take slaves into these regions in too precarious a condition. They swung, instead, behind the Southern Zachary Taylor and put the Whigs in control of the White House. Van Buren, however, had gathered in 300,000 votes, and the leaders of both major parties saw the lesson clearly: the issue of slavery extension had to be settled, or it would tear apart the political system. Whigs and Democrats had actually held their voters extraordinarily well in the election of 1848, demonstrating that party loyalties by this time were still too strong to pull voters away from their commitments on the basis of a single issue. But the territorial question could not be allowed to go on unresolved.[45]

If anything were needed to demonstrate the vigor of the Jacksonian party system, it may be found in the way that Whigs and Democrats, in the long congressional session of 1850, worked out the Compromise of that year and preserved the political structure, as they believed, from dissolution. The Northern states, in that agreement, received a partial victory in the application of the principle of popular sovereignty to the new territories: slavery would be allowed only if the local residents established the system. In return, their legislators in Washington accepted a much stronger fugitive slave act to send black Americans, alleged to have fled their bonds, back to their Southern owners.*

Two years later, in the presidential election of 1852, the national balloting was everywhere seen as a national referendum on the Compromise of 1850. The Whigs ran General Winfield Scott, who acquiesced reluctantly in the agreement, while the Free Soilers nominated John P. Hale, who condemned it as "inconsistent with all the principles and maxims of Democracy." The Democratic party nominated a Northerner, Franklin Pierce from New Hampshire, who warmly supported the Fugitive Slave Act, popular sovereignty in the new territories, the principle of strong states' rights, and the continued existence of slavery. He won an enormous victory in the electoral college (though a narrow one in the popular vote) that gave the Democrats all but four states. The white population of the Northern states seemed ready now to accept the arrangement that had been worked out on the slave question. Abolitionism was everywhere shrunken in power and influence, and slavery appeared solid and secure. Within two more years, however, this apparent political consensus would be shattered. In the uproar, the Jacksonian party system would be destroyed, and when it fell to pieces, it would come apart with startling speed.

---

*Joel Silbey observes,
 [It] is true that in the three years following the introduction of the Proviso and the question of slavery in the territories into Congress, some leaders actively tried to change the political context in which Congress specifically and politicians generally operated. And they had a high degree of success. The constant propaganda on the question of slavery extension and the failure to solve the issues raised by the Wilmot Proviso did lead many people to react sectionally, and their congressmen, in response, did also. But, at the same time, national party leaders forcefully resisted the sectionalizing of American politics and managed to keep parties as the most effective influence operating on issues not connected with slavery. Furthermore, when sectional sensitivity grew among some elements, other groups and leaders moved to end the slavery-extension dispute and thus remove the one possible destructive force countering the Democratic and Whig parties. The moderate leaders were, in large part, successful. During 1850 Congress passed a series of measures designed to solve the outstanding sectional disputes. (_The Shrine of Party_, pp. 143–144.)

part three

THE
CIVIL WAR
PARTY SYSTEM:
1856=1894

VII

First Phase: Realignment and Disunion, 1856-1860

The Jacksonian party system broke apart rapidly in the 1850s because it was overwhelmed by swiftly moving cultural tides. Each enhanced the intensity of the others, and they rushed together with such violence that, in the presence of a national mood like that in Revolutionary times, the national institutional structure was torn apart. Irish and German immigrants fleeing the potato famines of western Europe in the 1840s poured into the Northern states in numbers so enormous that a panic arose in Yankee America that steadily mounted, for the "Great Migration" continued year after year. The political parties heaved and buckled in the face of this immigrant influx, which to thousands of Americans posed a fundamental threat to the national way of life. Then the apparent agreement between North and South over slavery in the territories ripped apart in circumstances condemned by multitudes in the Northern states as dishonest, corrupt, and evil. The outcome placed Northern civilization, many believed, under an even graver threat than that embodied in the Catholic, alien invasion. A series of events then convinced Yankees that a "Slave Power Conspiracy" had seized control of the national government. They rallied, unified as never before, behind a new political movement, the wholly northern

Republican party, dedicated to the cause of free society. Southerners, on their side, believed that the Republicans were secretly under the control of an "Abolitionist Conspiracy" aimed at freeing the slaves and releasing mass pillage, murder, and rape in the South.

In this charged and violent atmosphere, Yankees and Southerners faced off as in ultimate combat against forces that they feared would otherwise destroy them. This time, they found their enemy not in Great Britain but in each other, as for many years radicals on both sides had said that they would. The first event to occur in this cascade of cultural shifts and transformations was the shattering of the Whigs and the Democrats and a continental realignment of the parties; the second was secession and war.

The Northern states were already in a confused and troubled mood in the 1850s and given to sharp reactions to every new issue. Hundreds of millions of dollars in gold from California were pouring rapidly into the Northern economy, fueling an almost convulsive burst of industrialization that accelerated as immigration provided bountiful supplies of cheap labor. A boom-and-bust cycle that produced economic slumps and unemployment in 1851, 1854, and 1855 —to be followed by the Panic of 1857—was accompanied by massive programs of regional railroad construction. Trunk-line roads connecting the Atlantic Coast with the midwestern interior were completed, bringing with them rapid dislocations in hundreds of local economies. Thousands of workers lost jobs in the older forms of transport; unpredictable freight rates produced almost daily fluctuations in price levels and major shifts in demand and markets; competitive forces from distant producers endangered local crafts and industries; and river traffic rapidly declined. Local foundries were wiped out by cheaper iron from distant factories, and the livelihoods of many craftsmen—tailors, cobblers, butchers—were endangered.[1]*

*Writing of the "industrial revolution of the 1850s," Allan Nevins observed that the steady rise of the corporation was one great fact of the period. . . . New York's general incorporation act of 1811 had been liberal for its time; but the famous law of 1848 . . . roughly marked the beginning of an epoch. Within the next dozen years all the Northern and Northwestern States took similar action, and the corporations set up under these new laws were numbered by tens of thousands. Of all the

Furthermore, in the aftermath of the Mexican War, many were uneasy about the American experiment in republican self-government. Northern Democrats and Whigs had attacked that conflict as a violation of American values. Now it was no longer so easy to associate the growth of the United States with the expansion of freedom in the world. There was an embarrassment with expansionist spread-eagle oratory, accompanied by a sense, now that the surge to the Pacific Coast was finished, that the United States was territorially complete. National attentions formerly directed outward turned inward, producing a deflation in mood. The failure of the democratic revolutions of 1848 in Europe intensified this sense of unease. Despotism seemed as powerful in the world as ever, despite the example set by the American republican government, now more than half a century old. Most of the social crusades of the Jacksonian years—for peace, penal reform, and the labor movement—went into decline, their energies sapped. Abolitionism remained a tiny, internally torn movement, much condemned.[2]

In these circumstances, when in the eyes of thousands of Northern Americans the Republic itself seemed to have lost its momentum and to be in a time of grave testing, the Roman Catholic hierarchy launched an offensive against the public schools. This attack touched a central nerve in American republicanism, for the schools were conceived as the principal training grounds for democratic citizenship and sturdy, morally conscious individualism. In an overwhelmingly Protestant country, the schools were essentially state-supported, ꞌnondenominational Protestant parochial institutions. They openly taught Protestant values, requiring children to listen to readings of the King James Bible daily and to say prayers. No theme in American schoolbooks was more universally prominent than anti-Catholicism. The Catholic faith was regularly depicted "not only as

---

business corporations of the country in the first half of the nineteenth century, *nearly half were established during the fifties* [italics added].... In a sprawling, inchoate nation, industrialism was by far the most powerful force making for a greater degree of organization ... [for] business alone was developing organization on a general scale and of a powerful type. The first trunk-line railroads, the strongest banks ... the Trenton and Pittsburgh iron corporations, were islands of organization in a restless sea of multitudinous unorganized activities.... The capital invested in manufacturing ... almost doubled between 1850 and 1860, rising from $533,200 to $1,009,000, or by 89.4 per cent. This increase represented the largest ten-year investment thus far made in American history. Not even in the Civil War decade was so high a *percentage* of growth attained. (*Ordeal of the Union* [New York, 1947], II, pp. 242–248.)

a false religion, but as a positive danger to the state; it subverts good government, sound morals, and education."³*

Catholics bitterly condemned these public-school practices and set off a great uproar in the early 1850s by demanding public funds for the building of their own schools. A Protestant newspaper in Michigan cried out that the "Jesuitical Hierarchy," with its massed Catholic voters at their instant command, "seem determined to carry the war 'to the knife.' We propose to give them 'the knife to the hilt.'" The First Presbyterian Church of Detroit protested that the Catholic assault would subvert "the very citadel of Republican strength in the free education of youth and the consequent independence of mind." "Every Christian," a Michigan woman wrote to her son, "has to buckle on his Armour—& keep it Bright—The Battle of the Lord of Hosts has begun."⁴ When the Papal Nuncio Gaetano Bedini arrived in America in 1853 for a visit to the Catholic hierarchy, he was accused of being "an agent of the papal plot to subvert American freedom," and anti-Catholic riots erupted. At the same time that anti-Catholicism was flaring up in the United States, an equally violent outburst against Catholicism was sweeping Protestant Europe. Belief in a Catholic plot against freedom in every Protestant country had not been so widespread for many generations.⁵

Out of these alarums sprang the American party, a secret political organization devoted to anti-Catholicism, whose members were called "Know-Nothings" because they denied all knowledge of their party's nature. The fastest-growing political force in the country in the years 1853–1856, the Know-Nothings swiftly gained major strength in states like New York, Massachusetts, and Pennsylvania,

---

*David Potter observed of anti-Catholicism:

> In the 1850s, religious toleration was regarded more as an arrangement among the Protestant sects than as a universal principle. . . . Though it is largely forgotten today, and has consistently been minimized in American history, it is nevertheless true that for a considerable part of the nineteenth century the Catholic church was chronically under fire. Its beliefs were denounced; its leaders were assailed; its convents were slandered, and its property was threatened or even attacked. With both the Protestant press and the secular press keeping up a constant barrage of abuse, mob action sometimes resulted. Between 1834 and the end of the fifties, serious riots, with loss of lives, occurred in Charlestown, Massachusetts, in Philadelphia, in Louisville, and elsewhere. Convents were attacked, and one in Charlestown was burned to the ground, while probably as many as twenty Catholic churches were burned in cities or towns from Maine to Texas. (*The Impending Crisis 1848–1861*, completed and edited by Don E. Fehrenbacher [New York, 1976], p. 243.)

See also Ray Allen Billington, *The Protestant Crusade 1800–1860: A Study of the Origins of American Nativism* (New York, 1938; Chicago, 1964).

where Irish Catholics were concentrated in numbers. In 1854 the Know-Nothings carried both houses of the Massachusetts legislature and controlled its delegation to Congress, in addition to taking a third of the vote in Pennsylvania. Perhaps the immediate stimulus for these events lay in the fact that after 1851 the five-year waiting period required in many states for naturalization and voting was being completed by the immigrants, and they began to cast ballots in large numbers. It seemed to Protestants that Catholic immigrants voted in unthinking blocs, slavishly following the orders of their priests. Furthermore, the new arrivals were heavy drinkers; they crowded together in the slums, rapidly growing in numbers with each boatload; their families were large; they recreated freely on the Sabbath; they committed crimes against property at an alarming rate; and they seemed to fill the jails and pauper houses.[6]

There is a sense in which the Know-Nothing party was a precursor to the Progressive movement that arose half a century later. American party voters felt themselves to be engaged in a fight to save pure and honest republican government. Thousands of them were former Whigs who, more than Democrats, had always prized personal independence from party discipline and had been hostile to the "slavery" of party membership.* Now their antipartyism directed itself against the Irish Catholic Democrats, who massed in army fashion behind their party banner, handed out public offices to one another, and monopolized nominations to office by their tight ward organizations and state conventions. From Know-Nothings came the first demands for direct primaries, which would enable the people at large rather than party bosses in state conventions to nominate candidates. Feeding upon a widespread loss of confidence in the established political

---

*Ronald P. Formisano's discussion of antipartyism is instructive:

Antiparty thinking tended to be related to ideas about government that began with society rather than the individual, with the corporate organic whole rather than its atomic parts. If this thought pattern assumed a hierarchy of classes, it also assumed social harmony, not conflict. Men who desired society unified by shared moral codes tended to assume that government and society possessed organic unity. Party organization contradicted these assumptions and mocked the idea that government existed to promote the commonweal and by sufferance of the commonality. "Party" suggested the promotion of the particular, artificial, and selfish, unnaturally and unconstitutionally. (*The Birth of Mass Political Parties: Michigan, 1827–1861* [Princeton, 1971], p. 74.)

The Liberty Party, a tiny abolitionist movement, had been filled with antipartyism and a pride in independence of views and action: "religious men, moralists in politics, men of principle not expedience, men sure of their rightness, and therefore less flexible, less compromising" were hostile to party (p. 77).

leaders of both parties—everywhere a demand was heard for new leaders and new faces—the Know-Nothings soon not only had control of most of New England but had become the principal party in opposition to the Democrats in the Middle Atlantic States and much of the South. They absorbed into their ranks thousands of ex-Whigs who had left the party because Whig leaders like William H. Seward of New York and Abraham Lincoln of Illinois were trying to damp down nativism. The Know-Nothings took in perhaps even more Democrats in the Yankee-settled counties of western New York, in the Northern Tier of counties in Pennsylvania, and in the Middle West. Many leaving the Democratic party were Methodists and Baptists who had long been Democrats on personal liberty grounds and had opposed the state-churchism of the Calvinists. Now, however, they were alarmed at the sight of an increasingly Catholic Democratic party and the threat this posed to Protestant America.[7]

The German ethnic community grew with great speed in the 1850s. German immigrants arrived in the United States during that decade in larger numbers than even the Irish. There were 600,000 German-born people in the country in 1850; by 1860 there were 1.3 million. They generally avoided Yankee country, forming large colonies in New York City, Buffalo, and Baltimore and migrating into the interior of the country. They settled in Wisconsin and the northern Middle West; in northern Illinois, especially in and around Chicago; in the St. Louis area; and in southern Ohio, where Cincinnati became a flourishing German city. Their impact upon the national German community was electrifying. They included not only thousands of Catholics from Bavaria, but a new wave of Lutherans whose religious commitments were far more intense than those of the German Lutherans who had been part of American life for many generations. German Lutheranism in the United States had been losing its distinctiveness, practically merging with Episcopalianism in New York and sharing hymnals and catechism with the German Reformed of Pennsylvania. The new Lutherans, however, fleeing from anti-Lutheran decrees in Prussia, insisted upon denominational loyalty and doctrinal purity. They established their own parochial schools to maintain their separateness, and they spread an argumentative, aggressive spirit through the American Lutheran community.

The failure of the 1848 democratic revolution in Germany sent another surge of immigrants to America. Unlike the devout, hardworking farmers and artisans who had composed the earlier German migrations, these immigrants were political activists, radical reformers, lawyers, scientists, professors, writers, musicians, and journalists. Only the impact of the immigration of intellectuals forced out of Germany in Hitler's time can be compared with that of the '48ers, whose extraordinary intellectual vitality exerted an invigorating influence upon American life. The immigrants of 1848 galvanized the German communities, greatly broadening their cultural life, especially in the field of journalism. However, the "Grays," as Germans of pre-1848 immigrations called themselves, drew back from the "Greens," as they termed the new liberals, who were eager to achieve in America the reforms they had failed to win in the mother country. In response, the '48ers disparaged the earlier comers as provincial, conservative, and apathetic. Bringing with them the rationalism and anticlericalism of the 1848 revolutions, they rejected orthodox Lutheranism. Appalled at the slums, political corruption, and above all at the slavery disfiguring the land of Jefferson, they had little interest in temperance and Sunday closing laws and were passionately committed to antislavery.

Liberal German newspaper editors so vigorously threw their support behind Abraham Lincoln in the election of 1860 that it has traditionally been said that he owed his election to German support. However, the voting masses among the Germans held strongly to their Democratic partisanship in most states. Like the Dutch, who also had a "great migration" of their own beginning in the 1840s (though the numbers involved were tiny by comparison) and who established settlements in Michigan and Iowa, the Germans disliked the Yankee temper in politics. They were offended by Whig and Republican campaigns against drinking and the informal, Continental style of Sunday relaxation. Even in such divergent matters as proper farming techniques and the dress and domestic habits of women, the Dutch of Iowa found cause to be irritated with the Yankee majority. The Germans and Dutch were aware that they were among the targets of the Know-Nothings, and as the nativism of the Know-Nothings was absorbed by the Republicans, they voted massively Democratic. Neither group cared very deeply about the cause of black America. They wished, instead, to be themselves freed of Yankee oversight and condescension.[8]

National attention centered far more on the Irish Catholics than on the Germans. The Celtic flight from Ireland to America after the potato famines had been so massive that for every Irish immigrant in the United States in 1860, only five Irishmen remained behind in the homeland. A third of the Boston electorate in 1855 was Irish Catholic, their numbers having tripled since 1850. This was why, said one politician, the Yankees "want a Paddy hunt & on a Paddy hunt they will go."⁹* The Irishman's hero in national politics was Senator Stephen A. Douglas of Illinois, the "Little Giant." He was a pugnacious, combative politician driven by dreams of greatness and of the White House. A Jacksonian Democrat, he attacked banks, tariffs, and paper money. The cause to which he gave himself most passionately, however, was the expansion of the frontier of settlement into the immense territories beyond the bend of the Missouri. As early as 1844, Douglas had introduced a bill that would have opened the Nebraska region to settlement by providing a territorial government. He called for the building of a railroad to the Pacific and persistently advocated homesteading bills to make the public domain free to settlers.

Reared in a part of Vermont that had been raided by British forces in the War of 1812 and of Scottish descent, Douglas hated the English, ranting against them year after year on the floor of Congress to Irish Catholic cheers. His constant cry was that plots were being hatched in London to hem in the United States by ringing it round with British possessions and fortifications that would halt the growth of democratic institutions and dim the glory of the great Republic. "While I would not violate the laws of nations," he said in 1845, "I would exert all legal and honorable means to drive Great Britain and the last vestiges of royal authority from the continent of North America, and extend the limits of the republic from ocean to ocean." Perhaps it was this aspect of expansion that appealed to the Irish, who warmly supported the cause of Manifest Destiny in the 1840s. Michael Walsh, the first Catholic Irishman elected to Congress, insisted that he was also the first man to call for the acquisition of Texas.¹⁰

The Irish agreed, too, with Douglas' attitude toward black Americans. He refused to condemn slavery in the South. What he instead

---

*David Potter, commenting on Irish migration, pointed out that

It is widely known, of course, that migration to America at the time of the Irish famine was very heavy. But it is seldom realized that, proportionately, *this was the heaviest influx of immigrants in American history* [italics added]. The total of 2,939,000 immigrants in the decade between 1845 and 1854 was less than one-third of the number in the decade before the First World War, but the total population was also much smaller.... Moreover, this riptide of immigration between 1845 and 1854 struck with severe shock in a society with a very small proportion of foreign-born members. Total immigration had never reached 100,-000 before 1842, nor 200,000 before 1847, but it exceeded 400,000 three times in the four years between 1851 and 1855. In addition to the general fact that immigration was extremely heavy, there was a further, more specific feature: no less than 1,200,000 of the immigrants of 1845–1854 came from a single country— Ireland. (*The Impending Crisis*, pp. 241–242.)

condemned was any notion of racial equality. "We do not believe in the equality of the negro, socially or politically, with the white man [in Illinois]," he said in 1856. "Our people are a white people; our State is a white state; and we mean to preserve the race pure, without any mixture with the negro." As to slavery, it was a local institution, he said in 1848, and its "burdens or advantages . . . belong to those who chose to retain it, and who alone have the right to determine when they will dispense with it."[11] Around Douglas centered a "Young America" movement, a loose coalition of young men who between 1849 and the mid-1850s agitated for further American expansion. They called abolitionism a British plot, spawned in England as a means of breaking up the American Union and halting its spread westward into regions coveted by London.[12]

Irish Catholics nourished a deep-rooted animosity toward black Americans. Violence between the two groups was a regular feature of urban life in the North in the 1840s, particularly but not only in Philadelphia. The Irish were desperately poor, and they competed with blacks for the same unskilled jobs. Furthermore, the Irish were greeted with attacks on their patriotism. Were not Catholics inherently disloyal, it was asked, since they lived in a Protestant country yet were loyal to the Pope? Thus, the last thing the Irish desired was to become entangled in abolitionism, a movement widely condemned as composed of fanatics who wanted to disrupt the Union. As early as the 1840s, the Irish press in America described abolitionists as lunatics and infidels. The *New-England (Catholic) Reporter* said that the abolitionist William Lloyd Garrison should "be immediately transported to Ethiopia, there to dwell in love and harmony with the wild negroes." Together with the Northern labor movement, the Irish asked why abolitionists were not interested in the industrial exploitation of workingmen in the North. They insisted that their situation was, if anything, worse than that of slaves. So moved, Irishmen opposed abolition as certain to flood Northern labor markets with released slaves. Also, their enemies, the Yankees—who backed temperance and anti-Catholicism—seemed to be friendly toward emancipationist movements. The Roman church, furthermore, found nothing wrong in slavery. Pius IX (1846–1878) was a determined enemy of liberalism and all social reform, having been made so by the attacks of liberal revolutionaries in Italy upon the power of the Vatican. The Catholic Irish, therefore, were encouraged in their views by their own priests.[13]

These attitudes toward black Americans were not, of course,

confined to Democrats. They were widely shared among whites of
both parties. In practically every sphere of life in the Northern states,

> Negroes found themselves systematically separated from whites. They
> were either excluded from railway cars, omnibuses, stagecoaches, and
> steamboats or assigned to special "Jim Crow" sections; they sat, when
> permitted, in secluded and remote corners of theaters and lecture
> halls; they could not enter most hotels, restaurants, and resorts, except
> as servants; they prayed in "Negro pews" in the white churches, and
> if partaking of the sacrament of the Lord's Supper, they waited until
> the whites had been served the bread and wine. Moreover, they were
> often educated in segregated schools, punished in segregated prisons,
> nursed in segregated hospitals, and buried in segregated cemeteries.[14]

Only in New England, where they were few in number, were blacks
allowed to vote. The Middle Atlantic States were determinedly segregationist, but it was in the Middle West, among northern sections,
that antiblack feelings were strongest. "Our people [of Indiana],"
said George W. Julian, a leading antislavery congressman, "hate the
Negro with a perfect if not a supreme hatred." The Middle Western
States refused to lift antiblack laws in the 1850s, and several of them
in these years even made it a crime for blacks to settle within their
borders. In some strongly Yankee areas, as in northeastern Ohio, the
mood was somewhat less antiblack, and Quakers were especially
hospitable to black Americans. In general, however, midwestern
racism was unrelenting—even though less than 1 percent of the
population was nonwhite. During the Civil War, hatred of black
people would intensify.[15]

On January 4, 1854, Stephen A. Douglas rose on the Senate floor
to propose his Kansas-Nebraska bill. If passed, the bill would provide
the remaining portion of the Louisiana Purchase (save for the area
of present-day Oklahoma) with territorial governments and thereby
open it to settlement by American citizens. The country was electrified by the bill. It would repeal the Missouri Compromise of 1820,
which banned slavery north of 36° 30" in the Louisiana Purchase,
and allow settlers to decide the question for themselves. Thus, the
Kansas-Nebraska bill would open this enormous region to the possibility of slavery. The bill "brought virtually the entire North to its
feet in indignant protest. . . . 'We went to bed one night,' " wrote the
wealthy Whig Amos A. Lawrence of Massachusetts, " 'old-fashioned,

conservative, compromise, Union Whigs, and waked up stark mad Abolitionists.' "[16] After four months of debate in Congress, during which hundreds of angry protest meetings were held in the Northern states and the Kansas-Nebraska bill was unceasingly condemned, a crucial vote in the House revealed the shape of the future: Southern Democrats and Whigs voted almost as a solid bloc in favor of the bill; Northern Whigs separated entirely from Southern Whigs to vote unanimously against it; and Northern Democrats, deeply split along the pro-Southern (Hunker) and anti-Southern (Barnburner) fissure that for years had existed within the party, divided equally. By a narrow margin, the Kansas-Nebraska bill passed, and soon the Senate gave its approval as well.[17]

Already breaking apart under the impact of anti-Catholicism, the Jacksonian party system now disintegrated. Thousands of Northerners were infuriated to see the South, which with few interruptions since Jefferson's election in 1800 had been in effective control of the national government, once more getting its way. Slavocracy seemed to be remorselessly advancing, with no regard for Northern sensibilities. Northerners were enormously offended by what to them was Southern arrogance, the "overbearing nature these nabobs have acquired in their custom of giving commands to their miserable serfs." "They are intolerant," wrote the *Christian Herald* on March 26, 1854, "not occasionally, nor by accident . . . but habitually, and on principle. . . . It is the slave driver's lash, differing a little in shape, and applied to Northern white men, instead of Southern slaves, but wielded for the same end, the enforcement of their will, and by essentially the same means—brute force instead of reason and justice."[18] Now, in various Northern states, an anti-Democratic coalition began to form, pouring scorn upon "the timid, weak-minded, servile, fawning, venal spirit" of Northern Democrats who voted for the Kansas-Nebraska bill and supported Southern interests. A fusion meeting of so-called Free Democrats and Whigs, calling themselves "Republicans," gathered in Jackson, Michigan, on July 6, 1854, to adopt a bold platform statement. Demanding repeal of the Kansas-Nebraska Act and reinstatement of the prohibition of slavery in those territories, the convention went on almost recklessly to assert:

> That after this gross breach of faith and wanton affront to us as Northernmen, we hold ourselves absolved from all "compromises," except those expressed in the Constitution, for the protection of slavery and slave-owners, and we now demand protection and immunity for ourselves; and among them we demand the Repeal of the Fugitive Slave

Law, and an Act to abolish slavery in the District of Columbia. . . . That we notice without dismay certain popular indications by slaveholders on the frontier of said Territories of a purpose on their part to prevent by violence the settlement of the country by non-slaveholding men. To the latter we say: Be of good cheer, persevere in the right, remember the Republican motto: "The North will defend you."[19]

That those forming the new party should reach back to the time of the Revolution, take the term "republican," and apply it to their organization profoundly reveals how they conceived of this national crisis; that is, as if it were a reenactment of that Revolution. Use of the name "Republican" sprang up almost spontaneously, "instinctively, with obvious fitness," Horace Greeley said. It evoked the sainted name of Thomas Jefferson, whom Whigs, as well as Democrats, had always sought to claim, and the hallowed Ordinance of 1787, attributed to Jefferson, by which slavery had been excluded from the Northwest Territories. Republicans insisted that the Democrats had fallen into the hands of slavery and lost all ties with Jefferson, the great philosopher of freedom. It was their own party, Republicans insisted, that was Jefferson's true inheritor.

In this assertion, we see a historic shifting in the national ideological balance. The two political traditions as they formed in the 1790s were both "republican," each drawing upon differing modes of the national ideology. Jeffersonian Republican leaders had seized upon the libertarianism and egalitarianism that republicanism contained, and behind them rallied the ethnocultural outgroups whose interests these values supported. Federalists had been moralistic and nationalistic republicans, as befitted spokesmen of the predominantly Yankee, elitist, development-oriented coalition that gathered behind the Federalist banner. In the second party system, Jacksonian Democrats and Whigs again divided the republican ideology in this fashion.

The Republican party born in the 1850s was clearly in the Federalist-Whig line of descent, as its concentration in the Yankee heartland revealed, but it was more libertarian than its predecessors. The national enemy as Republicans conceived of it was slavery—and not simply slavery in the South, but the slavery implied in submission to Southern arrogance in national affairs, the "slavery" of Roman Catholicism, the slavery of drink, and the slavery of boss-dominated partisan politics. Since freedom was the issue, Republicans could reach over boldly to appropriate the libertarianism that Democrats had traditionally claimed as their special inheritance from Thomas Jefferson. In their national platforms, Republicans praised the Declaration of Independence and its ringing affirmation of human rights. In order to attack the Fugitive Slave Law, they even stressed the primacy of states' rights. Republicans insisted that every state had the rightful power to interfere with the enforcement, within its borders, of so tyrannical an enactment, which they likened to the Alien and Sedition Acts. After the Dred Scott decision was issued in 1857, which held that Congress had no power to legislate upon slavery, Republicans again turned to Jefferson's words, this time to attack the Supreme Court's usurpations of power in relation to personal liberties. In 1859 hundreds of Republicans gathered in Washington to listen to a reading of the Declaration of Independence and to a recounting of Jefferson's antislavery record. At the same time, hundreds more in Boston cheered assertions that Jefferson had led the first two American revolutions in 1776 and 1800, that Jackson had led the third against the Money Power, and that now they were leading the fourth and most crucial, the revolution against the Slave Power.[20]*

The Republicans were too reformist and Jeffersonian in their rhetoric to be able easily to attract many Whigs. Thousands, like the Whig leader Amos Lawrence of Massachusetts, held back from merger. They moved instead for a time into the Know-Nothing party, lured by its nativist anti-Catholicism. There was in fact, however, a special link between the anti-Catholic movement and the antislavery campaign, and fusion of both under the Republican banner was the next step. Yankee New Englanders were the Protestants most obsessed by the threat of Catholicism, perhaps because their region received the largest proportion of Irish Catholics. They were also the Northerners traditionally most hostile to the South, their ancient rival for national supremacy. When the Know-Nothing party dissolved in 1856 over its failure to find a common ground on the slavery issue that would hold its Northerners and Southerners together, it was natural, therefore,

---

*It is important to observe here that the Jefferson position on liberty, blacks, and slavery was highly ambivalent, a fact well established in historical literature. Republicans in these years were practicing selective emphasis. The South and the Democratic party still tried to make use of the Jefferson image, but engaged in their own tortured selectivity. The truth is that Jefferson, like Henry Clay, Lincoln, and most other American public leaders, was never able to resolve the paradox implicit in his republicanism, with its emphasis upon human rights, and his fear of the freed black person. See Merrill D. Peterson's discussion in *The Jefferson Image in the American Mind* (New York, 1962), pp. 92–93, 167, 172, 175–176.

that Yankee Know-Nothings moved over to join the Republicans. For this reason, the Republican party was more homogeneously Yankee in spirit and membership than the Whigs had ever been. The crisis of the 1850s unified New Englanders as they had never been before, in both New England and the western states to which they had migrated. Baptists and Methodists now joined their Congregationalist and New School Presbyterian countrymen. This process of Yankee fusion welded a hard core within the Republican party that, because it lacked the Southern wing that Whiggery had possessed, made it a powerful instrument of Yankee civilization. The universal Yankee nation that in Revolutionary times Sam Adams had envisioned—the Christian Sparta of his dreams—could once again seem an imminent reality.[21]

The end was in sight for the Whig party. It was known to be friendly to antislavery, and as early as the presidential balloting of 1852, its vote in the South had fallen off sharply. Then, when nativism in the North drained off thousands of former Whig voters to the Know-Nothings, the party slowly collapsed. As former Whigs in the North began moving in growing numbers into the Republican party after 1856, they took with them their economic activism; that is, their belief that the government should encourage industrialization and national self-sufficiency by turning away from Adam Smith's notion of laissez faire and adopting Henry Clay's American System: protective tariffs, a centralized banking system, and federally assisted internal improvements.[22] Thus the Republicans were not simply the party of anti-Southernism but the party of "improvement." They held to "a dynamic conception of the economy that at its core valued highly the expansion of economic opportunity and the promise of success." They idealized not the simple farmer but the man who rose from humble origins by hard work to power, wealth, and place. The term "self-made man" came from Henry Clay and carried with it a heavy freight of democratic meaning. From this perspective, commercialism was to be not a monopoly of the wealthy but an opportunity for the whole people, or rather, for those among them who were progressive-minded and entrepreneurial.[23]

The Republicans' biting edge, however, derived from those among them who were called Radicals. They were not concerned with economic policy but rather with the evils that lay in the South. For them the formation of the Republican party as a strong coalition of formerly divided antislavery groups was the culmination of whole lifetimes of political labor. Radicals were not really party men, for principles, not organization, absorbed them. They had moved about from party to party in their search for a vehicle that would assault the South. In the Liberty party and then among the Free Soilers, they had preached uncompromising hostility to the South on every possible question concerning slavery. Profoundly New England in origins, they were such anti-Southern zealots that Republican leaders regarded them warily, worried that their radicalism would drive away voters. The leadership knew, however, that the Radicals would quickly bolt the party if it became too conservative on slavery questions. Without New England and the populous Yankee settlements thickly scattered through the Middle West, where moral issues were paramount, the leadership knew that they could not win. Thus the Radicals, whose personal courage and strong anti-Southern language appealed strongly to Republican voters, had a powerful influence in the party.[24]

The anti-Southern mood was not so intense in the Lower North as it was in Yankee-settled country. In this east-west band of territory, roughly below the forty-first parallel, lay the great port cities of New York and Philadelphia, with their strong economic ties to the South and their masses of antiblack Irish Catholics. The Lower North also encompassed the bulk of Pennsylvania and New Jersey, with their traditionally Democratic Scotch-Irish and German peoples, and southern Ohio, Indiana, and Illinois, where Southern ancestry was strong. Antislavery agitators found it risky to engage here in anti-Southern declamation. Whig leaders in the Lower North had been nationalist disciples of Henry Clay and his strong Unionism, and with him they had struggled to keep the slavery issue out of national politics. They were reluctant to move rapidly over to join the Republicans as their party dissolved, because the formation of a wholly sectional party in the North seemed to be the first step in breaking up the Union. When the Whigs of the Lower North finally joined up, they brought into the Republican party a moderate and gradualist attitude toward slavery and its abolition.[25]

The thousands of ex-Democrats from all over the Northern states who joined the Republicans comprised perhaps one-fifth of the Republican vote.[26] Especially after 1856, when the Democratic national convention endorsed the Kansas-Nebraska Act, nominated pro-Southern James Buchanan of Pennsylvania, and seemed to tilt finally and irrevocably southward, Northern Democrats began decamping to the Republicans in a massive exodus. Maine's Democratic senator, Hannibal Hamlin, rose in the Senate to announce that he could no longer be a Democrat. "The old Democratic party," he said, "is now the party of slavery." Having long and unsuccessfully battled

Southerners for control of the Democratic party, seceding Democratic leaders left it with bitterness and harsh recrimination. They
were soon close allies of the Radicals within the Republican ranks.
Indeed, in many states Democrats actually played a leading role in
forming the Republican party. They had always been more obsessed
with politics than the Whigs, who retained a strong antiparty strain.
In fact, the Democrats seemed to enjoy political combat and had a
lot of experience in it. They were especially valued by Republicans
for their fighting spirit. "My observation," remarked an Illinois Whig,
"is that we old line whigs in the Republican ranks are not worth a
curse to carry on a campaign and its only life is in the Democratic
party of the ranks." Throughout the Middle West, Democratic leaders and newspaper editors switched to the Republicans. In New York
State, there was a similar shifting. The venerable Jacksonian editor
of the *Evening Post* in New York City, William Cullen Bryant, led
a large group of Democratic intellectuals into the Republican party.
Self-styled "heirs of Jackson" who insisted that only the Republicans
could now claim that lineage, they brought a fervent egalitarianism
into the new party, as well as a distrust of banks and protective tariffs.
In most states, half the Republican nominees were former Democrats, as were about half the members of Abraham Lincoln's presidential cabinet.[27]

Among the Republicans, the party of anti-Southernism, the most
prominent Radical was Charles Sumner of Massachusetts, Free Soil
senator from 1851 and upon the Republican party's formation one of
its leading members. Tall, imperious, learned, and eloquent, Sumner
was as passionate in his hatreds as he was in his affections. In the
mid-1850s, after a series of spectacular oratorical encounters on the
Senate floor with a group of Southern senators, he became a national
figure, cherished in the North for his violent anti-Southern rhetoric
and hated in the South as a "serpent," a "filthy reptile," and a
"leper." In Sumner converged a revealing combination of transatlantic cultural influences. New Englanders tirelessly aped English ways,
and Sumner was an Anglophile so fervent that his friends sometimes
called him "the Earl." In slavery politics, this was a crucial influence.
Southern Democrats, who scorned Southern Whigs' fondness for
London magazines and styles, had insisted for many years that abolitionism was spawned in England and supported by English money.
In the larger sense they were right, for abolitionism was distinctively
a transatlantic crusade. American abolitionists drew constant aid,
comfort, and inspiration from England, and they annually com-

memorated the date upon which the British in 1833 abolished slavery in their empire. When the abolitionist William Lloyd Garrison was made much of during his first English visit, his prestige in the American movement soared.[28]

Being an Anglophile meant being able to move out of the American value system to stand in judgment upon the United States from a wider and higher vantage point. The strongest antislavery workers —the abolitionists—were in this sense the most unnational in their sympathies, the most devoted to the universal cause of humankind and not simply to the stability or even the survival, in its existing form, of the American republic. Garrison thought the Constitution a compact with the devil; he urged a boycott of voting and American politics and called for breaking up the Union by expelling the slave states. Like most Radical Republicans, Charles Sumner held close and friendly relations with the abolitionists. He was too loyal to the nation that New England had done so much to create to join them in their extreme stand, but he was passionately in love with England, the "land of my studies, my thoughts, and my dreams," and like the abolitionists was offended by his country's ills from a standpoint that was transnational. Lionized as a young man by the British aristocracy and even by royalty, he spent much of his time in that country in 1838, feeling embarrassed for his nation and for Americans. Seen from western Europe, the United States appeared to him lawless, crude, narrow, and lacking in culture. Furthermore, everywhere he went while abroad, he learned that slavery was a stench in European nostrils, that it was regarded as his country's greatest disgrace.[29]*

---

*I have not given close attention in this narrative to abolitionism as a movement and a world view because my principal focus is upon the two larger parties. A sensitive, recently published analysis of the abolitionist mentality is Ronald G. Walters' *The Antislavery Appeal: American Abolitionism after 1830* (Baltimore, 1976), which explores the subtle relationship between abolitionists and entrepreneurial capitalism as well as the sense in which abolitionists wished to "Yankeeize" the South in both its economy and attitudes toward work, and the special form of their nationalism. The more extreme among them were disunionists who hoped by that step to render slavery defenseless before the world and doomed. At the same time, however, abolitionists conceived of themselves as national statesmen working to preserve the sainted Union that had been born in the Revolution, an event to which they constantly returned in their rhetoric. "Abolitionists relished their self-cast role of redeemer of the South, the Union, and the Nation." This meant, of course, the spreading southward of Northern ideals. "In picturing the perfect Union as a Yankee one abolitionists were more naïve than culpable." They believed America had a divine destiny in the world to exemplify freedom, and they yearned to bring humanity together in moral fellowship. Slavery was a *national* responsibility made even more compelling by this sense of the American mission. They believed that the victory of their cause would create national unity in freedom, their ultimate goal. (Pp. 129–145.)

Formerly an indifferent Unitarian, while in Europe Sumner
learned that William Ellery Channing, the spiritual leader of New
England Unitarianism, had an enormous international reputation.
When he returned, Sumner became a devoted disciple of that almost
ghostly old saint, now in his last years. Unitarians rejected the Calvinist view that human nature is foul and corrupt. As "Liberal Congregationalists," they had taken control of Harvard in 1803 and subsequently of the established Congregational Church in Massachusetts.
(Calvinist Congregationalists thereupon angrily withdrew, building
their own churches and insisting that they were the true Congregationalists. In 1837, working with the Baptists and Methodists, they
got the Unitarian-controlled Congregational Church disestablished,
thus ending church-state ties in Massachusetts. After the Civil War,
Unitarians finally organized themselves as a sect under that name.)
Preaching the message of love and the New Testament, Unitarian
reformers focused on social evils—that is, on the way people treat
each other—rather than on the sins of personal behavior in relation
to drink, dress, sexual relations, and Sabbath activities. Having inherited the Puritan sense of the corporate community, Unitarians believed that governments must work actively to heal public ills. As
preached by William Ellery Channing, therefore, Unitarianism was
impatient with materialism and the search for wealth. The important
question, Channing said, is what do we do with our freedom and
riches? Thus, the inner dynamic of Unitarian ideals was naturally
reform-oriented. It moved away from wealth and toward human
rights; toward radical positions in social questions.

The Unitarians stood in a paradoxical relation to mid-nineteenth-
century American life. Powerful cultural influences kept them
Whigs, and yet equally powerful national issues kept tugging their
most ardent spirits in another direction. As people who loved England and stayed in close touch with the currents of European
thought, Unitarians had bitterly opposed the War of 1812, viewing
it as an aid to Napoleonic tyranny and a shameful attack upon England, the champion of liberty. Their organic sense of community led
them to support the notion of protective tariffs and national banks
to make the United States strong, cohesive, and subject to appropriate leadership by the elite. In 1846 the war with Mexico continued
to keep Unitarians within the Whig party, for they supported the
party's condemnation of the war as an outrage against humanity.
They had long disapproved of the westward movement, not only
because it meant a progressive diminution of Yankee influence in the
nation at large, but because to Unitarians the West stood as a corrupt-

ing temptation to ordinary persons to "leave behind them all the means and appliances of civilization" and take on the intemperate license and anarchy of barbarism. Yet they felt an equal distaste for the speculative "passion for easy money" of entrepreneurial capitalism. Dr. Joseph Tuckerman, one of Unitarianism's leading figures, greeted the Panic of 1837 with a stern jeremiad: "Infinitely better for us would it be that our commercial embarrassments . . . should indefinitely be increased, than that returning prosperity should bring with it increasing luxury and extravagance, . . . recklessness and depravity."[30]

Unitarians believed in the limitless perfectibility of all persons, provided they were given the means and the opportunity for self-development. This conviction brought William Ellery Channing finally and at long last to speak out against slavery. In so doing, he broke sharply with tradition. Unitarians were genteel, upper-class gentlemen and ladies, and they looked upon William Lloyd Garrison and his loud abolitionist declamations with distaste. Thoughtful, calm reflections upon life and absorption with books and timeless learning marked the Unitarian style. Their fundamental optimism about human nature led them to think of slavery with Olympian detachment as an evil certain to disappear almost of its own volition. Unitarians traditionally drew back from aggressive debate; the zealous fervency of the evangelicals, with their huge revivals, was enough in itself, theology aside, to keep them out of the religious battles of their era. Toward slavery, therefore, Unitarians had been quietistic and retiring, even though they thought of themselves as the conscience of the community. But slavery could not, ultimately, be avoided by so compassionate and principled a man as Channing. "A condition under which a human being is kept from progress is infinitely wrong," he decided. A "rational, moral being [must not] be converted into a mere instrument of others' gratification." In 1835 he gave witness to this conviction in a quiet-voiced, slim volume entitled *Slavery,* which condemned the institution, in the light of calm, reasoned human values, as an atrocity. In response, Channing's colleagues in Boston and even his own parishioners shunned him, an experience that left him deeply wounded and sympathetic toward the much-maligned abolitionists.[31]

It was to this aroused and determinedly antislavery Channing that Charles Sumner came in the late 1830s, to sit at his feet and learn of the ills of the age: war, the inhumanity of the prisons, illiteracy and ignorance among the masses, and slavery. Sumner eagerly took up these causes and, after Channing's death in 1842, threw himself with his characteristic passion into campaigns for pacifism, better schools and prisons, and the abolition of slavery. He was a Conscience Whig in the 1840s, urging his party to lay aside its fascination with economic development and economic policies and turn to the age's pressing issue: human freedom. In time Sumner became so angered by the indifference of the wealthy to social justice that, as a Free Soiler after 1848, he developed close political relations with Northern Democrats, securing his Senate seat in 1851 with their support.

Both Channing and Sumner interpreted the Constitution as giving the federal government no direct power over slavery within given states. Nonetheless, Sumner was also convinced that the Founding Fathers had intended to indicate, in their writing of that document and in their subsequent actions, that freedom was to be national. Therefore, he called for an attack upon slavery where Congress's powers seemed beyond question: in the District of Columbia, in the territories, and in interstate commerce. Sumner insisted, as had Channing, that the most powerful weapon against slavery was the force of moral condemnation and that the Southern states must be surrounded with a *"moral blockade."* Eventually, he said, the "Slave-holding Oligarchy, banished from the National Government, and despoiled of ill-gotten political consequence, without ability to punish or reward," would sink into impotence, and nonslaveholders in the South would throw off the institution.

After the passage of the Kansas-Nebraska Act, Sumner attacked the South with a slashing, caustic vituperation that made even his Republican colleagues wince, although the Northern masses were delighted with their champion and the *New York Times* lauded his "matchless eloquence and power." In a two-day speech given in May 1856, he vilified individual Southern senators so woundingly that Preston Brooks, a South Carolina congressman, subsequently confronted Sumner while he sat working at his Senate desk and beat him unmercifully about the head with a heavy cane, driving him half-conscious and bleeding from the chamber. For three years Sumner was unable to return to his seat. The event produced an enormous outburst of rage and condemnation in the North and righteous gratification in the South. Since it occurred just as a proslavery armed force was completing its "sack" of the antislavery capital of Lawrence, Kansas, the attack upon Sumner convinced millions of Northerners that a moment of crucial testing had arrived: the South intended by naked force to put down all resistance to its continued dominance in the country and to the outward spread of slavery. In

Massachusetts, wrote Henry Adams in later years, "one lived in the
atmosphere of the Stamp Act, the Tea Tax, and the Boston Massacre." The mood of the American Revolution was once more fully
alive in Yankeedom.[32]

At the same time, the Northern mind was steeping itself in lurid
tales recounting the evils of slavery. The publication in 1852 of Har-
riet Beecher Stowe's *Uncle Tom's Cabin* was an electrifying cultural
event. The first novel ever to make black people its subject—and
moreover to take them seriously—it became a best seller overnight.
Within a year, 300,000 copies had been sold in America. When it was
published in England, in 1855, a million copies were snapped up in
eight months. Ultimately, more than six million copies were purchased in the United States and abroad, making the novel more
widely read than any other American book, then or since. Its fascination arose not simply because it dramatized the cruelties of slavery
but because by delicate implication it touched upon the moral issue
of sexual relations within the slave system, which so titillated the
Northern mind.

The cousinship of antislavery and anti-Catholic nativism—a remarkable conjunction—was revealed by the huge contemporary
popularity of another novel, *The Awful Disclosures of Maria Monk*.
Anti-Catholics had traditionally alleged that priests, using the power
of the confessional, reveled in sexual congress with penitent Catholic
women and made use of nuns as well to satisfy their lust. Now in *The
Awful Disclosures of Maria Monk* sensational "proof" of sensuality
within convents was revealed:

> Endangered chastity—whether of lovely octoroon girls or of virginal
> nuns—was a vital part of the message of reform. If the escape of a
> mulatto girl was the high point of *Uncle Tom's Cabin,* the escape of
> a nun from the convent was the high point of *The Awful Disclosures
> of Maria Monk*. If *Uncle Tom* outsold *Maria, Maria* outsold everything
> else, and was called, with perhaps more significance than was in-
> tended, "the *Uncle Tom's Cabin* of Know-Nothingism." If Wendell
> Phillips [the abolitionist] said that the slaveholders had made the entire
> South "one great brothel," the *American Protestant Vindicator* said
> that an unmarried priesthood had converted whole nations into "one
> vast brothel."[33]

Thus, spectacularly, the forces that together tore apart the Jacksonian parties in the 1850s combined even in popular literature to
shape the national consciousness.

By 1858 the work of scrapping the old party system and building a new one was largely complete. The American party in the Northern states was being rapidly absorbed into Republican ranks. The Republicans in four years of swift growth had become a powerful, continental political movement driving purposively toward its goal: seizing control of the national government to bring to fruition the cause of the North.[34]

What was that cause? Southerners called party members "Black Republicans" and linked them with abolitionism. The fact of the matter was different, however. The Republican party was not primarily an antislavery party; rather, it was anti-Southern and pro-Yankee. For generations, the kind of people who became Republicans had watched with almost morbid interest the evolution below the Mason and Dixon line of a way of living that was deeply repellent to them. The Southern culture seemed to the Yankee temper, and also to Whigs in the Lower North and even in the South, to be in opposition to everything America should be and should symbolize to the world. Its central institution, slavery, was in every way an appalling curse, brutalizing blacks and whites alike. Slavery bred an arrogant habit of authority among white Southerners, an instinctive reaction to reach for guns or whips to get one's way, to wrestle and gouge, use knives, or murder one's adversary with elaborate courtesy at twenty paces. The black laboring force was kept ignorant and without incentive, which insured stagnation and inefficiency. For the poor whites, there were no schools, no nearby towns in which to learn industrial skills, and therefore no hope of getting ahead as Yankees conceived of that process. A small aristocracy of great planters monopolized both the wealth and the government. Sloth, decay, unshakable poverty, crudity, and violent barbarisms—these, to Republicans, were the distinguishing marks of Southern civilization.

If Southernism were indeed to grow so powerful that it would spread slavery and its associated way of life throughout the territories and possibly into the Northern states themselves—as many in the North warned was in the future—then every hope that Republicans entertained for America as a land of true morality and industrious freedom for the common people would be destroyed. For many years abolitionists had preached that a Slave Power Conspiracy was at work in Washington to subvert the Constitution, destroy freedom, and make America a slave country, but few had believed them. After the events of the mid-1850s, and especially after the issuance of the

Dred Scott decision, in which collusion between the newly elected President, James Buchanan, and the Southern-dominated Supreme Court seemed evident, Republican leaders like Lincoln and Seward began to agree with the abolitionists and talked publicly of a Southern conspiracy in the national capital. "It is now demonstrated," announced the moderate Cincinnati *Commercial,* "that there is such a thing as the Slave Power."[35]

By contrast with what they saw in the South, Republicans envisioned Northern society as vigorous, enterprising, educated, and progressive. Their goal, they said, in protecting that society was to keep labor honorable: to protect the continued growth of a dynamic, capitalistic, expanding economy in the North in which ordinary men could get ahead and in which, unlike white Southerners, they were proud to toil with their hands. Republicans believed that Yankee virtues of honesty, self-denial, diligence, and sobriety, when combined with an eagerness for education and a "true" Protestant faith, would build an open, optimistic, and sturdily competitive social order. Out of such a way of life, Republicans believed, came strong character and a healthy nation. Individuals who failed in this social order could find the cause in their own moral failings. If there was poverty, as among the Irish, it was rooted in drunkenness, laziness, extravagance, and an "un-Biblical" religion.[36]

Two images of the South had until these crisis years contended in the Northern mind. In one, Southerners had been seen as a cultivated and kindly aristocratic people, concerned for the welfare of their slaves and surrounded by loyal, nodding black retainers. In the other, they had been viewed as violent, quarrelsome, arrogant slave drivers who were determined to have their own way, in all things and at all costs.[37] Now, as Northern Republicans became convinced that the South was launching its final and climactic assault upon Northern freedom and that by closing the North out of the territories the South intended to throttle the North's growth and render it fatally weakened, the latter vision of the South dominated the Republican consciousness. The fighting that erupted in Kansas in 1855 and persisted year after year confirmed thousands of Northerners' conception of the essential Southern character, for proslavery men in Kansas used fraud and violence to get what they could not win by honest votes. The heart of republicanism was being attacked and negated.[38]

The enforcement of the Fugitive Slave Act of 1850 had for years profoundly offended and alarmed Northern sensibilities. The sight of black Northerners being dragged off to slavery, sometimes with bod-

ies of federal troops marching around the prisoners to insure their
delivery southward (and to protect their captors), was a shocking
northward extension of the slave system. Clearly, the system was
developing powerful arms that could reach even into New England
to claim its victims. Slavery was becoming *national*. Every case of a
black Northerner being taken into slavery became a sensationally
publicized cause célèbre that refreshed the sense of outrage. "The
Fug. Slave bill," wrote the abolitionist Lewis Tappan to a friend, "is
awakening the country to the horrors of slavery & creating widespread sympathy for the slaves." A new willingness to resort to violence entered even the abolitionist movement, which had long
proclaimed its pacifism, its reliance upon moral condemnation and
the Holy Word rather than force. Theodore Parker, a muscular theological activist and abolitionist, preached in hundreds of addresses to
Northerners that the sword was as much a symbol of a true, avenging
Christianity as the Bible. Parker was a direct descendant of men who
had fought at Lexington and Concord against the British, and
through him the antislavery cause was widely cast among religious
Northerners in the imagery of the Revolution.[39]

The evangelical ministry of the North threw itself fervently into
the anti-Southern cause. Through the 1840s the Second Great Awakening had fallen quiet, but in the 1850s there was again a tidal
quickening of pietism, especially in the hitherto ignored cities of the
North. Congregationalists, Methodists, Baptists, and New School
Presbyterians exhorted a national pentecost of the spirit in order to
destroy drink, poverty, greed, and, above all, slavery. The temperance crusade caught fire again. Fed by evangelicals' fears of heavy-
drinking immigrants, it built up such momentum that between 1846
and 1855 thirteen states followed Maine's lead and passed prohibition enactments (most of them soon struck down by court decisions).
Then, following the Kansas-Nebraska Act, evangelical ministers
seized upon the Northern cause as they had nothing else since the
Revolution itself.[40]

The ministry's outcry, raised in a fervently religious age, produced
seismic reactions in the South, where Protestantism in its various
embodiments had become a faith almost tribal in its commitment to
the cause of Southern civilization. The outcry also gave a crusader's
iron to the will of the Republican North. Charles G. Finney and
Henry Ward Beecher were only the most prominent of the many
Northern evangelicals who called upon the North to strengthen itself
for stern tests and to go to war, if necessary, in a great sacrifice for
a holy cause. Untroubled by the constitutional and practical difficul-

ties that puzzled others, the evangelical ministry was inspired by
transcendent moral conviction and a confidence that the Lord would
provide. Early in the decade Methodist editor William Hosmer had
stated the issue with stark power and simplicity in his book *The
Higher Law* (1852):

> The fact that a law is constitutional amounts to nothing, unless it is also
> pure; it must harmonize with the law of God, or be set at naught by
> all upright men. Wicked laws not only may be broken, but absolutely
> must be broken; there is no other way to escape the wrath of God. . . .
> When the fundamental law of the land is proved to be a conspiracy
> against human rights, law ceases to be law, and becomes a wanton
> outrage on society.[41]

Democrats who remained in their party bitterly complained, as
they had for generations, about the Yankee "political clergy" who
once again were intruding into public affairs. Old School Presbyterians in the Middle Atlantic states and in the South condemned the
evangelists' assault on the South, thus continuing their ancient battle
against everything that emanated from Yankee Congregationalists
and New School Presbyterians. Episcopalians also held back from the
antislavery cause, as did the other "church" denominations, the Lutherans and Roman Catholics, that historically had advocated separation between church and state (in America) and had rejected pietist
campaigns for social reform.[42]

In 1858 a sudden surge of evangelical revivalism swept the Northern states. Even Old School Presbyterians, Episcopalians, and Unitarians joined in, and in Chicago and New York thousands of
worshippers jammed churches and impromptu meeting places. City-
wide campaigns stimulated the formation of ecumenical organizations that survived after the "year of wonders" had passed, ready to
focus the assault against the high crime of slavery. The great revival
of 1858 seemed to many ministers a "careful preparation for some
overwhelming manifestation . . . [in which the] strong towers of sin
shall fall, the glory of the Lord shall be displayed, and the millenial
[*sic*] glory shall dawn upon the earth."[43]

The weapon of the Lord in this holy cause, however, was the
Republican party, and purity of soul and purpose is rarely the property of political parties. Although the evangelical ministry in their
pulpits could describe the cause in transcendent terms as a great new

work of freedom, the central question was the Republican view of black persons and what they thought should be done about the blacks' condition. This was an extremely sensitive issue in 1850s politics. What, precisely, did Republicans intend? Only a tiny number of them were abolitionists, and as a party they had in mind no direct action against slavery where it existed in the Southern states. However, Republicans genuinely felt a moral repugnance toward the institution, and they hoped that, by closing it in and denying it any shred of recognition or support by federal action, it would eventually die of its own accursed weight. Republicans were in fact notable for agitating the cause of improved rights for blacks even in the North. They advocated giving blacks the vote, providing schools, and repealing segregationist laws. Even so, it was the rare Republican who had social equality in mind. They thought, as did practically all whites, that black persons were inherently inferior as human beings. And yet, Democrats constantly attacked and ridiculed Republicans for being problack, and Republicans worried persistently about this popular image of their party. Salmon P. Chase remarked in 1855 that the Democrats seemed to talk of nothing but "the universal nigger question, as they called it." In response to Democratic criticism, Republicans turned in many different directions in their search for a means of shaking off the issue.[44]

Republicans were actually, their party leaders said, the true white man's party. It was their purpose, in resisting the expansion of slavery into the territories, to keep them open to whites. "I want to have nothing to do either with the free negro or the slave negro," said Lyman Trumbull, a Republican senator from Illinois of Yankee antecedents, who in 1864 would author the Thirteenth Amendment abolishing slavery. "We wish to settle the Territories with free white men." It was the Democrats, Republicans insisted, who wanted to flood the country with blacks by spreading slavery. When accused of advocating race mixture, Republicans replied that slavery, not freedom, caused miscegenation, as the enormous mulatto population in the South demonstrated. They continually proposed colonization in Africa for free black Americans as the solution to the race problem. In a time of huge transoceanic population movements, reverse immigration seemed not so extraordinary.

In relative terms, however, the difference between Republicans and Democrats on the race issue was clear for all to see. Democrats continually ranted white supremacist slogans, pouring scorn upon the idea of ending slavery and the notion of the common humanity of blacks and whites. By contrast, the Republican position was clear and positive. They believed that black Americans "were human beings and citizens of the United States, entitled to the natural rights of humanity and to such civil rights as would protect the natural rights of life, liberty, and property." Blacks must, however, prove themselves equal before being treated as such. Republicans accepted the idea of the "equal chance": breaking down the barriers before black Americans to let them engage in self-improvement and character building in a free condition. If they then demonstrated their worth, the question of equal relationships would be reopened. It was this basic position that underlay Radical Republican Reconstruction after the Civil War.[45]*

In this ambivalent state of mind, pulled both toward ideas of equality and inferiority for the black person, Abraham Lincoln of Illinois puzzled over the race question.[46] Lincoln must be seen, first of all, as a Southerner who revolted against Southern values and who, if he had remained in slave country, would have been part of the "Other South"—the pro-Yankee world represented by Henry Clay, Lincoln's idol. Lincoln and his family had early migrated northward from Kentucky, where he had been born in 1809, into that distinctively Southern world that had formed in southern Indiana and Illinois. Illinois came close to reestablishing slavery after its admission to the Union, and its antiblack laws made Afro-Americans almost slaves again within its borders. Abolitionists lived dangerous lives in

---

*A recent work that explores in detail the complexities of the Republican position on black Americans is Richard H. Sewell's *Ballots for Freedom: Antislavery Politics in the United States 1837–1860* (New York, 1976), pp. 321–342. Following the story from the appearance of the Liberty party, Sewell finds much to dispute the revisionist view that even the Free Soilers were simply a racist white man's party.

Without question, some Free Soilers despised blacks and championed the [Wilmot] Proviso as a means of "keeping the territory clean of negroes." . . . Yet for all their racial prejudice . . . most . . . Free Soilers . . . responded primarily to the menace of *slavery* and the "Slave Power," and only fitfully and secondarily to the "curse" of degraded blacks . . . [and they] managed to a remarkable extent to transcend the racism of the age. Far from seeking to strengthen or extend discrimination against blacks, many Free Soilers went out of their way to debunk conventional stereotypes of Negro inferiority and to preach the "equality of all men, of every climate, color, and race. . . ." Free Soilers often took the lead in defending—and extending —the civil rights of black Americans . . . [though] notably reticent on the question of social equality. (Pp. 171–176.)

Most believed the Wilmot Proviso, by shutting off westward migration, "would leave slaveholders only one option—emancipation" (p. 191). So, too, with the Republicans, "too much can be made of [the] . . . racist element in the Republican party. . . . What is surprising . . . is that nearly all Republicans defended the Negro's manhood and insisted that he be accorded those inalienable rights set forth in the Declaration of Independence" (pp. 326–327).

Lincoln's country. The abolitionist editor Elijah Lovejoy was murdered in Alton, Illinois, just two years after Lincoln entered the state
legislature in 1834. Jacksonian Democrats of the most outspoken,
anti-Yankee, expansionist, and pro-Southern type were powerful in
Illinois politics. Lincoln's own family was of the faith.

It was a revealing act of conscious choice, therefore, for Lincoln to
become a Whig. Much of his motivation was frankly economic. To
open and develop the country, he incessantly advocated the development of canals, railroads, and banks. "My politics," he had said in his
first political speech in 1832, "are short and sweet. . . . I am in favour
of the internal improvement system and a high protective tariff." It
was important to him that America be a country where poor men
could rise from poverty to wealth and standing. A self-trained lawyer,
by the 1850s he was regularly fighting major cases for the Middle
West's largest corporations, factories, and railroads.

Lincoln's Whiggery, however, was much more than simply an
outlook on the national economy. It involved his entire approach to
life, his sense of the good and fruitful moral order. Even as a young
man Lincoln was a teetotaler in a hard-drinking frontier world. He
wrote essays condemning alcohol, joined temperance societies, and
as a politician spoke repeatedly on the subject. Surrounded by cigar
smoke and spittoons, he neither smoked nor chewed tobacco. He
disliked crudity in personal behavior and would not swear. As a boy,
Lincoln was considered lazy and was mocked by his neighbors, who
were generally illiterate, for he read constantly, even when ostensi-
bly at work. In New Salem, as a teen-ager, he sought out a debating
society led by a Yankee doctor trained at Dartmouth College; he
seemed naturally to gravitate to the living rooms, libraries, and favor
of the local gentry. Though not an active church-goer, Biblical imagery colored his otherwise simple, spare oratory, for he had a strong
sense of humanity's immediacy to God and to divine judgment. In a
violent society obsessed with guns, Lincoln would not use them even
to shoot animals. When running for office in 1836, he publicly favored the vote only for those who paid taxes or served in the militia,
thus disapproving of the universal white manhood suffrage praised
by Jacksonian Democrats. He even advocated votes for women.

Surveying the riotous disorders of the Jacksonian years in 1837—
the assassination of Elijah Lovejoy appalled him—he cried out in
classic Whig fashion against the "mobocratic spirit which . . . is now
abroad in the land," appealing eloquently for law and order. No
republic, he warned, could long survive such turbulence. For his
wife, Lincoln chose a young woman from the cultivated elite of

Springfield, the capital city, and they had the first Episcopalian wedding in that community. At one point, he was even denied a local Whig nomination because he was thought to be too close to the circles of wealth, pride, and aristocratic family distinction. Abraham Lincoln, in short, chose Whiggery for much more than economic reasons. He rejected the cultural values of Jacksonian Democracy, Southern style, for a different and—Whigs would say—more civilized way of living.

It is not surprising, therefore, that Lincoln was one of the small number of persons of Southern antecedents who deplored slavery and that, rarer still, he was an Illinois legislator driven to oppose that institution long before the Civil War. He was a compassionate man, given to deep moods of melancholy, and he brooded over the dilemmas posed by the race question. He looked in this, as in economic matters, to Henry Clay for guidance, "my beau ideal of a statesman, the man for whom I fought all of my humble life." The Kentuckian's belief that slavery was a curse, and his hope that it would disappear, strengthened Lincoln's outlook. Yet both men thought that racial equality was impossible, and they could only conceive of colonization in Africa as a final solution.

Lincoln was especially shy and sensitive toward women, and the sight of young black women stripped naked and coarsely examined, which he observed during his travels on the Ohio and the Mississippi, offended him, as did the entire situation of black men and women in slavery. "[It] was a continual torment to me," he wrote to his close friend Joshua Speed, a proslavery man, after a trip into the South. When the Illinois legislature passed a proslavery resolution in 1837, as a member of that body Lincoln protested against it. In Congress in 1847–1849, he proposed the gradual and compensated extinction of slavery in the District of Columbia and voted scores of times for the Wilmot Proviso. Yet he disliked abolitionists, refused to back the use of force in the antislavery cause in Kansas, and supported firmly, if reluctantly, the Fugitive Slave Law.

The status that Lincoln envisioned for black Americans was the possession of an equal right, as he put it, to eat the bread they had earned by the sweat of their brow, to enjoy freely the fruits of their own toil. But how could this status of effective freedom be preserved for them unless they were given full participation in the national society and government? Lincoln did not know. He observed in 1858 that "there is a natural disgust in the minds of nearly all white people at the idea of an indiscriminate amalgamation of the white and black men," and this universal sentiment, he believed, could not be ignored. Facing this unresolvable dilemma—the central paradox in American race relations—he found no usable solution.

Nevertheless, Lincoln insisted repeatedly upon one central point: slavery must be placed "in the course of ultimate extinction." This called for placing it back where he believed the Founding Fathers, by their actions, had intended to place it: marked out as an evil institution and closely bound by strong proscriptions. They had banned it from the Northwest Territories, given it reduced representation in Congress, and in 1808 provided for an end to the slave trade. Were slavery to be confined to the South, Lincoln believed, it eventually would die. To this end, in the 1850s he took as his greatest task the fighting down of what he feared to be a growing national indifference to the moral evil of slavery. Things were so bad, he said, that those who condemned the institution were ridiculed and that "if one man chooses to enslave another, no third man shall have the right to object." Little by little, the nation seemed to be giving up on what Lincoln called its "central idea": its belief in equality. In 1859 he published one of the most eloquent tributes ever made to Thomas Jefferson, whose Declaration of Independence, for Lincoln, was the lodestone for all political belief. In the late 1850s he traveled about the nation appealing to the national conscience. Using the language of Biblical prophecy, which struck so sensitive and reactive a chord among Northerners in these evangelical years, Lincoln called upon Americans never to forget that slavery was wrong.

Pennsylvania's role in the realignments of the 1850s was crucial. In a sense, the state was a microcosm of the North as a whole. Its southern counties had intimate ties to the South, for just over the border was slavery. Thousands of Germans and Scotch-Irish in the Appalachian region looked southward down the long valleys that reached for hundreds of miles into the upland South, where their own ethnic countrymen had migrated. A rich farming state, and the location for one-third of the distilleries in the United States, Pennsylvania by the 1850s had also become the nation's major industrial state. Just behind New York in banking and commerce, Pennsylvania produced five times more pig iron than any other state; its output, amounting to half of that produced nationwide, was exceeded in the world only by that of Great Britain and France. The industrial revolution that was underway in the Northern states in the 1850s centered in Pennsylvania. This made the tariff and other economic issues topics of intense controversy between Whigs and Republicans, on the protective side, and Democrats, with their traditional bent toward free trade and anticapitalism.

The southeastern counties around Quaker Philadelphia were traditionally Whig, and so was Pittsburgh. Along the New York border were the Northern Tier counties, settled by Yankee Baptists and Methodists. These counties were solidly Democratic, as were most of those bordering Maryland. Pennsylvania as a whole was with rare exceptions Democratic in presidential balloting, for with its Scotch-Irish, German, and Baptist population, the state had been Jeffersonian and Jacksonian for decades. Industrialization, however, made the Whig position on the tariff ever more attractive, especially in times of economic slump, and the Republicans inherited this advantage. In the late 1840s and after the Panic of 1857, Pennsylvania Democrats fought desperately against the charge that they were the party of low tariffs and unemployment. In 1859 they lost heavily in the industrial counties.

Pennsylvania was engaged, however, in a cultural as well as an economic revolution. It had more than fifty thousand blacks in its population, the largest such group in any Northern state, and their presence was regarded with mounting distaste. In 1838 Pennsylvanians adopted a new constitution that excluded blacks from the vote. When in 1851 the Christiana riot erupted, in which Southerners attempting to recover a group of fugitive slaves were shot down by blacks barricaded within a house well known as a station on the underground railroad, antiblack sentiment erupted throughout the state. Though Pennsylvanians generally opposed the expansion of slavery into the territories, most accepted the Compromise of 1850 and the Fugitive Slave Act as welcome settlements insuring North-South peace. The state had heavy economic commitments southward, through nearby Baltimore and through Philadelphia and Pittsburgh, and wished no further dissension to disrupt that trade. Indeed, the Democrats constantly justified their low-tariff policy on the ground that it insured good North-South economic relations.[47]

Another source of growing cultural tension within Pennsylvania was the huge invasion of Roman Catholic immigrants that had begun in the 1840s and swelled further in the 1850s. Among Pennsylvania's 2.3 million people in 1850, 300,000 were foreign born. Most of them came from Germany and Ireland, and they converged in the two industrial centers. In Philadelphia County alone, there were more than 100,000 aliens, heavily Roman Catholic. As elsewhere, it was primarily the Irish, not the Germans, who aroused the most bitter hatred among the native-born Protestants, just as it was the Irish, far more than the Germans, who were likely to react violently to slights and prejudicial treatment. The Irish were at the center of the alarming violence that flared in Philadelphia in the 1840s and culminated in the Kensington and Southwark riots of 1844—disorders so destructive that the city established, for the first time, a regular police force to keep the peace.[48]

The Irish brought with them their centuries-old hatred of Protestant governments, and they transferred that feeling to the Protestant majority that surrounded them in Philadelphia. On theological grounds the Irish were skeptical of social reform. They vigorously condemned every hint of Yankee cultural imperialism, especially in the public schools. Antiliquor agitation led them to fear that even the use of wine in religious observance would be outlawed. Around their church, the tavern, and the firehouse, the Irish built their tightly knit communities, concentrated in the factory districts. Their self-imposed isolation—the first such instance of ethnic ghettoization (save for that of blacks) in American urban life—alarmed native Americans. This refusal to assimilate seemed an arrogant denial of the American community. The fact that Catholic priests, anxious to protect their flock from corrupting religious influences, worked actively to achieve this separateness and were leaders in political controversies deepened the sense that the Irish were a permanently foreign bloc at war with American republicanism. At the same time, the Irish were so monolithically Democratic in voting loyalties, so obedient to their party leaders, that in the Irish wards Democrats sometimes ran entirely unopposed. A crucial voting bloc that could swing elections, the Irish played a highly prominent role in Philadelphia politics. In labor disputes, as well, their quickness to use disruption, destruction, and intimidation to get what they wanted made them much disliked. Thus, the Irish seemed to native-born Americans almost a nation within a nation, contemptuous of lawful authority, anarchic, and frightening.[49]

A nativist American Republican party sprang up in Philadelphia in the 1840s to combat what was perceived as the Irish menace. Its membership was largely composed of Protestant craftsmen and artisans. These workingmen regarded the immigrants as a source of cheap, unskilled labor for their capitalist enemies, who were turning ever more to mechanization. Nativists also dealt heavily in anti-Catholic rhetoric, talking endlessly of a conspiracy launched from Rome to subvert the American republic. The American Republican party itself concentrated primarily upon the political dangers emanating from the Catholic presence; the vilification of Irishmen on

Sabbatarian, temperance, and Biblical grounds was left to a hard core of evangelical Protestant clergymen in Philadelphia. "The outright slanders heaped on Catholic religious beliefs," writes Michael Feldberg, "spewed forth from the pulpits and religious presses of the city rather than from its political soapboxes."[50]

The American Republicans stood for "good government," for the suppression of political corruption from any source whatever. The intrusion of Catholic priests into American politics, the voting en masse for the Irish boss's choice, the handing out of patronage and graft to fellow Irishmen when in power—these, rather than alleged moral evils, made the Irish Catholics seem, to political nativists, an antirepublican force ready to subvert the democratic process. Thus, the American Republican party advocated a simple platform: increasing the naturalization period, electing only the native-born to office (even if they were the children of immigrants), and rejecting all foreign interference (i.e., by the Pope) in American institutions. In the 1850s, therefore, there were strong economic and cultural reasons why Philadelphia and its environs voted Whig and then, after the collapse of that party, became strongly Republican.[51]

In the western part of the state, Pittsburgh's politics revealed the same differences between Whigs and Democrats over economic issues that existed in Philadelphia and in the Northern states generally. The city, with its burgeoning industries, consistently supported the protectionist, development-oriented Whigs, whose leaders were considerably wealthier than those of the Democrats and more typically native-born and Protestant. Despite the efforts of Democrats to describe themselves as the party of the workingmen against their employers, the Whig party actually drew a large number of Protestant and native-born mechanics and workingmen into its ranks. So strong were Protestant Irishmen and Germans in their anti-Catholicism that they belonged to the rabidly antipapist Protestant associations.[52]

When Know-Nothingism emerged in 1853 and began swiftly growing, it was the native-born Protestants in the working- and middle-class districts of Pittsburgh who flocked to the American party with the greatest enthusiasm. Then, when the American party broke apart on the slavery issue after 1856, these same Protestant voting groups flooded into the new Republican party in Pennsylvania. In fact, the Republicans in Pennsylvania were not so distinctively the party of wealth as had been the Whigs, for the Republicans were much more successful in attracting the working classes. Heavily Presbyterian, they also benefited from the fact that Northern Tier Baptists and Methodists—who, though Yankee in origin, had long voted Democratic—were also moving toward the Republican party because they feared Irish Catholicism.

The Republican party in Pennsylvania, of course, also inherited the Whigs' strong anti-Southernism. Whig newspapers had continually ridiculed Democrats as allies of slavery and toadies to Southern slaveholders. Republican resolutions, in turn, attacked "the organized conspiracy of the slaveholders of Missouri backed by the public opinion of the whole South . . . to force slavery into Kansas. . . . [The battle of Kansas free-state settlers] is ours, and . . . if we would continue free, we must look at once to our weapons and see that our powder is dry." In reply, Democratic editors condemned their opponents as "Black Republican abolitionists," fanatical warmongers who would tear apart the Union. They cared only for blacks, the Democratic *Post* said in Pittsburgh. Their aim was to abolish slavery and bring "the Negroes into the Northern States to take the places of white laborers."[53]

By 1860 the Republican coalition in Pennsylvania was complete and solid. Abraham Lincoln was able to carry Pennsylvania by a large majority. In the voting for state offices, the Republicans won the most decisive victory over the Democrats that had ever been achieved. They swept the Northern Tier, carried every county along the Ohio River, and even took Democratic strongholds along the southern border. The land of the Scotch-Irish, who in Pennsylvania were by this time voting Republican, as they were wherever the Catholic Irish had arrived in numbers, had tipped the national balance. The South's great ally in the North, Pennsylvania, had finally gone over to the other side.[54]

With rising alarm, the South watched the events of the 1850s in the Northern states. Never before had the national scene changed as swiftly in directions so threatening to Southern life. Arguments over slavery had occurred before, but they had taken place within a political system in which the South's declared enemies could find no position of power to achieve their goal. The Whig party was strong in both North and South, and antislavery politicians within the party were always in a powerless minority, unable to make the issue an effective anti-Southern vehicle. The Liberty and Free Soil parties had, if anything, confirmed the inability of antislavery Northerners to muster more than a small following. They might tip an election in key states, but they could never take over Washington. Yankeeism, the great enemy of the South, seemed isolated and ineffective.

Thus, with the national government essentially under Southern control from the time of Jefferson's election in 1800, and with the leaders of the Whigs and Democrats in the Jacksonian years working successfully to keep slavery out of politics, sectional issues had been of secondary importance. Northern ideologists of antislavery and Southern advocates of an aggressive Southernism had been persistently frustrated by this tacit bipartisan agreement to keep the nation's most divisive question in the margins of politics. For long periods, as we have seen, Southerners were as absorbed by the great questions of national economic development as were Northerners, and they worked together cooperatively across sectional lines on these issues. The Whig party, with its organic nationalism and its commitment to Yankee, Anglicized ways of living and thinking, was powerful in the South for more than twenty years. When South Carolina and Mississippi, the chief centers of anti-Yankeeism in the South, agitated secessionism during the slavery extension crisis of 1850–1851, it was primarily the Unionist stance of the great majority of Southerners that kept the nation together.[55] Southerners were profoundly patriotic. They had led in the nation's founding, had been a dominant influence in its government for most of its history since 1789, and had provided most of its Presidents. The readiness with which they returned to the Union after the Civil War, as David Potter observed, can only be understood against this background. It was this instinctive loyalty to the United States of America, a feeling never obliterated during the Civil War, that gave the conflict "its peculiarly tragic tone—its pathos as a 'brothers' war.' "[56]

In the 1850s, that basic sense of ultimate security within the American Union that was the foundation stone for Southern loyalty began rapidly to erode. Southerners were fully aware that the Republican party was far more Yankee than Northern Whiggery had been, that it was the vehicle for New England hegemony that Yankees had sought for many decades. At the same time, Southerners were keenly conscious of the booming industrial growth of the North, its rapidly spreading railroad net, and the influx of immigrants who avoided the South but flocked to Northern states. In the days of Thomas Jefferson, the slave states had been equal in population to the North, and they had held 40 percent of the nation's white people. By the 1850s, however, the Northern population—including both whites and blacks—was half again as large as the population of the South. The number of white people in the North was more than double (in a ratio of seven to three) the number in the South.[57] If Southerners had been concerned about Yankees in John Adams' time, now they were faced with a colossus of the North that had enormous strength if it were concentrated and turned in one direction—as now it seemed to be.

The Southern states became freshly and fearfully obsessed with *The Yankee*. It was probably for this reason that Southerners in the 1850s turned almost en masse to the Democratic party and Whiggery rapidly declined, for the Democrats were anti-Yankee and the Whigs supported New England ways. Both Northern and Southern Democrats had long aimed their bitterest attacks at the archetypical Yankee. In the 1850s it mattered little where the Democratic newspaper was published, whether in Texas or Alabama, in Illinois or New York; everywhere the anti-Yankee invective that Democratic editors poured out in an uninterrupted stream was practically identical.[58]

"The people of the New England States," observed a Texas editor in 1856, "have been as remarkable in their history, for the violence of their fanaticism and proclivity to superstition and intolerance on all subjects connected with religion as they have been for their intelligence, energy, and enterprise on all other subjects."[59] As they observed the Yankees in politics, Democrats singled out for particular condemnation, as they had for generations, the Yankee "practice of dragging politics into the pulpit." New England ministers, they said, were the moving force in the crusade to shape the nation in the Yankee image. "The Puritans of today," wrote a Tennessee editor, "like the Puritans of 1700, conceive themselves to be better and holier than others, and entitled—by divine right as it were—to govern and control the actions and dictate the opinions" of their fellow men. New England was "always putting itself forward as the accuser & maligner of its brethren, the marplot & busybody of the confederacy, always crying over its grievances & always arraigning the other states for pretended usurpations. . . . They are unhappy unless they can persecute, either some unprotected class of their own people, or their colleagues in the confederacy." Intolerance, an arrogant belief that they had a monopoly upon truth, and "a fanatical zeal for unscriptural reforms" characterized Yankees in the present scene, as in the past when they "burnt old women for witches, banished the Quakers, tore down Catholic convents, or gathered together a blue light Hartford Convention."[60]

New Englanders had "persuaded themselves that they had a prescriptive right to impose their politics, their habits, manners and dogmas on the sister States and aspired to convert the whole people of the United States to Yankeedom." For them, "nothing exists that may not be improved." The ominous fact was that all the various New England radicalisms were coalescing within one powerful party, the Republicans, "composed of Free Soilers, Abolitionists, Maine-Lawites [prohibitionists], Free-Negroes and Spirit Rappers." Like smoldering logs brought together to catch fire, their conjunction was giving an intense new flame to revived Puritanism. The whole nation, not simply the South, was threatened by this revitalized New England imperialism, for "abolition is but a small part of their programme and probably the least noxious of their measures." The chief nature of Republicanism was "to meddle with everything —to meddle with the domestic institutions of other States, to meddle with family arrangements in their own States—to force their harsh and uncongenial puritanical creed down the throats of other men."[61]

The Whigs' activist philosophy of government, inherited by the Republicans, now became a crucial issue once more. Government intervention, said Democrats, was apparently no longer just to be applied in economic matters at the national level. The Republicans' combined warfare against Catholicism, drink, and slavery demonstrated that the strong government ideal would be turned in cultural directions as well. What New Englanders intended to do, if they got power in Washington, seemed to be abundantly demonstrated by their record at the state level, where for years they had agitated for Sabbath laws, used the public schools to Protestantize Catholic children, exerted strict controls over marriage relationships, and tried to stop the use of alcohol. In short, Democrats formed their image of the Republican party, not from single issues, but rather from a combination of them all. What emerged was the threat of aggressive Yankee Republicanism, a revival of the Puritanism of old, which came, said Democrats, from the Republicans' forgetting basic concepts of liberty. The moment that "democratic principles [are ignored], that men are to be let alone unless they invade the rights of others, and States allowed to govern themselves . . . we know not to what vagaries and inconsistencies communities may run."[62]

Republican government would be Puritan government, and to Southerners this meant, sooner or later, an assault upon slavery. It "*meant* the ascendancy of abolitionists to national power—*meant* convulsive slave insurrection—*meant* emancipation of the Negro hordes with the political, social, and economic chaos that must follow the breaking of those bonds." A hammer blow to the South and its state of mind came in 1858 when William Seward, at that time perhaps the foremost figure in Republicanism, spoke of an "irrepressible conflict" existing between slavery and freedom. The anguished subtleties of attitude toward black persons and slavery that Republicans had struggled over had always seemed irrelevant to Southerners. Seward's words meant only one thing: an attack upon slavery was coming.[63]

If Yankees believed in a Slave Power conspiracy at work in Washington, Southerners had their own conspiratorial delusions. Abolitionists, they were convinced, secretly controlled the Republican party. Southern whites fantasized that lavishly financed organizations existed to lure slaves northward and direct Northern resistance to the Fugitive Slave Law. They believed that nests of abolitionists were placed in Kansas to prey upon Missouri, Arkansas and Texas; regarded Northerners traveling through the South as abolitionist agents "tampering" with the slaves; circulated stories of poisonings and burnings on the plantations, allegedly plotted by Northern, even English, elements; and conceived of Yankees as "shifty, cowardly hypocrites [who] concealed their aggressive designs behind a mask of pious benevolence."[64]

Stung by Northern contempt for their ways of life, Southerners fashioned their own philosophy of anti-Northernism and pro-Southernism. George Fitzhugh's 1854 book, *Sociology for the South: or The Failure of Free Society,* held that it was Yankeedom, not the South, that was cruel, heartless, exploitive of its workers, money-mad, criminal, violent, acquisitive, and lost in an anarchy of selfish individualism.[65]* With regard to slavery, there was much less soul-searching in the South in the 1850s than there had been after the Denmark Vesey and Nat Turner slave conspiracies of the 1820s and 1830s. For many years Southern ministers and publicists had reassured the South that slavery was Biblical, ordained by God, and the most natural and beneficent form of human society for black Africans, who were not human beings in the usual sense. Slavery was believed to gentle, elevate, and Christianize creatures who were

---

*C. Vann Woodward observes,

> If it is impossible to imagine either of the two old racial components of the South without the other, or the peculiar regional subculture they produced without the combination, it is quite as difficult to conceive of the distinctiveness of American life and national history without the presence of both or without the North-South polarity that presence proclaims and the myths it inspires. The South has been almost as essential to the North and North to South in the shaping of national character and mythology as the Afro-American to the Southern-American and vice versa. North and South have used each other, or various images and stereotypes of each other, for many purposes ... occasionally ... to define their identity and to say what they are *not*, [and] ... to escape in fantasy from what they *are*. (*American Counterpoint: Slavery and Racism in the North-South Dialogue* [Boston and Toronto, 1971], p. 6.)

essentially brutes. Thus, white Southerners had little painful sense of being party to a moral wrong. White Southerners believed that slavery made black people productive; left to themselves, as the history of the Caribbean islands was taken by white Southerners to demonstrate, blacks became slothful, unreflective, and wholly lacking in productive skills.

The owning of slaves was also said to ennoble the white population. It made them honest, prideful of character, honorable, concerned for the welfare of others, and trained to leadership. Freedom for black people, furthermore, would expose them to their natural weaknesses and condemn them to poverty, crime, and death. There were some Southern Whigs of the Other South who expressed a concern for black people and described slavery as economically and socially harmful, but they were restricted to the upper South, primarily places like western Virginia and eastern Tennessee, where mountainous conditions made for few slaves. These Whigs usually had first-hand contacts with the North, often having gone to college there, and thus were led to make unfavorable comparisons between Northern industriousness and Southern aversion to work.[66]

From its first appearance in the 1820s, Southern whites regarded abolitionism as an unthinkable horror. It was not simply that slaves were profitable to own or that whites were reluctant to give up the joys of mastery, for only a fraction of white Southerners actually possessed slaves. Rather, the white South, especially in places like South Carolina where blacks were often overwhelmingly in the majority, was terrified by the prospect of the blood bath that it believed would instantly follow general emancipation. Books on this theme were widely read, and the subject was constantly discussed. Slavery, as whites conceived of it, was their great protector, a barrier standing between themselves and the barbaric tribe in their midst. Although they insisted publicly that black people were naturally docile and warm-hearted persons who loved their masters, Southern whites secretly feared the hatred for all whites that they believed must be rooted in the black consciousness.[67]

Slavery was therefore the only conceivable relationship that most Southern whites could understand as a basis for their society. This was why they reacted in such exaggerated fashion to every antislavery development in the North and why they came to so furiously hate Northerners. How could white people so endanger those who shared their race and culture? In October 1859 came the thunderous event that sent Southerners in such especially tense locations as South Carolina into a hysteria of fear: John Brown's raid at Harper's Ferry.

Though Brown's attempt to set off a mass insurrection of the slaves failed, the raid confirmed Southern fears that abolitionists would one day strike directly against the South.

> To be sure, life went on in South Carolina after October 1859. Ships sailed out from Charleston with their rich cargoes of cotton and rice, and the endless round of sowing and harvesting turned its slow cycle from hilly farms to lush plantations. But the atmosphere was different. John Brown had plunged a knife deep into the psyche of Southern whites, and life would never be quite the same again.[68]

People in South Carolina were reported actually to have become deranged because of fears of a slave uprising and abolitionist invasion. Alleged agents of John Brown were arrested all over the South. Mysterious fires in the distance were linked to his mythical army, whose detachments were believed to be everywhere. A witch hunt was set in motion against free blacks. Vigilance committees were formed, men suspected of being incendiaries were arrested, and public meetings involving the great mass of the white population were held. The "base line of race fear stretched unbroken across the state, embracing patrician planter and yeoman farmer." Patrols were formed, slaves were freely arrested and punished on the public roads, visitors were often violently seized and interrogated, white men talking to black persons were jailed, mail was taken and opened, people were tarred and feathered, and Northern birth was sometimes enough to lead to expulsion from communities. The populations of entire towns were gathered together for questioning, to see if they were completely in support of the Southern cause. Everyone whose ideas had been suspect in the past was condemned as a "hidden abolitionist." A conviction was widespread that, by covert means, abolitionist literature and ideas were being regularly fed to the slaves. There was constant fear of fire, and arson plots were rumored. South Carolina's blacks, it was said, were growing freer in their speech and dress. They were allowed too much liberty to travel and engage in skilled trades, and they were given too much education. Now a massive determination surfaced to turn back this trend and make slavery once more an iron and unyielding institution.

When the Democratic party split nationally into Northern and Southern segments in the summer of 1860, unable to agree upon a presidential candidate, alarm surged through the South. Then, as the election itself approached, tension mounted again. Running through these events was "the profound and inescapable fact of massive African slavery, and a dread of the potential disaster arising out of that presence. . . . [In] the end fear of the Negro—physical dread, and fear of the consequences of emancipation—would control the course of [South Carolina]."[69]

In the presidential election of 1860, four candidates were presented to the American people. When Southern Democrats walked out of the national Democratic nominating convention rather than agree to the choice of Stephen Douglas, who had turned against the South on the Kansas issue, they formed their separate convention and nominated John Breckinridge of Kentucky. In Chicago, the Republicans settled upon Abraham Lincoln, whose relatively moderate position on slavery and whose popularity in the Middle West promised victory. Douglas was the nominee of the Northern Democrats. The Constitutional Union party, hastily gathered in convention by despairing ex-Whigs from the Upper South who feared a breakup of the Union if either of the other three were elected, presented John Bell of Tennessee. In the balloting, a national shift of historic proportions took place. Since 1800 enough Middle Atlantic and Middle Western states in the region of the Lower North had voted for Southern-supported candidates to give them the victory in most elections. Now, however, the Lower North moved to the other side, giving the Republican party, within six years of its founding, control of the national government.

South Carolinian whites now believed they were faced with a choice between remaining in the Union and suffering, sooner or later, the blood bath that would follow general emancipation or leaving the Union and keeping their slaves in subjection. They could see only one conceivable course: secession. A massive folk movement within the state swept South Carolina out of the Union within weeks of Lincoln's election. Before he was inaugurated, in March 1861, the six other states of the Lower South had seceded, and the Confederate States of America was formed. Then came the firing upon Fort Sumter, a federal installation placed as if by historic design under the eyes of the South Carolinians, the most determined of the seceders. President Lincoln, the ultimate republican—in the Revolutionary sense—now began his long struggle to prove, as he said, that republicanism was not too weak, by being founded in the popular will, to survive. His call for troops precipitated the agonized, reluctant secession of the four states of the Upper South, who then joined the Confederacy. And the war came.[70]

VIII

Second Phase:
Civil War
and Reconstruction,
1860=1877

The North responded to Lincoln's call and through four years of war
fought to put down secession for reasons too complex to catalogue,
although the issue has called forth more than a century of speculation. Within the context of this book, which is concerned with understanding the nation's larger experiences as they are mediated and
explained by the history of the parties, it is important to begin first
with the fact that the Civil War was a Republican war. As in the case
of the wars fought against Britain in 1812 and Mexico in 1846, the
decision to fight the Civil War was made by one of the two political
parties, and that party carried on the fighting in the face of unrelenting criticism from the other side. Federalists in 1812 had condemned
the war against Old England; Whigs in 1846 had denounced the war
to seize immense new western territories; and now Democrats attacked a Yankee war against the South that midway in its course also
became a war to free four million black Americans.

The Republicans directed the national government, guided the
conflict, dominated Congress, officered the army, and received the
soldier vote during the war and the veteran vote thereafter. Claiming then and afterward that theirs was the party of patriotism, Republicans fashioned both the policies and the means by which the
Union was reconstructed.[1] Though many Democrats supported the

fight to restore the Union, they assented to little else. "Peace Democrats" condemned the entire enterprise. Within the Republican
party there were many "Democratic-Republicans"—former Democrats who had joined the party in the realignments of the 1850s—and
strong efforts were made to hold them. In 1864 Lincoln renamed his
party the "National Union" party, selecting a former Jacksonian
Democrat from the South, Andrew Johnson of Tennessee, as his
running mate. The war effort, however, resulted in a strong national
surge toward policies of centralism that Democratic-Republicans instinctively opposed, and their allegiance to the Republican party
became ever more tenuous.[2]

Indeed, even by 1860 the Republican party, for all its gestures
toward the Democrats within its ranks, was being largely taken over
by former Whigs. All gubernatorial nominees in the Middle West on
the Republican ticket were ex-Whigs. The very mood in which the
North justified the need for going to war was Whiggish in temper.
Whigs had always called themselves the party of law and order.
Criminality, violence, and a disdain for law were said to be Democratic qualities. Now, in the secession crisis, Northern newspapers
said time and again that if secession were accepted, the country at
large would be overwhelmed by "disorder, anarchy, and a general
disrespect for democratic government." The *North American* in
Philadelphia greeted secession with the headline, "Lawlessness on a
Gigantic Scale." The firing on Fort Sumter was the capstone to these
events, for it was the ultimate challenge to lawful authority. Now,
throughout the North, warnings of anarchy multiplied. In Chicago:
"Without a Union that is free, without a Constitution that can be
enforced . . . our Republic ceases to be a government, our freedom
will be quickly supplanted by anarchy and despotism"; in Madison,
Wisconsin: "This contest is not so much about territorial limits as to
demonstrate whether we have government or not"; in Roxbury,
Massachusetts: "Every man instinctively feels that the moment has
at last arrived for crushing treason and asserting the supremacy of
law and the constitution"; in Cincinnati: "If [the] doctrine of secession as illustrated and enforced by [its] practice, is true, then there
is no such thing as government authority or social obligation. . . . *A
surrender to Secession is the suicide of government.*" A Philadelphia
newspaper called for establishing "the authority of the Constitution
and laws over violence and anarchy." Lifelong Democrat Robert J.
Walker, formerly Polk's secretary of the treasury, cried out to a rally
of 200,000 people at Union Square in New York City that "we must

resist and subdue [secession] or our government will be but an organized anarchy." The New York *Tribune* on April 17, 1861, put the
matter simply: "The Chief Business of the American people must be
proving that they have a Government, and that freedom is not another name for anarchy." If the Southern challenge were successful,
it would open the door to further secessions, and the whole nation
would break into fragments, taking self-government and republicanism with it into oblivion.[3]

This reaction, so instantaneous and widespread in the North, had
been in preparation for many years. Long before 1860, Northern
Whigs had been alarmed at what seemed to them to be dangerously
mounting levels of disorder in American life. Everywhere, angry
men were taking the law in their own hands. The rioting that had
erupted in Northern streets in the Jacksonian years and such events
as the assassination of the abolitionist Elijah Lovejoy awakened deep
fears that the republic was in danger. Unchecked individualism appeared to be evolving into so explosive a force that it would tear
apart the social order. There had been indeed a powerful anti-
institutionalist impulse within Jacksonian reformism. The old restric-
tive regime controlled by established elites was to be broken apart
so that ordinary individuals could be liberated from its restraints and
find new lives. Ralph Waldo Emerson and the Transcendentalists
preached an almost ecstatic individualism. Henry David Thoreau's
voice was but one of many crying for a kind of anarchistic personalism that would hold out against the corruptions of power and the
dead hand of government.

By the 1850s, a mood of caution and disillusion was emerging in
the North. Jacksonian reforms had not created the utopia that many
envisioned. Thousands of public schools now existed in the Northern
states, the prisons and the legal system had been liberalized in major
ways, the economy had been thrown open to individual initiative in
unprecedented fashion, the currency system had been transformed,
and yet the country still suffered from persistent social ills. When
Nathaniel Hawthorne, scoffing at reformism and insisting that un-
happiness and anxiety lay within human nature itself, turned away
from his Transcendentalist friends, he was taking a stance toward
which many in the North were moving. The events of the 1850s
intensified this mood. Urban violence seemed to be escalating as the
influx of Irish Catholics persisted, and from the South came violence
that was directly aimed at the nation itself. The fighting in Kansas

that broke out in the mid-1850s and seemed to go on endlessly convinced Northerners that Southerners intended to get their way by any means or destroy the republic.

From the Yankee intellectual community came ever more powerful appeals for a return to traditional ways. Congregational and Unitarian ministers, writers, and journalists called for order and concentration in public life, rather than diffusion and spontaneity. They condemned the anarchic personalism which seemed to be rending the nation and called sternly for strengthening those institutions which disciplined individual appetites and kept order: church, courts, and government. Even the national prophet of unrestrained individualism, Ralph Waldo Emerson, turned in the new direction. As the Republican party in the mid-1850s became a supremely Yankee organization, intellectuals in the Northern states joined in a rush. Among them were not only Emerson but the Transcendentalist philosopher Bronson Alcott; the editor of *Harper's Weekly,* George William Curtis; the editor of the *Atlantic Monthly,* James Russell Lowell; the Ohio poet William Dean Howells (in later years Lowell's successor as editor of the *Atlantic*); and E. L. Godkin, who in 1865 would found *The Nation*—for decades the most influential Republican journal.[4]

When secession occurred, Republican intellectuals were quick to support military coercion of the South, whose very nature, as Yankees, they had long condemned. Then, as scholars whose intellectual lineage reached back to John Adams and the Revolutionary New Englanders, they welcomed the fighting, not simply as a holy war against Southern slavery, but as a "chastening calamity" that would purge the Northern soul of its selfishness, materialism, and disorderly individualism. The Christian Sparta of which Sam Adams had long ago dreamed would be forged in the sufferings of a war whose fires would burn away the dross.

When in the first battle at Bull Run the Northern army was forced ignominiously to flee in panic—Congressmen, journalists, and hysterical soldiers stampeding in a pell-mell rush back to Washington— Yankee intellectuals were almost delighted. The disgrace, they said, would prove the folly of existing ways. It would induce discipline, obedience to those in lawful authority, and the submergence of individualism in the common enterprise. Horace Bushnell, a nationally prominent Congregational clergyman from Hartford, Connecticut, exulted that Bull Run was God's punishment for atheism and irreverence. As the war grew bloodier, he insisted that "adversity kills only where there is weakness to be killed. Real vigor is at once tested and fed by it." The army was a fine school, many said, for training Americans to take orders. With their Yankee urge to create that organic sense of community symbolized by traditional New England, Republican intellectuals responded warmly to war-induced centralization under a vigorous and powerful national government. They were especially fascinated by the promise that such an enhancement of the national government held out for the future. In this spirit, Emerson called for the creation of a national cultural authority to set standards of taste and fitness in literature and the arts.[5]

The war was not long in motion before the Republicans began turning away from Thomas Jefferson. "The first gun fired at Fort Sumter," Merrill D. Peterson has written, "smashed the old Union and with it the political design of Thomas Jefferson." Now the author of the Declaration of Independence was seen also as the author of the concept of states' rights. His ideas, never congenial to moralistic republicans, were once more viewed as an exhortation to anarchy in all aspects of life. Jefferson was replaced by Alexander Hamilton, rediscovered as the honored prophet of American nationalism. So obsure had he become in the long Jeffersonian and Jacksonian years that, when his name began appearing in dispatches from the United States, Englishmen were said to have asked in bewilderment who he was. "Have you thought what a vindication this war is of Alexander Hamilton?" asked George William Curtis. Certainly, "he was one of our truly great men, as Jefferson was the least of the truly great." Books appeared telling of Hamilton's life and ideas; Republicans studied his works; and he emerged as "nation-builder" where Jefferson was seen as "nation-destroyer."[6]

If the Republicans directed the Civil War in a mood of moralistic republicanism, its immense demands upon the North opened the door to that nationalist republicanism that was their Federalist and Whig inheritance. Midway in its course, the conflict had become a revolutionary force in Northern life. Raising, equipping, supplying, and transporting an armed force of more than a million men taught Northerners lessons of efficient social organization that Northern entrepreneurs and Republican leaders never forgot. Large-scale economic enterprises directed from central locations emerged out of the chaos of thousands of localized businesses with which the North had entered the struggle. Plan and system, and a recognizably modern economic system, made their appearance.[7] It was a spectacle Henry Clay would have greeted enthusiastically.

The Union government, which needed money in huge quantities, was directed by men who for many years had advocated a national banking system. The result was a revolution in the country's banking and currency arrangements. For twenty years the Democrats had ensured that banking questions were kept in the states. Now the federal capital took them up once again. The ideological battle lines were familiar. Democrats, in classic Jacksonian style, were hostile to banks and bankers and fearful of price inflation. They continued to believe in sound currency and insisted that Congress had no powers either to authorize a national paper currency or to charter banks. In 1862, however, the Republican-dominated Congress voted the creation of a national currency. Hundreds of millions of dollars in "greenbacks" were issued—and promptly stigmatized by Democrats as "rag money." The epithet was not wholly inaccurate, for the greenbacks were issued without backing in gold (i.e., they were not convertible to gold upon demand) but were based simply upon the federal government's assurance that they were "legal tender" for all debts, public and private.

The Republicans created a national banking system during the war, but not around the concept of a central "national bank." Rather, their legislation authorized the federal chartering of existing state-chartered banks, designating them "national banks" and empowering them to issue currency (convertible upon demand into gold) according to the amount of federal bonds they purchased. Then the paper money issued by the more than sixteen hundred state-chartered banks under the authority of state-originated chartering documents was taxed out of existence. By this stroke, the United States finally came into the possession of a single national currency.

This was not conceived simply as a wartime measure to raise money (the system by its provisions created an instant market for federal bonds). Instead, Republican leaders envisioned the new banking and currency systems as permanent contributions toward building that stronger, more unified national community of which nationalist republicans had always dreamed. By "so simple and popular a measure as that of a National Currency," observed Republican Senator John Sherman of Ohio, "[we] teach the people that we are a Nation. . . . If we [are] . . . dependent upon the United States for a currency and a medium of exchange, we would have a broader and more prosperous nationality." The long argument over national banking policy, with all that it implied concerning localism and nationalism, was finally concluded in a Yankee victory. The new system that the Republicans created would survive with little change for half a century.[8]

The Republican Thirty-seventh Congress then went on to complete what Leonard P. Curry has called its "blueprint for modern America." It erected a protective tariff; passed the Pacific Railroad Act to build a line to the Pacific Coast, thus taking steps both to unify the nation and to provide further lavish government assistance to corporations over the succeeding years; and by means of federal land grants prevailed upon the states to establish public universities devoted to teaching the agricultural, mechanical, and liberal arts. These land grant universities were essentially an elitist achievement, for the people at large had not asked for them. Most Americans were hostile to higher education as aristocratic and impractical, and they distrusted intellectuals and scientists. So, rather than the people, it was the college-bred Yankee leadership of the Republican party that gave the program impetus. The purpose of the universities was to train an educated national leadership and to provide the experts and professionals needed to direct the industrial system whose growth the Republican program was designed to stimulate. Upon completion of this historic spate of lawmaking, Senator Sherman remarked that the new enactments "will be a monument of evil or of good. They cover such vast sums, delegate and regulate such vast powers, and are so far-reaching in their effects, that generations will be affected well or ill by them."[9]

The two-party system did not die during the Civil War, but remained fully alive. The Democratic party, strong and active despite the constant charge that it was the party of traitors, both North and South, dropped only to a 43.8 percent share of the Northern vote even in 1872, its lowest post-1860 point.[10] Voters kept voting the Democratic ticket because they were hostile to the war or because they were alarmed by the swift strides toward national centralization taken by the Republicans in Washington. Above all, Democrats were able to keep up their voting strength in the Northern states because so many thousands hated black Americans and detested the idea of abolition. Peace Democrats, alive to this sentiment, warned that abolition was certain to choke Northern labor markets with freed slaves. Thus, they called up an anxiety that had long circulated within the Northern working class. When the Emancipation Proclamation was issued, the Sheboygan, Wisconsin, *Journal,* in words that echoed hundreds of similarly negrophobic editorials in the Middle West, burst out in harsh condemnation:

> All the support the war has ever received from the Democrats was originally obtained by a base cheat, an infamous swindle, a damnable deception. . . . The Democratic party trusted and was betrayed. "The war for the Union" was cordially supported by Democrats all over the North. It turned out to be a war of abolition, of violation of the Constitution, a war by the Eastern oligarchy.[11]

The war brought many dramatic changes to the Northern states, changes that Peace Democrats—called "Copperheads" by their Republican enemies—resisted bitterly: threats of racial equality, a powerful central government, the violation of states' rights, swift victories for industrialists and financiers in the form of high tariffs and the new national currency and banking legislation, and a President who made free use of his powers as Commander in Chief to imprison his critics and keep them confined without habeas corpus. The greatest strength of the Copperhead movement lay in Ohio, Indiana, and Illinois, where Peace Democrats could draw heavily upon what was called the "Butternut Democracy": those rural areas in the lower Middle West settled predominantly by Southerners who used the bark of the butternut tree to color their homespun clothes. Usually Methodists or Baptists of Southern rather than Yankee origins, Butternut Democrats were held in contempt by Republicans. In return Butternut Democrats hated Yankee Congregationalists and blamed them bitterly for the war and its sufferings.[12]

Clement Vallandigham, the Ohio Democratic congressman who gave a spectacular national leadership to the Peace Democrats, assailed the Yankees vigorously, saying that he was "inexorably hostile to Puritan domination in religion or morals or literature or politics." When Congress passed the Morrill Tariff of 1862, Vallandigham, along with the Democratic newspapers of the Middle West, attacked the tariff as a graphic demonstration of what would happen to the western states in a nation dominated by New England. "She is determined," observed the Cincinnati *Enquirer,* "that the whole country shall be subservient to the interests of her manufacturers; and, having driven the South out of the Union, she wants additional burdens put upon the West to make up for the loss of the Southern market."[13]*

German-language and Irish-Catholic newspapers, firmly Democratic, played upon the theme that New England Puritans wanted to make their own church the church of the entire nation. The fact that Congregational clergymen were so vocal and prominent in the leadership of the Republican party ensured that Irish and German Catholics would hold to their Democratic loyalties. The military draft, which was instituted in 1863, created an enormous uproar, for through conscription the Yankees were apparently forcing Democrats to carry out their national goal: the freeing of the blacks. The draft law was in fact class legislation and unfair to the predominantly immigrant poor, for it allowed anyone with three hundred dollars to buy an exemption. Enforcement of conscription led to wholesale arrests for draft resistance in Kentucky, Missouri, and states in the Middle West. Defiant Democrats nominated imprisoned resisters for public office, read the Declaration of Independence at antidraft rallies, and gave heroes' welcomes to freed prisoners upon their return to their homes.[14]

In the cities, the Irish Catholics were the backbone of the Copper-

*Received too late for use in the writing of this narrative is a valuable new work by Joel H. Silbey, *A Respectable Minority: The Democratic Party in the Civil War Era, 1860–1868* (New York, 1977). Though by design he does not seek to explore the party's ethnic and other cultural roots, Silbey confirms the picture given here of the wartime Democrats' anger at "the Puritan spirit of New England"; at the encroachments of federal power upon liberty, states' rights, and freedom; at the Republicans' "radicalism"; at Lincoln and his "nigger-crazed counselors" (p. 81); and at the drive not simply to "scatter" the rebel armies, but to transform the South. Those whom Silbey terms "Legitimists" were willing to support the war (thus serving as a "legitimate" loyal opposition) if little else, but "Purists" condemned the war as an obstacle to peace and opposed the Republicans' every policy. "The peace group was convinced that the Legitimists deluded themselves if they believed it possible to support the war and still preserve the Constitution" (p. 102). As to voting strength, the Democratic party's surprising ability to continue to attract voters is the key point to remark. This was primarily due, Silbey believes, to what he calls the "partisan imperative"; that is, a habitual, traditional loyalty to one's party that by these years had developed a power of its own. Thus, the outstanding characteristic of "Northern voter behavior in the Civil War years was that the electorate had neither fragmented nor become volatile. Neither the geography of each party's vote nor its size relative to the other had moved markedly. There had been little conversion of voters to new political habits. . . . When people cast their ballots they remained in accustomed partisan grooves. . . . By 1860 the electorate had become locked in" (pp. 156–157). That is, the great realignments of the mid-1850s were completed, and the third, or Civil War, party system simply endured in its essential form through the conflict and the succeeding decades.

head movement, and they led the protests against the draft. Though they had volunteered by the thousands in the early stages of the war, they now recoiled. Bringing with them from Ireland an ancient distrust of governments directed by Englishmen, they refused to be coerced by Yankees into fighting a war that had become a struggle to free a race whom they hated. Irish Catholics had always been especially violent in their opposition to abolition, and in their present mood they set off antiblack riots in Detroit, Chicago, and Cincinnati. Terrorism in Ireland had been their only means of fighting back against their enemies, and now they reverted to traditional tactics. Rioting, in fact, had been endemic in New York City since their arrival in the 1830s, and it was to recur frequently until the 1870s, with especially fierce fighting between Protestant Irishmen and their Catholic countrymen. Slum gangs fought constantly, and battles raged between competing fire companies. Indeed, communal violence was so incessant that thousands of Catholics regularly guarded their churches. During the war, they had the warm support of newspapers in their homeland, where the treatment of the Catholic Irish was watched with consuming interest. "Our countrymen," said the *Cork Examiner* in autumn, 1872, "have played the part of the dwarf in this war, to the giant—the Native Americans—the Know-Nothings —the abolitionists. They have fought the battles, got the blows, and bear the wounds, while their companions receive the glory and the plunder." In these circumstances, when the draft was inaugurated in mid-July 1863, the Irish Catholics set off a riot in New York City that raged for a week, the bloodiest race riot of the century.[15]

Abolitionists subjected the Irish to continual barrages of derision. Among the Northern elite, Irish opposition to abolition almost by itself made that cause fashionable. If the Irish were opposed to the blacks, what educated Protestant gentleman and lady could not be for them? Yankee intellectuals became obsessed by Irish "disloyalty." They attacked the Copperheads, supported campaigns to throw them into jail, and established "Loyal Publication Societies." A flood of sermons, speeches, and articles demanded absolute and unqualified loyalty to the United States government. The President, it was now said, must be obeyed, right or wrong, for he was responsible only to God. Government by consent, it was asserted, was a meaningless abstraction.[16]

The war ended with Republicans talking exultantly of "the nation" and speaking the language of a triumphant centralism. "I turn," said the Republican scientist John W. Draper, "from the hideous contemplation of a disorganization of the Republic, each state, and county, and town setting up for itself . . . to a future [of] . . . an imperial race organizing its intellect, concentrating it, and voluntarily submitting to be controlled by its reason." When E. L. Godkin founded his new magazine to lead Republican opinion, its name, *The Nation,* sprang instantly to his mind. For the Republican clergy, the rebirth of the American republic after years of war and disunion opened the vision of a New Jerusalem, "the glory of our age and country, and the marvel of the civilized world." "A new nation has been born," said the chaplain of the House of Representatives, "a nation that embodies . . . the spirit of the Gospel." Across the Atlantic, members of Britain's Liberal party viewed the United States and the Republican party with enthusiastic approval, for they had apparently proved the vigor of democratic government and of liberty. The North's victory, it was said in England, was "the event of the age. The friends of freedom everywhere should thank God and take courage."[17]

Radical Republicans now had before them the task for which their past had prepared them: remaking the South in the Yankee image. As soon as the war had begun, the question of reconstruction had been immediately agitated in the North, and throughout the four years of fighting the issue had rarely receded from center stage.[18] The Lower North was essentially concerned with bringing the errant states back into the Union in an atmosphere that would foster harmony between Northern and Southern whites now that slavery had been ended. But for those of a more Yankee outlook, the chief objective of the war had not been to rebuild what had existed before but to transform Southern society. It was this desire to remake the South in some fundamental sense that identified politicians as *radical* Republicans. Within that world of radical politics, abolitionists remained as active in the cause of justice for black people during and after the war as they had been in the antebellum years.[19]

Radical Reconstruction, therefore, was undertaken in a mood of triumphant Yankeeism. As the Congregationalist *Independent,* the most influential religious periodical in Yankeedom, put the issue, "There is one, and only one, sure and safe policy for the immediate future, namely: the North must remain the absolute Dictator of the Republic until the spirit of the North shall become the spirit of the whole country." "It is intended," said caustic, passionate Thaddeus Stevens, New England–born leader of the Radical Republicans in the House, "to revolutionize [the South's] . . . principles and feelings . . . [to] work a radical reorganization in Southern institutions, habits, and manners."[20]

The events of Reconstruction are familiar and often told: President
Andrew Johnson's abortive attempt in 1865 to reconstruct swiftly the
Southern states on the basis of white supremacy and black exclusion;
the massive response of Northern voters in the election of 1866,
angered at the apparent revival of arrogant white Southernism and
concerned that black Southerners not be thrust back into a form of
involuntary servitude; and the establishment, primarily under the
control of moderate Republicans, of what history has come to call
"Radical Reconstruction." These events led to the creation, under
military controls, of new state governments in the South founded in
black as well as white voters, the continuance of the Freedmen's
Bureau, the building of thousands of schools and hospitals, and the
emergence of a Republican party in the South, which in several
states achieved a brief ascendancy.[21]

The Yankee thrust of this extraordinary campaign was abundantly
clear. The building of public schools was a direct expression of this
impulse: an attempt to re-create in the South the basic building block
of Yankee democracy. The New England town system of local government was even pressed upon South Carolina. In Willie Lee Rose's
Rehearsal for Reconstruction: The Port Royal Experiment (1967), we
are able to follow the Yankee impulse at work from its high expectations at the outset of Reconstruction to its final defeat. "Gone were
the grand claims," she writes, "of making a new New England of the
South" as Reconstruction faded. By 1870 the burst of Radical reform
in the South had passed its peak. In 1877 all occupying troops were
withdrawn from the few states where they still remained, and the
South and its race relations were returned to the hands of Southern
whites.[22]

Through all of these years, the crucial question for Republicans to
solve was a deceptively simple one: What was to be done with the
freed slaves? Republicans deplored the Black Codes, enacted by the
state governments that President Johnson had briefly erected, for
they established a form of quasi-slavery denying black people freedom of movement, excluding them from many occupations, denying
them the vote and equality before the law, and thus giving whites
complete dominance. But if what the Southern whites had in mind
for the freed slaves was not to be allowed, what was in fact to follow?
This was an enormously difficult dilemma for Republicans to resolve
in any consistent way. It filled the Yankee mind with contradictions
and misgivings and clouded the Reconstruction years with agonized
doubts and erratic swervings. In some sense, Republicans were
agreed that black and white Southerners must be placed on an equal
footing, but they did not know exactly in what way. The topic was

clearly political dynamite in the Northern states. In the fall elections that had followed Lincoln's issuance of the Emancipation Proclamation in 1863, Republicans had lost disastrously at the polls. Everywhere north of the Mason-Dixon line was the brooding fear, constantly verbalized by Democrats, that emancipation would flood the North with freed slaves. This possibility appalled Northerners, for, despite their opposition to slavery, they remained fundamentally racist and segregationist, with few and scattered exceptions.[23]

"*Equality before the law* is to be the great cornerstone," said Isaac N. Arnold, a leading Republican in Illinois, and this expressed succinctly the position upon which Republicans could generally agree.[24] They had a genuine concern for black Americans, had thought slavery repugnant, and were deeply moved after the war by news of atrocities committed against black Southerners by vengeful whites. Such reports accentuated Northern fears of a black inundation, for they raised the possibility that the former slaves would be driven northward by the oppression. Few Northerners agreed with Thaddeus Stevens and Charles Sumner, who so sympathized with the plight of black Americans that they wanted to grant full and complete equality. At the least, however, Northern whites wished the blacks' situation improved sufficiently to keep them in the South. Salmon P. Chase, Lincoln's secretary of the treasury and chief justice of the United States from 1864 to 1873, believed that if conditions in the South could be made attractive enough for the black Americans, those in the North might flee the prejudice they encountered there and return to their "natural and congenial environment" in the South.[25]

Equality before the law, to Republicans, meant insuring black persons' civil rights. They should not be subject to special legal restrictions not applicable to whites. They should be able to testify in court, sit on juries, move freely about the country, take up any occupation, and give up one job for another. No crimes should exist for which only black persons would be arrested and imprisoned, and when convicted of crimes, their punishment should be the same as that given to whites. Freedmen should be able to own land, in whatever part of the country they chose. They should not be singled out for imprisonment for unpaid debts, and when in prison, they should not be hired out to labor. Apprenticeship laws should not be so drawn up to limit their freedom, and curfew and vagrancy laws especially designed to apply to black people should be inadmissible.

Republicans were also in reasonable agreement that there should be not only civil equality but equality in politics and government.

Black Southerners, as American citizens, should be free to vote, to work in public causes, to stand for and be elected to public office, and to hold government positions. A few Radical Republicans went even further: they supported social equality as well, in personal relationships, schooling, housing, and public accommodations. Most radical of all was the demand, emanating from those Radical Republicans among whose leadership former abolitionists were prominent, that a solid base for economic equality be established. This would require more than providing schools and skills to freedmen. It would require the confiscation of rebel-owned plantations to give them land. Such schemes, however, attempted only in a few locations, did not meet with lasting success.

Southern whites responded to Radical Reconstruction with accusations of hypocrisy. When the Republican-dominated Pennsylvania legislature turned down by more than a two-to-one vote a proposal for giving the franchise to blacks in that state, the Southern white community bitterly ridiculed this action, for at that moment it was having black suffrage forced upon it by the Radical Republican federal Congress.[26] Northern Democrats joined this outcry of condemnation. Samuel Tilden, now chairman of the Democratic party in New York, insisted that the whole enterprise of Radical Reconstruction aimed, not at uplifting the black person, but at giving Yankees full power to run the country in their characteristic dictatorial style. "The grim Puritan of New England," he said, "whose only child, whose solitary daughter is already listening to the soft music of [an Irish] . . . wooer . . . stretches his hand down along the Atlantic coast to the receding and decaying African and says: 'Come, let us rule this continent together.' "[27]

When in 1870 the Fifteenth Amendment was ratified, making it illegal to keep the vote from any American citizen on the ground of race (disfranchisement on other grounds being specifically left open), Northern Republicans regarded their crusade as nobly finished. Black Americans had civil rights under the Fourteenth Amendment, and now they had and presumably would keep the ballot. Schools were being widely provided. In short, black people had their "equal chance." It was now up to them, in what Republicans confidently believed to be traditional American fashion, to fend for themselves, to become "self-made men."[28]

About all of these matters we have been abundantly informed. What is less noticed, however, is that Radical Reconstruction was not concerned simply with black Southerners. It had another large objective: the reconstruction of Southern *white* society. The Civil War had been fought in good part to put down "Southernism," an attitude of mind that existed in the white community. The reunited nation could not look to the future in confidence, however, if the way of thinking that had led to secession and war were allowed to persist. Yankees had always believed that if slavery could be terminated, the Southern whites could be taught to build a progressive society founded on the virtues of diligence, austerity, frugality, and, above all, hard work. "The conversion of the Southern whites to the ways and ideas of what is called the industrial stage in social progress," observed E. L. Godkin, was a "formidable task." But it must go forward, mockingly said Horatio Seymour—a former Democratic governor of New York and the party's presidential candidate in 1868 —"until [the South's] ideas of business, industry, money making, spindles and looms were in accord with those of Massachusetts." In C. Vann Woodward's words, Southern whites were urged to "put behind them the 'irrationality' of the Old Order, outmoded notions of honor, chivalry, paternalism, pride of status, and noblesse oblige, together with all associated habits of indolence, extravagance, idle sports, and postures of leisure and enjoyment."[29]

Within the South there was a strong cultural base for the new outlook to build upon, for the Other South had always leaned toward Yankee values. It is usually little noted that within the borders of what became the Confederacy, 49 percent of those casting ballots in the 1860 presidential election had voted either for John Bell (Constitutional Union candidate) or for Stephen A. Douglas (Northern Democratic candidate), thus implicitly rejecting disunion. Thousands of white Southerners—almost ninety regiments—had served in the Union army during the Civil War, a gesture reminiscent of the Loyalists during the Revolution. Appalachia had remained a hotbed of Unionism during the conflict. West Virginia had separated from Virginia in order to form a separate state and remain with the North, and eastern Tennessee had been practically in a state of insurrection against the Confederate government. The first congressional elections to the Confederate Congress had sent two former Whigs to that body for every three Democrats, and during the Civil War the Democratic party in the South rapidly lost favor with the voters. Former Whigs probably commanded a majority in the Confederate Congress from 1863 onward, and they swept to victory in North Carolina, traditionally the most Unionist of the Southern seaboard states.[30]

The Civil War in important ways had been as revolutionary an experience for the South as it had been for the North, for its every impulse had thrust Southern life away from tradition and toward modernization. "The very acts of making a nation and fighting a war," Emory Thomas remarks, "constituted an external revolution. . . . [Then] the external revolution, the revolt against Yankee ways and a Yankee Union . . . wrought an internal revolution." It had been necessary to create a strong central government, readying Southerners for an enhanced centralism after the conflict. An army had to be raised, troops conscripted, martial rule established, and the economy closely managed. In "terms of industrial strength the Confederacy was born with little and died with less," but between 1860 and 1865 "the Southern economy experienced a period of intense industrial growth . . . [that accomplished] little short of an industrial revolution. . . . At the end the supposedly agrarian nation had supplied its principal army with no food, but there were seventy-five rounds of manufactured ammunition for each man." During the Civil War, in reluctant recognition of the South's needs, Jefferson Davis not only had fostered manufacturing and centralized governing institutions but had turned away from the Southern Rights activists and the plantation gentlemen to give authority to those former Whigs who came from the business community.[31]

To the North's appeal at the war's end that the South take on Northern virtues, the Southern business community burst "into effusions of assent and hosannas of delivery."[32] To distinguish themselves from the Radical Republicans of the North and the Democrats of the South, who during the war had often been called "radicals," Southern Whigs took the name "Conservatives." When in 1869 the Conservatives won control of the Virginia state government, the newly elected governor, who felt a close affinity to the Northern party of industrialization and progress, suggested that his party take on the name "Liberal Republicans." While in office, Virginia Conservatives worked hard to foster industry and "the economic regeneration of Virginia on Northern capitalist lines."

With many young Confederate army officers in their leadership, the Conservatives separated from traditionalism and the old Southern slogans. They proclaimed their loyalty to the American Union, supported free public schools for whites and blacks, and even advocated a modicum of civil rights for the freed slaves. In national elections Conservatives aligned themselves with the Northern Democrats, for Radical Republicanism was categorically rejected by most Southern whites as too Yankee and too problack. The Conservatives of Virginia, however, were clearly reborn Whigs and in essential matters more Yankee in outlook than the antebellum Whigs whose role in Southern life they were now taking.[33]

A Republican party also sprang into being in the South after 1867, during the period when Radical Reconstruction installed military occupation and gave the vote to freed slaves. The party was primarily black, but thousands of white Southerners also joined—that is, became "scalawags"—making up perhaps one-fifth of the white vote. The whites who became Southern Republicans were often men from poor counties, with little former reputation in government. Angry at the old elite, they condemned the "bombastic, high falutin, aristocratic fools" who had dragged the South into a disastrous war and had driven "negroes and poor helpless white people until they think they can control the world of mankind." Many of these new Republicans doubtless came from the parts of the South where resistance to Confederate authority had been strongest: the pine barrens, the swamps, and the hill country of Appalachia. They firmly approved of Republican notions of economic development sponsored by governmental assistance; they wanted railroads and jobs; and they called for social reforms. The Reconstruction governments that they controlled in the South made local government more democratic and spread free public education, as much or more a boon to poor whites as it was to poor blacks.[34]

Scalawags saw Republicanism sweeping into the South as the wave of the future, and they joined it in the conviction that its supremacy was lasting. Especially after Ulysses Grant won his sweeping victory in the presidential election of 1868, the new regime seemed a fixed element in Southern life. By the mid-1870s, however, the North lost its interest in reforming the South, and Republicanism in that region began its lengthy decline into a position of permanent minority. The Democratic party, with the adherence of the South's Conservatives, swept back into control of the Southern states as the symbol of white supremacy and Southern identity. Nonetheless, thousands of white Southerners were to continue voting Republican until well into the twentieth century. The one-party "Solid South," traditionally thought to have appeared at the end of Reconstruction, in fact took many years to evolve. It required a massive disfranchisement of black voters in the 1890s and thereafter the establishment of a white primary system to complete the transformation.[35]

The immediate postwar years were an exciting period for young Northern Republicans like Henry Adams, grandson and great-grandson of Presidents. The United States, they believed, was now entering upon a new day of reform and national vitalization under the leadership of the victorious Republican party. Never comfortable with the localized and disorderly nation of Jeffersonian ideology, they were inspired by the new vision of a unified country under strong central direction. In such a reborn United States, the role they conceived for themselves, as young Yankees of education, good family, and moral sensitivity, was to provide intellectual guidance through a dynamic Republican party. Henry Adams had spent the war years in England—where his father, Charles Francis Adams, had been the American ambassador to Britain—observing in and around Parliament and Whitehall the brilliant young Liberals who helped to guide and govern the British empire. Now, writing home in an exultant mood, Adams declared, "We want a national set of young men like ourselves or better to start new influences not only in politics, but in literature, in law, in society, and throughout the whole social organism of the country—a national school of our own generation."[36]

E. L. Godkin shared these great hopes. A Protestant Irishman, he had arrived in the United States in the 1850s as a firm disciple of William Gladstone and British Liberalism. He had gravitated to the Republicans because, he said, they were "the party of good government, of virtue, of knowledge, and understanding"—a position understandable in a man who must have watched with distaste as Irish Catholics flocked into Democratic ranks. The Democrats, Godkin went on, were the party of "the most ignorant and vicious elements in the community." John Stuart Mill, the philosopher of Liberalism, wrote to him from England in encouragement, saying that "the great concussion which has taken place in the American mind must have loosened the foundations of all prejudices, and secured a fair hearing for impartial reason on all subjects such as it might not otherwise have had for many generations."[37]

The immediate problem that called for centrally directed reform was that of the South. However, young Radical Republicans paid close attention to their own Northern states as well. In this undertaking, the shaping influence was often not so much the socially conscious Unitarianism that had impelled Charles Sumner, or transatlantic Liberalism and the example of Britain, as it was the war itself and modern science. Having served as commissioned officers, men like the Middle Westerner James A. Garfield, a man of firm Yankee lineage, had been trained in discipline, responsibility, corporate loyalty, and logical organization. Toughened by what they had seen and experienced, they had become men of purposive achievement. In states like Ohio, they worked hard to reshape the structure of the postwar Republican party along these lines.[38]

Radical Reconstruction, in such hands, was firmly statist. Radical Republicans thought it quite proper that white Southerners should have governments imposed upon them that they had not chosen. In the North, they were ready to use similar centralizing tactics to find the means for ending waste through social efficiency. The New York City scientist-physician John Draper, who directed the medical school of the University of the City of New York, typified the kind of Radical Republican who would be prominent in this effort. He wrote lengthy books on the conflict between science and religion and insisted that scientists and technicians must take the role in public life formerly occupied by clergymen. August Comte, not yet a decade in his grave, had called in France for the elevation of what he called a Positivist priesthood of this scientific type to take over the direction of the state. Now, in America, the same appeal was being heard.

In the Northern states, the most ambitious of the Radical Republican campaigns to bring order and system into local institutions took place in Draper's state of New York. New York City, with its teeming immigrant population, corruption, appalling disease rates, congestion, crime, and tragic vulnerability to fire, both fascinated and alarmed the Radical Republican mentality. The city, of course, was too overwhelmingly immigrant and Democratic to be effectively governed by Republicans. There was another avenue open, however, and Radical Republicans quickly put it to use. Since American cities did not yet have home rule—nor were they to have it for many decades—they could be governed through the state capitals. Here, in the legislatures, the native Protestant Americans of the countryside and small towns had a disproportionate weight of representation, based upon earlier distributions of population. Their hatred of the city, with its Catholic immigrants and its saloons, was traditional, and they produced consistently strong Republican, antiurban majorities. With this force behind them, Radical Republicans gained control of Albany and began reconstructing New York City.[39]

First the city's police force was regularized and placed under public authority. Then the fire-fighting system was transformed from a volunteer force into a paid, centrally directed system. This made for much more efficient fire control, lowered taxes, and provided a better-equipped force. However, the changes set off a political uproar among the Irish Catholics. Volunteer fire departments were integral elements in Democratic ward organizations. They provided impromptu living accommodations for party workers and a promotion ladder by which the most talented could be selected for the party hierarchy. Fire companies fought with each other over factional rivalries within Democratic politics and were closely identified with particular bosses.

Democrats of all varieties attacked the Republican tactic of using the Albany legislature to control New York City affairs, saying that it mirrored the controls being exerted over the defeated Southern states by the Republican-dominated government in Washington. In both cases, Democrats insisted, local rights were being overborne by autocratic centralism. The Radical Republican crusade, however, continued, involving statewide as well as urban reforms. With the urging of the ex-Democrats within their party, Republicans enacted far-reaching reforms in New York's public education system, making the schools more accessible to the poor, expanding facilities for teacher education, and founding Cornell University—partially as a land-grant institution—along the model of the "new universities." Cornell was to be removed from sectarian influences; to stress the sciences, modern history, the most advanced studies; and to be rationalistic in temper.

At the same time, a determined assault was made upon disease in New York City, reputedly western civilization's filthiest city. Open sewers, tanning yards, roaming hogs, broken outhouse vaults spewing waste into yards and alleys, mounds of organic waste in the streets erratically and indifferently hauled away by private contractors (whose contracts were political plums), thousands dying annually from disease: to Radical Republicans these conditions cried out for reform. From the immigrant wards, however, came strong Democratic protests. The germ theory of disease, only recently developed by Louis Pasteur, was widely thought ridiculous. Democrats found the notion of Republican physicians from elite colleges running the city in presumed accordance with scientific knowledge highly offensive and distrusted their motives. They fought fiercely to have laymen, rather than professionals, in control of public health. Despite this resistance, a pioneering sanitary district and board of health was established in New York, which began an immediate city cleanup and achieved dramatic reductions in disease. Following this, an eight-hour law for workingmen was enacted (although relatively weak and ineffective), and measures were passed to reform congested living conditions in the tenements.[40]

This burst of reform ended when Radical Republicans proposed to the voters a new state constitution that would give the vote to black

New Yorkers. "The 'great mission' of the Republican Party," said the Democrats' leading newspaper, the New York *World,* was "to erase the word *white* from the vocabulary of politics." Since Radicals at the same time were proposing that the period of residence required for immigrant aliens to receive citizenship be lengthened, the instinctive Know-Nothingism that Democrats had always accused them of harboring seemed exposed. The proposed constitution was turned down in 1869 by the voters, Democrats took control of the state legislature, and the Radical Republican experiment in state centralism and the use of experts in social reforms was terminated.

New York City Democrats dulled the impact of the health regulations and ended enforcement of the Tenement House Law. The notion of an efficient civil service had been inaugurated by the Republicans within the new agencies, but the Irish had angrily denounced the idea as an assault against democracy, local self-government, and the poor, whose lack of education would keep them from passing tests of fitness. Boss politics was restored. Meanwhile, regular Republicans observed with some asperity that reformism did not attract Democratic votes, as the young Radicals had forecast. In fact, especially when applied to race relations, reformism lost elections. Regular Republicans swung, therefore, in other directions: toward helping the business community and the railroads and receiving in return their financial support.[41]

As the 1870s proceeded, humanitarian impulses faded rapidly in the Northern states. For most Americans, the Civil War had drained away the spirit that had inspired abolitionism and the holy Yankee crusade against Southernism. The conflict's enormity simply had left them exhausted. After the sharp anti-Southern impulse of the 1866 congressional election, which had triggered Radical Reconstruction, Northerners wanted only to get on with the business of their own private lives. In 1873 Mark Twain and Charles Dudley Warner published a novel whose title historians now take to represent the entire period of the 1870s and 1880s: *The Gilded Age.* Although the title implies that this was a period of shallow glitter and mercenary appetites, for most Americans these years were characterized by a struggle to rise from poverty, open the nation's still little-tapped resources, and build a better life.

Charles Darwin's *Origin of Species,* which had appeared in 1859 just before the war, had a profound influence upon the Northern educated mind because it seemed to describe with arresting accuracy the trends actually at work in American life. Capturing the new universities and the journals of opinion, Darwinism predisposed those influenced by its hypotheses to turn away from further social reforms. Natural selection and evolution convinced them that the wisest course would be to require the disadvantaged of whatever race and culture to solve their own problems without government aid. Charles Sumner sensed early in the postwar years a shift in his party's mood. Its affairs were drifting into the hands of men "whom Sumner did not understand and for most of whom he had little liking." He had conceived political parties to be justified only as instruments to achieve high moral reforms, but the new Republicans were party men who thought only of patronage, contracts, and discreet graft. In the best of circumstances, the United States had never been comfortable with the Puritans. They demanded too much of human nature and were too confident of their superior virtue. Now the Republican party was taken over by public men who stressed the need for practicality and for close ties between government and business. Sumner watched the nomination of Ulysses S. Grant in 1868 and remarked that the event would begin "the gradual disintegration of the Republican party."[42]

The Republican party became, in any event, a different party than the one Sumner had known. Giving way to the demands for vigorous economic development, the Republican party by the 1870s was so deeply involved with the country's entrepreneurs that an odor of corruption pervaded the nation. At every level of government, from Grant's White House to a thousand city halls, the buying of favors seemed to be imperiling the American experiment in democracy. Of all politicians, the Yankee Republicans experienced the greatest difficulties and conflicts as they observed this ugly spectacle in which their own party was so deeply implicated. As we have seen, there had always been an ambivalence toward wealth and power among New Englanders. The part of them that was Yankee applauded industrious, productive enterprise encouraged and guided by a strong central government. John Quincy Adams, with his Kentucky lieutenant Henry Clay, had labored for this cause while President at great cost to his national reputation. The part of them that was Puritan, however, recoiled from avarice and luxury, sought to discipline such appetites, and preached the politics of civic virtue. In the Revolutionary years, Yankee republicans had been appalled at the political corruption that had flourished in London, for it had seemed not only an offense to public morals but the means by which Tories undermined liberty and lined their pockets. By buying votes in Parliament, the status and powers of that body had been diminished, while the royal ministry had grown ever more aggressive and authoritarian. It had been in part to keep out this corrupt system, which linked government and greedy capitalists, that Yankees had become rebels. In later years, it had been inevitable that John Adams and Alexander Hamilton would rend the Federalist party between them, for an Adams could not have helped but find distasteful the elegant Hamiltons of this world, with their frilled shirts and high aristocratic style, their close links to wealth, bankers, and speculative enterprise.

After 1800 Liberal Congregationalism (i.e., what was eventually to be called Unitarianism) had taken over the church in Massachusetts and spread through the younger elite. With it had gone a kind of social moralism that had been wider in its concerns than the obsession with private morals that had absorbed most moralistic republicans. In the Jacksonian years a small but highly visible company of Yankee intellectuals in New England had begun calling for social reforms. With William Ellery Channing, they had fought such social evils as slavery, maltreatment of the insane, illiteracy, and cruelty in the prisons. In so doing they had been much closer in spirit to Thomas Jefferson, the classic social moralist—and also a Unitarian—than to Alexander Hamilton. They had grown understandably impatient with the Whig party for its refusal to fight the anti-Southern cause. Never good party men, since they had prized principle and independence more highly than partisan loyalty, Yankee intellectuals had remained for a while as restive Conscience Whigs and then had begun searching within the Liberty party and the Free Soil movement for a morally more responsible role. There had been powerful cultural reasons why such men could not have become Democrats: they could not have joined the Catholics, Baptists, Southerners, Anglophobes, and Manifest Destiny enthusiasts in that party. Yet Charles Sumner's anger at the indifference of the Whigs to social oppression finally had led him, before the war, to move into close relations with Northern Democrats, who helped elect him to the Senate.

Then came the creation of the Republican party, satisfyingly anti-Southern in its outlook, and the war itself, riveting Yankees within that party. In these years, British Liberals could reasonably regard the Republicans as their counterparts, as Godkin's gravitation to the Republican party after his migration to the United States demonstrates. But in the Gilded Age, as the social moralism of the Republican party faded and an aura of corruption and involvement with venal capitalists took its place, the partisan location of the Yankee Republicans became increasingly uncertain. In the mid-1870s they took the name "Independent Republican" and once more began to search for a role in American life that would let them work for a more enlightened social order. In 1872, unable to accept Ulysses Grant on the Republican ticket for a second term, some of them staged an abortive revolt, forming the "Liberal Republican" party. In confused and ultimately disastrous circumstances, the Liberal Republicans joined forces with the Democrats; that is, they jointly chose as their presidential nominee the quixotic Horace Greeley. The result was politically catastrophic. Greeley was known as an advocate of temperance, women's rights, black equality, and a variety of socialism. To most voting Americans, he was impossibly radical, and Grant defeated him overwhelmingly.[43]

For the next dozen years, the Independent Republicans, who rarely held elective office, hung suspended between the parties, uneasily voting Republican but ready again to bolt. Predominantly Yankee and northeastern, urban and college educated, they were overwhelmingly Unitarian, Congregationalist, or Episcopalian. For political guidance, Independent Republicans looked to Godkin's *Nation* and his New York *Evening Post,* both of which he edited until his death in 1902. "To my generation," wrote the Harvard philosopher William James, "Godkin's was certainly the towering influence in all thought concerning public affairs, and indirectly his influence has certainly been more pervasive than that of any other writer of the generation."[44]

Through Godkin, Independent Republicans could stay in close intellectual contact with the world that meant so much to them: the world of British Liberalism. From the beginning of national history, in fact, Yankee intellectuals had looked eastward across the Atlantic to the English homeland for ideological and cultural nourishment. By this means, they could feel part of the larger cosmopolitan world of thought and civilized moral value. Their principal point of contact was the Liberal England of the Dissenting Protestant faiths, of Unitarianism and sober mercantile enterprise. England seemed, by contrast with crude America, so cultivated, enlightened, and in touch with the sanctified traditions of the past.

It was inevitable that William Gladstone would emerge as the Independent Republicans' inspiration in public life. Founder and leader of the Liberal party from the 1850s to the 1890s, he towered over British political life. Gladstone was a compassionate and charismatic figure who possessed a hypnotizing oratorical power and a personal magnetism that inspired multitudes of Britons either to love or to hate him. Indeed, he was the Thomas Jefferson of Victorian Britain (a deeply religious, church-going Thomas Jefferson, however, if such may be imagined). He battled the cause of Catholic Ireland, although he was an Anglican Scot of wealthy parentage. With Robert Peel, Gladstone was the hero of the long and arduous struggle to establish free trade, a struggle conceived of as an assault upon economic privilege and a massive stroke for social justice. The aristocracy hated him, for he seemed almost instinctively to attack every pillar that underpinned their social supremacy (although in this reading of him, the aristocracy wildly exaggerated his radicalism). They were particularly alarmed at his democratizing the style of British politics. Long before American presidential candidates were to adopt the practice, Gladstone was stumping the countryside and speaking to enormous audiences. Above all, he attacked privilege and championed the cause of the British religious and ethnic outgroups, who idolized him; he opposed militarism as morally criminal; and he stood out as the preeminent trans-European figure in the struggle for liberty.[45]

Through the pages of the *Nation,* Godkin urged classic Gladstonian Liberalism upon Independent Republicans. In the heyday of Radical Republicanism, he called for black equality. Then, as that issue faded, he advocated low tariffs, honest and abstemious government, the withholding of all aid to business enterprise, sound money, and hostility to imperialism. These were principles that with each year stood in sharper contrast with mainstream Republicanism. Furthermore, Godkin again and again returned to Gladstone's basic principle: every public issue must be judged by *moral* standards, by which was meant a concern not with private but with social morals. Gladstone was concerned with expunging the social evils of oppression and exploitation, not those of drink and Sabbath recreations.*

*In *The Transatlantic Persuasion: The Liberal–Democrat Mind in the Age of Gladstone* (New York, 1969), I have described the British Liberals and the American Democrats as parallel movements, outcroppings of the same political strata on either side of the Atlantic. My point is that in both cases the two parties represented the outgroups, and in their ideologies both drew upon Adam Smith's critique of mercantilist capitalism (government assistance to business enterprise) and stressed egalitarianism and cultural laissez faire. During the Civil War era, however, the slavery issue attracted Liberals to Radical Republicans like Charles Sumner, whom they saw as their counterpart in American politics and with whom they maintained close ties. On every other ground, however, Liberals and Democrats were in ideological agreement. When in Grover Cleveland's time the Independent Republicans swung over to join the Democratic party in giving him enthusiastic support, the transatlantic political relationship was clarified. The accession of Woodrow Wilson to the presidency in 1913 confirmed the existence of a Liberal–Democratic community, for Wilson was the transcendent Gladstonian in his domestic and, above all, in his foreign policy.

Independent Republicans remained, therefore, in the ambivalent position that they had occupied for many years, pulled intellectually toward the Democrats but culturally unable to move to the party of the Irish Catholics and the South. Thus, they held aloof. Their role was little understood or approved of by the rest of political America, for the Gilded Age was a time of intense partisanship. Being "independent" simply meant being unreliable and untrustworthy. Charles A. Dana, cynical editor of the *New York Sun,* satirically called the Independent Republicans "Mugwumps," using an Indian term meaning great men who were rather self-important.[46] This name reflected the resentment non-Yankees had long felt toward puritanical Yankees, who seemed to recoil superciliously from the natural imperfections of this world, and ensured that the Mugwumps were the butt of endless jibes. To one side of them lay the Democrats and the Irish-Catholic corruption in the cities, hardly a sight to attract a gentleman. To the other side were the railroad scandals and the high tariffs of the Republicans. Not until the mid-1880s would the Mugwumps find, in Grover Cleveland, their model of excellence in American politics. In a mass insurgency, they would then decamp to the Democratic side.

Within six months of Grant's second inaugural, the Panic of 1873 created a major national slump in the economy, a slump that developed into one of the longest and most severe depressions of the nineteenth century. A downward spiral set in, lasting for more than five years—longer than that of the post-1929 depression. It hit the poor with especially cruel force, for no efforts were made to provide publicly supported jobs or to aid the unemployed in any way save through local charity. Layoffs and reductions in wages embittered labor-management relations. As early as the spring of 1874, the premonitory tremors were appearing; the trade journal *Iron Age* observed that relations between workers and employers were close to "guerrilla warfare." These tensions culminated in the most destructive labor outbreak in American history, the national railway strike of 1877.[47]

The great depression of the 1870s, unlike those of the 1890s and 1930s, did not reshape party allegiances and initiate a new party system. Perhaps political identities, so recently hardened during the Civil War, were too deeply ingrained. The Civil War party system, with its characteristic pattern of cultural and economic groups aligned behind the two parties, would persist into the mid-1890s.

Nonetheless, the national political argument was profoundly affected. The cultural issues that had obsessed the country since the mid-1850s—the conflict between Yankee and Southerner and the question of race relations—receded, and economic questions seized center stage. The Democratic vote rebounded in practically every state from its low point in 1872, especially in those states that were becoming industrialized. As the depression worsened, Republican economics came under an increasingly powerful attack.[48]

For years, in fact, Republican leaders had worried about a slow erosion in their party's voting strength. Even in the strongest midwestern Republican counties, where Lincoln had won eight out of ten votes, there was a decline. Seeking to hold fast to its western base, the Republican party consistently chose its presidential candidates from the Middle West, that swiftly growing region where so many New Englanders had gone to find their fortunes. The vice presidency would be left to the northeastern states. Despite these gestures, the Republican voting decline in midwestern constituencies continued. This loss of support had an important effect upon the "party-in-office," as distinct from the "party-in-the-electorate"—the mass of the voters. Those elected to Congress on the Republican ticket from the Middle West were able to hold their seats only for relatively short periods. This, in turn, meant that those who were elected from "safe" constituencies, primarily in New England, came ever more to dominate the party. They confidently proclaimed Republican policy from positions so secure that party leaders could exert little influence over them. Furthermore, they proclaimed that policy not from Mugwump perspectives—Independent Republicans were not a mass movement—but from the perspectives of the anti-Catholic, proindustrial New England Protestant masses. Thus a small group of New Englanders, who were rock-ribbed "regular" Republicans of firm Whiggish and Hamiltonian views as to the government and business enterprise, eventually fixed so strong a grip upon national policy that it could rarely be shaken. Men like Nelson Aldrich of Rhode Island, Orville H. Platt of Connecticut, and James G. Blaine of Maine believed that a more abundant life for all lay in entrepreneurial capitalism. In the 1870s the Republicans' tilt toward New England's industrial interests was already making itself evident. Non–New England voters in the Republican party were restive, and the decline in party strength west of the Appalachians grew more serious.

Party workers made vigorous efforts in the 1870s to attract Democratic voters to the Republican column to compensate for these difficulties, but Northerners who had voted Democratic in the presidential election of 1864 remained solidly with that party there-after. At the same time, immigration was surging again, bringing in more Irish Catholics and Germans, so that the Democratic voting base was swelling. Since the Republican constituency seemed unable to expand, party orators in the depression of the 1870s turned ever more desperately to "waving the bloody shirt"; that is, linking Demo-crats with Southern treason. Charging the Democrats with subver-sion was not, in truth, a new tactic. Since Jefferson's time, the Democratic political tradition had been accused of disloyalty, for it leaned toward French radicalism, relied upon Catholic votes, and in economics opposed the "patriotic" high-tariff position. Republican Governor Oliver P. Morton of Indiana, unable to restrain his con-tempt for Democrats, called their party "a common sewer and loath-some receptacle, into which is emptied every element of treason North and South, and every element of inhumanity and barbarism which has dishonored the age."[49]

It was impossible in the depression of the 1870s, however, for Republicans to continue relying upon Civil War emotions and the slavery cause. Nationwide, the same kinds of economic questions that had obsessed American voters in Andrew Jackson's time were insis-tently raised. In fact, the Gilded Age witnessed a full-scale revival of Jacksonian politics, with all that this meant in the topics being de-bated, in political behavior, and in national mood. Instinctively, the Democrats began reaching back to the Jacksonian years for instruc-tion and leadership. Now Samuel Tilden, that venerable Jacksonian who in the mid-1870s was the Democratic governor of New York, received his opportunity to win the White House. His party col-leagues knew that he had been a close economic adviser to Martin Van Buren, his scholarly turn of mind gave him a broad command of current economic thought in the transatlantic community, and among Democrats he had an almost unassailable authority in such matters. In addition, Tilden had won national eminence for his ear-lier campaign against corruption in New York City, successfully bat-tling that prince of corruptionists, Boss William Marcy Tweed.

Political corruption had become a piercing issue in American pub-lic life. It seemed to be sapping the whole experiment in republican self-government, reaching into every community and disgracing the federal government. "It is not necessary for me to attempt to paint the state of political corruption to which we have been reduced," the political reformer Henry George said in California as he called for the election of Samuel Tilden to the presidency in 1876.

It is the dark background to our national [centennial] rejoicing, the skeleton which has stood by us at the feast. Our Fourth of July orators do not proclaim it; our newspapers do not announce it; we hardly whisper it to one another, but we all know, for we all feel, that beneath all our centennial rejoicing there exists in the public mind today a greater doubt of the success of Republican institutions than has existed before within the memory of our oldest man.[50]

It was "not to ourselves alone," said Tilden in 1875, "that we are to look when we consider what is involved in this controversy. The whole United States, and indeed other countries, are interested in it. The cause of free government has been dishonored and imperilled by the abuse, maladministration, and peculations that have recently prevailed in the country."[51]

What was the cause of political corruption? From the time of the radical British Whigs in eighteenth-century England, the answer given by the Jeffersonian side of American politics had been simple and direct: corruption was inevitable whenever businessmen and government were interlinked. The proper position for government was to stand in critical judgment of capitalists and to protect the public welfare rather than private profit. Federalists, Whigs, and Republicans had consistently taken the opposite view—that close ties between enterpreneurs and government were beneficial to the entire community—and on this ground Jeffersonian Republicans and Jacksonian Democrats had attacked them year after year as the servants of the wealthy and toadies to the powerful. Now, in the Gilded Age, the cry was again raised that political corruption was a national disgrace, making the United States the mock of Europe and its republican creed once more a synonym for greedy, undisciplined democracy. Corruption, moreover, was said to be the principal means by which the wealthy robbed the common people. Jacksonians had insisted that clever businessmen lived by their wits, while laborers and farmers had to live by the sweat of their brow. Unscrupulous enterpreneurs were able to persuade gullible (and probably corrupt) legislators to grant tariffs, bounties, chartered monopolies, and other special privileges, which were justified on the ground that they would make the nation strong and prosperous.

Democrats had another venerable Jeffersonian explanation for political corruption: centralism. The nation's ills, said Samuel Tilden, flowed directly out of a perverted concentration of power, both in Washington and in the states. In Albany and other state capitals dominated by Republicans, legislators refused to allow cities to govern themselves democratically. Instead they established powerful commissions, independent of local control, to administer urban affairs. When seized by corrupt interests, said Tilden, as in the case of Boss Tweed, the commissions were used to take out enormous sums in graft. "The cancer which reached a head in the municipal government [of New York City]," he insisted, "gathered its virus from the corrupted blood which pervades our whole country."[52]

Tilden's role was not simply to discourse upon corruption's cause and cure. Rather, as the party's chief link with its golden age during Jackson's time, he was counted upon to lead Democrats in money issues—a topic that bewildered most people. "The man who attempted to thread [the money question's] twists and turns . . . [that] intellectual labyrinth that easily confused the untrained and the ill-informed," Irwin Unger has written, "risked finding himself hopelessly befuddled."[53] The depression, Tilden observed, had a simple cause: it lay in the soft money policy that the Republicans had initiated by printing greenbacks without backing in gold and continued with their banking and currency reforms of 1862. The effect of the policy was greatly to inflate the currency. The postwar boom had been artificially stimulated by this inflation, and the collapse of 1873 was inevitable. "The fruits of a false and delusive system of government finances are everywhere around us," Tilden said in 1873. "All business is in a dry-rot. . . . Inflation no longer inflates. . . . The truth is that our body politic has been overdrugged with stimulants."[54]

The answer, according to Tilden, was to return to sound money. This would restore confidence and prosperity. Democratic party workers knew, however, that within their own party following sound money had become a risky appeal. In Andrew Jackson's time, when American farmers had not been so closely tied to commercial agriculture, it had been possible for the sound-money principle to have wide appeal in the countryside. Conservative in habits and outlook, agrarian people had distrusted paper money in any form and hoarded gold coin. Now, however, the huge expansion of grain farming that had occurred in the Middle West in the 1850s and produced by 1860 an enormous outflow of American grain to the British market, and a heavy dependence upon such sales, made farmers more sophisticated about currency questions. Many of them recognized the link that seemed to exist between an inflated currency supply and high grain prices. In the mid-1870s, Middle Western farmers were suffering from drastic slumps in the price of grain abroad, and Tilden was urged to stop his militant demands for sound money. He refused, however, insisting as his political tradition had insisted since

Jackson's time that sound money was essential to keep the price level low and ease the condition of the working poor. He would rather lose a million votes, he said, than allow that "the mechanics, the servant girls and laboring men should be robbed of their earnings." Equally important, according to Tilden, was for the federal government drastically to reduce its spending. The weight of taxation that private citizens bore in order to produce lavish aid to capitalists and to pay for the costly Reconstruction efforts in the South must be sharply cut back. Then, consumers would again have money to spend and trade would revive. As Gladstone had said in his now famous dictum, money left in the pockets of private citizens would "fructify."[55]

As the Democratic party surged, the image of Thomas Jefferson was rehabilitated. Tilden appealed constantly to Jefferson's words, insisting that the Republic would find its true salvation when it returned to his teachings and rejected Hamilton's tutelage. "Thomas Jefferson," Tilden said in 1873, "founded and organized the Democratic party. He stayed the advancing centralism. He restored the rights of the States and the localities. He repressed the meddling of government in the concerns of private business, remitting the management of the industries of the country to the domain of the individual judgment and conscience."[56] A tide of Jeffersonianism swept through Tilden's party, expressing itself in campaign buttons, banners, medallions, party magazines, pilgrimages to Monticello, and verse and song. Democrats came to have an almost mystic belief that by "touching the bones" of the sainted Virginian, their party would be restored to the power and potency which for so long it had enjoyed:

> Jefferson, like the Messiah, would rise again. Jefferson was the Christ of the American government; they were his latter-day apostles. The mildest jest at Jefferson they regarded as blasphemous; the gentlest criticism they took as a personal insult. There were only two ways in American politics: Jeffersonian and Hamiltonian.[57]

So inspired, Democrats in the Gilded Age called not simply for states rights, localism, and limited government, but for a renewed Jeffersonian attack upon the conspiracies they believed to exist among the wealthy. According to Democrats, the objective of the elite was to appropriate the power of government for their own enrichment. The Hamiltonian spirit that dominated Republicans, Tilden said, was simply the belief that "our American people must be governed, if not by force, at least by appeals to the selfish interests of classes, in all the forms of corrupt influence." By this means, greedy men had gained control of the national government:

> The myriads of officeholders, with enhanced salaries, and often with illicit gains; the contractors and jobbers; the beneficiaries of Congressional grants of the public property or of special franchises; the favored interests whose business is rendered lucrative by legislative bounties or legislative monopolies; the corporations whose hopes and fears are appealed to by the measure of the government; the rapacious hordes of carpet-baggers who have plundered the impoverished people of the South at least ten times as much as Tweed's Ring did the rich metropolis, and whose fungus growth is intertwined with the roots of the Republican party; all these classes are not only interested in perpetuating existing wrongs, but they are the main agencies and instruments by which that work is done.[58]

For their reply to this Democratic assault, Republicans turned to their most honored economist, Henry C. Carey. One of the rare Irish Catholics who voted Republican, Carey's father, Mathew, had been hounded from Dublin to the United States in the 1790s as a seditious journalist. Soon after his arrival, Mathew Carey had become a leading advocate of protective tariffs in order to insure American nationalism by encouraging its industries. In the 1840s, young Henry had done the same, founding the "American School" of political economy to provide intellectual support for Henry Clay's "American System" of national policy. By the Gilded Age, Carey had become an economist internationally honored, though rarely in England. Scorning Adam Smith and his disciples, Carey denounced world free trade and the system of gold-standard-based sound money as simply English propaganda. British theorists had persuaded Americans to believe in low tariffs and sound money in order to keep the United States in a subordinate, colonial status in the transatlantic economy.

Thus, in this subordinate position, the United States would continue to produce raw materials. These would then be sent to factories in Britain to be turned into finished products, whose purchase would place Americans at a constant financial disadvantage. Gold-standard-based sound money would require Americans always to be in debt to English bankers, who held the greatest store of gold in the world. What was instead needed, as Mathew Carey and Henry Clay had said, was to build barriers against British goods and make America self-sufficient. British products were cheap, Henry Carey insisted, because the British already had their factories, and they paid their workmen wages no American would accept. Special assistance was needed, therefore, to aid American capitalists in starting new industries—out of which would flow jobs, excellent wages, and opportunity for all.

Henry Carey was so far from being a sound money advocate that he called for keeping the Civil War–originated greenbacks in circulation even without providing for them a backing in gold. This system would constitute, in effect, what modern economists call a managed currency. That is, since greenbacks were not limited in volume by the amount of gold available in the country, they could be printed by the government in whatever volume was needed to meet industry's needs. Capital could be made available, as required, for investment and industrialization. Passionate in his cause, Carey fantasized that British agents were working in American politics at the behest of British monopolists and using such prominent reform groups as the Free Trade League to subvert American opinion and keep British interests safe. As one of Carey's colleagues put the matter, "The whole system of [British] political economy, from beginning to end, is an apology for tyranny, and the whole tribe of political economists are humbugs. . . . [At] their head stands the prince of humbugs, John Stuart Mill," whose *Principles of Political Economy* (1848 and many later editions), which restated and further developed Adam Smith's ideas, was authoritative for Mugwump and Democratic economists.[59]

In popular votes, Samuel Tilden won the presidential election of 1876 against Rutherford B. Hayes of Ohio. In the electoral college, however, as a result of the most disputed and confused electoral count in American history, Tilden was defeated. C. Vann Woodward has pointed to one powerful influence that, in the months of debate in Washington, helped speed the result. Southerners, anxious to receive federally supported public works to open their war-ravaged ports, restore their rivers, and build railroads, recognized in Tilden too loyal a Jeffersonian. His gubernatorial performance had shown that he meant what he said about opposing government expenditures on public works, for he not only crushed the Tweed Ring, but he rooted out the Canal Ring, a corrupt organization of contractors, and sharply cut expenditures on the Erie Canal. As a result, New York's taxes were soon one-third their former level. The Republican party, by contrast, had been lavishly scattering public works throughout states in the North and West. To Southerners in Washington, many of them former Whigs, the choice seemed clear. Indeed, as

Carl Harris has recently shown, even among Democrats in the South there was probably not much enthusiasm for Tilden. As early as the mid-1870s, Southern Democrats, eager for higher cotton prices, were beginning to vote with midwestern legislators in favor of soft money. Most Southerners wanted inflation, believing that their region suffered from a currency shortage. In response to Republican assurances that the South would have reason to be pleased with a continuation of Republican rule in the White House, Southerners appear to have promised their assistance in securing an electoral count victory for Hayes.[60]

Hayes' victory, however, may already have been dictated by the tide of events. Tilden gave the Democrats in Congress almost no leadership during the crucial weeks of negotiation over electoral count procedures. The Republicans and the shrewd Hayes—whose tactical moves were skilled and effective—were free to direct affairs as they wished.[61] Ironically, the South derived small advantage from the Hayes presidency. He did little more than withdraw the last occupying Northern troops, thus bringing a final end to Reconstruction—a gesture that Tilden, too, had pledged to carry out. Little federal money went southward for public works. The "New South" of rapid commercial and industrial development would remain only a dream for many years into the future.

part four

IN RETROSPECT

IX

The First Century:
The Era of Bipolar Politics

My purpose in this book has been to examine the first century of American politics from the perspective of cultural history in order to see if the familiar story takes on a different aspect from this vantage point. The new political history, which highlights the role of ethnic and other culture groups, has provided me with a rich body of materials to draw upon in searching out larger patterns, but so too has a mass of political history written from more traditional standpoints. Intellectual historians have for many years been exploring ideology, one of cultural history's central concerns, and social historians work in a field that yields much that is useful in this context. Indeed, since it is in the nature of the historical discipline to deal broadly with human affairs, the scholar sensitive to cultural issues will rarely emerge empty-handed from reading even the most strictly political narrative.

By shifting the angle of vision so that we focus upon ethnicity, religion, group relationships, myths and images, life styles, and ideology, we get a different picture of the American past. This picture is more complex than our earlier views of our past, for it has become clear that we can no longer describe the conflict of economic interest groups and assume that the story is complete. Cultural politics is not a side show that occasionally attracts our attention with odd issues like temperance and Sabbatarianism; it is as pervasive and powerful in shaping public life as is the impact of economic politics. Although the two forms of politics originate in separate spheres of human experience, they continually flow into each other, creating cultural dimensions to essentially economic questions and economic outcomes of cultural facts.

The American people bring to their politics a set of attitudes that spring from the fact that they represent not one kind, but many different kinds of peoples. They live in different ways, speak different languages (or speak with different accents), worship differently and harbor different beliefs, and think in different images and myths about the nation they inhabit, its past, and its hoped-for future. We are familiar with tribal conflict in primitive societies; what we must now recognize is that tribalism is present even in modern societies. Every people has a sense of "the other," the tribe across the boundary line with whom relations are uncertain, precarious, and always complicated. Each culture group believes that its customs are natural and proper and tends in varying degrees to regard those of other peoples as either comic or harmful. In every setting in which different kinds of peoples must be in contact, power relationships emerge, involving superiority and inferiority, which induce feelings of arrogance, fear, and resentment. For each group, the enemy is omnipresent and must be guarded against and watched warily.

At the same time, relations between culture groups can involve quite another emotion—that of admiration, which brings in turn its correlate, emulation. The relations of the peoples that form the hierarchy of every nation can be either benevolent or malevolent. The more two peoples intermix, the more individuals from one group decide that they like the ways of living and the values of the other and move toward them. Thus, as we have seen, in the Southern states there has always been an Other South which has looked northward for example and inspiration. Similarly, within the transatlantic Anglo-American community there were many colonials who looked admiringly to London and worked to Anglicize the colonies. During the nineteenth century there were thousands of Northerners and Southerners who shaped their ideas and lifestyles according to the English model. Cultural politics involves, therefore, not only hostilities, but also attachment.

When culturally pluralistic societies adopt democratic politics, people who share common enemies come together to form political parties. At the apex of each party is a small elite that provides not only leadership, but ideology. In certain aspects ideology has to do with God, humanity, society, and nature, and is the property of clerics, scientists, and the intellectual class in society at large. In other aspects, ideology has to do with visions of the nation itself—what it should be, where its dangers lie, and in what directions it should move. In determining this ideology of the nation, a major role is assumed not only by key intellectuals like Adam Smith, but also by leading political personages. These political figures both symbolize political traditions and articulate them. The Thomas Jeffersons and Henry Clays are ideologues as well as charismatic political chiefs. They have been frequently referred to as "masters" by their many "disciples," and their maxims are pored over and memorized.

The union of leaders and followers is never an easy one, and ruptures are in the nature of the relationship. However, the basic outlook of each cultural community remains relatively stable over long periods of time, and out of this consensus grows a party system that, in its ideologies, alignments, and leadership, is remarkably long-lived. As soon as national politics began, American public life fell into a pattern of political relationships between kinds of peoples and ideologies, and this pattern still endured, in basic outline, a hundred years later. It is not, however, a simple pattern, and in its larger nature it is relatively new and unfamiliar in historical writing. To clarify its chief features, therefore, we will, in this concluding chapter, look back briefly through the narrative of the first century. Then, we will glance forward through the nation's second century in order to determine in a preliminary way whether the pattern persists.

We have seen that American politics took form in the context of the British empire. A complex community centered in England, the British empire had for centuries been developing within itself a many-sided conflict among ethnic and religious communities. The Scots, Scotch-Irish, Welsh, and Catholic Irish were the principal ethnic outgroups in a United Kingdom dominated by the English, a powerful, numerous, and wealthy people. The American colonists shared this outgroup status, being looked down upon with distaste by the English in the mother country. In religious terms, the British empire was run by members of the Church of England, or Anglicans, whose role and established links to constitutional power were resented by all non-Anglicans—Scottish and Scotch-Irish Presbyterians, Irish Catholics, and the Dissenting Protestants within England itself (the Congregationalists, Baptists, and English Presbyterians).

When democratic politics emerged in America in the eighteenth century, the colonials immediately fell into alignments that mirrored these larger cultural divisions within the empire. Catholics, however, were not represented in sizable numbers in either the colonies or in their successor, the United States of America, until well into the nineteenth century. This meant that before the 1840s, when Irish Catholics began arriving in North America in great multitudes, politics in America were essentially between various kinds of British Protestants. Generally joining the side of the British outgroups were Dutchmen and Germans, who were present in the colonies in large numbers, and who shared the outgroups' dislike of the English, with their superior and arrogant ways toward non-English minorities.

One fact, however, became obvious as soon as the rebelling colonials began to gather in a common consultative body, the Continental Congress. Two home-grown ethnic communities existed within the new United States: the Yankees of New England and the white Southerners, who lived widely distributed over an immense region south of Pennsylvania. Within Congress a culturally charged confrontation immediately sprang up between Yankee and white Southerner, and it continued to be the nation's central political conflict until these two peoples settled their account in open warfare a century later.

At first, Yankee and white Southerner shared much—a common enemy in the royal government in London, a common sense of anger at English affectations of superiority, and a common fear that the tie to England would ultimately be a destructive one. Thus, in the larger political framework of the British empire, Yankees and Southerners were both outgroups; they were on the same side of the political argument and could join forces in building an independent American nation. While struggling against the monarchists of Britain, Yankees and Southerners were united as passionate republicans who dispensed with kings, feudal lordships, and concentrated authority. Each envisioned a new country that would be simple, austere, and democratic, one in which the people, not royalty, were sovereign.

Once the imperial framework was cast aside, however, and the Americans' political life was contained within the boundaries of the new nation, the former allies found in each other the enemy that, doubtless, they already knew was there; that, perhaps, it is humanity's deepest impulse in politics to locate and fix upon. Yankees and white Southerners had had more than a century and a half to develop their separate North American cultures. Their concepts of themselves and of life differed sharply, as did their speech, ways of living, guiding principles, and historical memories. They were American-grown ethnic communities who found each other as distasteful as Highlander and Lowlander found each other in Scotland. Once begun, their rivalry grew in bitterness and distrust as each came to regard the other as the enemy of true republicanism.

In the Americans' new political setting there was a crucial question: Which group was now the outgroup, and which one was the center? This, in turn, led to other, more fundamental questions: What was America to be? Where was its cultural and economic center of gravity, and who would occupy it? If the new republic was to be defined as the antithesis of the older civilization across the Atlantic—that is, as a nation of self-sufficient (white) yeomen farmers living in conditions of widely scattered rural independence—then its center of gravity would be found by plunging into the interior, breaking free of the Atlantic world, and forging a distinctively American culture. If America was to be defined instead as a purer and better England, if its destiny was to move in England's direction of urbanization, industry, intellectual sophistication, and power, then its center of gravity would remain the northeastern seaboard, its future would be Atlantic, and it would continue to look to the older culture. The former choice was the South's; the latter, New England's. The issue between the two would be settled by the Middle Atlantic states, which looked both eastward and westward.

The seacoast mercantile and financial elite of New York City and Philadelphia were primarily English in ethnic identity, Episcopalian and Quaker in faith, and cosmopolitan. Anglicized in way of life and closely tied to the English trading empire, they had been reluctant to break their tie with England. Many in fact had been Loyalists, and like the New Englanders they envisioned an Atlantic future for the United States. However, New York and Pennsylvania also opened westward through the Mohawk valley of New York to the Great Lakes, and from Pennsylvania's Pittsburgh down the Ohio River. In succeeding generations both states would labor mightily to develop and dominate the interior, using first canals and then railroads to increase trade. New York and Pennsylvania also contained large non-English ethnic minorities who hated the English—the Scotch-Irish, the Dutch, and the Germans. For them, America was to be a new world, not a purer and better England. It was to be multiethnic, egalitarian, and agrarian, a land where English pretensions of superiority were excluded. It was the non-English minorities, driven by these impulses, who had taken over the governments of the Middle Atlantic colonies in the 1770s and had wrenched them out of the British Empire.

Would the Middle Atlantic states lean toward New England or toward the South? In the answer to this question lay the future course of American history, for it would determine which of the nation's polar cultures would dominate the national government. The decisive factor lay in the character of the Yankee and how he was perceived by the rest of the society. Something within New England made it confident, in a way denied to the other regions, that it was the host culture for the new American nation. Was not the United States' predominant language English? Were not its common law and institutions the mainstream of American Republicanism? Was not New England the most homogeneously English part of the country and therefore the region most suited to lead? After the Revolution New England kept close ties with Old England, perhaps to counter-balance the vast West into which the other states were pouring their energies, and this bond gave Yankee society a continuing sense of cultural superiority. The Yankees were certain that New England's common schools and colleges, its scholarship, its learned Congregational ministry, its libraries and journals demonstrated that they, not Thomas Jefferson and his French radicalism, provided the nation's intellect. Furthermore, the Yankees' fervent Puritanism, roused to a new militancy by the Revolutionary struggle against Anglican England, convinced them that New England ways were closer to God and more upright and wholesome than Southern ways. New Englanders, therefore, were certain of themselves and their mission; they were to be the righteous fragment, the few who could save an America sorely needing instruction in true republicanism and moral virtue. Their task, a divine one, was to remake America in the Yankee image.

The culturally aggressive Yankees were disliked everywhere outside of New England. Baptists and Methodists were angered by the supercilious Congregational clergymen, who were disdainful of an unlearned and plebeian clergy.Within New England itself, generations of Baptists had struggled against the hostility of established Congregationalism. The Dutch in New York State, inundated by thousands of westward-migrating Yankees, could not abide them, nor could the Scotch-Irish Presbyterians and German Lutherans of Pennsylvania. These ethnic groups took the Yankees, in fact, at their own estimation, seeing them as the American representatives of England and English culture. Thus, in the Middle Atlantic states there emerged an anti-Yankee coalition that swung its support to Thomas Jefferson and the South, allowing Southerners effectively to dominate the federal government for sixty years, from 1800 to 1860.

As America's cultural communities drew apart, they divided between them their common ideology, republicanism. As a political world view, republicanism had been the shared perspective of the entire Revolutionary generation. After independence, however, it was soon clear that republicanism was not a single outlook, but a broad spectrum of belief in which it is possible to discern at least four different modes.

One of these flourished among the New Englanders. A pious and moralistic people for whom the politics of virtue was of paramount concern, they dreamed of building a Christian Sparta in their new country. Instinctively, New Englanders viewed the nation at large as they did their Puritan villages—as an organic community united by a shared way of life or one in need of being put into that condition. Their central concern was the moral purity of the whole society, which they considered an offering to God and an example to the world. To them government was a divine institution which, like the Calvinist God Himself, should be strong and active. Magistrates were His representatives. Their task was to bring order where human chaos always threatened and righteousness and discipline where impurity and waywardness constantly impended.

In Yankee republicanism, therefore, government should guide the nation toward moral as well as economic health by direct intervention, fostering both godly living and industrious habits. The American people should be self-disciplined, self-denying, and hardworking, though uncorrupted by the fruits of their labors. They should be energetic, upright, and engaged in furthering God's business. From the beginning Congregational New Englanders had made their sect the established church in Massachusetts, Connecticut, and New Hampshire, and the state-church mentality was natural to them. It was wholly appropriate, in their view, for the lay government, guided by ministers of the true faith, to supervise the private morals of its citizens. Throughout the first century of American politics and afterwards, their temperance, Sabbatarian, and other moral crusades, urged by Congregational clergymen, would polarize the nation's politics.

The republicanism of white Southerners emphasized liberty, not moral purity. All but a tiny urban minority among them lived in rural isolation. A rambling, spacious openness characterized Southern life, save in the folded hills of Appalachia. Lacking any experience of the corporate village and town discipline so common in New England, Southern whites held fast to a belief in the right of white persons to live their lives as they saw fit. Government should be small and inactive, not strong and interfering. Assertive manliness and arrogant gentry imperiousness were much admired. Slavery hardened the Southern dogma that government should be limited and locally controlled, for no external authority should be allowed to impede white authority. As commercial farmers, Southern planters were also hostile to distant bankers and merchants. Thus Southern republicanism distrusted close links between businessmen and the central government. With Thomas Jefferson, Southerners found in the Scotsman Adam Smith's *Wealth of Nations* (1776) their bible in political economy, for Smith insisted that businessmen always conspire against the common interest by raising prices and lowering wages; that they are always scheming to get government aid, through tariffs and other bounties, which gives them an unfair advantage. Government-business cooperation, said Smith, is inherently corrupt. Justice for all will emerge only when everyone is forced in an open market place to compete equally for the public's favor. Then consumers will have the lowest prices, and supplies of necessaries will be abundant.

In the Middle States, the republicanism that claimed the support of the Scotch-Irish Presbyterians and their allies—the Calvinists and Lutherans among the Germans, the farmers among the Calvinist Dutch, and the small but increasingly vocal and politically mobilized urban artisan and working classes—emphasized egalitarianism. Social rank and economic power meant English privilege and exploitation. The crucial issues were English arrogance and the fact that Englishmen seemed to monopolize wealth and positions of power and prestige. The outgroups felt an urgent need to establish that un-English did not mean unequal; that a strange language, a strange church, strange dress, and strange ways of recreation were not signs of inferiority. Identifying itself with the "people" rather than the elite, the republicanism of the ethnic outgroups had a populist quality. It demanded loudly and insistently that government be kept close to the people by frequent elections, and that each people be allowed to live according to their own customs by maintaining a national policy of *cultural* laissez faire in concert with the *economic* laissez faire of Adam Smith. The Scotch-Irish shared the belief that close ties between government and the economically powerful inevitably led to political corruption and social exploitation. In Pennsylvania politics, their enemy in the Revolutionary years had been Robert Morris and his Bank of North America.

There were, of course, thousands in the Middle States who hated the Scotch-Irish and their egalitarian republicanism. Ethnically English, these individuals were led by the Anglicized and cosmopolitan merchant and financial elite of Philadelphia and New York City. The elite had won great profits from the huge trading network of the empire, which was centered in London. They had observed that the economic prosperity of that empire seemed to arise largely from the leadership of London and the Bank of England. For them the Navigation Acts, which had established protected markets for American produce, had been an aid, not a hindrance. They preferred the mercantilist policy of the English rather than the laissez-faire theories of Adam Smith. The notion of a strong government intervening actively in economic life to exclude the products of foreigners and foster domestic industry was an article of faith. Now that the United States was independent, the capitalist elite of the Middle States intended to create within the new nation, with its immense continental expanse, the same kind of setting that had existed in the older colonial regime. Investment and entrepreneurship were to be encouraged.

Such men, in short, were nationalist republicans. They envisioned an America that was centrally organized, economically activist and commercialized, orderly and obedient to elite leadership. The crucial point for them was the continued predominance in the new nation of an elite generally English in cultural origin, modern in its large vision and developmental values, urban and imperial in outlook and style. Thus, in the Northern states, capitalism achieved a cultural character. From the beginning, Englishness in mood as well as in actual ethnic identity was linked to entrepreneurial capitalism, if not exclusively—there were wealthy Scotch-Irish, Dutch, and Germans within the elite—at least predominantly.

These were the materials with which the American people constructed their two major political parties and political traditions. The moralistic republicans of New England and the nationalist republicans of the Middle States, both Anglophile, cosmopolitan, and economically developmental, formed the Federalist party, with its heartland among the Yankees. The egalitarian republicans of the Middle States and the libertarian republicans of the South, both Anglophobe, localistic, and distrustful of entrepreneurial economics, gathered within Thomas Jefferson's Republican party, its heartland south of the Mason and Dixon line. The two parties faced off against each other as if in ultimate combat. It was this sense of a common enemy that gave each party its most enduring strength. Indeed, in politics the image of "the enemy" plays a subtle and complex role. One of its major functions is as an aid to self-definition. Virginians and South Carolinians discovered their common identity as Southerners when they learned that they had a common adversary in New England. Yankees considered the nature of Southern civilization, and knew what they themselves were; that is, they defined themselves as in every way the opposite of the other side. Cultural politics always contains this centrifugal tendency, forcing its antagonists away from each other and toward polar extremes. So it was that North-South tensions carried ominous overtones of danger to the republic itself. Eventually, the clash of cultural antipathies would lead, if indirectly, to the destruction of the republic. The fears and angers to which they gave rise cannot be separated from the coming of the Civil War.

It is important, however, to remember that whatever its politics, each side considered itself republican; common to both parties was an American consensus in opposition to Europe. Both believed in a nation governed not by a monarch and a titled aristocracy but by its people and their representatives. Both believed in freedom of religion and belief, at least at the national level where the Constitution provided for a complete separation of church and state. All the marks and practices of feudalism, whether in land tenure, government, or social relations, were to be eradicated. Both parties believed in guaranteed civil rights and in a government controlled by a constitution that, because it was adopted by the people, would be beyond the reach of that government. Republicanism called for a separation of powers, frequent elections, and a widespread, eventually universal (white, male) suffrage. It demanded that the economic and educational means for personal independence and well-being be made available to every white person. American republicanism envisioned an austere, simple, and honest government freed of the awesome trappings and complications of monarchy, and a social order that fostered individual self-respect, personal autonomy, moral wholeness, and public virtue.

These values made the United States, during its first century, a precarious experiment in a western civilization still largely feudal, monarchical, aristocratic, and culturally authoritarian. In Europe, the United States was hated by the privileged and idolized by radicals. Americans were keenly conscious that they lived in an unfriendly world and that their experiment in republicanism was uncertain. This consciousness, which became a continuing national anxiety, created the mood within which all of American politics took place during its first century. Were the common people in fact capable of virtuous self-government, as republicanism insisted? Could they practice the self-denial that orderly government requires and give primacy to the public welfare instead of their own selfish appetites? Or were they so ignorant and selfish, so given to self-indulgence, unthinking passions, internecine violence, and a sour envy of their superiors that they needed the stable, independent, and strong government that only a hereditary order of noblemen and monarchy could provide? Generations of European observers who traveled the United States shook their heads in disapproval and returned to their native countries to write that America was a failure, a mistake, a disaster for all those in Europe who advocated republicanism. Generations of Americans read these accounts avidly, for they were painfully sensitive to European criticism, and their private anxieties were reawakened by these widely published condemnations.

In each period after the Revolution, Americans faced a new challenge to republicanism, a new testing of the national political faith. This produced enormous pressures within public life, for each party freely predicted the downfall of the republic if the other side won control. The politics of the 1790s, the nation's first decade under the federal Constitution, were uniquely embittered and violent. Each party was convinced that the other was subversive; that enemies within the country conspired to revive monarchy or to induce total national anarchy and thus a popular swing toward rule by a Napoleonic dictator. In the Jacksonian years, another period of especially fevered politics erupted. This was followed in the 1850s by a total rupture of the party system, leading to secession and civil war. In the name of republicanism as conceived of by a political party which had just taken that term as its own designation, Abraham Lincoln would reunite the nation by force of arms.

Foreign policy, particularly the American relationship with England, was a powerfully reactive element in these party battles. Here, too, ideology was linked to cultural constituency. The Jeffersonians and their inheritors, the Jacksonian Democrats, were the party of the Scotch-Irish and the other Anglophobic ethnic minorities. They were also the party of the South, whose fears for slavery, as well as its large settlements of Scotch-Irish and Germans, made it hostile to England and its abolitionism. The Federalists and their inheritors, the Whigs, were the party of the English and the Anglicized. It is not surprising, in light of these considerations, that the second war against the English, the War of 1812, was declared and pursued by Jeffersonian Republicans, the Scotch-Irishman Andrew Jackson winning its culminating victory, and passionately opposed by the Federalists. The Democrats eagerly pushed for westward expansion, not only to expand Jefferson's agrarian "empire for liberty" but to repel the "encirclements" of British power and make North America predominantly American. New England's Federalists and Whigs, conversely, resisted westward expansion. They saw it as an influence that would isolate New England from the trajectory of American growth and culture and make the country more savage and uncivilized. Such advocates as the Indians had in American politics were Whigs. At the advent of the war with Mexico, New England and Whiggery stood apart in harsh condemnation. More culturally cosmopolitan than Democrats, Whigs maintained much closer ties with English thought. Thus they were better able to view their country from a transatlantic perspective, especially in the matter of slavery, and to be ashamed for its crudities and excesses. Even in the South with its traditional Anglophobia, Southern Whigs closely followed English styles and English politics and kept English magazines in their parlors. Democrats tended to scoff at such refinements.

Economic ideology was similarly related to cultural constituency. The ethnically English predominated among the wealthier classes; the ethnic minorities predominated among those of modest incomes. As we have seen, the agrarian South distrusted bankers, the manipulation of currency, and Northern capitalists. Its opposition to protective tariffs was a matter of principle. Although Henry Clay of Kentucky, a Southern Whig who rejected the name of Southerner, advocated Yankee civilization and, in his American System, called for protective tariffs and a central bank, the country as a whole was moving away from his position. In Andrew Jackson's time, Democratic economic thought came to a sharp focus in the Bank War. Hostile to government assistance for entrepreneurs, Jacksonian Democrats eliminated the national bank, threw open the power of incorporation to everyone, and slashed the tariff. They worked toward price stability and a manageable cost of living for the consuming masses by advocating sound money (currency backed by gold). This, they believed, would eliminate the booms and busts brought on by speculators and break up what they saw as the capitalist conspiracy that exploited the nation. Jacksonian Democrats, as disciples of Thomas Jefferson, believed that the social classes were inherently in conflict; that the wealthy, working incessantly to their own advantage, profited at the expense of the community. The government, therefore, should be separated from the economy and ensure that all compete equally. By the 1850s this economic ideology was supreme in the nation. Both in the United States and in Great Britain, where the free trade revolution was winning its final victories, Adam Smith had become the Anglo-American patron saint of economics. The mercantilism of Alexander Hamilton and his Federalist-Whig inheritors had lost the battle.

The cultural pattern in Jeffersonian and Jacksonian politics was not a simple and monolithic one. There were many Democratic Yankees and many Whig Southerners. New Hampshire contained strong Baptist and Scotch-Irish settlements, and its chief city, Portsmouth, was economic rival to Boston. The state, in consequence, was possibly the most fervent Democratic state in the Union. In New York's banking community, there were Scotch-Irishmen who would never vote for Andrew Jackson. In the South there were Federalists in Jefferson's time, and multitudes of Whigs in Jackson's. Indeed, there was always the Other South, which admired Yankee ways, deplored Southern crudities and violence, and identified with the United States as a whole. In 1860 only slightly more than half of the Southern voters supported the Southern Democratic candidate. The rest, though they could not bring themselves to vote for Lincoln, supported candidates who were opposed to secession. In Jacksonian America, in short, Whigs and Democrats contended on practically even terms in almost every state in the Union. Even in religious matters, a rough balance existed. Although the Whigs claimed that they were uniquely the party of true piety and in the name of Christian morality fought year after year for temperance and Sabbath laws, the Democrats had their own devout Christians in the Baptists, Scotch-Irish Presbyterians, and Catholics.

Nonetheless, a pattern of strong cultural polarities and images existed, and Americans clearly perceived and used them. Although there were both Whig and Democratic New Englanders, the term "Yankee" seemed to apply primarily to Whig New Englanders, not to their political opponents. Although there were both Whig and Democratic Southerners, the term "Southerner" was perhaps most proudly and consistently used by Democrats. When Andrew Jackson was trumpeted as the champion of Scotch-Irishmen, no one would have suggested that this meant he championed the cause of Presbyterian financiers in New York City. Whig political picnics were like revival meetings, but few would expect to see many Baptists there. The broad outlines, in short, were widely recognized, the overall character of each party and its followers was apparent, and stereotypes were freely used. Whigs blamed all violence upon the ethnic minorities and termed themselves the party of law and order, sober living, proper manners, and steady habits—as, apparently, they were. The Scotch-Irish with their whisky and the Germans with their beer made the Democrats immovably anti-temperance. Whigs, exaggerating, commonly identified the Democrats with the village drunk. Since Jefferson's time Democrats were known to be the party of religious free-thinkers, and the issue of cultural laissez faire, of absolute separation between church and state, was incontestably their ideological property.

In the 1850s a new era of revolutionary spirit and turbulence seized the country and transformed the party system. An enormous inflooding of Irish Catholics and Germans, comprising in relative terms the heaviest influx of immigrants in American history, produced a wave of alarm and cultural hysteria in the Northern states. Catholics had never played a large part in American life. The nation's politics until this time had been almost exclusively between Protestants. Now all that was changed by the arrival of a people widely held in contempt. The British peoples, whether English, Scots, Scotch-Irish, or Welsh, had always thought the Catholic Irish practically a subhuman people, immoral, violent, undisciplined, and their Catholicism and their priests historic and bloody enemies to Protestantism. They were contemptuous of the illiteracy and ignorance of the Catholic Irish, despite the fact that these were the fruits of British laws. Britons regarded the Irish, in fact, as white Americans viewed blacks, and Irish Catholics fully returned this malevolence. Centuries of oppression, murderous warfare, and degradation had made them a people bound monolithically by their hatred of Englishmen and especially of the Scotch-Irish.

For half a century after the Revolution, the Scotch-Irish had determined the tone and form of American politics. Their ancient hostility toward Englishmen had driven them over to the side of the South, thus allowing that region to dominate national politics. Now, however, the Catholic Irish assumed that central role in American public life. As they lined up massively within the Democratic party—the party of the outgroups, and of religious toleration and cultural laissez faire—their arrival drove the Scotch-Irish in the Northern states out of that party. The same happened to Baptists and Methodists, who detested Catholics much more than they did Congregationalists.

Where did these peoples go? At first they went to the American or Know-Nothing party which sprang up in the 1850s to fight Catholicism. Then when the slavery expansion issue erupted after the passage of the Kansas-Nebraska Act in 1854, the Know-Nothings broke apart because they could not unite their Southerners and Northerners on the issue. A wholly Northern party, the Republicans, appeared. It drew the anti-Catholics decamping from the now dying Know-Nothings; the entire Whig coalition—nationalist republicans of Henry Clay's lineage and moralistic republicans from New England and that broad band of Yankee settlement running through upstate New York and Pennsylvania out into the upper Middle West; and all militant anti-Southerners, especially from the Democratic party.

We observe several outcomes of these events. The accession of anti-Catholic Scotch-Irish to the Republican party meant that the British peoples, whose mutual hostilities had previously done so much to shape American politics, were now relatively unified within the Republican party. A *British* monolith had formed where formerly there had been an *English* one. Similarly, when the Baptists and Methodists, many from New England, swung over to join the Congregationalists within the Republican party, Yankeedom and Protestantism in the Northern states were unified as never before. All of this was intensified by anti-Southernism, now concentrated within one party to an unprecedented degree.

In the 1850s, therefore, the cultural pattern shifted sharply, and this was to have a powerful impact upon all subsequent events. For many years the most pressing cultural issue to thousands of Northerners had been how to resist the crusade of Congregational (and New Light Presbyterian) Yankees to build a purer America in their image. Now that enemy was replaced by a new and greater threat —Catholicism. At the same time Southern expansionism seemed to be surging so threateningly that republicanism itself, as embodied in the free states of the North, appeared to be in grave danger. Swiftly moving events combined in the Northern states to induce a paranoid belief that a Slave Power conspiracy had seized Washington.

Now the Republican party could insist that it incorporated the libertarian republicanism that Democrats had always claimed as their inheritance from Jefferson. Though in truth profoundly ambivalent about the status of black persons—Republicans were surrounded by a racist Northern population that hated blacks—they persistently held that slavery was morally wrong and that the slave system must be confined within its existing territory, clearly made anathema to all humankind, and thus put on the road to extinction. Those who remained in the Northern Democratic party countered with great vehemence that black people were inferior; that slavery was not a moral evil, but simply a local institution within the free choice of white Southerners (to this position had cultural laissez faire proceeded); and that Republicans were all abolitionists bent on destroying the Union.

The fundamental concern of Republicanism, however, was not the cause of black America. Indeed, so strong was Northern racism on both sides of the political fence that Republican leaders argued that theirs was the true white man's party and that by keeping the territories free of slavery they were saving them for white settlers and free labor. Their deepest concern was the cause of Yankee America, in their eyes a uniquely moral and Protestant civilization, hardworking, progressive, and thriving. By contrast, the South and its way of life seemed stagnant and slothful, degraded by the whites' distaste for manual labor, improvident, violent, and made immoral and unChristian by slavery. Republicans feared that a militant, expansionist South intended to destroy Yankee civilization, and hence the cause of true republicanism, by making slavery nationwide.

The Lower North was the fulcrum in the national balance of power as it had been from the nation's beginnings. Lying roughly below the 41st parallel, this band of east-west territory contained the great port cities of New York and Philadelphia, and the southern parts of Pennsylvania, Ohio, Indiana, and Illinois. The larger cities were ethnically mixed; the countryside was Scotch-Irish, Dutch, and German; and the Middle Western segment had been settled by Southerners. The Lower North traditionally leaned southward, for it distrusted Yankees and was strongly anti-abolitionist. However, since the arrival of the Catholic Irish had pushed the Scotch-Irish, as well as Baptist and Methodist New Englanders, over to the Republican side, the Lower North went for Abraham Lincoln. Henceforth, the national balance of political power would lean toward the North. The Yankees had won; leadership was finally theirs.

As a result of these swiftly moving events, the South found itself isolated as never before and confronted by a newly powerful and unified Yankee North. Southern allies in the North were no longer Protestants of British descent, but the Irish Catholics, a despised minority. The South's feeling of fundamental security within a Union in which slavery was not directly threatened began rapidly to dissolve. Yankeedom had always been a brooding hostile presence, but one kept successfully at a distance. To alarmed Southerners the government in Washington was now in Puritan hands, and sooner or later this would mean the abolition of slavery. Had not the Yankees used the government everywhere it was in their hands to carry out their moral reforms? Formerly, Yankee power in these matters had been kept at the state level and within the North. Now, Yankees had the federal government in their grasp.

Whether in Texas or Illinois, South Carolina or New York, Democratic editors burst into passionate attacks upon Yankee fanaticism, intolerance, and intrusion into the affairs of others. To Southern whites, abolition had been an unthinkable horror since it was first broached. They were convinced that, once freed, the slaves would take vengeance on their former masters as well as on their wives and children. Thrown into hysteria by John Brown's raid upon Harper's Ferry, South Carolina concluded upon Lincoln's election that it had no choice but to secede. To South Carolina, secession seemed to be the only way it could keep in subjection the enormous world of black Americans within its borders. Secession spread across the South, and war was close behind.

Thus the party system founded in the 1850s repeated the cycle of the first system: revolutionary crisis, war, a period of confusion in which the nation was reconstructed along new lines, and the tilting of the political balance toward one of the nation's poles. This time, the dominance and leadership swung to New England. Now there was a great surge of nationalism, and fundamental new legislation embodying that nationalism was enacted. The nation emerged from the Civil War and Reconstruction altered in many ways. During the war, the Yankee preeminence in Congress had resulted in the establishment of Henry Clay's American System so firmly that it held sway for the next half century. After the war, Yankee republicanism sought to remake the South, both black and white, in the Yankee image. The building of public schools, the establishment of a functioning local democracy where earlier there had been elite rule, and the effort to bring to the freed slave civil and political equality as well as education: these were the chief objectives of Radical Reconstruction. With the ratification of the Fifteenth Amendment in 1870 making it illegal to deny the vote on the ground of race, Republicans regarded the edifice as complete. It was believed that black Americans in the South and the North now had the "equal chance," which had always been the principal goal of Republican race policy. Meanwhile, the Other South had been encouraged to move strongly toward economic modernization—industrialization and urbanization.

In the 1870s humanitarian concerns faded in the face of national depression, and the North turned away from the Yankee effort to remake the South. The Gilded Age burgeoned. The Republican party tilted heavily toward giving lavish aid to entrepreneurs, and it acquired a disabling involvement with corruption. The Independent Republicans of the northeastern states—the Mugwumps—drew back in distaste. Since the days of John and John Quincy Adams, their tradition had been ambivalent toward economic development. As Yankees and nationalist republicans, they had approved of government leadership in the building of a vigorous national economy. As Puritans and moralistic republicans, they had been hostile to greed and avarice and distrustful of the Alexander Hamiltons of the world with their close links to financiers and speculative entrepreneurism.

After the shifts of the 1850s, the coalitions on each side remained fixed. Then, in the depression of the 1870s, national concern shifted from cultural (racial) questions back to economic ones, and the Democrats shifted the focus of their attack. Buoyed by increasing national disenchantment with Republican economic policies and a renewal of heavy German and Irish immigration, they reached back to the Jacksonian era for ideas and fresh vigor. A renewed debate over currency and taxation erupted, and the image of Thomas Jefferson, whose states-rights philosophy had been blamed for the Civil War, was rehabilitated. Democrats began once more to attack the close Republican links between business and government in exactly the terms which had served them so well a generation before. Corruption, the Democrats insisted, was more than simply a political disgrace. It was the principal means by which the wealthy bought government favors and secured special privileges—tariffs, land grants, and other bounties—which enabled them to exploit the community at large. By the Republicans' skillful maneuvering of the disputed electoral count in 1877, the venerable Jacksonian Democrat Samuel Tilden did not receive the presidency to which his popular vote majority entitled him, losing instead to the Republican Rutherford B. Hayes. However, the Democrats had clearly regained a position of parity in presidential elections with their Republican enemies. Then came the final withdrawal of federal troops from the South, a development that gave the Democrats free reign to dominate Southern congressional elections. Thereafter, in the houses of Congress, there was an even balance between Republicans and Democrats.

Thus, the end of the nation's first century of national politics coincided with the reemergence of an evenly balanced two party system.

But what happened thereafter? Did the essential pattern we have observed to this point continue to form the larger framework for politics in the United States?*

From the 1870s to the mid-1890s, the balance between the parties persisted, and a virtual impasse at the national level ensued. In the presence of massive voter turnouts unmatched in the twentieth century, the Republicans and the Democrats traded the presidency back and forth, and Congress was evenly divided. For only four years of this period did one party control both Congress and the White House —the Republicans from 1889 to 1891 under Benjamin Harrison and the Democrats from 1893 to 1895 under Grover Cleveland. Thus, from the 1870s to the mid-1890s, the fundamental structure of the third, or Civil War, party system endured as it had been established in the mid-1850s.

During this apparent stasis, however, a new United States was making its appearance, and with it a significantly modified setting for national politics. The appeal of America was reaching ever deeper into eastern and southern Europe, and immigrants of new ethnic stocks began to appear on North American shores. By the opening of the twentieth century, this new tidal wave of immigration, larger than any of its predecessors, meant that the ethnic minorities in American politics were not simply German and Irish, with small additions of Dutch and Scandinavian, but Italian, Polish, Russian, Jewish, Hungarian, and Greek, to mention only the most prominent of the new peoples. An explosion of urban and industrial growth, lurching and ill-balanced, transformed the country during the Gilded Age, appalling traditional Americans in the small towns and countryside. Crop prices for cotton producers in the South and grain farmers on the High Plains began a long decline, inaugurating an upsurge of agrarian radicalism. The economy went through an alarming sequence of erratic swings from brief prosperity to serious recession, social protest mounted, and class conflict between labor and capital became endemic. "Our era . . . of happy immunity from those social diseases which are the danger and the humiliation of Europe is passing away," observed a writer in the *Atlantic Monthly* in 1882. American confidence in the future, a spirit that had infused the Northern states and the West for many years, even in the depres-

*Because the preceding pages in Chapter Nine distill the narrative of this book, I have made no effort to footnote relevant scholarly works. However, from this point on the chapter breaks new ground. For documentation, refer to my article, "Ideology and Political Culture from Jefferson to Nixon," *The American Historical Review,* 82 (June 1977), 547–562.

sion of the 1870s, gave way in the 1880s, the decade to which recent scholarship increasingly points as the watershed years between the old and the new America.

The essential fact that had underlain American politics until this time necessarily lost its primacy. As the United States became more complex and multipolar, it passed out of the era in which the Yankee-Southerner confrontation, which had begun a century before in the eighteenth century, provided the fundamental shaping influence of its politics. Whether the nation would be dominated by the South or the North was no longer a matter for debate; that question had been settled at Appomattox. The Yankee culture which flourished in New England, with its ethic of orderly behavior, self-discipline, hard work, and an enterprising, get-ahead outlook, had spread westward through New York State and northern Pennsylvania into the Middle West. Indeed, Yankeedom had become the host culture toward which the rest of America was gravitating. When soldiers from the United States went out to the world in the two great wars of the twentieth century, they were called "Yanks," though Southern whites might demur. Even within the South itself, the "New South" ideology trumpeted about in the Gilded Age embodied Henry Clay's message: the South should become industrial, progressive, and urban like New England. European radicals correctly perceived, from the 1880s onward, that the United States was no longer the classless and egalitarian utopia of their dreams; instead, it was becoming ever more capitalistic, elitist, and plutocratic, ever more under the domination of Hamiltonian entrepreneurs. Free schools, free votes, free churches, and free land had not worked the republican magic that had so long been promised.

The second century of American national politics was, therefore, different in important respects from the first. Northern predominance was settled and secure; a powerful industrial order had emerged. During the great depression of the 1890s, a political earthquake occurred that solidified Yankee preeminence: the ethnic minorities in Northern cities suffered cruelly from unemployment and began voting Republican, for that party had always insisted upon active government intervention in the economy to create jobs and economic well-being. The national balance between the two parties that characterized the Gilded Age and the earlier Age of Jackson was replaced by a system of regional one-party predominance. Although the Democrats held on to their Solid South, in the North and West the Republican party was so triumphant from William McKinley's election to Herbert Hoover's (save for Woodrow Wilson's two terms) that Democrats could hardly mount a believable challenge. The demographic core of the Republican party expanded to comprise not simply British Protestant America, but Northern WASP (white Anglo-Saxon Protestant) America—a broad coalition of German Prot- estants, Dutchmen, Scandinavians, Britons from Canada and the British Isles, and those of Yankee stock whether in New England, the Middle West, or the Pacific Coast. Indeed, the years of the fourth, or Progressive Era, party system (1894–1930) were the years of North- ern WASP ascendancy in all things, including government, litera- ture, scholarship, the arts, and the economy.

Republicanism, the national ideology of the first century, was re- born after 1900 as "progressivism," a broad and bipartisan political consciousness that set the mood for an entire generation in rebellion against an older regime and culture. It existed, furthermore, in the same four modes—nationalist, moralistic, libertarian, and egalitarian —we have observed in the republicanism of the first century. The first two modes may be seen in Theodore Roosevelt's New National- ism and in his Yankee following. The latter two are evident in Wood- row Wilson's New Freedom and in the Democratic party's Southern and reemerging urban ethnic following. The trend toward an ever stronger national government continued, however, under both Re- publican and Democratic progressives.

During the 1920s, American politics swung back strongly toward a party system like that of Thomas Jefferson's time. Republicans fueled a massive campaign of moral reform that focused upon the refusal of the ethnic minorities to obey prohibition (this particular campaign angered the Germans, who decamped in a flood to the Democrats) and the supposed threat of the minorities' Jewishness, Catholicism, and urbanism. Republicans emphasized that further immigration of these ethnic groups must be ended. The Ku Klux Klan, traditionally thought to be primarily Southern, was actually strongest and most active in Northern and Western Republican dis- tricts, especially in the small towns and cities where WASP America predominated. Thus, a swing of tidal proportions toward the Demo- cratic party was already in evidence among the ethnic peoples in large Northern cities before the great depression of the 1930s pro- duced F.D.R.'s nationwide sweep. The revival of the first party sys- tem was complete in the fifth, or New Deal, party system (1932 to the present), for by this time the ethnic minorities of the North had again joined with the white Democratic South to dominate the na- tional government and rule the country. In the White House there was once again an egalitarian national leader who distrusted bankers and talked, in the Jeffersonian idiom, of the common folk being exploited by special interests and of the virtues of farming and country life, while also appointing Jews and Catholics in great numbers to high national office. Like the Virginian, F.D.R. was skeptical of orthodox opinions, uninterested in moralistic reforms, idolized by multitudes, and regarded as a traitor to the American way of life by his enemies. Jefferson was thought to be the advance agent of revolutionary French radicalism; Franklin Roosevelt was said to take his orders from Moscow.

Looking further ahead, it becomes clear that major features of the two party system that took shape in the 1790s persisted into the days of John Kennedy, Lyndon Johnson, and Richard Nixon. In the 1960s and 1970s, as in the nation's beginnings, the Irish Catholic and the Southerner were on one side, the Quaker was on the other. The Harvard graduate, with his intellectuality and his cosmopolitan life style, and the Texan with his ethnic accent and his down-home manners, were Democratic, perpetuating their party's tradition of identifying with ways of life frowned on by the puritanical and genteel, and with those peoples thought of as outsiders by the host culture. Speaking for the ignored and the exploited, Kennedy and Johnson labored for minority rights and social justice. The California WASP from a moralistic small town who symbolized what in the 1960s was called the square majority, identified by its preference for close-cropped hair and methodical ways, was Republican. He was swept to the White House in a national upwelling of anti-minority, law and order sentiments, and he promptly instituted a regime friendly to corporations and big business. Intellectuals, he said, had corrupted American values; the nation had lapsed into a slack and permissive frame of mind. What was needed, Richard Nixon believed, was a renewed dedication to hard work and self-denial.

In 1976, it was the Republican national convention that busied itself with moral issues—drugs and abortion—and that nominated an archetypical Northern WASP from a Middle Western Dutch constituency, Gerald Ford. He had warm personal relations with the wealthy, and in a long congressional career had devoted himself unswervingly to the needs of the entrepreneurial community. It was the Democratic national convention that talked about the poverty-stricken and the minorities and nominated a Baptist from the Deep South, Jimmy Carter, whose speech and customs, like those of outgroups everywhere, were ridiculed outside his region. Carter's rhetoric resounded with the populist values of the Jacksonian years. His victory in the election was the result of the same alliance between the South and the ethnic minorities of the Middle Atlantic and Middle Western states that had placed Jeffersonians and Jacksonians in the White House. Just as the massive pro-Jefferson vote of the Scotch-Irish, the most militant outgroup in 1800, put the Virginian into the presidency, so the massive pro-Carter vote of black America, the most militant outgroup in the 1970s, delivered the presidency to the Georgian.

The basic pattern endured, but much, of course, had changed. The United States was a profoundly different country at the end of two centuries than it had been in its beginnings. It had lost its youthful buoyant optimism and simplicity of purpose, and the national setting for cultural and economic politics was far more complex. Bipolarity was replaced by multipolarity. The nation's population climbed from four million in 1790 to fifty million at the end of the first century and to more than two hundred million in the 1970s. A cycle of great wars after 1900 and a series of technological revolutions transformed the national way of life. That there were major shifts in the country's cultural politics was demonstrated by the fact that black Americans were voting heavily Democratic at the end of the second century, whereas at the end of the first they had been solidly Republican.

The meanings of liberty, equality, morality, and nationalism grew more complicated. Was a Democratic party that took over from its Republican adversary the concept of a strong and intervening national government during the New Deal leaving libertarianism behind, or redefining it? When it stimulated the great boom of the 1960s by spending and taxing policies, could it any longer be thought of as standing in judgment upon aggressive capitalism? In the 1960s the Democrats (against strong opposition from white Southerners in their party) led the effort to prevent not only local government, but private citizens, from discriminating against non-whites and women. Was it, then, still the party of cultural laissez faire?

Which party was the modernizing influence, and which looked backward in dismay at a lost way of living? Which turned toward Europe for models and cultural sustenance, and which looked inward, hoping to close out transatlantic influences and root the nation's spirit in the continental heartland? How may we explain the fact that, in 1972, the one state that held out against the national landslide for the Republican candidate, Richard Nixon, and voted for the Democrat, George McGovern, was Massachusetts—that ancient heartland of Federalism, Whiggery, and Republicanism?

To look at another dimension, we have seen that the two parties differed in their foreign policies during the first hundred years. In the

second century the Republicans continued to be the voice of nationalism and "America First." In the years of Woodrow Wilson and
Franklin Roosevelt, the Democrats, with their minority group constituency and their egalitarian and libertarian tradition, insisted
upon the equality of all nations, asserted the right of self-government
by nationality groups, and called for an international structure of
collective security to control great power aggressiveness and protect
the smaller nations. Wilson and Roosevelt transformed American
involvement in the two world wars into crusades to spread liberty
around the world. In the latter decades of the second hundred years
did Democrats and Republicans still diverge in their views of the
world at large, Cold War tactics, and the military-industrial complex?
If they did, how can we account for the bipartisan tragedy of the
Vietnam War?

A remarkable fact in the politics of recent decades is the decline
of party membership and a turn, by voters, toward independence.
Since the decline has been heaviest among Republicans, is it related
to the ever-widening diffusion of the WASP life style in the population at large, a diffusion so extensive that those who used to be
Republicans and now declare themselves independents may be doing so because they have lost their sense of having a cultural enemy?
Certainly anti-Catholicism has lost most of its virulence, as has anti-
Semitism. In the 1970s it has often been said that the parties are
blurring into each other; that the basis for partisanship is dying.

In light of these complexities, my sense that the essential cultural
pattern of our politics is still that of the nation's beginnings is probably an assertion meriting the Scottish verdict "not proven." There is
much that remains to be explored and explained in the troubled and
complex second century of American public life before we can gain
a sufficient understanding of our politics at present and, accordingly,
of ourselves as a people. There must be profound differences between the first and second centuries of this country's politics, just as
there are between the nature and behavior of an individual as a child
and as an adult. However, the past is in us, and it will be strange
indeed if we find that it does not shape American political behavior
in its second century in ways similar to its influence during the first.
Cultural identities seem to have faded as national culture moves
increasingly toward an apparent uniformity, but they continue to
express themselves in politics in strikingly persistent ways.

White Southerners still have ancient memories of and resentments
toward Yankee predominance; the division between North and
South is finding a new terminology in "sunbelt" and "frostbelt"; Jews

remember centuries of oppression and massacre and still vote en bloc; and Irish and Polish Catholics, though no longer so monolithic, continue to line up strongly behind the Democrats. It may be difficult in the mid-twentieth century to tell a German from a Yankee, but the Lutheran community is still overwhelmingly German (or Scandinavian) in ethnic nature, and its attitudes tend to follow common alignments toward the nation's larger issues. Traditional cultural identities flourish, as in Texas, new ones appear to be forming, as in California, and others, as in the case of Chicanos, have only recently entered national politics in force. We cannot forget, furthermore, the division between black and white, modern America's counterpart in intensity to the North-South and Protestant-Catholic divisions in the nation's first century.

Until the unlikely time when cultural differences between the nation's peoples disappear, all communities share equally in power and status, our systems of moral values and ideologies are identical, and historical memories of hostility and oppression fade because they no longer relate to life as it is daily experienced, cultural politics, in its paradoxical interrelationship with economic politics, will continue powerfully to shape American public life.

Notes

The following journals will be abbreviated as follows:

The American Historical Review: AHR
Civil War History: CWH
The Journal of American History: JAH
The Journal of Southern History: JSH
Political Science Quarterly: PSQ
William and Mary Quarterly: WMQ

Introduction

1. J. Morgan Kousser, "The 'New Political History': A Methodological Critique," *Reviews in American History,* 4 (1976), 1–14.
2. Richard Hofstadter, *The Progressive Historians: Turner, Beard, Parrington* (New York, 1968).
3. For this shift in mood, see John Higham's two chapters, "Crisis in Progressive History" and "A Search for Stability," in John Higham, Leonard Krieger, and Felix Gilbert, *History* (Englewood Cliffs, N.J., 1965), pp. 198–232.
4. Robert Allen Skotheim, *American Intellectual Histories and Historians* (Princeton, N.J., 1966), p. 149. See also, for developments in intellectual history in recent years, John Higham's essays "Intellectual History and Its Neighbors" and "The Study of American Intellectual History," in his

Writing American History: Essays on Modern Scholarship (Blooming-
ton, 1970), pp. 27–72.
5. See Stanley Elkins and Eric McKitrick, "Richard Hofstadter: A
   Progress," in the book these two historians edited, *The Hofstadter
   Aegis: A Memorial* (New York, 1974), pp. 300–367, and Richard Gillam,
   "Richard Hofstadter, C. Wright Mills, and 'The Critical Ideal,'" *The
   American Scholar,* 47 (1978), 69–85.
6. Robert F. Berkhofer, Jr., has described the impact of cultural anthropology upon historiography in his "Clio and the Culture Concept:
   Some Impressions of a Changing Relationship in American Historiography," *Social Science Quarterly,* 53 (1972), 297–320. Especially valuable
   is this issue of *SSQ,* which is devoted primarily to a symposium of nine
   articles by such figures as Talcott Parsons and Kenneth E. Boulding on
   the general theme, "The Idea of Culture in the Social Sciences."
7. *The Social Sciences in Historical Study: A Report of the Committee on
   Historiography,* Social Science Research Council Bulletin 64 (New
   York, 1954).
8. Hays's most influential writings were "The Politics of Reform in Municipal Government in the Progressive Era," *Pacific Northwest Quarterly,*
   55 (1964), 157–169, and "The Social Analysis of American Political History, 1889–1920," *PSQ,* 80 (1965), 373–394.
   In an extraordinarily concentrated burst of scholarly achievement,
   from 1969 onward there appeared in quick succession the leading
   works in the new political history and a literature upon their implications: Michael F. Holt, *Forging a Majority: The Formation of the Republican Party in Pittsburgh, 1848–1860* (New Haven, 1969); Frederick C.
   Luebke, *Immigrants and Politics: The Germans of Nebraska, 1880–
   1900* (Lincoln, Neb., 1969); Paul Kleppner, *The Cross of Culture: A
   Social Analysis of Midwestern Politics, 1860–1900* (New York, 1970);
   Ronald P. Formisano, *The Birth of Mass Political Parties: Michigan,
   1827–1861* (Princeton, 1971); Richard Jensen, *The Winning of the Midwest: Social and Political Conflict, 1888–1896* (Chicago, 1971); John M.
   Allswang, *A House for All Peoples: Ethnic Politics in Chicago, 1890–
   1936* (Lexington, Ky., 1971); Samuel T. McSeveney, *The Politics of
   Depression: Political Behavior in the Northeast, 1893–1896* (New York,
   1972); and William Gerald Shade, *Banks or No Banks: The Money Ques-
   tion in the Western States, 1832–1865* (Detroit, 1973).
   Essays analyzing the new political history are Robert P. Swierenga,
   "Ethnocultural Political Analysis: A New Approach to American Ethnic
   Studies," *Journal of American Studies,* 5 (1971), 59–79; Paul Kleppner,
   "Beyond the 'New Political History': A Review Essay," *Historical Meth-
   ods Newsletter,* 6 (1972), 17–26; Samuel T. McSeveney, "Ethnic Groups,
   Ethnic Conflicts, and Recent Quantitative Research in American Politi-
   cal History," *International Migration Review,* 7 (1973), 14–33; Rudolph
   J. Vecoli, "European Americans: From Immigrants to Ethnics," in Wil-

liam H. Cartwright and Richard L. Watson, Jr. (eds.), *The Reinterpretation of American History and Culture* (Washington, D.C., 1973), pp. 81–112.

9. Richard Hofstadter, "Pseudo-Conservatism Revisited: A Postscript," in Daniel Bell (ed.), *The Radical Right: The New American Right —Expanded and Updated* (Garden City, N.Y., 1964), p. 99.

10. Berkhofer, "Clio and the Culture Concept," *Social Science Quarterly,* p. 303.

11. Clifford Geertz, *The Interpretation of Cultures* (New York, 1973), p. 12. I have been much aided by Hatch's *Theories of Man and Culture* (New York, 1973), in this and the following discussion. The quotation is from p. 6. See also the classic work, A. L. Kroeber and Clyde Kluckhohn, *Culture: Critical Review of Concepts and Definitions* (New York, 1952).

12. Hatch, *Theories of Man and Culture,* pp. 158, 340.

13. *Ibid.,* pp. 162–213.

14. Clifford Geertz, "The Impact of the Concept of Culture on the Concept of Man," in Yehudi A. Cohen (ed.), *Man in Adaptation: The Cultural Present,* 2nd ed. (Chicago, 1974), p. 20.

15. Michael Kammen, "The American Revolution as a *Crise de Conscience:* The Case of New York," in Jack P. Greene, Richard L. Bushman, and Michael Kammen, *Society, Freedom, and Conscience: The American Revolution in Virginia, Massachusetts, and New York* (New York, 1976), pp. 126–131.

16. *AHR,* 82 (June 1977), 580–581. The controversy in *CWH* between Eric Foner and Ronald P. Formisano may be read in connection with Foner's essay "The Causes of the American Civil War: Recent Interpretations and New Directions," 20 (September 1974), 197–214, which has recently been republished in Robert P. Swierenga (ed.), *Beyond the Civil War Synthesis: Political Essays of the Civil War Era* (Westport, Conn., 1975), and an exchange of letters to the editor in the "Communications" section, 21 (June 1975), 185–190. Professor Rose's full critique may be read following the published version of my address, "Ideology and Political Culture from Jefferson to Nixon," in *AHR,* 82 (June 1977), the words quoted appearing on pp. 580–581.

17. Richard L. McCormick, "Ethno-cultural Interpretations of Nineteenth-Century American Voting Behavior," *PSQ,* 89 (1974), 351–377. Other critiques of method in relation to the new political history may be found in Allen G. Bogue, "United States: The 'New Political History,' " *Journal of Contemporary History,* 3 (January 1968), 22–24; James E. Wright, "The Ethnocultural Model of Voting," *American Behavioral Scientist,* 16 (May–June 1973), 653–674; and James R. Green, "Behavioralism and Class Analysis: A Review Essay on Methodology and Ideology," *Labor History,* 13 (Winter 1972), 89–106.

18. For this general position, to which I have also referred in the introduction to a former book, *The Transatlantic Persuasion: The Liberal-*

Democratic Mind in the Age of Gladstone (New York, 1969), see William Dray, *Laws and Explanation in History* (London, 1957), particularly chapter 5, "The Rationale of Actions."

19. V. O. Key, Jr., "A Theory of Critical Elections," *Journal of Politics,* 17 (1955), 3–18. In the fifth edition of his text *Politics, Parties, and Pressure Groups* (New York, 1958), Key observes that "a conception of the party system must take into account its dimension of time. It may be useful to think of the party system as an historical process rather than as patterned and static institutional behavior" (p. 222).

20. The book that most successfully brings together the work that followed Key's pronouncement and creates out of it a new synthesis is Walter Dean Burnham, *Critical Elections and the Mainsprings of American Politics* (New York, 1970). I have relied in the above passage upon his first chapter, "Toward a Definition of Critical Realignment," pp. 1–10. See also another fundamental work, William Nisbet Chambers and Walter Dean Burnham (eds.), *The American Party Systems: Stages of Political Development,* 2nd ed. (New York, 1975). Burnham's summary statement in *Critical Elections* (p. 10) is useful:

> To recapitulate, then, eras of critical realignment are marked by short, sharp reorganizations of the mass coalitional bases of the major parties which occur at periodic intervals on the national level; are often preceded by major third-party revolts which reveal the incapacity of "politics as usual" to integrate, much less aggregate, emergent political demand; are closely associated with abnormal stress in the socioeconomic system; are marked by ideological polarizations and issue-distances between the major parties which are exceptionally large by normal standards; and have durable consequences as constituent acts which determine the outer boundaries of policy in general, though not necessarily of policies in detail.

21. See Burnham, *Critical Elections,* pp. 11–33, for a detailed statistical presentation and analysis of the five party systems and their chronology.

22. Basic works in the genre of modernization are Walt W. Rostow, *The Stages of Economic Growth: A Non-Communist Manifesto,* 2nd ed. (Cambridge, Eng., 1971); Daniel Lerner, *The Passing of Traditional Society: Modernizing the Middle East* (Glencoe, Ill., 1958); Gabriel A. Almond and Sidney Verba, *The Civic Culture: Political Attitudes and Democracy in Five Nations* (Princeton, N.J., 1963); Samuel Huntington, *Political Order in Changing Societies* (New Haven, 1968). It is interesting that Huntington has recently taken the view that the modernization concept does not apply within American history, though the command of that history that he reveals in his essay would not be persuasive, as regards depth and knowledge of present-day scholarship, to historians. See his essay "Paradigms of American Politics: Beyond the One, the Two, and the Many," *PSQ,* 89 (March 1974), 1–26.

23. The foregoing passage draws upon C. E. Black, *The Dynamics of Modernization: A Study in Comparative History* (New York, 1966), the quotation being from p. 27.

24. See Richard D. Brown, *Modernization: The Transformation of American Life 1600–1865* (New York, 1976), pp. 3–22. For a recent critique of Brown's book, see James A. Henretta, " 'Modernization': Toward a False Synthesis," *Reviews in American History,* 5 (December 1977), 445–452.

25. A valuable critique of modernization analyses is in Dean C. Tipps' "Modernization Theory and the Comparative Study of Societies: A Critical Perspective," *Comparative Studies in Society and History: An International Quarterly,* 15 (March 1973), 199–226. The quotation is from page 199. A recent effort at close analysis and controlled quantification is Allan Schnaiberg, "Measuring Modernism: Theoretical and Empirical Explorations," *American Journal of Sociology,* 76 (November 1970), 399–425.

26. In his Commentary upon my bicentennial address and article, published in *AHR,* 82 (1977), pp. 568, 572.

27. For a position similar to my own on the South, see George B. Tindall's presidential address before the Southern Historical Association, "Beyond the Mainstream: The Ethnic Southerners," *JSH,* 40 (1974), 3–18, and his *The Ethnic Southerners* (Baton Rouge, 1976).

28. Lawrence M. Fuchs (ed.), *American Ethnic Politics* (New York, 1968), p. 1. For a fuller discussion of ethnicity, see Cynthia H. Enloe, *Ethnic Conflict and Political Development* (Boston, 1973).

29. Edgar Litt, *Beyond Pluralism: Ethnic Politics in America* (Glenview, Ill., 1970), pp. 5–6.

30. *Ibid.,* p. 6.

31. R. A. Schermerhorn, "Minorities: European and American," in Milton L. Barron (ed.), *Minorities in a Changing World* (New York, 1967), pp. 5–14.

32. Milton L. Barron, "Ethnic Anomie," in Barron, *Minorities in a Changing World,* pp. 15–39.

33. Carl N. Degler, *The Other South: Southern Dissenters in the Nineteenth Century* (New York, 1974).

34. Mark R. Levy and Michael S. Kramer, *The Ethnic Factor: How America's Minorities Decide Elections* (New York, 1973), p. 9.

35. See Richard Gillam, "Richard Hofstadter, C. Wright Mills, and 'The Critical Ideal'," *The American Scholar,* 47 (Winter 1978), pp. 73–81.

Chapter One

1. My treatment of this period draws upon Bernard Bailyn's picture of mid-eighteenth-century colonial public life in his *The Origins of American Politics* (New York, 1968), pp. 59–105. The literature on these topics is rich, diverse, and like that on the entire Revolutionary period, rapidly growing. Among other works of fundamental importance are Jack P. Greene's *The Quest for Power: The Lower Houses of Assembly*

in the Southern Royal Colonies, 1689–1776 (Chapel Hill, N.C., 1963) and his essay "The Social Origins of the American Revolution: An Evaluation and Interpretation," *PSQ,* 88 (March 1973), 1–22. The political system in a Northern colony may be seen in Richard D. Brown, *Revolutionary Politics in Massachusetts: The Boston Committee of Correspondence, 1772–1774* (Cambridge, Mass., 1970).

2. Bailyn, *Origins of American Politics,* p. 64; Gary B. Nash, "The Transformation of Urban Politics 1700–1765," *JAH,* 60 (1973), 605–632. Richard L. Bushman's *From Puritan to Yankee: Character and the Social Order in Connecticut, 1690–1765* (Cambridge, Mass., 1967), pp. 3–21, is central to understanding this entire transformation. Other important works are: Michael Zuckerman, *Peaceable Kingdoms: Massachusetts Towns in the Eighteenth Century* (New York, 1970); Kenneth A. Lockridge, "Social Change and the Meaning of the American Revolution," *Journal of Social History,* 6 (1973), 403–439; John B. Kirby, "Early American Politics—The Search for Ideology: An Historiographical Analysis and Critique of the Concept of 'Deference,' " *The Journal of Politics,* 32 (1970), 808–838.

3. For an extended exploration of the British ethnic, religious, political, and intellectual background to American public life, see Robert Kelley, *The Transatlantic Persuasion: The Liberal-Democratic Mind in the Age of Gladstone* (New York, 1969).

4. I am presenting the simplified conceptions that Revolutionary-era patriots held of Whigs and Tories, not the complex reality that existed in Britain. Esmond Wright asserts that the analyses of Whig and Tory by Bernard Bailyn and Edmund Morgan are too steeped in the pamphlet literature of the period. They are "apt to see the events of 1776 in terms of the stereotypes of those pamphleteers and sermon-writers . . . [that is] as an American replica of 1649, with George III sometimes appearing to some contemporaries indeed as a latter-day Charles I [though he] . . . was in fact no tyrant, and . . . his limitation was executive weakness, vacillation and inconsistency rather than the reverse. . . . The intellectual conflict of 1776 was in fact not between Whig and Tory but between Whig and Whig, or, to use Burke's language—between Old Whig and New," each emphasizing different sides of John Locke's ideology. (See Wright's "The Loyalists," in H. C. Allen and Roger Thompson [eds.], *Contrast and Connection: Bicentennial Essays in Anglo-American History* [Athens, Ohio, 1976], pp. 131–132.)

J. G. A. Pocock has observed that there

> weren't any Tory governments after 1714, until a date well subsequent to the American Revolution; neither North nor the younger Pitt would have accepted the label; and the regime which the Revolutionaries and Founding Fathers opposed is best described as that of the Court Whigs or the Whig oligarchy, thrown into disarray but not yet replaced in consequence of the political initiatives of George III, leaving the term "Whig" applicable to the Americans in the sense of "Old Whig," "Country," or

more simply (but still Whiggishly) "Patriot." I argue that the Revolution is a schism in the Whig political culture. (Letter to the author, August 24, 1977.)

That is, as Pocock explains in the concluding pages of his remarkable work, *The Machiavellian Moment: Florentine Political Thought and the Atlantic Republican Tradition* (Princeton, 1975), the American Whigs discovered after independence that a society freed of tyranny did not naturally form itself into hierarchical classes in which the Few led the Many in a relationship of virtuous regard for each other, but became a diverse, multi–interested People. A revolutionary conception emerged in America, that of grounding government in a sovereign people who chose representatives without releasing to them that sovereignty, and put these representatives at work within a constitutional structure whose internal balance of powers was to be the safeguard for virtue. In Britain, Whiggery continued to conceive of sovereignty as lodged not in the people but in *Parliament,* a constituent part of which was the executive. Although British Whigs differed from the Tories in their sense of Parliament's relationship to the people and of its obligations to consider public opinion and work for the general welfare, they still assumed the rightful existence of a hierarchical set of "orders." The natural elite, the Few, should be in a trustee relationship to the Many. (See pp. 506–552.)

5. Carl Bridenbaugh, *Mitre and Sceptre: Transatlantic Faiths, Ideas, Personalities, and Politics: 1689–1775* (New York, 1962).
6. Jack P. Greene, "An Uneasy Connection: An Analysis of the Preconditions of the American Revolution," in Stephen Kurtz and James Hutson (eds.), *Essays on the American Revolution* (Chapel Hill, N.C., 1973), pp. 47–53; Michael Kraus, *The Atlantic Civilization: Eighteenth-Century Origins* (Ithaca, N.Y., 1949); Alison Gilbert Olson, *Anglo-American Politics, 1660–1775: The Relationship Between Parties in England and Colonial America* (New York, 1973); Richard Maxwell Brown, "The Anglo-American Political System, 1675–1775: A Behavioral Analysis," in Alison Gilbert Olson and Richard Maxwell Brown (eds.), *Anglo-American Political Relations, 1675–1775* (New Brunswick, N.J., 1970), pp. 2–28.
7. James G. Leyburn, *The Scotch-Irish: A Social History* (Chapel Hill, N.C., 1962); E. R. R. Green (ed.), *Essays in Scotch-Irish History* (London, 1969); Robert Henry Billigmeier, *Americans from Germany: A Study in Cultural Diversity* (Belmont, Calif., 1974); Richard L. Merritt, *Symbols of American Community, 1735–1775* (New Haven, 1966); Robert McCluer Calhoon, *The Loyalists in Revolutionary America 1760–1781* (New York, 1973), pp. 364–365; R. J. Dickson, *Ulster Emigration to Colonial America 1718–1775* (London, 1966).
8. Cushing Strout, *The New Heavens and New Earth: Political Religion in America* (New York, 1974), pp. 29–55, and Alan E. Heimert, *Religion*

and the American Mind, from the Great Awakening to the Revolution
(Cambridge, Mass., 1966).

9. Kenneth A. Lockridge, "Social Change and the Meaning of the American Revolution," *Journal of Social History,* 6 (Summer 1973), 403–439.
Joyce Appleby writes,

> Recent scholarship has begun to coalesce around a new interpretation of prerevolutionary society. Instead of the slowly diverging process of cultural differentiation [from England] associated with the colonial maturity view, there is now evidence of a disjuncture in colonial life in the second quarter of the eighteenth century. A social order of due subordination incumbent in varying degrees upon all members of the community gave way in the decades after 1730 to an atomized society. . . . This new social situation made contemporaries peculiarly sensitive to threats against their personal freedom. Among the many satisfying human goals, liberty came to overshadow all others. . . . Why did the group-centered social organization, the deferential political system, and the orthodox congregational establishments . . . fail to survive intact through the second third of the eighteenth century? A tentative answer is that demographic and economic changes overwhelmed these communities' adaptive capacities. ("Liberalism and the American Revolution," *The New England Quarterly,* 49 [March 1976], 7–9.)

Professor Appleby has subtly argued the interrelations of economic modernization and Revolutionary-era political thought in a series of recent essays: "Ideology and Theory: The Tension between Political and Economic Liberalism," *AHR,* 81 (June 1976), 499–515; "Locke, Liberalism and the Natural Law of Money," *Past and Present,* 71 (May 1976); "The Social Origins of American Revolutionary Ideology," *JAH,* 64 (1978), 935–958. "My point," she has written, ". . . is not that the Revolution made the modernization process possible so much as it is that the economic changes of the eighteenth century must be seen as a cause of a new social theory which gave the discontented colonists a way of looking at reality which explained and justified the declaration of independence." (Letter to author, August 3, 1977.) See also Bushman, *From Puritan to Yankee,* passim. Stephen E. Patterson, in his important work, *Political Parties in Revolutionary Massachusetts* (Madison, Wis., 1973), pp. 63–65, makes an intriguing use of modernization concepts.

10. Greene, "An Uneasy Connection," in Kurtz and Hutson, *Essays on the American Revolution,* pp. 65–68; John C. Miller, *Origins of the American Revolution* (Boston, 1943), pp. 204–206; "A Letter to John Farr and John Harris, Esquires, Sheriffs of Bristol, on the Affairs of America, April 1777," in Elliott Robert Barkan (ed.), *Edmund Burke on the American Revolution: Selected Speeches and Letters* (New York, 1966), p. 195.

11. For the classic analysis of this type of political behavior, see Richard Hofstadter, *The Paranoid Style in American Politics and Other Essays* (New York, 1967), pp. 3–40.

12. Miller, *Origins of the American Revolution,* pp. 186–197.

13. Caroline Robbins transformed the history of eighteenth-century British and American public life when in 1959 she published her study *The Eighteenth-Century Commonwealthman* (Cambridge, Mass.). The quotation is from p. 380.
14. *Ibid.*, pp. 134–136, 177–179, 221–233, 381–385.
15. In this discussion of republicanism, the "Tory Plot," and the radical British Whigs, I have relied upon J. G. A. Pocock's *The Machiavellian Moment: Florentine Political Thought and the Atlantic Republican Tradition,* which is now the fundamental work on republicanism as an ideology and especially on republicanism's obsession with the potential for corruption that exists in close relations between governments and entrepreneurial capitalism, and three landmark studies, Bernard Bailyn's *The Ideological Origins of the American Revolution* (Cambridge, Mass., 1967) and *The Origins of American Politics,* and Gordon S. Wood's *The Creation of the American Republic* (Chapel Hill, N.C., 1969).

    A valuable overview of the new literature on the theme of republicanism is Robert E. Shalhope, "Toward a Republican Synthesis: The Emergence of an Understanding of Republicanism in American Historiography," *WMQ,* 3d Series, 29 (January 1972), 49–80. See also H. Trevor Colbourn, *The Lamp of Experience: Whig History and the Intellectual Origins of the American Revolution* (Chapel Hill, N.C., 1965), and Lance Banning, "Republican Ideology and the Triumph of the Constitution, 1789–1793," *WMQ,* 3d Series, 31 (April 1974), 167–188.
16. Eric Foner, *Tom Paine and Revolutionary America* (New York, 1976); Bailyn, *Ideological Origins,* pp. 94–131; Wood, *Creation of the American Republic,* pp. 36–65, 107–123; Strout, *New Heavens and New Earth,* pp. 52–57; Patterson, *Political Parties in Revolutionary Massachusetts,* pp. 63–65.
17. William G. McLoughlin, "The Role of Religion in the Revolution: Liberty of Conscience and Cultural Cohesion in the New Nation," in Kurtz and Hutson, *Essays on the American Revolution,* pp. 206–208.
18. See Alfred F. Young (ed.), *The American Revolution: Explorations in the History of American Radicalism* (DeKalb, Ill., 1976).

Chapter Two

1. In the following discussion, I am greatly indebted to Stephen E. Patterson's recent study, *Political Parties in Revolutionary Massachusetts* (Madison, Wis., 1973), upon which I've drawn heavily. Of value to me also has been "A New Look at the American Revolution: An Environmental Theory," a paper he delivered before the Ninth Annual Conference of the Canadian Association for American Studies, October 14, 1973.

2. Jackson Turner Main, *Political Parties Before the Constitution* (Chapel Hill, N.C., 1973), pp. 93–94.
3. On unanimity, see Michael Zuckerman, *Peaceable Kingdoms: Massachusetts Towns in the Eighteenth Century* (New York, 1970). For other aspects see Rowland Berthoff and John M. Murrin, "Feudalism, Communalism, and the Yeoman Freeholder: The American Revolution Considered as a Social Accident," in Stephen Kurtz and James Hutson (eds.), *Essays on the American Revolution* (Chapel Hill, N.C., 1973), pp. 256–288; Gary B. Nash, "The Transformation of Urban Politics 1700–65," *JAH*, 60 (December 1973), 605–632; Robert Zemsky, *Merchants, Farmers, and River Gods: An Essay on Eighteenth-Century American Politics* (Boston, 1971), pp. 66–72; Patterson, *Political Parties in Revolutionary Massachusetts*, pp. 41–48.
4. Richard L. Bushman, *From Puritan to Yankee: Character and the Social Order in Connecticut, 1690–1765* (Cambridge, Mass., 1967), pp. 286–288.
5. Zemsky, *Merchants, Farmers, and River Gods*, pp. 254–255.
6. Patterson, *Political Parties in Revolutionary Massachusetts*, pp. 70, 87–124, 203–209, 245–251. On the desire of colonial merchants to gain sovereignty over American economic life, see Marc Egnal and Joseph A. Ernst, "An Economic Interpretation of the American Revolution," *WMQ*, 3d Series, 29 (January 1972), 15–24.
7. In this and the following discussion of Massachusetts and "slavery fears," I have drawn from Richard L. Bushman's McLellan Lecture at Miami University, Ohio, "Massachusetts Farmers and the Revolution," in Jack P. Greene, Richard L. Bushman, and Michael Kammen, *Society, Freedom, and Conscience: The American Revolution in Virginia, Massachusetts, and New York* (New York, 1976), pp. 81–122.
8. See Main's *Political Parties Before the Constitution,* pp. 265–287, for his discussion of localism and cosmopolitanism. His work strongly supports the view, traditional among historians at least since Frederick Jackson Turner and Charles Beard, that these alignments are to be explained primarily by residential location and economic influence, together with the impact of world views taken up by men because of their situation and life experience. Professor Main finds ethnocultural influences of little significance. He gives religion a role only in the cases of Episcopalians and Quakers, dismissing the heavy Presbyterian and Baptist alignment on the localist side as caused by place of residence. These judgments remind us that predispositions about human life and motivation lead scholars to take widely divergent views of the same evidence. In the above précis of localist/cosmopolitan characteristics, the references to Anglicization, English descent, Dissenters, the Scotch-Irish, and the relation of Loyalism to cosmopolitanism were my own interpolations. They seem to me to be indicated by the cultural elements that

Professor Main identifies and by my work in other sources. Professor Main has observed:

> most loyalists didn't belong to that class even in the north, and the state-
> ment or inference that most loyalists followed cosmopolitan leaders is a
> pretty big mouthful to digest.... Religious and ethnic divisions probably
> were more important in Pennsylvania than I indicated and you could
> make a case for New Jersey. But I found people dividing over the same
> issues, in much the same way, in states where religious and ethnic divi-
> sions did not exist at all (N.J., Conn., Del., Mass., R.I., Md., Va.) or where
> they did not compare in explanatory power with other factors (practically
> all the rest). Frankly I do not think you can ignore these. (Letter to the
> author, October 20, 1975)

9. Bernard Bailyn, *The Ordeal of Thomas Hutchinson* (Cambridge, Mass., 1974); Patterson, "A New Look at the American Revolution: An Environmental Theory," p. 18. On the rise of a radical working class movement, see Jesse Lemisch, "The American Revolution Seen from the Bottom Up," in Barton J. Bernstein (ed.), *Towards a New Past: Dissenting Essays in American History* (New York, 1968); Lemisch, "Jack Tar in the Streets: Merchant Seamen in the Politics of Revolutionary America," *WMQ*, 3d Ser., 25 (1968), 371–407; and especially Alfred F. Young (ed.), *The American Revolution: Explorations in the History of American Radicalism* (DeKalb, Ill., 1976). Especially relevant here is Gary B. Nash, "Social Change and the Growth of Prerevolutionary Urban Radicalism," pp. 6–36, which concentrates illuminatingly on Boston and Hutchinson, and Dirk Hoerder, "Boston Leaders and Boston Crowds, 1765–1776," pp. 233–272.
10. Rhys Isaac, "Religion and Authority: Problems of the Anglican Establishment in Virginia in the Era of the Great Awakening and the Parson's Cause," *WMQ*, 3d Series, 30 (January 1973), 3–36. See also his general discussion of Virginia in these years in his "Preachers and Patriots: Popular Culture and the Revolution in Virginia," in Young, *The American Revolution*, pp. 125–156.
11. Edmund S. Morgan, *American Slavery American Freedom: The Ordeal of Colonial Virginia* (New York, 1975), pp. 363–387.
12. *Ibid.*, pp. 376, 380.
13. Charles S. Sydnor, *Gentlemen Freeholders: Political Practices in Washington's Virginia* (Chapel Hill, N.C., 1952).
14. Egnal and Ernst, "An Economic Interpretation of the American Revolution," *WMQ*, pp. 24–28; Joseph Ernst, " 'Ideology' and an Economic Interpretation of the Revolution," in Young, *The American Revolution*, pp. 159–186.
15. George William Pilcher, *Samuel Davies: Apostle of Dissent in Colonial Virginia* (Knoxville, Tenn., 1971), pp. 158–169.
16. See Isaac, "Religion and Authority," and his "Evangelical Revolt: The Nature of the Baptists' Challenge to the Traditional Order of Virginia, 1765 to 1775," *WMQ*, 3d Series, 31 (July 1974), 345–368.

17. *Ibid.*
18. Gordon S. Wood, *The Creation of the American Republic* (Chapel Hill, N.C., 1969), p. 109; Merrill D. Peterson, *Thomas Jefferson and the New Nation: A Biography* (New York, 1970), p. 41.
19. See note 15 and Carl Bridenbaugh, *Mitre and Sceptre: Transatlantic Faiths, Ideas, Personalities, and Politics: 1689–1775* (New York, 1962), p. 131.
20. Peterson, *Thomas Jefferson and the New Nation,* p. 38; Main, *Party Politics Before the Constitution,* p. 245.
21. Patricia U. Bonomi, *A Factious People: Politics and Society in Colonial New York* (New York, 1971), pp. 24–26; Robert McCluer Calhoon, *The Loyalists in Revolutionary America 1760–1781* (New York, 1973), pp. 364–365; Nash, "The Transformation of Urban Politics 1700–1765," pp. 609–611; John A. Neuenschwander, *The Middle Colonies and the Coming of the American Revolution* (Port Washington, N.Y., 1973). With more than sixty congregations in the 1760s, the Presbyterians had twice the number of the Anglicans or the Dutch Reformed; the German Lutherans, who took little role in New York's politics, had twenty. The similarly quietistic Quakers had twenty-six, and the Baptists sixteen (see Bonomi, *A Factious People).*
22. John W. Pratt, *Religion, Politics and Diversity: The Church-State Theme in New York History* (Ithaca, N.Y., 1967), pp. 37–77.
23. Professor James S. Olson has made a roll-call analysis of votes in the Assembly during the years 1768–1771, finding the two factions to be loyal at about the 75 percent level on nineteen issues, which shows a high degree of party development. The Livingston group in the Assembly included three Presbyterians, five Dutch Reformed, a Lutheran, and a Quaker; the De Lancey faction included ten Anglicans, six Dutch Reformed, and a Presbyterian. All but two of the Anglicans became Loyalists; all members of the Livingston coalition were rebels in the Revolution, being joined by most of the Dissenters in the former De Lancey group. See Professor Olson's "The New York Assembly, the Politics of Religion, and the Origins of the American Revolution, 1768–1771," *Historical Magazine of the Protestant Episcopal Church,* 43 (March 1974), 21–28.
24. H. James Henderson, *Party Politics in the Continental Congress* (New York, 1974), p. 86; John C. Miller, *Origins of the American Revolution* (Boston, 1943), pp. 195–196.
25. For the foregoing discussion of the Scots, Presbyterianism, and America, see James G. Leyburn, *The Scotch-Irish: A Social History* (Chapel Hill, N.C., 1962), pp. 208, 235–346, 285–286; Cushing Strout, *The New Heavens and New Earth: Political Religion in America* (New York, 1974), pp. 47, 52–54; Sidney E. Ahlstrom, *A Religious History of the American People* (New Haven, 1972), pp. 265–279; Robert Kelley, *The Transatlantic Persuasion: The Liberal-Democratic Mind in the Age of*

Gladstone (New York, 1969), pp. 105–106; Douglas Adair, " 'That Politics May Be Reduced to a Science': David Hume, James Madison, and the *Tenth Federalist,*" *Huntington Library Quarterly,* 20 (1957), 343–360; Neuenschwander, *The Middle Colonies and the Coming of the American Revolution,* p. 107; Douglas Sloan, *The Scottish Enlightenment and the American College Ideal* (New York, 1971).

26. Alfred F. Young, *The Democratic Republicans of New York: The Origins, 1763–1797* (Chapel Hill, N.C., 1967), pp. 34–39, 66.

27. *Ibid.,* pp. 14, 66–68; Calhoon, *The Loyalists in Revolutionary America, 1760–1781,* pp. 24–25, 371, 408–421; William H. Nelson, *The American Tory* (New York, 1961), pp. 2–20, 85–95; Wallace Brown, *The King's Friends: The Composition and Motives of the American Loyalist Claimants* (Providence, R.I., 1965), pp. 256–283. See also Mary Beth Norton, *The British-Americans: The Loyalist Exiles in England, 1774–1789* (Boston, 1972), and Ronald Hoffman, "The 'Disaffected' in the Revolutionary South," in Young, *The American Revolution,* pp. 273–316.

28. Young, *The Democratic Republicans of New York,* pp. 34–39, 66; Main, *Political Parties Before the Constitution,* pp. 124, 137–47; Edwin G. Burrows, "Military Experience and the Origins of Federalism and Antifederalism," in Jacob Judd and Irwin H. Polishook (eds.), *Aspects of Early New York Society and Politics* (Tarrytown, N.Y., 1973), pp. 83–92, a quantitative study of voting in the New York ratifying convention (of the federal Constitution) of 1788; John Shy, "The American Revolution: The Military Conflict Considered as a Revolutionary War," in Kurtz and Hutson, *Essays on the American Revolution,* pp. 121–156. Valuable too is Alfred F. Young, "George Clinton: Democratic, Middle-Class Prototype of the Revolution," a paper presented to a conference, "New York in the New Nation," at State University College at Oneonta, April 26–27, 1974, especially for its comments upon Clinton's Scotch-Irish Presbyterian background and his links to the Dutch and other groups.

29. Young, *The Democratic Republicans of New York,* pp. 1–10, 32, 39–42, 51–52, 66–68, 74–79. This rich study is essential to any understanding of New York's complex politics. Its vantage point is not by means of ethnic and religious groups, but by class analysis, though as Professor Young writes, "I am always puzzled by scholars who interpret analysis of class as being economic. I have never thought of it that way." (Letter to the author, May 26, 1976.) See also Main, *Political Parties Before the Constitution,* p. 130.

30. Robert Henry Billigmeier, *Americans from Germany: A Study in Cultural Diversity* (Belmont, Calif., 1974).

31. In my discussion of the Scotch-Irish and their characteristics, I have drawn upon James G. Leyburn's revealing study, *The Scotch-Irish: A Social History,* as well as two studies in E. R. R. Green (ed.), *Essays in Scotch-Irish History* (London, 1969): Esmond Wright, "Education in the American Colonies: The Impact of Scotland," pp. 18–45, and E.

Estyn Evans, "The Scotch-Irish: Their Cultural Adaptation and Heritage in the American Old West," pp. 69–86. Leyburn, on p. 186, gives approximate percentages of Scotch-Irish settlement by state in 1790. The quotations in the above passage are from: pp. 329, 241, and the information on New Hampshire and Maine on pp. 236–242.

32. Leyburn, *The Scotch-Irish*, pp. 140–153, 305, 330.
33. In the foregoing and following discussion of Pennsylvania politics, I have drawn heavily upon James H. Hutson, *Pennsylvania Politics 1746–1770: The Movement for Royal Government and Its Consequences* (Princeton, N.J., 1972).
34. *Ibid.*, pp. 98–105.
35. *Ibid.*, pp. 105–243. A detailed quantitative study of voting in the Pennsylvania Assembly over the years 1755 to 1780 by Wayne L. Bockelman and Owen S. Ireland is reported in their essay: "The Internal Revolution in Pennsylvania: An Ethnic-Religious Interpretation," *Pennsylvania History*, 41 (January 1974), 125–159. See also William S. Hanna, *Benjamin Franklin and Pennsylvania Politics* (Stanford, Calif., 1964), pp. 13–14. As to the Philadelphia merchants and bankers, Professor Owen S. Ireland observes that there

> is some evidence to suggest that the cosmopolitan, urbanized, merchant and financial community of Philadelphia was not a homogeneous group with identical political interests. [Scotch-Irishman] McClenanchan and [Englishman] Morris did not readily eat out of the same dish; dry goods merchants differed from wet goods merchants in their response to both domestic and imperial issues; and West India men often differed with those involved in the direct trade with England or Europe.

Furthermore, "urban professional business groups were not totally free of the divisive influence of ethnic-religious identifications: Presbyterians Reed, McKean, Pettit and McClenanchan lined up against Anglican/Quaker Morris, Wilson, Clymer, Bingham, Willing, etc." (Letter to the author, February 3, 1976.)

36. Hutson, *Pennsylvania Politics, 1746–1770*, pp. 105–243. The role of the German Lutherans is not easily established. As Professor Ireland writes,

> There is some evidence of bitter political rivalry between Scotch-Irish and Germans, including German Lutherans, on the local level before 1776. . . . George III and the House of Hanover in general appear to have been rather "soft on" Lutheranism and I have seen some accounts which suggest that the Lutheran church in America received both moral and financial support from London. In the 1780's the German Lutherans tended to align with the Anglicans and the Quakers against the Scotch-Irish Presbyterians and the German Reformed. (Letter to the author, February 3, 1976.)

37. Eric Foner, *Tom Paine and Revolutionary America* (New York, 1976), pp. 41–66; Hutson, *Pennsylvania Politics 1746–1770*, pp. 105–243. See also Foner's essay "Tom Paine's Republic: Radical Ideology and

Social Change," in Young, *The American Revolution: Explorations in the History of American Radicalism,* pp. 187–232. Valuable, too, as a summing-up of the scholarship presently available on the role of the working class in the Revolution is Professor Young's concluding essay in this book, "Afterword," pp. 447–462.

38. Neuenschwander, *The Middle Colonies and the Coming of the American Revolution,* p. 72.
39. Foner, *Tom Paine and Revolutionary America,* pp. 74–78.
40. Wood, *Creation of the American Republic,* pp. 82–90, 131–162, 226–238; Main, *Political Parties Before the Constitution,* pp. 174–200; Bockelman and Ireland, "The Internal Revolution in Pennsylvania," pp. 141–156; Foner, *Tom Paine and Revolutionary America,* pp. 131–134.
41. Owen S. Ireland, "The Ethnic-Religious Dimension of Pennsylvania Politics, 1778–1779," *WMQ,* 3d Series, 30 (July 1973), 423–448; Main, *Political Parties Before the Constitution,* pp. 177–206.
42. Consult Ireland, "The Ethnic-Religious Dimension of Pennsylvania Politics," and Main, *Political Parties Before the Constitution,* pp. 175–176, 207, 210–211. The strong emphasis herein on these alignments as ethnocultural in nature is not to be found in Professor Main's work but derives from my own interpretive standpoint.

Chapter Three

1. H. James Henderson, *Party Politics in the Continental Congress* (New York, 1974), pp. 432–434. My formulation of the four varieties of republicanism has been much aided by Henderson's superb study, which has broken quite new ground, and by his essay "The Structure of Politics in the Continental Congress," in Stephen Kurtz and James Hutson (eds.), *Essays on the American Revolution* (Chapel Hill, N.C., 1973), pp. 157–195.
2. For the foregoing and following discussion of the parties and their attitudes, see Henderson, *Party Politics in the Continental Congress,* pp. 24, 44, 47, 75–77, 85–88, 100–124, 171–182, 218–239. For Paine and Morris, see Eric Foner, *Tom Paine and Revolutionary America* (New York, 1976), pp. 189–203.
3. Henderson, *Party Politics in the Continental Congress,* p. 78.
4. *Ibid.,* pp. 90–91, 246–377; Merrill Jensen, *The American Revolution Within America* (New York, 1974), pp. 142–145, 147–148.
5. For the foregoing discussion of the mounting crisis, consult Gordon S. Wood, *The Creation of the American Republic* (Chapel Hill, N.C., 1969), pp. 163–173, 321–322, 362–415; Jensen, *The American Revolution Within America,* pp. 100–108; Jack P. Greene, "The Role of the Lower Houses of Assembly in Eighteenth-Century Politics," *JSH,* 27 (October 1961), 451–474; William G. McLoughlin, *New England Dissent, 1630–1833: The Baptists and the Separation of Church and State*

(Cambridge, Mass., 1971), pp. 547–594, and *Isaac Backus and the American Pietistic Tradition* (Boston, 1967), pp. 110–170.

6. Jensen, *The American Revolution Within America,* p. 157.

7. Wood, *Creation of the American Republic,* pp. 393–493.

8. Consult Jensen, *The American Revolution Within America,* pp. 167–220, for a valuable discussion of the debates in the Constitutional Convention and Madison's role.

9. Wood, *Creation of the American Republic,* pp. 493–564; Henderson, *Party Politics in the Continental Congress,* pp. 413–415, 435; and Henderson, "The Structure of Politics in the Continental Congress," in Kurtz and Hutson, *Essays on the American Revolution.*

10. James G. Leyburn, *The Scotch-Irish: A Social History* (Chapel Hill, N.C., 1962), p. 305.

Chapter Four

1. Arthur Schlesinger, Jr., "America: Experiment or Destiny?", *AHR,* 82 (June 1977), 507–509. This general picture of the national mood in its first generation is widely available in historical literature. Roger H. Brown, *The Republic in Peril: 1812* (New York, 1964), finds this fear for the survival of republicanism to lie at the root of the decision to go to war with Great Britain again in 1812.

2. Ronald P. Formisano, "Deferential-Participant Politics: The Early Republic's Political Culture, 1789–1840," *The American Political Science Review,* 68 (June 1974), 473–487, provides a keen analysis of whether or not the Jeffersonian or first party system was in fact a "party system" in any modern sense. "I personally do not now believe in a first party system of Federalists and Republicans as conventionally portrayed." An institutionalized party, he writes, involves activists and organizers who run it as a permanent organization; a "party in office," consisting of its officeholders who consistently wear its distinguishing name and vote in some disciplined fashion; and a "party in the electorate," which must be not simply just "ticket voting" but self-conscious, enduring, and organized in detail from precinct to state and national nominating conventions. By these standards, Formisano holds, the first party system was highly transitional, retaining much of the preparty ethos of individualism and antipartyism. Only in fragmentary fashion did it take on the full attributes of mass-party, participant politics—and then for but brief periods in key states. "The Federalist and Republican 'interests'—a very accurate contemporary word—rather remained much closer to 'relatively stable coalitions' than to durable cadre parties of regular internal organization and fairly stable, self-conscious mass followings." Not until the 1840s would political party "systems," from this perspective, appear. For the general question of hostility to the idea of party, see Richard Hofstadter, *The Idea of a Party System: The Rise of Legitimate Opposition in the United States, 1780–1840* (Berkeley,

Calif., 1969); Michael Wallace, "Changing Concepts of Party in the United States: New York, 1815–1828," *AHR,* 74 (December 1968), 453–491; Daniel Sisson, *The American Revolution of 1800* (New York, 1974).

3. Merrill D. Peterson, *The Jefferson Image in the American Mind* (New York, 1962), is especially skillful in tracing the domination over politics and political thought, for many generations, of Jefferson, Hamilton, and the heroic period of foundings.

4. In the early years of the 1790s, the Middle States, then dominated by nationalist republicans, tended to side with New England, but later on, as Jeffersonian Republicanism began gaining strength in Pennsylvania and New York, they shifted to support of the South. The voting picture in Congress has been made clear in a detailed quantitative study of voting in the House of Representatives by Rudolph M. Bell, *Party and Faction in American Politics: The House of Representatives 1789–1801* (Westport, Conn., 1973), pp. 18–31, 117, 128–129. An average of three out of four New Englanders opposed an average of two out of three Southerners. The South, however, was too huge and varied to hold together consistently. The aristocratic nature of its representatives made them prickly and individualistic and not good candidates for party discipline. When roll calls were held, Southerners voted together, to the level of four-fifths of their number, only one-third of the time, while New Englanders, with their far more homogeneous culture and interests, voted together, to the same level, in two-thirds of the ballots. The Middle States had a polarized level of only 24 percent. On the rare occasions when Southern representatives could get together, they usually got their way.

5. Massachusetts and Connecticut politicians were obsessed by what they called the "Virginia interest." In the Yankees' view, that huge state, with its large population, western dreams, and arrogant aristocracy, dominated all of national affairs and had to be fought at every turn. See James Banner, *To the Hartford Convention: The Federalists and the Origins of Party Politics in Massachusetts, 1789–1815* (New York, 1970), pp. 99–100; Linda K. Kerber, *Federalists in Dissent: Imagery and Ideology in Jeffersonian America* (Ithaca, N.Y., 1970), pp. 26–34; Richard Buel, Jr., *Securing the Revolution: Ideology in American Politics, 1789–1815* (Ithaca, N.Y., 1972), p. 80.

6. John C. Miller, *Alexander Hamilton and the Growth of the New Nation* (New York, 1964), pp. 404–414; Harry Marlin Tinkcom, *The Republicans and Federalists in Pennsylvania 1790–1801: A Study in National Stimulus and Local Response* (Harrisburg, Pa., 1950), pp. 91–112; Eugene Perry Link, *Democratic-Republican Societies, 1790–1800* (New York, 1965).

7. Adrienne Koch, *The Philosophy of Thomas Jefferson* (Chicago, 1964), pp. 91–95; Kerber, *Federalists in Dissent,* pp. 68–71; Miller, *Alexander Hamilton and the Growth of the New Nation,* p. 406.

8. Link, *Democratic-Republican Societies,* pp. 71–99; Bell, *Party and Faction in American Politics,* pp. 46–50.

9. John C. Miller, *The Federalist Era 1789–1801* (New York, 1960), p. 168; Banner, *To the Hartford Convention,* p. 21; Alfred F. Young, *The Democratic Republicans of New York: The Origins, 1763–1797* (Chapel Hill, N.C., 1967), p. 447; Bell, *Party and Faction in American Politics,* pp. 132–181; Linda K. Kerber, "The Federalist Party," in Arthur M. Schlesinger, Jr. (ed.), *History of U.S. Political Parties* (New York, 1973), I, 13–14. That this process had been underway for some time is shown in the fact that during Washington's second administration, Republicans and Federalists in the House opposed each other 70 percent of the time; by Adams' administration, this rose to 90 percent. (Bell, *Party and Faction in American Politics,* pp. 183–190.) See also Mary P. Ryan's pioneering study, "Party Formation in the United States Congress, 1789–1796: A Quantitative Analysis," *WMQ,* 3d Series, 38 (October 1971), 523–542. On the question of whether or not the Federalists and Republicans were continuous with the Federalists and Antifederalists of the 1787–1789 period, see Buel, *Securing the Revolution,* p. 86; David Hackett Fischer, *The Revolution of American Conservatism: The Federalist Party in the Era of Jeffersonian Democracy* (New York, 1965), p. 222; Noble E. Cunningham, Jr., *The Jeffersonian Republicans: The Formation of Party Organization, 1789–1801* (Chapel Hill, N.C., 1957), pp. 256–257; Jackson Turner Main, *Political Parties Before the Constitution* (Chapel Hill, N.C., 1973), p. 387; Young, *The Democratic Republicans of New York,* pp. 566–567.

10. Miller, *Alexander Hamilton and the Growth of the New Nation,* p. 228; Jerald A. Combs, *The Jay Treaty: Political Battleground of the Founding Fathers* (Berkeley, Calif., 1970), p. 34.

11. Gerald Stourzh, *Alexander Hamilton and the Idea of Republican Government* (Stanford, Calif., 1970), p. 39; Richard B. Morris (ed.), *The Basic Ideas of Alexander Hamilton* (New York, 1957), p. 440.

12. Combs, *The Jay Treaty,* p. 65.

13. Cunningham, *The Jeffersonian Republicans,* p. 20.

14. Henry Adams, *History of the United States: During the Administrations of Jefferson and Madison,* abridged by George Dangerfield and Otey M. Scruggs (Englewood Cliffs, N.J., 1963), p. 14. These general views, well known, may be consulted in Dumas Malone's multivolume biography of Jefferson; Koch's *The Philosophy of Thomas Jefferson* and *Jefferson and Madison: The Great Collaboration* (New York, 1953); and Merrill D. Peterson, *Thomas Jefferson and the New Nation: A Biography* (New York, 1970). I have explored them also in *The Transatlantic Persuasion: The Liberal-Democratic Mind in the Age of Gladstone* (New York, 1969), Chapter 4, "The Inherited World View: Thomas Jefferson and the Ideology of Conflict."

15. Peterson, *Thomas Jefferson,* pp. 434–436; Kelley, *The Transatlantic Persuasion,* pp. 55–79 (re Adam Smith).

16. Morton Borden, *Parties and Politics in the Early Republic, 1789–1815* (New York, 1967), p. 54; Fischer, *The Revolution of American Conservatism,* pp. xv, 187–201.

17. Manning J. Dauer, *The Adams Federalists* (Baltimore, 1968), pp. 116, 190; Alexander DeConde, *The Quasi-War: The Politics and Diplomacy of the Undeclared War with France 1797–1801* (New York, 1966), pp. 30–85.

18. John R. Howe, Jr., "Republican Thought and the Political Violence of the 1790s," *American Quarterly,* 19 (1967), 150–163; Banner, *To the Hartford Convention,* p. 23.

19. David Brion Davis (ed.), *The Fear of Conspiracy: Images of Un-American Subversion from the Revolution to the Present* (Ithaca, N.Y., 1971), pp. 35–65; Banner, *To the Hartford Convention,* pp. 152–167; Young, *The Democratic Republicans of New York,* p. 570.

20. Kerber, *Federalists in Dissent,* pp. 22, 173–178; Banner, *To the Hartford Convention,* pp. 32–35; Young, *The Democratic Republicans of New York,* pp. 363–364.

21. Fischer, *The Revolution of American Conservatism,* p. 24.

22. Bell, *Party and Faction in American Politics,* p. 78; Banner, *To the Hartford Convention,* pp. 93, 111.

23. Peterson, *Thomas Jefferson and the New Nation,* pp. 247–254; Kerber, *Federalists in Dissent,* p. 91.

24. Kerber, *Federalists in Dissent,* pp. 21, 67–94.

25. *Ibid.,* p. 130. I have drawn heavily upon Professor Kerber's brilliant study in these passages. It is focused on the years after 1800 but reveals a fundamental outlook that certainly was present among Federalists in 1798. Many case studies of individual Federalists exist that, as in Morton Borden's revealing book, *The Federalism of James A. Bayard* (New York, 1955), flesh out the general picture. Bayard's feeling toward England and France, his hatred of Jefferson, and his belief that "aliens cannot be considered as members of the society of the United States" eloquently support the Kerber narrative.

26. Banner, *To the Hartford Convention,* pp. 90, 97; Fischer, *The Revolution of American Conservatism,* p. 164.

27. DeConde, *The Quasi-War,* p. 98; U.S., *Statutes at Large,* vol. 1, pp. 570ff and 596–597.

28. Kerber, *Federalists in Dissent,* pp. 22, 26–27, 31; Norman K. Risjord, "The Virginia Federalists," *JSH,* 33 (November 1967), 486–517.

29. The preceding account of federalism in the South has been drawn from Lisle A. Rose, *Prologue to Democracy: The Federalists in the South, 1789–1800* (Lexington, Ky., 1968), and James H. Broussard, "Regional Pride and Republican Politics: The Fatal Weakness of Southern Feder-

alism, 1800–1815," *The South Atlantic Quarterly,* 73 (Winter 1974), 23–33.

30. Buel, *Securing the Revolution,* p. 89; Fischer, *The Revolution of American Conservatism,* pp. 211–214.
31. Young, *The Democratic Republicans of New York,* pp. 113, 398–407.
32. Banner, *To the Hartford Convention,* pp. 258–267, 302–303, 329–332, 345–348, 398–409, 427, 504, 566–572; Cunningham, *The Jeffersonian Republicans,* p. 222; Alfred F. Young, "The Mechanics and the Jeffersonians: New York, 1789–1801," *Labor History,* 5 (1964), 247–276.
33. Tinkcom, *The Republicans and Federalists in Pennsylvania,* p. 71.
34. *Ibid.,* passim, especially p. 234.
35. *Ibid.,* p. 256.
36. This general discussion of Massachusetts has been drawn from Banner, *To the Hartford Convention;* Paul Goodman, *The Democratic-Republicans of Massachusetts: Politics in a Young Republic* (Cambridge, Mass., 1964); William G. McLoughlin, *Isaac Backus and the American Pietistic Tradition* (Boston, 1967), p. 170, and *New England Dissent, 1630–1833: The Baptists and the Separation of Church and State* (Cambridge, Mass., 1971), pp. 547–594.
37. Noble E. Cunningham, Jr., makes clear how assiduously Jefferson worked at being party leader in *The Jeffersonian Republicans,* pp. 116–143, 211.
38. Sisson, *The American Revolution of 1800,* passim.
39. Peterson, *Thomas Jefferson and the New Nation,* p. 667; Cunningham, *The Jeffersonian Republicans,* p. 22.
40. Banner, *To the Hartford Convention,* pp. 48–51, 86–89, 100–107; Kerber, *Federalists in Dissent,* pp. 135–172.
41. Brown, *The Republic in Peril,* pp. 14–15. In these passages on the War of 1812, I have relied heavily upon this extraordinary book, one of the first to awaken historians to the central role of "republicanism" in the American mind during the generation of turmoil that began with the Revolution.
42. *Ibid.,* pp. 16–43.
43. William Gribbin, *The Churches Militant: The War of 1812 and American Religion* (New Haven, Conn., 1973), p. 61; Banner, *To the Hartford Convention,* pp. 307, 317–318.
44. Banner, *To the Hartford Convention,* pp. 327–344.
45. Shaw Livermore, Jr., *The Twilight of Federalism: The Disintegration of the Federalist Party 1815–1830* (Princeton, N.J., 1962), pp. 12, 219.
46. *Ibid.,* pp. 86–89; 211–215; 349–350.
47. Paul Goodman, "The First American Party System," in William Nisbet Chambers and Walter Dean Burnham (eds.), *The American Party Systems: Stages of Political Development,* 2nd ed. (New York, 1975), p. 87; Harry Ammon, *James Monroe: The Quest for National Identity* (New York, 1971), p. 377.

48. Ammon, *James Monroe,* pp. 366–379.
49. *Ibid.,* p. 380.
50. See James Sterling Young, *The Washington Community, 1800–1828* (New York, 1966). I have drawn the preceding discussion of the political community in Washington from this unusual book.
51. *Ibid.,* p. 186.

Chapter Five

1. Douglas T. Miller, *The Birth of Modern America 1820–1850* (Indianapolis, 1970), pp. 31, 83; Peter Temin, "The Anglo-American Business Cycle, 1820–60," *Economic History Review,* 27 (May 1974), 207–221; W. Elliot Brownlee, *Dynamics of Ascent: A History of the American Economy* (New York, 1974), pp. 85–99.
2. John Higham, *From Boundlessness to Consolidation: The Transformation of American Culture 1848–1860* (Ann Arbor, 1969), p. 8. Higham writes,

> The limits of ascribed status yielded to an egalitarian celebration of the self-made man. The limits of history dissolved in an ecstatic dedication to the future. The limits of reason were metamorphosed into the infinite possibilities of knowledge and the intuitive truths of the heart. The limits of human nature faded before a glowing promise of liberation from sin and social iniquity. The limits of nature itself receded in a new dynamic world-picture overflowing with vitality and undergoing endless growth. It would be absurd to suppose that these expansive sentiments and ideas ever overwhelmed more cautious and traditionalist views. The point is rather that their explosive thrust defined the great issues of the age.

3. Alex Inkeles, "Making Men Modern: On the Causes and Consequences of Individual Change in Six Developing Countries," *American Journal of Sociology,* 75 (1969), 210. (Re: the modern personality.)
4. C. E. Black, *The Dynamics of Modernization: A Study in Comparative History* (New York, 1966), p. 27.
5. Walter E. Houghton, *The Victorian Frame of Mind, 1830–1870* (New Haven, Conn., 1957); Robert Kelley, *The Transatlantic Persuasion: The Liberal-Democratic Mind in the Age of Gladstone* (New York, 1969), pp. 3–10; Marvin Meyers, *The Jacksonian Persuasion: Politics and Belief* (New York, 1960); Peter Temin, *The Jacksonian Economy* (New York, 1969). The view that individual fortunes gyrated alarmingly, long a staple in the historical picture of the Jacksonian years, has been challenged by Edward Pessen, who has extensively explored social stratification in New York and Boston and concludes that the rich simply got richer, and social stratification became more rigid. See his "Who Governed the Nation's Cities in the 'Era of the Common Man'?", *PSQ,* 87 (December 1972), 591–614; "The Wealthiest New Yorkers of the Jacksonian Era: A New List," *New York Historical Society Quarterly,* 54

(April 1970), 145–172; "Moses Beach Revisited: A Critical Examination of His *Wealthy Citizens* Pamphlets," *JAH,* 58 (September 1971), 415–426; "Did Fortunes Rise and Fall Mercurially in Antebellum America?", *Journal of Social History,* 4 (Spring 1971), 339–354; "The Egalitarian Myth and the American Social Reality: Wealth, Mobility, and Equality in the 'Era of the Common Man,' " *AHR,* 76 (October 1971), 989–1034. Consult also Pessen's larger work, *Jacksonian America: Society, Personality, and Politics* (Homewood, Ill., 1969).

6. David Grimsted, "Rioting in Its Jacksonian Setting," *AHR,* 77 (April 1972), 361–397; Arthur M. Schlesinger, Jr., *The Age of Jackson* (Boston, 1945), p. 210. Schlesinger's rich and fascinating book remains a principal source for every scholar who explores the Jackson years, although major aspects of its interpretive stance require supplementing by more recent studies.

7. Richard H. Brown, "The Missouri Crisis, Slavery, and the Politics of Jacksonianism," *South Atlantic Quarterly,* 65 (Winter 1966), 55–72.

8. George A. Lipsky, *John Quincy Adams: His Theory and Ideas* (New York, 1950, 1965), pp. 116–140.

9. James Parton, *Life of Andrew Jackson* (New York, 1860), I, vii–viii.

10. John William Ward, *Andrew Jackson: Symbol for an Age* (New York, 1962); Schlesinger, *The Age of Jackson;* Parton, *Life of Andrew Jackson,* III, 695–699.

11. Parton, *Life of Andrew Jackson,* III, 685; I, 33.

12. It is important to understand that these party names did not yet reflect the existence of organized national parties in the modern sense or even consistency of usage. William G. Shade has written to me that the word *party*

> has many meanings and can be associated with many kinds of groups. At the time "the Great States Rights party of the South" about which Calhoun talked so much did not function as a political party nor did the abolitionists. What can Webster mean when he says that there were "three parties in Congress" on the French question? Certainly he is not talking about political parties. In most cases the usage of "party" during the period until the late thirties was in this generalized sense. (Letter to author, June 4, 1976.)

In a paper presented at the 1974 (Chicago) Annual Meeting of the American Historical Association, "Two Stages of Party Development in Early American History: A Quantitative Description," Professor Shade argued for a division of the political history of the period 1824–1852 into Phase I (through the election of 1832), 1836 being a transitional election, and Phase II (from the election of 1840). In the former phase, politics remained nonparty and personalized; in the latter, "fragmented politics of place gave way to a relatively well integrated politics of party" (p. 27). Phase I politics were "represented by ... short lived, loosely knit cliques," while Phase II politics saw the appearance of regular nomination procedures and recognizable labels, as well as a great deal of interstate uniformity on issues (p. 18). However, "This is not to say that there wasn't talk about the 'great Republican party,' the 'feds,' the 'Anti-Masons' or 'our party,' but rather that the use of the word was so loose that one cannot assume any institutional relationship" (fn. 11).

On the other hand, the information Robert Remini has presented in *The Election of Andrew Jackson* (Philadelphia, 1963), and "Election of 1828," in Arthur M. Schlesinger, Jr., and Fred L. Israel (eds.), *History of American Presidential Elections 1789–1968* (New York, 1971), I, 413–436, makes it hazardous summarily to dismiss the reality of parties as institutional entities even in the election of 1828. There was clearly underway a great deal of organizing activity and the defining of issues at the national level.

13. As observed earlier, Thomas Jefferson claimed Welsh descent to disassociate himself from the English, but his time did not conceive of him as what we would call an ethnic or minority person. "Welshness" had no particular resonance then in American public life, while to be a Scotch-Irishman, even in Jackson's time, was still a distinctive identity.

14. Remini, *The Election of Andrew Jackson,* p. 105; Lee Benson, *The Concept of Jacksonian Democracy: New York as a Test Case* (New York, 1964), p. 321; Philip S. Klein and Ari Hoogenboom, *A History of Pennsylvania* (New York, 1973), pp. 118–124.

15. Remini, *The Election of Andrew Jackson;* Schlesinger, *The Age of Jackson,* pp. 3–6.

16. Merrill D. Peterson, *The Jefferson Image in the American Mind* (New York, 1962), pp. 18–29.

17. Meyers, *The Jacksonian Persuasion,* p. 103.

18. Peter Temin's *The Jacksonian Economy* is essential on these points, especially as to popular ignorance and misconceptions. See also Brownlee, *Dynamics of Ascent,* pp. 141–149. On the yellow fever controversy, see Martin S. Pernick, "Politics, Parties and Pestilence: Epidemic Yellow Fever in Philadelphia and the Rise of the First Party System," *WMQ,* 3d series, 29 (October 1972), 559–586.

19. Asa Briggs, *The Making of Modern England, 1783–1867: The Age of Improvement* (New York, 1965), pp. 201–205, 294–344; Elie Halevy, *The Liberal Awakening, 1815–1830* (New York, 1961), pp. 196–202, and *Victorian Years, 1841–1895* (New York, 1961), pp. 97–99, 206–211.

20. Kelley, *The Transatlantic Persuasion,* pp. 186–188, 247–249, 256–260.

21. James D. Richardson (comp.), *A Compilation of the Messages and Papers of the Presidents* (Washington, D.C., 1913), II, 576–590. John McFaul, *The Politics of Jacksonian Finance* (Ithaca, N.Y., 1972), is the essential guide through these complicated matters.

22. The various writings of Glyndon G. Van Deusen provide the best guide to general Whig history. See his "The Whig Party," in Arthur M. Schlesinger, Jr. (ed.), *History of U.S. Political Parties* (New York, 1973), I,

333–363, together with its extensive appendices and bibliography. The book that first established the notion of party systems for historians is Richard P. McCormick, *The Second American Party System: Party Formation in the Jacksonian Era* (Chapel Hill, N.C., 1966), and it is the essential source on all these matters.

Joel Silbey has put the new political situation, which emerged after the election of 1836, concisely:

> A new political era was obviously taking shape in 1836, despite local deviations; a second American party system was crystallizing. The sectional, local quality of voting had largely disappeared. Both parties were becoming national in scope, penetrating into the traditional strongholds of their opposition, and establishing new and enduring voting patterns. Almost everywhere the differences between the two parties were close, unlike the one-sided margins of previous elections.... The voting patterns which appeared so dramatically in the 1836 election proved to be fairly stable.... Until 1952, 53 of Tennessee's 65 counties continued to vote for the same party they had supported in 1836. Six of the remaining 12 remained consistently Democratic when [Hugh] White [a favorite son] was no longer a candidate. Only six counties shifted their vote from election to election. The same phenomenon was common throughout the South and, to a lesser extent, nationally.

See Silbey's "Election of 1836," in Schlesinger and Israel, *History of American Presidential Elections,* I, 598–599.

William N. Chambers, in a work he coedited with Walter Dean Burnham, *The American Party Systems: Stages of Political Development* (New York, 1975), observes that voting turnout, stimulated by this two-party competition, jumped from the 26.9 percent of white adult males that turned out in 1824 to 57.8 percent by 1832 and to the remarkable level of 80.2 percent in the election of 1840 (p. 12).

23. Ronald P. Formisano, in a brilliant demonstration of the revelatory power of the case study method, superbly evokes the party atmosphere of the time and its cultural origins. See his *The Birth of Mass Political Parties: Michigan, 1827–1861* (Princeton, N.J., 1971), pp. 22, 57–58, 70, 77–78. Perry M. Goldman, "Political Virtue in the Age of Jackson," *PSQ,* 87 (March 1972), 46–62, is also valuable, as is Michael Wallace, "Changing Concepts of Party in the United States: New York, 1815–1828," *AHR,* 74 (December 1968), 453–491.

The question of whether the Whigs were wealthier than Democrats is closely argued among scholars. The issue arose when Lee Benson, in his study of ethnocultural patterns in New York Jacksonian politics, held that the *leaders* of both parties came from similar socioeconomic backgrounds and challenged the traditional historical view, founded in the work of Charles Beard and Frederick Jackson Turner—indeed, in the rhetoric of the Jacksonian Democrats themselves—that the Democrats were the party of the farmers, artisans, and laborers, while the Whigs were the party of the wealthy (*The Concept of Jacksonian Democracy:*

New York as a Test Case, pp. 64–85). Ronald P. Formisano, in *The Birth of Mass Political Parties,* his study of Michigan politics, has taken the same position with regard to party leaders (drawing upon the work of other scholars in this connection). Burton W. Folsom, II, in a recent study of the situation in Tennessee, agrees ("The Politics of Elites: Prominence and Party in Davidson County, Tennessee, 1835–1861," *JSH,* 39 [August 1973], 359–378).

This position, in turn, has tended to support the interpretation of the Jacksonians advanced by Richard Hofstadter in his *The American Political Tradition and the Men Who Made It* (New York, 1948) and Bray Hammond in his *Banks and Politics in America from the Revolution to the Civil War* (Princeton, N.J., 1957). Hofstadter and Hammond held that Democratic party rhetoric that described them as battling the common people's cause against exploitive bankers was only that: rhetoric. Democrats were really eager, upwardly mobile entrepreneurs who wanted to break apart the controls exerted by the Second Bank of the United States in order to make themselves wealthier. If the Benson thesis was correct, and the Democrats were just as wealthy as the Whigs, then Democratic hypocrisy on economic matters would seem even more likely.

However, we now have research on the "party in the electorate," the party masses as distinct from leadership. Michael F. Holt has found that the Whigs had far more wealth in their ranks than did the Democrats in Pittsburgh in the 1850s (*Forging a Majority: The Formation of the Republican Party in Pittsburgh, 1848–1860* [New Haven, 1969], pp. 43–48). Frank Otto Gatell, on the basis of a close study of the New York City wealthy, has found the more than six hundred persons he studied among the very rich to have been more than 80 percent Whig ("Money and Party in Jacksonian America: A Quantitative Look at New York City's Men of Quality," *PSQ,* 82 [June 1967], 235–252). Gatell has persuasively refuted the Hofstadter-Hammond thesis in his "Sober Second Thoughts on Van Buren, the Albany Regency, and the Wall Street Conspiracy," *JAH* (June 1966), 19–40. So have other historians, such as John McFaul in his *The Politics of Jacksonian Finance.* Robert Rich has found Boston's wealthy to have been about 90 percent Whig (" 'A Wilderness of Whigs': The Wealthy Men of Boston," *Journal of Social History,* 4 (Spring 1971), 263–276). There would seem to be a question of timing involved, with the wealthy being much more evenly divided between Jackson and his enemies in the early stages and polarized and pushed away when his economic policies became clear.

It is persuasive that the popular rhetoric of the Jacksonian years also depicted Whigs as the party of the wealthy. However, this does not negate what I have taken to be Professor Benson's larger thesis: that historians must take account of the fact that both parties obviously drew about half the voting population into their ranks, for the margins of victory were narrow. The parties seem to have divided fairly equally the mass of the people. If the Whigs had been simply the party of the wealthy, as the traditional version held, how could they ever have won elections? It is in demonstrating that ethnocultural motivations were also a powerful, often deciding, factor, whether or not the voters concerned were rich or poor, that Professor Benson's book has made its striking contribution to historical thinking.

24. Formisano, *The Birth of Mass Political Parties;* Goldman, "Political Virtue in the Age of Jackson." See also Robert F. Dalzell, Jr., *Daniel Webster and the Trial of American Nationalism 1843–1852* (Boston, 1973), ix–xv. In 1967 Richard Hofstadter, in his introductory remarks to a collection of his writings (*The Paranoid Style in American Politics and Other Essays* [New York, 1967]), observed, "People respond ... to the great drama of the public scene. But this drama, as it is set before them and as they perceive it, is not identical with questions involving material interests and the possession of power. Even those who exercise power are not immune to the content of the drama.... The political contest itself is deeply affected by the way in which it is perceived and felt" (pp. ix–x).

25. Glyndon G. Van Deusen, "Some Aspects of Whig Thought and Theory in the Jacksonian Period," *AHR*, 58 (1958), 305–322; Schlesinger, *The Age of Jackson*, p. 274; Holt, *Forging a Majority*, pp. 49–50. "Instead of abdicating responsibility," Lee Benson writes, "as the Locofocos and Radical Democrats demanded, [Whigs believed] the state had a positive responsibility to act. It must regulate society so as to promote the general welfare, raise the level of opportunity for all men, and aid all individuals to develop their full potentialities" (*Concept of Jacksonian Democracy*, pp. 102–103). New York Whig legislators in 1838 said, "We hold it to be the wisest and soundest political prudence, to apply the means of the state *boldly and liberally to aid those great works of railroads and canals which are beyond the means of unassisted private enterprise*" (pp. 104–105, italics added). "The Whig modernists looked forward to an increasingly dynamic, complex, and industrialized society. To use twentieth century terms to state their conception of their party's mission: they thought the party should help to provide the political, social, and cultural conditions necessary to launch the United States on the 'take-off' stage of economic growth" (p. 105). See also Professor Benson's extended discussion of the Whigs, pp. 237–253.

26. Herbert Ershkowitz and William G. Shade, "Consensus or Conflict? Political Behavior in the State Legislatures During the Jacksonian Era," *JAH*, 58 (December 1971), 591–621.

27. McFaul, *The Politics of Jacksonian Finance*, traces these progressions in national currency policy.

28. "Address to the Farmers, Mechanics and Workingmen of the State of New York, Tammany Hall, February 26, 1838," in John Bigelow (ed.),

The Writings and Speeches of Samuel J. Tilden (New York, 1885), I, 79–87.

29. Frank Thistlethwaite, *America and the Atlantic Community: Anglo-American Aspects, 1790–1850* (New York, 1964), pp. 40–43. See also David Paul Crook, *American Democracy in English Politics 1815–1840* (Oxford, 1965). I fully recognize that in using the term "British Liberal," I am simplifying a complex situation. The term "Liberal" was being used in the 1830s, but so were "Whig" and "Radical" to refer to other segments of what in the 1850s came together to form the Liberal party. For convenience, I am using the term here to refer to all three groups. See my *Transatlantic Persuasion,* pp. 180–201.

30. Martin Van Buren, "The Autobiography of Martin Van Buren," John C. Fitzpatrick (ed.), *Annual Report of the American Historical Association for the Year 1918,* II, 460–461, 465, 481–484, 493.

31. Benson, *Concept of Jacksonian Democracy,* p. 161.

32. Charles Sellers, *James K. Polk: Continentalist 1843–1846* (Princeton, N.J., 1966), pp. 327–330, 451–468; Thistlethwaite, *America and the Atlantic Community,* pp. 157–172; James P. Shenton, *Robert John Walker: A Politician from Jackson to Lincoln* (New York, 1961), pp. 74–85; Glyndon G. Van Deusen, *The Jacksonian Era 1828–1848* (New York, 1959), pp. 200–204.

33. Schlesinger, *The Age of Jackson,* pp. 314–315.

Chapter Six

1. Marvin Meyers, *The Jacksonian Persuasion: Politics and Belief* (New York, 1960), pp. 10–11, 26.

2. Robert Kelley, *The Transatlantic Persuasion: The Liberal-Democratic Mind in the Age of Gladstone* (New York, 1969), pp. 55–79, 238–293; Hammond, *Banks and Politics in America from the Revolution to the Civil War;* Richard Hofstadter, *The American Political Tradition and the Men Who Made It* (New York, 1948), pp. 44–66.

3. Lynn L. Marshall, "The Strange Stillbirth of the Whig Party," *AHR,* 72 (January 1967), 445–468, demonstrates how the Jacksonians began taking away the aristocratic monopoly of government offices and breaking down the ethic that supported it. They instituted what amounted to civil service procedures: auditing accounts, establishing regulations that creating the functions of key offices, and dismissing those who did not come up to the mark—actions regarded as "insolent" by the former governing elite.

4. Lee Benson, *The Concept of Jacksonian Democracy: New York as a Test Case* (New York, 1964), p. 64; Frank Otto Gatell, "Money and Party in Jacksonian America: A Quantitative Look at New York City's Men of Quality," *PSQ,* 82 (June 1967), 246–252. In the sample of wealthy men Gatell studied, there were 157 Episcopalians, 118 Presbyterians (in New York State, Congregationalists and Presbyterians were both in-

cluded in the latter designation), 45 Quakers, and 33 Dutch Reformed, as against 4 Catholics, 7 Baptists, 8 Jews, and 9 Methodists. There was only 1 Irish Catholic, no French Canadians or Welsh, 11 Germans, 226 of British or English descent, 102 of Dutch descent, 147 from New England, 13 from the Southern states, 26 from Pennsylvania or New Jersey, 15 from Germany, and 12 from France.

5. Richard P. McCormick, *The Second American Party System: Party Formation in the Jacksonian Era* (Chapel Hill, N.C., 1966), pp. 35–76.

6. Dixon Ryan Fox, *Yankees and Yorkers* (New York, 1940), pp. 199–221; Meyers, *The Jacksonian Persuasion*, pp. 57–100.

7. William Gerald Shade, *Banks or No Banks: The Money Question in the Western States, 1832–1865* (Detroit, 1973), pp. 136–144, 159, 163. The findings of a similar study by James Roger Sharp, *The Jacksonians Versus the Banks: Politics in the States after the Panic of 1837* (New York, 1970), confirm this picture with remarkable fidelity. The Democratic party's appeal, Sharp writes,

> was in the nature of a plaintive warning against the increasing commercialization and vulgarization of American life. . . . The commercialization of the country and the extension of the market economy were major innovative factors that stimulated profound and unsettling economic and social changes in ante-bellum America. The Panic of 1837 threw these changes into sharp relief. . . . The Democratic party became the instrument through which protest against this change was funneled. (pp. 321–322)

> The Germans in particular were antibank on these grounds. "Clannish, industrious, and frugal, these stolid folk were extremely suspicious of anything that smacked of speculation. . . . Communities that were established by the Germans . . . were 'heavily weighted in economic fields toward tradition and continuity' " (p. 326). See also Richard Lyle Power, *Planting Corn Belt Culture: The Impress of the Upland Southerner and the Yankee in the Old Northwest* (Indianapolis, 1953), for a valuable exploration of the cultural conflict between these groups.

8. Donald G. Mathews, "The Second Great Awakening as an Organizing Process, 1780–1830: An Hypothesis," *American Quarterly*, 21 (Spring 1969), 23–43; Whitney R. Cross, *The Burned-Over District: The Social and Intellectual History of Enthusiastic Religion in Western New York, 1800–1850* (New York, 1965), pp. 198–208.

9. John L. Thomas, "Romantic Reform in America, 1815–1865," *American Quarterly*, 17 (Winter 1965), 656–681; Bertram Wyatt-Brown, "Prelude to Abolitionism: Sabbatarian Politics and the Rise of the Second Party System," *JAH*, 58 (September 1971), 316–341. The essential work to consult is Clifford S. Griffin, *Their Brothers' Keepers: Moral Stewardship in the United States, 1800–1865* (New Brunswick, N.J., 1960).

> These would-be overseers of their brethren's conduct believed themselves the stewards of heavenly commands and the trustees of the Lord.

They were the nineteenth-century exemplars of men who throughout American history have claimed the right and alleged their duty to tell other men how to behave.... [They] were heirs of the stewardship tradition of the Calvinistic past. (pp. x–xi)

10. William Gribbin, "Antimasonry, Religious Radicalism, and the Paranoid Style of the 1820s," *The History Teacher,* 7 (February 1974), 239–254; Michael F. Holt, "The Antimasonic and Know Nothing Parties," in Arthur M. Schlesinger, Jr. (ed.), *History of U.S. Political Parties,* I, 575–740; Ronald P. Formisano, *The Birth of Mass Political Parties: Michigan, 1827–1861* (Princeton, N.J., 1971), pp. 60–67; Benson, *Concept of Jacksonian Democracy,* pp. 18–22, 186–197. See also Lorman Ratner, *Antimasonry: The Crusade and the Party* (Englewood Cliffs, N.J., 1969).
11. Formisano, *The Birth of Mass Political Parties,* p. 133. The study by Herbert Ershkowitz and William G. Shade, "Consensus or Conflict? Political Behavior in the State Legislatures During the Jacksonian Era," *JAH,* 58 (December 1971), 591–621, demonstrates also how the voting of Whigs supported these cultural crusades.
12. Formisano, *The Birth of Mass Political Parties,* pp. 124, 149.
13. Benson, *Concept of Jacksonian Democracy,* pp. 198–207; Formisano, *Birth of Mass Political Parties,* p. 171.
14. Bertram Wyatt-Brown, "Prelude to Abolitionism: Sabbatarian Politics and the Rise of the Second Party System," *JAH,* 58 (September 1971), 322–337; Gribbin, "Antimasonry," pp. 239–254. The Presbyterians and the Congregationalists in New York, observes Whitney R. Cross, were at "the fountainhead of all the streams of intolerance." They were the best educated among the Protestants, the most prosperous, and socially the most established, save for the Episcopalians (who regarded all this activist moralism with distaste). The Congregationalists and Presbyterians assumed a "strongly inbred" sense of superiority. The northern Presbyterian church was simultaneously involved, in the 1830s, in Antimasonry, Bible and tract circulation, Sunday-school campaigns, Sabbath-observance crusades, and appeals to the New York legislature to adjourn for three days in support of their temperance effort (*The Burned-Over District,* pp. 46–47, 131). See also Lois W. Banner, "Religious Benevolence as Social Control: A Critique of an Interpretation," *JAH,* 60 (June 1973), 23–41, which explains how historians have far overrated Ely and his call for a Christian party in politics and wrongly depicted evangelicals as monolithically on the side of government supervision of morals.
15. Formisano, *Birth of Mass Political Parties,* pp. 155–161.
16. For the larger history of Presbyterianism in this period, see Kelley, *The Transatlantic Persuasion,* pp. 308–311; Fox, *Yankees and Yorkers,* pp. 209–210; Cross, *The Burned-Over District,* pp. 14–22, 163, 259–261; Elwyn A. Smith, "The Role of the South in the Presbyterian Schism of 1837–38," *Church History,* 29 (March 1960), 44–63; C. Bruce Staiger,

"Abolitionism and the Presbyterian Schism of 1837–1838," *Mississippi Valley Historical Review,* 26 (December 1949), 391–414.

17. Robert W. Doherty, "Social Bases for the Presbyterian Schism of 1837–1838, The Philadelphia Case," *Journal of Social History,* 2 (Fall 1968), 69–79.

18. In Michigan, "Presbyterians more than any other denomination occupied leadership positions in benevolence, reform societies, and Whiggery. By the late 1830s Presbyterianism appeared to be in almost open alliance with Whiggery. The Michigan Synod repeatedly made policy statements intended for the ears of rulers and politicians." Whig meetings were often held in Presbyterian churches, and Presbyterian newspapers were often published at the offices of the Whig newspaper. (Formisano, *Birth of Mass Political Parties,* pp. 104, 112–113.)

19. Cross, *The Burned-Over District,* pp. 168, 270; Arthur M. Schlesinger, *The Age of Jackson* (Boston, 1945), pp. 138–139; Merrill D. Peterson, *The Jefferson Image in the American Mind* (New York, 1962), pp. 69–86.

20. Kelley, *The Transatlantic Persuasion,* pp. 238–292; Schlesinger, *The Age of Jackson,* pp. 317–320; Meyers, *The Jacksonian Persuasion;* Edward K. Spann, *Ideals and Politics: New York Intellectuals and Liberal Democracy 1820–1880* (Albany, N.Y., 1975), pp. 130–131.

21. See also Joseph G. Rayback, "The American Workingman and the Antislavery Crusade," *Journal of Economic History,* 3 (1943), 152–164.

22. Edward M. Levine, *The Irish and Irish Politicians: A Study of Cultural and Social Alienation* (Notre Dame, Ind., 1966), pp. 53–75: Allen Jones Maldwyn, *American Immigration* (Chicago, 1960), pp. 107–176.

23. The literature on the Irish is voluminous. Valuable general works are William V. Shannon, *The American Irish* (New York, 1963), and John B. Duff, *The Irish in the United States* (Belmont, Calif., 1971). For the ancient roots to these feelings between English and Irish, see David Beers Quinn, *The Elizabethans and the Irish* (Ithaca, N.Y., 1966).

24. Thomas T. McAvoy, "The Formation of the Catholic Minority in the United States—1820–1860," *Review of Politics,* 10 (January 1948), 13–34; Michael F. Holt, *Forging a Majority: The Formation of the Republican Party in Pittsburgh, 1848–1860* (New Haven, 1969), p. 33; Formisano, *Birth of Mass Political Parties,* pp. 222–238; Levine, *The Irish and Irish Politicians;* Shannon, *The American Irish,* pp. 29–131.

25. Benson, *Concept of Jacksonian Democracy,* pp. 166–171.

26. *Ibid.,* pp. 171–173.

27. Robert Henry Billigmeier, *Americans from Germany: A Study in Cultural Diversity* (Belmont, Calif., 1974), pp. 29–61; Benson, *Concept of Jacksonian Democracy,* pp. 173–174.

28. William G. Shade, "Pennsylvania Politics in the Jacksonian Period: A Case Study, Northampton County, 1824–1844," *Pennsylvania History,* 39 (July 1972), 313–333.

29. *Ibid.*
30. Benson, *Concept of Jacksonian Democracy,* pp. 293–304.
31. Formisano, *Birth of Mass Political Parties,* pp. 81–90, 93, 44, 166, 179–182. Professor Formisano finds that the following percentages of particular ethnic groups and religious denominations in Michigan were Democratic: Catholic Irish, 95; New Dutch, 90; Catholic Germans, 80; Protestant Germans, 65; New British, 40; Yankees, 35; Yorkers (Old Dutch and Old British), 65; Pennsylvania Dutch, 65; Churched Protestants, 40; Evangelical Protestants, 20; Quakers, 5 (p. 192).
32. McCormick, *The Second American Party System,* pp. 310–320.
33. Burton W. Folsom II, "The Politics of Elites: Prominence and Party in Davidson County, Tennessee, 1835–1861," *JSH,* 39 (August 1973), 359–379. The ethnic and religious affiliations of the leadership that Folsom uncovers are interesting: two out of three of the Scotch-Irish in the political elite voted Democratic; the English leaned slightly Whig; and the Germans and Dutch were unanimously Whig. The Presbyterians among the leadership were evenly divided, as were the Episcopalians, but the Baptists and Church of Christ members were Whig by a margin of three to two.
34. On Kentucky voting, see McCormick, *The Second American Party System,* pp. 209–222. Concerning Henry Clay, see Clement Eaton, *Henry Clay and the Art of American Politics* (Boston, 1957), and Glyndon G. Van Deusen, *The Life of Henry Clay* (Boston, 1937).
35. Eaton, *Henry Clay,* p. 21.
36. The evidence as yet on Southern voting is fragmentary, especially concerning the pre-war period. See Folsom, "The Politics of Elites"; Charles G. Sellers, Jr., "Who Were the Southern Whigs?" *AHR,* 59 (January 1954), 335–346; Carl N. Degler, *The Other South: Southern Dissenters in the Nineteenth Century* (New York, 1974), pp. 106–110, 115–116. The German settlements in Texas were later a strong Republican voting group.
37. William R. Taylor, *Cavalier and Yankee: The Old South and American National Character* (Garden City, N.Y., 1963), pp. 138, 189.
38. Sellers, "Who Were the Southern Whigs?" p. 336.
39. Joel H. Silbey, *The Shrine of Party: Congressional Voting Behavior 1841–1852* (Pittsburgh, 1967).
40. Frederick Merk, *Manifest Destiny and Mission in American History: A Reinterpretation* (New York, 1966), pp. 24–40.
41. *Ibid.,* pp. 40–60.
42. John H. Schroeder, *Mr. Polk's War: American Opposition and Dissent, 1846–1848* (Madison, Wis., 1973); Chaplain W. Morrison, *Democratic Politics and Sectionalism: The Wilmot Proviso Controversy* (Chapel Hill, N.C., 1967).
43. Thomas H. O'Connor, *Lords of the Loom: The Cotton Whigs and the Coming of the Civil War* (New York, 1968), p. 78. See also Kinley J.

Brauer, *Cotton versus Conscience: Massachusetts Whig Politics and Southwestern Expansion, 1843–1848* (Lexington, Ky., 1967).

44. Joseph G. Rayback, *Free Soil: The Election of 1848* (Lexington, Ky., 1970); Peterson, *The Jefferson Image in the American Mind,* pp. 189–191.

45. Morrison, *Democratic Politics and Sectionalism,* pp. 165–173. Joseph G. Rayback has written,

> The strength of [party loyalty] . . . in the presidential election of 1848 was the largest single factor contributing to the results. In an election in which divisive forces were very powerful, the overwhelming majority in both parties remained loyal to party. Taylor retained 98.23 percent of the Whig vote in the whole nation and 95.26 percent of the Whig vote in the free states. Cass held 85.91 percent of the Democratic vote in the nation, 81.40 percent in the free states and 93.78 percent in the slave states. (*Free Soil,* p. 288.)

Chapter Seven

1. Michael F. Holt, "The Politics of Impatience: The Origins of Know Nothingism," *JAH,* 60 (September 1973), 309–331. W. Elliot Brownlee, *Dynamics of Ascent: A History of the American Economy* (New York, 1974), p. 160, comments upon the "acceleration of urbanization" being "clearly associated with the thrust of industrialization, which was also rapidly increasing in tempo during the boom of the late 1840s and early 1850s."

2. John Higham, *From Boundlessness to Consolidation: The Transformation of American Culture 1848–1860* (Ann Arbor, Mich., 1969), pp. 18–28.

3. Ruth Miller Elson, *Guardians of Tradition: American Schoolbooks of the Nineteenth Century* (Lincoln, Neb., 1964), pp. 47–62.

4. Ronald P. Formisano, *The Birth of Mass Political Parties: Michigan, 1827–1861* (Princeton, N.J., 1971), pp. 224–225.

5. Vincent P. Lannie, "Alienation in America: The Immigrant Catholic and Public Education in Pre-Civil War America," *Review of Politics,* 32 (October 1970), 503–521; William G. McLoughlin, "The Role of Religion in the Revolution: Liberty of Conscience and Cultural Cohesion in the New Nation," in Stephen Kurtz and James Hutson (eds.), *Essays on the American Revolution* (Chapel Hill, N.C., 1973), p. 254; Michael F. Holt, *Forging a Majority: The Formation of the Republican Party in Pittsburgh, 1848–1860* (New Haven, 1969), p. 133; Formisano, *Birth of Mass Political Parties,* pp. 222–238.

6. Holt, "The Politics of Impatience," pp. 309–324; Eric Foner, *Free Soil, Free Labor, Free Men: The Ideology of the Republican Party Before the Civil War* (New York, 1970), pp. 237–260.

7. Holt, *Forging a Majority,* pp. 9, 139–141, and "The Politics of Impatience," pp. 318–322; personal communication from Paul Kleppner,

May 4, 1976, concerning Democratic secessions to Know-Nothings. On the Progressive analogy, Richard Jensen has observed that "I see the Know-Nothings as an anti-party, anti-corruption middle-class civic reform movement that was strong in all states to 1860." (Letter to the author, June 14, 1976.) His views thus coincide with those of Professor Holt, in the works cited above.

8. James M. Bergquist, "People and Politics in Transition: The Illinois Germans, 1850–60," in Frederick C. Luebke (ed.), *Ethnic Voters and the Election of Lincoln* (Lincoln, Neb., 1971), pp. 196–226; Robert Henry Billigmeier, *Americans from Germany: A Study in Cultural Diversity* (Belmont, Calif., 1974), pp. 62–81; George H. Daniels, "The Immigrant Vote in the 1860 Election: The Case of Iowa," *Mid-America*, 55 (July 1962), 146–162.

9. For the Germans, the ratio was 1 : 33; for the English, 1 : 42. Joseph M. Hernon, Jr., *Celts, Catholics, and Copperheads: Ireland Views the American Civil War* (Columbus, Ohio, 1968), p. 11. On Boston, see Michael F. Holt, "The Antimasonic and Know Nothing Parties," in Arthur M. Schlesinger (ed.), *History of U.S. Political Parties* (New York, 1973), I, 575–620.

10. Robert W. Johannsen, *Stephen A. Douglas* (New York, 1973), p. 162; William V. Shannon, *The American Irish* (New York, 1963), pp. 54–58.

11. Johannsen, *Stephen A. Douglas*, pp. 233, 340, 501.

12. David B. Danbom, "The Young America Movement," *Illinois State Historical Society Journal*, 67 (June 1974), 294–306.

13. Hernon, *Celts, Catholics, and Copperheads*, pp. 65–75; Gilbert Osofsky, "Abolitionists, Irish Immigrants, and the Dilemmas of Romantic Nationalism," *AHR*, 80 (October 1975), 900; Joseph G. Rayback, "The American Workingman and the Antislavery Crusade," *Journal of Economic History*, 3 (January 1943), 152–164; Williston H. Lofton, "Abolition and Labor," *Journal of Negro History*, 33 (June 1948), 249–283.

14. Leon F. Litwack, *North of Slavery: The Negro in the Free States, 1790–1860* (Chicago, 1961), p. 97. See also George M. Fredrickson, *The Black Image in the White Mind: The Debate on Afro-American Character and Destiny, 1817–1914* (New York, 1971).

15. V. Jacque Voegeli, *Free but Not Equal: The Midwest and the Negro During the Civil War* (Chicago, 1967), pp. 1–6.

16. Thomas H. O'Connor, *Lords of the Loom* (New York, 1968), p. 98.

17. Mark L. Berger, *The Revolution in the New York Party Systems: 1840–1860* (Port Washington, N.Y., 1973), p. 10.

18. Formisano, *Birth of Mass Political Parties*, p. 244.

19. *Ibid.*, pp. 242–243.

20. Merrill D. Peterson, *The Jefferson Image in the American Mind* (New York, 1962), pp. 199–206.

21. See Holt, "The Politics of Impatience," pp. 309–313, and O'Connor, *Lords of the Loom*, on the circuitous route to Republicanism taken by

many Whigs. On the rise of the Republican party, see Eric Foner, *Free Soil, Free Labor, Free Men,* pp. 106–108, 228–237; James L. Sundquist, *Dynamics of the Party System: Alignment and Realignment of Political Parties in the United States* (Washington, D.C., 1973), pp. 80–81; Potter, *The Impending Crisis,* pp. 251–265; Formisano, *Birth of Mass Political Parties,* pp. 295–324. On the shift in the Northern Tier Pennsylvania counties occupied by Yankees, see Walter Dean Burnham, *Critical Elections and the Mainsprings of American Politics* (New York, 1970), pp. 34–39. "Viewed in global terms, the decisive margins of Republican victory after 1856 were provided by the New England-origin counties —the only area in the state where pro-Republican conversion of former Democrats appears to have occurred on a mass scale—and by the two major urban centers" (p. 36).

William G. Shade observes:

> In its policies, its leadership, and its support, the Republican party was much more a continuation of the [Northern] Whig party than historians have been willing to admit. It found its greatest strength in economically dynamic areas and among groups of Yankee origin who were also Congregationalist, Quaker, or Presbyterian. To an even greater extent than the Whigs, the Republicans were the party of Yankee-Protestantism, and their opponents bitterly attacked the intrusion of "Puritanism in Politics." Nearly every county in Illinois, Indiana, and Ohio that shifted from Democratic to Republican allegiance could be distinguished by its economic dynamism and the Yankee rather than southern origins of its population. As has been argued, the partisan conflict of these years was essentially a cultural one based on ethnic and religious differences. This cultural conflict expressed itself in the major issues of the day: the veiled nativism of temperance and the antisouthernism implicit in opposition to slavery and slavery extension. (*Banks or No Banks: The Money Question in the Western States, 1832–1865* [Detroit, 1973], p. 197.)

22. Holt, *Forging a Majority,* pp. 184–189, 213–214, 303; Formisano, *The Birth of Mass Political Parties,* p. 294. The question of how much the Republican party was entrepreneurial and business-oriented not only in its policies but *in its membership in the voting public* and was composed of the wealthy is uncertain. "Like the Whigs," writes Holt, "the Republicans [in Pittsburgh] drew more of their leaders from the wealthier classes of society than did the Democrats. . . . As a group Republican leaders were richer." They drew heavily upon iron and glass manufacturers. However, business leaders split evenly, with manufacturers trending Republican and store owners stronger proportionately among Democratic candidates (*Forging a Majority,* pp. 184–189). In 1860 balloting, Republicans received less support from businessmen than had the Whigs. "Instead, the Republicans received their most solid support from poor Protestants," far more than Whigs ever had. Conversely, Democrats lost a good deal of working-class support in Pittsburgh and

even significant numbers of immigrants. "Both parties were broader
and more heterogeneous coalitions than the earlier organizations" (p.
303).

In Michigan, in the 1860 election, Formisano finds that Republicans
had higher status occupations than Democrats, more of them being
skilled workers. Democrats had twice as many foreign born in their
ranks, held the Germans fairly well, and continued to maintain their 95
percent hold among Irish Catholics. Two-thirds of the Presbyterians
were Republicans; 70 percent of that party were Yankee; and Yankees
made up 50 percent of the elite. (*Birth of Mass Political Parties,* pp.
295–324.) "Landowners again displayed a strong Democratic tendency.
Capitalist, entrepreneurial, and unspecialized business elements, with
the exception of bankers, tended to favor Republicanism as they had
earlier favored Whiggery. The association of 'businessmen' with Republicanism, however, was not as strong as it had been with Whiggery," for
the Whigs had been more elite in makeup, less successful in appealing
to the masses (p. 294).

23. Shade, *Banks or No Banks,* p. 198.
24. David Donald, "The Republican Party 1864–1876," in Schlesinger, *His-
    tory of U.S. Political Parties,* II, 1288; Foner, *Free Soil, Free Labor, Free
    Men,* pp. 103–147.
25. Foner, *Free Soil, Free Labor, Free Men,* pp. 186–216. James A. Rawley's
    Race and Politics: Bleeding Kansas and the Coming of the Civil War
    (Philadelphia, 1969), a book that is essential on the psychology of the
    1850s, points to the division along the line of the forty-first parallel (pp.
    168–172).
26. The proportion of the Republican vote that came from ex-Democrats
    is in dispute. Foner estimates, "Taking the North as a whole, the ex-
    Democratic portion of the Republican vote in 1856 may have been as
    much as 25 percent" (*Free Soil, Free Labor, Free Men,* p. 165). Richard
    Jensen estimates them to have comprised perhaps 20 percent (personal
    communication, June 14, 1976). Paul Kleppner has cited research that
    in the Midwest only 11 percent of the 1852 Democrats crossed to the
    Republicans by 1856, and only 2 percent of the 1856 Democrats moved
    to the Republicans in 1860 (letter to the author, May 4, 1976, referring
    to Ray Myles Shortridge, "Voting Patterns in the American Midwest,
    1840–1872" [unpublished Ph.D. dissertation, University of Michigan,
    1974]). William Shade observes, with regard to Illinois, that "Lincoln's
    belief that 'nine tenths of the anti-Nebraska votes have to come from
    old Whigs' was undoubtedly an over-estimate, particularly for 1856. But
    when one looks at the entire period from the late 1840s to 1860 and
    considers the Old Northwest as a whole, Lincoln's estimate is not far
    from the truth. It is also clear that by 1860 well over 90% of the Whig
    electorate had joined the new party" (*Banks or No Banks,* p. 196).
27. Foner, *Free Soil, Free Labor, Free Men,* pp. 144–185, discusses at length

the exodus of the Democrats, whom he terms thereafter "Democratic-Republicans."

28. David Donald, *Charles Sumner and the Coming of the Civil War* (New York, 1967), I, pp. 36, 57–61; David Brion Davis, *The Slave Power Conspiracy and the Paranoid Style* (Baton Rouge, La., 1969), pp. 43–47; Betty Fladeland, *Men and Brothers: Anglo-American Antislavery Cooperation* (Urbana, Ill., 1972).

29. Donald, *Charles Sumner,* pp. 51–98, 131. "Relations between abolitionists and radicals were very close," writes Hans L. Trefousse in *The Radical Republicans: Lincoln's Vanguard for Racial Justice* (New York, 1969). "Engaged in a similar cause, they associated and corresponded with one another. Sumner enjoyed a life-long personal friendship with Wendell Phillips, Garrison's aristocratic collaborator and later antagonist. He also communicated frequently with such abolitionists as John Jay, Thomas Wentworth Higginson, W. I. Bowditch, Oliver Johnson, Lewis Tappan, and Henry B. Stanton. Gerrit Smith admired him greatly and he reciprocated the compliment" (pp. 15–16). But "the radicals . . . were essentially free soilers rather than immediate abolitionists, foes of the expansion of slavery who also favored the extinction of the institution by constitutional means" (p. 20).

30. In this discussion of Unitarianism, I have drawn upon Daniel Walker Howe's important study, *The Unitarian Conscience: Harvard Moral Philosophy, 1805–1861* (Cambridge, Mass., 1970). Tuckerman's statement is on p. 234. In a later work that Howe edited, *Victorian America* (Philadelphia, 1976), he remarks upon the peculiarly transatlantic character of Unitarianism even after the Civil War (p. 83). In 1838 the *Edinburgh Review* could observe of religious Dissenters in their English strongholds, Liverpool and Manchester—the heart of England's industrial North Country—that they

> are allied by close mercantile ties to Boston and New York; and the alliance of mind is closer still . . . Affinity of opinion has produced between members of these parties on each side of the Atlantic, a sort of cousinship and similarity of manner and tone of thought, not to be met with between any other classes in the several countries. The slight peculiarities, both of habit and mind which appear to characterise well educated Americans of the Eastern States are more nearly to be matched among the higher classes of dissenters in the great provincial towns of England than anywhere else; and an English Unitarian, especially if connected by family and acquaintance with the select people of that sect in his own country, is pretty sure of meeting in America not only with the kind and hospitable reception which all travellers can procure, but with a sort of family greeting. (Frank Thistlethwaite, *America and the Atlantic Community: Anglo-American Aspects, 1790–1850* [New York, 1964], pp. 77–78.)

31. Howe, *The Unitarian Conscience,* p. 272.
32. George M. Fredrickson, *The Inner Civil War: Northern Intellectuals and the Crisis of the Union* (New York, 1965), p. 37; Donald, *Charles*

Sumner, pp. 99–114, 125–147, 180–203, 227–275. Sumner also became close to John Quincy Adams in Adams' last years. Sumner never thought himself an original thinker, likening himself to a cistern and not a spring. Through him, William Ellery Channing had a long and powerful influence upon the nation after his death in 1842, which affected Sumner more than the death of his own father. Massachusetts Whigs came to detest Sumner heartily. It was he who linked what he called the "lords of the loom" with the "lords of the lash" while still a Conscience Whig and trying to move his party away from its Southern links, and these words were never forgotten.

33. Potter, *The Impending Crisis,* pp. 140, 252.
34. Holt, "The Politics of Impatience," pp. 309–331, and "The Antimasonic and Know Nothing Parties," in Schlesinger, ed., *History of U.S. Political Parties,* I, 575–620.
35. Foner, *Free Soil, Free Labor, Free Men,* pp. 41–72, 96–98; Davis, *The Slave Power Conspiracy and the Paranoid Style.*
36. Foner, *Free Soil, Free Labor, Free Men,* pp. 41–72, 96–98.
37. *Ibid.,* pp. 1–39; William R. Taylor, *Cavalier and Yankee: The Old South and American National Character* (New York, 1961). W. J. Cash's *The Mind of the South* (New York, 1941) is the classic description of this duality in the Southern character.
38. Formisano, *Birth of Mass Political Parties,* pp. 239–245, 266–288; Rawley, *Race and Politics,* pp. 125–128.
39. Fladeland, *Men and Brothers: Anglo-American Antislavery Cooperation,* pp. 348–375; Bertram Wyatt-Brown, *Lewis Tappan and the Evangelical War against Slavery* (Cleveland, 1969), pp. 328–333; Michael Fellman, "Theodore Parker and the Abolitionist Role in the 1850s," *JAH,* 61 (December 1974), 666–684.
40. Formisano, *Birth of Mass Political Parties,* pp. 229–238; Timothy L. Smith, *Revivalism and Social Reform: American Protestantism on the Eve of the Civil War* (New York, 1957), pp. 45–62.
41. Smith, *Revivalism and Social Reform,* pp. 204–206.
42. *Ibid.,* pp. 208, 214–215.
43. *Ibid.,* pp. 63–79, 227, 232–237.
44. Foner, *Free Soil, Free Labor, Free Men,* pp. 261–300.
45. *Ibid.* Republicans "saw their anti-slavery program as one part of a world-wide movement from absolutism to democracy, aristocracy to equality, backwardness to modernity, and . . . [this conviction] did much to strengthen their resolve." (p. 72).
46. In the following discussion of Lincoln, I have been guided by: George M. Fredrickson, "A Man but Not a Brother: Abraham Lincoln and Racial Equality," *JSH,* 41 (February 1975), 39–58; Don E. Fehrenbacher, *Prelude to Greatness: Lincoln in the 1850's* (New York, 1964); Lord Charnwood, *Abraham Lincoln* (New York, 1917); Benjamin P. Thomas, *Abraham Lincoln: A Biography* (New York, 1852); Albert J.

Beveridge, *Abraham Lincoln, 1809–1858* (Boston, 1928), 4 vols.; Paul M. Angle (ed.), *Created Equal? The Complete Lincoln–Douglas Debates of 1858* (Chicago, 1958); Ronald D. Rietveld, "Lincoln and the Politics of Morality," *Illinois State Historical Society Journal,* 68 (February 1975), 27–43; Arthur Zilversmit (ed.), *Lincoln on Black and White: A Documentary History* (Belmont, Calif., 1971). On the question of the Founding Fathers and slavery, so important to Lincoln and recently understood anew, see William W. Freehling, "The Founding Fathers and Slavery," *AHR,* 77 (February 1972), 81–93.

47. In my general discussion of Pennsylvania and its politics, I have drawn upon John F. Coleman, *The Disruption of the Pennsylvania Democracy 1848–1860* (Harrisburg, Pa., 1975), and Holt, *Forging a Majority.*

48. For the Irish in Philadelphia, and the following discussion, see Michael Feldberg, *The Philadelphia Riots of 1844: A Study of Ethnic Conflict* (Westport, Conn., 1975).

49. *Ibid.,* pp. 19–38.

50. *Ibid.,* p. 59.

51. *Ibid.,* pp. 41–73.

52. Holt, *Forging a Majority,* pp. 40–83.

53. *Ibid.,* pp. 123–219, 300–313. The quotations are on pp. 195, 203.

54. Coleman, *The Disruption of the Pennsylvania Democracy,* pp. 103–144. It is my own conjecture, based upon what are to me convincing indications widely scattered in the literature, that the Scotch–Irish were now voting Republican. Detailed statistical studies on them have not been conducted.

55. Potter, *The Impending Crisis,* pp. 225–227; Carl N. Degler, *The Other South: Southern Dissenters in the Nineteenth Century* (New York, 1974), p. 113.

56. David M. Potter, *The South and the Sectional Conflict* (Baton Rouge, La., 1968), p. 78.

57. Potter, *The Impending Crisis,* p. 475.

58. In the following discussion of the Yankee image, I draw heavily upon "Social Conflict and the Coming of the American Civil War: The Perspective of the New Political History," a paper read by Joel H. Silbey on December 30, 1976, at the Annual Meeting in Washington, D.C., of the American Historical Association. To demonstrate the national spread of these Democratic attitudes, the location of the newspapers he cites are indicated in the notes.

59. *Ibid.,* p. 8, citing Galveston *Tri-Weekly News,* July 17, 1856.

60. *Ibid.,* pp. 7–9, citing newspapers in Tennessee, South Carolina, Georgia, Alabama, Albany (N.Y.), Illinois, Arkansas.

61. *Ibid.,* pp. 10–12, citing newspapers in New York, Washington, D.C., Virginia, Alabama, Illinois, and South Carolina.

62. *Ibid.,* pp. 13–16, citing newspapers in New York, Illinois, Texas, Washington, D.C., Alabama, and the *Congressional Globe.*

63. Steven A. Channing, *Crisis of Fear: Secession in South Carolina* (New York, 1970), p. 237.
64. Davis, *The Slave Power Conspiracy,* pp. 32–47.
65. C. Vann Woodward, *American Counterpoint: Slavery and Racism in the North-South Dialogue* (Boston and Toronto, 1971), pp. 107–130.
66. William W. Freehling, *Prelude to Civil War: The Nullification Controversy in South Carolina 1816–1836* (New York, 1968), pp. 328–329; Claude H. Nolen, *The Negro's Image in the South: The Anatomy of White Supremacy* (Lexington, Ky., 1967); Degler, *The Other South,* pp. 41–64, 75–110.
67. Stephen A. Channing, *Crisis of Fear: Secession in South Carolina* (New York, 1970), pp. 58–61.
68. *Ibid.,* p. 23.
69. *Ibid.,* pp. 23–46, 145–147, 178–188.
70. I have not here narrated the course of events, in themselves of very great historical interest, that occurred following Lincoln's election in November and the outbreak of war many months later. Indeed, a great deal was going on in the North and in the South that I have not sought to describe in these pages, for this book is not in fact a history of the Civil War, its occurrence and results, but rather an exploration of cultural patterns in the nation's politics and the states of mind associated with them. For an excellent commentary on the relevant historical literature upon the whole subject of the war's origins, see Eric Foner, "The Causes of the Civil War: Recent Interpretations and New Directions," *CWH,* 20 (September 1974), 197–214, and a subsequent exchange between Professors Foner and Formisano on the role of cultural factors in *ibid,* 21 (June 1975), 185–190.

Chapter Eight

1. Horace Greeley estimated that the pro-Republican soldier vote in 1864 was as high as 75 percent. The veterans' organization after the war, the Grand Army of the Republic, practically became an adjunct of the Republican party. On the Republican identity of the officer corps, see James L. Sundquist, *Dynamics of the Party System: Alignment and Realignment of Political Parties in the United States* (Washington, D.C., 1973), p. 87.
2. Eric Foner, *Free Soil, Free Labor, Free Men: The Ideology of the Republican Party Before the Civil War* (New York, 1970), pp. 181–185.
3. Philip S. Paludan, "The American Civil War Considered as a Crisis in Law and Order," *AHR,* 77 (October 1972), 1017–1018.
4. John Higham, *From Boundlessness to Consolidation: The Transformation of American Culture 1848–1860* (Ann Arbor, Mich., 1969); George M. Fredrickson, *The Inner Civil War: Northern Intellectuals and the Crisis of the Union* (New York, 1965), pp. 1–180.

5. Fredrickson, *The Inner Civil War*, pp.55–81.

6. Merrill D. Peterson, *The Jefferson Image in the American Mind* (New York, 1962), pp. 216–226.

7. Allan Nevins, *The War for the Union: War Becomes Revolution 1862–1863* (New York, 1960), pp. 483–511.

8. William Gerald Shade, *Banks or No Banks: The Money Question in the Western States, 1832–1865* (Detroit, 1973), pp. 216, 224–241. See also Bray Hammond, *Sovereignty and an Empty Purse: Banks and Politics in the Civil War* (Princeton, N.J., 1970).

9. Leonard P. Curry, *Blueprint for Modern America: Non-Military Legislation of the First Civil War Congress* (Nashville, 1968), pp. 244–249; Laurence R. Veysey, *The Emergence of the American University* (Chicago, 1965), pp. 1–18.

10. Paul Kleppner, *The Cross of Culture: A Social Analysis of Midwestern Politics 1850–1900* (New York, 1970), p. 6.

11. Frank L. Klement, *The Copperheads in the Middle West* (Chicago, 1960), p. 45.

12. *Ibid.*, pp. viii, 1–6, 32–35.

13. *Ibid.*, pp. 6–7.

14. *Ibid.*, pp. 13–14, 19–32.

15. *Ibid.*, p. 13; Joseph M. Hernon, Jr., *Celts, Catholics, and Copperheads: Ireland Views the American Civil War* (Columbus, Ohio, 1968), pp. 11–23, 65–75; Adrian Cook, *The Armies of the Streets: The New York Draft Riots of 1863* (Lexington, Ky., 1974), pp. 19–31. New York City's population of 813,662 held 383,717 foreign born. Of these, 119,984 were Germans, and 203,740 were Irish (Cook, *The Armies of the Streets,* pp. 19–31, 44–45).

16. Fredrickson, *The Inner Civil War,* pp. 115, 130–150.

17. Morton Keller, *Affairs of State: Public Life in Late Nineteenth Century America* (Cambridge, Mass., 1977), pp. 37–46.

18. Herman Belz, *Reconstructing the Union: Theory and Policy During the Civil War* (Ithaca, N.Y., 1969).

19. James M. McPherson, *The Struggle for Equality: Abolitionists and the Negro in the Civil War and Reconstruction* (Princeton, N.J., 1964), dispels the traditional notion that the abolitionists deserted the slaves after the war began, indifferent to their future in a freed condition. It "was in the 1860s," he writes, "that the abolitionist crusade reached the height of its power and saw the achievement of most of its objectives" (p. vii). It was their program for reconstruction that, save for confiscated land, became the core of Reconstruction as it was actually carried out.

20. Keller, *Affairs of State,* pp. 45–47; C. Vann Woodward, *American Counterpoint: Slavery and Racism in the North-South Dialogue* (Boston, 1971), p. 42.

21. It is not my intention to explore in detail either the nature of Radical

Republicanism in its almost limitless complexities or the progress of Radical Reconstruction. The works that seem to me of the greatest value on this period are David Herbert Donald, *The Politics of Reconstruction, 1863–1867* (Baton Rouge, La., 1965), a revealing quantitative study; the same author's *Charles Sumner and the Rights of Man* (New York, 1971), a judicious account of the great symbol of Radical Republicanism; Eric L. McKitrick, *Andrew Johnson and Reconstruction* (Chicago, 1960), a remarkable exploration of the Northern state of mind toward the resurgent white South. Two works that reveal how ambiguous in their attitudes all political groups were toward the question of race are John and La Wanda Cox, *Politics, Principle, and Prejudice, 1865–1866: Dilemma of Reconstruction America* (New York, 1963), and W. R. Brock, *An American Crisis: Congress and Reconstruction 1865–1867* (New York, 1963). The most important recent study is Michael Les Benedict, *A Compromise of Principle: Congressional Republicans and Reconstruction 1863–1869* (New York, 1975). For a broad review of the literature, see Richard O. Curry, "The Civil War and Reconstruction, 1861–1877: A Critical Overview of Recent Trends and Interpretations," *CWH,* 20 (September 1974), 215–238.

22. p. 388.
23. Woodward, *American Counterpoint,* p. 167.
24. V. Jacques Voegeli, *Free but Not Equal: The Midwest and the Negro During the Civil War* (Chicago, 1967), pp. 160–162.
25. Woodward, *American Counterpoint,* pp. 165–176.
26. *Ibid.,* pp. 175–181.
27. Speech delivered at the Democratic State Convention, Albany, March 11, 1868, in John Bigelow (ed.), *The Writings and Speeches of Samuel J. Tilden* (New York, 1885), I, 395–420.
28. William Gillette, *The Right to Vote: Politics and the Passage of the Fifteenth Amendment* (Baltimore, 1965), pp. 160–162. The Fifteenth Amendment had one historic effect: it enfranchised Northern blacks. The matter was in this fashion finally taken out of the hands of reluctant Northern state legislatures. Black voters immediately cast their ballots in the presidential election of 1872 for the Republican Ulysses S. Grant.
29. Woodward, *American Counterpoint,* p. 42.
30. Carl N. Degler, *The Other South: Southern Dissenters in the Nineteenth Century* (New York, 1974), pp. 163–164, 173–178; T. B. Alexander and Richard E. Beringer, *The Anatomy of the Confederate Congress: A Study of the Influences of Members' Characteristics on Legislative Voting Behavior, 1861–1865* (Nashville, 1972), pp. 43–45, 54, 331–334; Thomas B. Alexander, "Persistent Whiggery in the Confederate South, 1860–1877," *JSH,* 27 (August 1961), 205–229.
31. Emory Thomas, *The Confederacy as a Revolutionary Experience* (Englewood Cliffs, N.J., 1971), pp. 56–57, 70, 78, 87, 93–94, 98–99; Rai-

mondo Luraghi, "The Civil War and the Modernizatiōn of American Society: Social Structure and Industrial Revolution in the Old South Before and During the War," *CWH,* 18 (1972), 230–250.

32. Woodward, *American Counterpoint,* p. 42.

33. Jack P. Maddex, Jr., *The Virginia Conservatives, 1867–1879: A Study in Reconstruction Politics* (Chapel Hill, N.C., 1970), pp. xi–xv, 276–296. Maddex specifically rejects the traditional historical view that the pre-war plantation elite, the "Bourbons," quickly reassumed control after the Civil War.

34. Degler, *The Other South,* pp. 193–228; Otto H. Olsen, "Reconsidering the Scalawags," *CWH,* 12 (1966), 304–320; Thomas, *The Confederacy as a Revolutionary Experience,* p. 104. "Parts of eastern Tennessee were virtually 'no man's lands' in which no one wearing a military uniform was safe from 'bushwackers,' " writes Thomas. "The same was true of northern Alabama, northern Georgia, and the [French Cajun] swamps of southern Louisiana. Bands of deserters controlled areas in western North Carolina. It was difficult to distinguish West Virginia from portions of western Virginia, if the criterion was loyalty to the South" (p. 104).

35. Degler, *The Other South,* pp. 227–228; J. Morgan Kousser, *The Shaping of Southern Politics: Suffrage Restriction and the Establishment of the One-Party South, 1880–1910* (New Haven, Conn., 1974).

36. Ernest Samuels, *The Young Henry Adams* (Cambridge, Mass., 1948), pp. 145–146.

37. Morton Keller, Introduction to the John Harvard Library edition of *Problems of Modern Democracy: Political and Economic Essays* by E. L. Godkin (Cambridge, Mass., 1966), pp. xviii, xxxix, xiv–xv.

38. Felice A. Bonadio, *North of Reconstruction: Ohio Politics, 1865–1870* (New York, 1970), pp. 24–29; Fredrickson, *The Inner Civil War,* pp. 188–206.

39. The following discussion of New York City reform is drawn from James Mohr, *The Radical Republicans and Reform in New York During Reconstruction* (Ithaca, N.Y., 1973), pp. 1–29, 54–55, 153–201.

40. *Ibid.,* pp. 61–138.

41. *Ibid.,* pp. 202–270.

42. *Ibid.,* pp. 271–279; Fredrickson, *The Inner Civil War,* pp. 183–198; Donald, *Charles Sumner and the Rights of Man,* pp. 339, 349.

43. Richard Allan Gerber, "The Liberal Republicans of 1872 in Historiographical Perspective," *JAH,* 62 (June 1975), 41–73; Matthew T. Downey, "Horace Greeley and the Politicians: The Liberal Republican Convention in 1872," *JAH,* 53 (March 1967), 727–750; James M. McPherson, "Grant or Greeley? The Abolitionist Dilemma in the Election of 1872," *AHR,* 71 (October 1976), 43–61.

44. Quoted in Keller, Introduction to *Problems of Modern Democracy,* p. viii.

45. I have at length discussed the career and ideas of William Gladstone in *The Transatlantic Persuasion* (New York, 1969), pp. 145–237.
46. Gerald W. McFarland, *Mugwumps, Morals and Politics, 1884–1920* (Amherst, Mass., 1975), pp. 11–13. I have relied upon this work for much information upon the Mugwumps, as to ideas and cultural location. See also John G. Sproat, *"The Best Men": Liberal Reformers in the Gilded Age* (New York, 1968).
47. Paul Kleppner, "Parties, Voters, and Political Culture: The Third Party System, 1853–1892," an unpublished manuscript that Professor Kleppner allowed me to read.
48. *Ibid.*
49. David Herbert Donald, "The Republican Party 1864–1876," in Arthur M. Schlesinger, Jr. (ed.), *History of U.S. Political Parties* (New York, 1973), II, 1281–1289.
50. Henry George, *The Question Before the People. What Is the Real Issue in the Presidential Campaign?* (San Francisco, 1876), p. 5.
51. Speech delivered in Utica, N.Y., August 12, 1875, in Bigelow, *The Writings and Speeches of Samuel J. Tilden*, II, 227. I have examined at length the character, career, and ideas of Tilden in "Samuel Tilden: The Democrat as Social Scientist," Chapter 7 of *The Transatlantic Persuasion*, pp. 238–292.
52. "The New York City Ring: Its Origin, Maturity, and Fall," in Bigelow, *Writings and Speeches of Samuel J. Tilden*, I, 600; Municipal Reform Message to the Legislature, Albany, May 11, 1875, *ibid.*, II, 119–135.
53. Irwin Unger, *The Greenback Era: A Social and Political History of American Finance* (Princeton, N.J., 1964) p. 35. See also Walter T. K. Nugent, Money and American Society, 1865–1880 (New York, 1968), on this topic.
54. Address delivered in Syracuse, N.Y., September 17, 1874, in Bigelow, *Writings and Speeches of Samuel J. Tilden*, II, 9–14; First Annual Message, Albany, N.Y., January 5, 1875, *ibid.*, II, 23–74; Second Annual Message, Albany, N.Y., January 4, 1876, *ibid.*, 237–295; Address of Acceptance of Gubernatorial Nomination, September 17, 1874, *ibid.*, II, 10–11.
55. Alexander C. Flick, *Samuel J. Tilden* (New York, 1939), pp. 317–318.
56. Letter from Tilden to the New York State Democratic Committee, August 1873, in John Bigelow (ed.), *Letters and Literary Memorials of Samuel J. Tilden* (New York, 1908), I, 321.
57. Peterson, *The Jefferson Image in the American Mind*, pp. 250–265.
58. Bigelow, *Letters and Literary Memorials of Samuel J. Tilden*, I, 321–323.
59. Robert Sharkey, *Money, Class, and Party: An Economic Study of Civil War and Reconstruction* (Baltimore, 1959), p. 208.
60. C. Vann Woodward, *Reunion and Reaction* (New York, 1956), especially p. 228; Carl V. Harris, "Right Fork or Left Fork? The Section-

Party Alignments of Southern Democrats in Congress, 1873–1897," *JSH,* 42 (1976), p. 478.

61. Keith Ian Polakoff, *The Politics of Inertia: The Election of 1876 and the End of Reconstruction* (Baton Rouge, La., 1973). See also Allan Peskin, "Was There a Compromise of 1877," *JAH,* 60 (1973), 63–75.

Bibliography

BOOKS CITED

Adams, Henry. *History of the United States: During the Administration of Jefferson and Madison.* Abridged by George Dangerfield and Otey M. Scruggs. Englewood Cliffs, N.J., 1963.

Ahlstrom, Sidney E. *A Religious History of the American People.* New Haven, 1972.

Alexander, T. B., and Beringer, Richard. *The Anatomy of the Confederate Congress: A Study of the Influences of Members' Characteristics on Legislative Voting Behavior, 1861–1865.* Nashville, Tenn., 1972.

Almond, Gabriel A., and Sidney Verba. *The Civic Culture: Political Attitudes and Democracy in Five Nations.* Princeton, N.J., 1963.

Ammon, Harry. *James Monroe: The Quest for National Identity.* New York, 1971.

Angle, Paul A. (ed.). *Created Equal? The Complete Lincoln-Douglas Debates of 1858.* Chicago, 1958.

Apter, David E. *The Politics of Modernization.* Chicago, 1965.

Bailyn, Bernard. *The Ideological Origins of the American Revolution.* Cambridge, Mass., 1967.

——. *The Origins of American Politics.* New York, 1968.

——. *The Ordeal of Thomas Hutchinson.* Cambridge, Mass., 1974.

Banner, James. *To the Hartford Convention: The Federalists and the Origins of Party Politics in Massachusetts, 1789–1815.* New York, 1970.

Bell, Daniel (ed.). *The Radical Right: The New American Right—Expanded and Updated.* Garden City, N.Y., 1964.

Bell, Rudolph M. *Party and Faction in American Politics: The House of Representatives 1789–1801.* Westport, Conn., 1973.

Belz, Herman. *Reconstructing the Union: Theory and Policy During the Civil War.* Ithaca, N.Y., 1969.

Benedict, Michael Les. *A Compromise of Principle: Congressional Republicans and Reconstruction 1863–1869.* New York, 1965.

Benedict, Ruth. *Patterns of Culture.* Boston, 1934.

Benson, Lee. *The Concept of Jacksonian Democracy: New York as a Test Case.* Princeton, N.J., 1961.

Berger, Mark L. *The Revolution in the New York Party Systems: 1840–1860.* Port Washington, N.Y., 1973.

Berkhofer, Robert F., Jr. *A Behaviorial Approach to Historical Analysis.* New York, 1969.

Bigelow, John (ed.). *The Writings and Speeches of Samuel J. Tilden.* New York, 1885.

Billigmeier, Robert Henry. *Americans from Germany: A Study in Cultural Diversity.* Belmont, Calif., 1974.

Billington, Ray Allen. *The Protestant Crusade 1800–1860: A Study of the Origins of American Nativism.* Chicago, 1964.

Black, C. E. *The Dynamics of Modernization: A Study in Comparative History.* New York, 1966.

Bonadio, Felice A. *North of Reconstruction: Ohio Politics, 1865–1870.* New York, 1970.

Bonomi, Patricia U. *A Factious People: Politics and Society in Colonial New York.* New York, 1971.

Borden, Morton. *The Federalism of James A. Bayard.* New York, 1955.

——. *Parties and Politics in the Early Republic, 1789–1815.* New York, 1967.

Brauer, Kinley J. *Cotton Versus Conscience: Massachusetts Whig Politics and Southwestern Expansion, 1843–1848.* Lexington, Ky., 1967.

Bridenbaugh, Carl. *Mitre and Sceptre: Transatlantic Faiths, Ideas, Personalities, and Politics: 1689–1775.* New York, 1962.

Briggs, Asa. *The Making of Modern England, 1783–1867: The Age of Improvement.* New York, 1965.

Brock, W. R. *An American Crisis: Congress and Reconstruction 1865–1867.* New York, 1963.

Brown, Richard D. *Revolutionary Politics in Massachusetts: The Boston Committee of Correspondence, 1772–1774.* Cambridge, Mass., 1970.

————. *Modernization: The Transformation of American Life 1600–1865.* New York, 1976.

Brown, Roger H. *The Republic in Peril: 1812.* New York, 1964.

Brown, Wallace. *The King's Friends: The Composition and Motives of the American Loyalist Claimants.* Providence, R.I., 1965.

Brownlee, W. Elliot. *Dynamics of Ascent: A History of the American Economy.* New York, 1974.

————, and Mary M. Brownlee. *Women in American Economy: A Documentary History, 1675–1929.* New Haven, 1976.

Buel, Richard Jr. *Securing the Revolution: Ideology in American Politics, 1789–1815.* Ithaca, N.Y., 1972.

Burnham, Walter Dean. *Critical Elections and the Mainsprings of American Politics.* New York, 1970.

Bushman, Richard L. *From Puritan to Yankee: Character and the Social Order in Connecticut, 1690–1765.* Cambridge, Mass., 1967.

Calhoon, Robert McCluer. *The Loyalists in Revolutionary America 1760–1781.* New York, 1973.

Cash, W. J. *The Mind of the South.* New York, 1941.

Chambers, William N., and Walter Dean Burnham (eds.). *The American Party Systems: Stages of Political Development.* New York, 1975.

Channing, Steven A. *Crisis of Fear: Secession in South Carolina.* New York, 1970.

Charnwood, Lord. *Abraham Lincoln.* New York, 1917.

Colbourn, H. Trevor. *The Lamp of Experience: Whig History and the Intellectual Origins of the American Revolution.* Chapel Hill, N.C., 1965.

Cole, Donald B. *Jacksonian Democracy in New Hampshire, 1800–1851.* Cambridge, Mass., 1970.

Coleman, John F. *The Disruption of the Pennsylvania Democracy 1848–1860.* Harrisburg, Pa., 1975.

Combs, Jerald A. *The Jay Treaty: Political Battleground of the Founding Fathers.* Berkeley, Calif., 1970.

Cook, Adrian. *The Armies of the Streets: The New York Draft Riots of 1863.* Lexington, Ky., 1974.

Cox, John, and La Wanda Cox. *Politics, Principle, and Prejudice, 1865–1866: Dilemma of Reconstruction America.* New York, 1963.

Crook, David Paul. *American Democracy in English Politics 1815–1840.* Oxford, 1965.

Cross, Whitney R. *The Burned-Over District: The Social and Intellectual History of Enthusiastic Religion in Western New York, 1800–1850.* New York, 1965.

Cunningham, Noble E., Jr. *The Jeffersonian Republicans: The Formation of Party Organization, 1789–1801.* Chapel Hill, N.C., 1957.

Curry, Leonard P. *Blueprint for Modern America: Non-Military Legislation of the First Civil War Congress.* Nashville, 1968.

Curti, Merle. *The Growth of American Thought.* 3rd ed. New York, 1964.

Curtis, L. Perry, Jr. *Apes and Angels: The Irishman in Victorian Caricature.* Washington, D.C., 1971.

Dalzell, Robert F., Jr. *Daniel Webster and the Trial of American Nationalism 1843–1852.* Boston, 1973.

Dauer, Manning J. *The Adams Federalists.* Baltimore, 1968.

Davis, David Brion. *The Slave Power Conspiracy and the Paranoid Style.* Baton Rouge, La., 1969.

——— (ed.). *The Fear of Conspiracy: Images of Un-American Subversion from the Revolution to the Present.* Ithaca, N.Y., 1971.

DeConde, Alexander. *The Quasi-War: The Politics and Diplomacy of the Undeclared War with France 1797–1801.* New York, 1966.

Degler, Carl N. *The Other South: Southern Dissenters in the Nineteenth Century.* New York, 1974.

De Jong, Gerald F. *The Dutch in America, 1609–1974.* Belmont, Calif., 1974.

Dickson, R. J. *Ulster Emigration to Colonial America 1718–1775.* London, 1966.

Dinnerstein, Leonard, and David M. Reimers. *Ethnic Americans: A History of Immigration and Assimilation.* New York, 1975.

Donald, David Herbert. *The Politics of Reconstruction, 1863–1867.* Baton Rouge, La., 1965.

————. *Charles Sumner and the Coming of the Civil War.* New York, 1967.

————. *Charles Sumner and the Rights of Man.* New York, 1971.

Dray, William. *Laws and Explanation in History.* London, 1957.

Duff, John B. *The Irish in the United States.* Belmont, Calif., 1971.

Eaton, Clement. *Henry Clay and the Art of American Politics.* Boston, 1957.

Edward, Owen Dudley, Gwynfor Evans, Joan Rhys, and Hugh MacDiarmid. *Celtic Nationalism.* London, 1968.

Elson, Ruth Miller. *Guardians of Tradition: American Schoolbooks of the Nineteenth Century.* Lincoln, Neb., 1964.

Fehrenbacher, Don E. *Prelude to Greatness: Lincoln in the 1850's.* New York, 1964.

Feldberg, Michael. *The Philadelphia Riots of 1844: A Study of Ethnic Conflict.* Westport, Conn., 1975.

Fischer, David Hackett. *The Revolution of American Conservatism: The Federalist Party in the Era of Jeffersonian Democracy.* New York, 1965.

Fladeland, Betty. *Men and Brothers: Anglo-American Antislavery Cooperation.* Urbana, Ill., 1972.

Flick, Alexander C. *Samuel J. Tilden.* New York, 1939.

Foner, Eric. *Free Soil, Free Labor, Free Men: The Ideology of the Republican Party Before the Civil War.* New York, 1970.

————. *Tom Paine and Revolutionary America.* New York, 1976.

Formisano, Ronald P. *The Birth of Mass Political Parties: Michigan, 1827–1861.* Princeton, N.J., 1971.

Fox, Dixon Ryan. *Yankees and Yorkers.* New York, 1940.

Franklin, John Hope. *Reconstruction After the Civil War.* Chicago, 1961.

Fredrickson, George M. *The Inner Civil War: Northern Intellectuals and the Crisis of the Union.* New York, 1965.

———. *The Black Image in the White Mind: The Debate on Afro-American Character and Destiny, 1817–1914.* New York, 1971.

Freehling, William W. *Prelude to Civil War: The Nullification Controversy in South Carolina 1816–1838.* New York, 1968.

Gaston, Paul M. *The New South Creed: A Study in Southern Mythmaking.* New York, 1970.

George, Henry. *The Question Before the People. What Is the Real Issue in the Presidential Campaign?* San Francisco, 1876.

Gillette, William. *The Right to Vote: Politics and the Passage of the Fifteenth Amendment.* Baltimore, 1965.

Goodman, Paul. *The Democratic-Republicans of Massachusetts: Politics in a Young Republic.* Cambridge, Mass., 1964.

Green, E. R. R. (ed.). *Essays in Scotch-Irish History.* London, 1969.

Gribbin, William. *The Churches Militant: The War of 1812 and American Religion.* New Haven, 1973.

Griffin, Clifford S. *Their Brothers' Keepers: Moral Stewardship in the United States, 1800–1865.* New Brunswick, N.J., 1960.

Halevy, Elie. *Victorian Years, 1841–1895.* New York, 1961.

———. *The Liberal Awakening, 1815–1830.* New York, 1961.

Hammond, Bray. *Banks and Politics in America from the Revolution to the Civil War.* Princeton, N.J., 1957.

Hanna, William S. *Benjamin Franklin and Pennsylvania Politics.* Stanford, Calif., 1964.

Hatch, Elvin. *Theories of Man and Culture.* New York, 1973.

Heimert, Alan E. *Religion and the American Mind, from the Great Awakening to the Revolution.* Cambridge, Mass., 1966.

Henderson, H. James. *Party Politics in the Continental Congress.* New York, 1974.

Hernon, Joseph M., Jr. *Celts, Catholics and Copperheads: Ireland Views the American Civil War.* Columbus, Ohio, 1968.

Higham, John. *Strangers in the Land: Patterns of American Nativism 1860–1925.* New Brunswick, N.J., 1955.

———. *From Boundlessness to Consolidation: The Transformation of American Culture 1848–1860.* Ann Arbor, Mich., 1969.

———. *Writing American History: Essays on Modern Scholarship.* Bloomington, Ind., 1970.

———, Leonard Krieger, and Felix Gilbert. *History.* Englewood Cliffs, N.J., 1965.

Hofstadter, Richard. *Social Darwinism in American Thought.* Philadelphia, 1944.

———. *The American Political Tradition and the Men Who Made It.* New York, 1948.

———. *The Age of Reform: From Bryan to F.D.R.* New York, 1955.

———. *The Paranoid Style in American Politics and Other Essays.* New York, 1967.

———. *The Progressive Historians: Turner, Beard, Parrington.* New York, 1968.

———. *The Idea of a Party System: The Rise of Legitimate Opposition in the United States, 1780–1840.* Berkeley and Los Angeles, 1969.

Holt, Michael F. *Forging a Majority: The Formation of the Republican Party in Pittsburgh, 1848–1860.* New Haven, 1969.

Houghton, Walter E. *The Victorian Frame of Mind, 1830–1870.* New Haven, 1957.

Howe, Daniel Walker. *The Unitarian Conscience: Harvard Moral Philosophy 1805–1861.* Cambridge, Mass., 1970.

——— (ed.). *Victorian America.* Philadelphia, 1976.

Huntington, Samuel. *Political Order in Changing Societies.* New Haven, 1968.

Hutson, James H. *Pennsylvania Politics 1746–1770: The Movement for Royal Government and Its Consequences.* Princeton, N.J., 1972.

Jensen, Merrill. *The American Revolution Within America.* New York, 1974.

Johannsen, Robert W. *Stephen A. Douglas.* New York, 1973.

Keller, Morton. *Affairs of State: Public Life in Late Nineteenth Century America.* Cambridge, Mass., 1977.

Kelley, Robert. *Gold vs. Grain: The Hydraulic Mining Controversy in California's Sacramento Valley.* Glendale, Calif., 1959.

———. *The Transatlantic Persuasion: The Liberal-Democratic Mind in the Age of Gladstone.* New York, 1969.

Kerber, Linda K. *Federalists in Dissent: Imagery and Ideology in Jeffersonian America.* Ithaca, N.Y., 1970.

Key, V. O., Jr. *Politics, Parties and Pressure Groups.* New York, 1958.

Klein, Phillip S., and Ari Hoogenboom. *A History of Pennsylvania.* New York, 1973.

Klement, Frank L. *The Copperheads in the Middle West.* Chicago, 1960.

Kleppner, Paul. *The Cross of Culture: A Social Analysis of Midwestern Politics 1850–1900.* New York, 1970.

Koch, Adrienne. *Jefferson and Madison: The Great Collaboration.* New York, 1953.

———. *The Philosophy of Thomas Jefferson.* Chicago, 1964.

Kousser, J. Morgan. *The Shaping of Southern Politics: Suffrage Restriction and the Establishment of the One-Party South, 1880–1910.* New Haven, 1974.

Kraus, Michael. *The Atlantic Civilization: Eighteenth-Century Origins.* Ithaca, N.Y., 1949.

Kurtz, Stephen, and James Hutson (eds.). *Essays on the American Revolution.* Chapel Hill, N.C., 1973.

Lerner, Daniel. *The Passing of Traditional Society: Modernizing the Middle East.* Glencoe, Ill., 1958.

Levine, Edward M. *The Irish and Irish Politicians: A Study of Cultural and Social Alienation.* Notre Dame, Ind., 1966.

Levy, Mark R., and Michael S. Kramer. *The Ethnic Factor: How America's Minorities Decide Elections.* New York, 1973.

Leyburn, James G. *The Scotch-Irish: A Social History.* Chapel Hill, N.C., 1962.

Link, Eugene Perry. *Democratic-Republican Societies, 1790–1800.* New York, 1965.

Lipsky, George A. *John Quincy Adams: His Theory and Ideas.* New York, 1965.

Litt, Edgar. *Beyond Pluralism: Ethnic Politics in America.* Glenview, Ill., 1970.

Litwack, Leon F. *North of Slavery: The Negro in the Free States, 1790–1860.* Chicago, 1961.

Livermore, Shaw, Jr. *The Twilight of Federalism: The Disintegration of the Federalist Party 1815–1830.* Princeton, N.J., 1962.

Lubell, Samuel. *The Future of American Politics.* New York, 1952.

Luebke, Frederick C. (ed.). *Ethnic Voters and the Election of Lincoln.* Lincoln, Neb., 1971.

McCormick, Richard P. *The Second Party System: Party Formation in the Jacksonian Era.* Chapel Hill, N.C., 1966.

McFarland, Gerald W. *Mugwumps, Morals and Politics, 1884–1920.* Amherst, Mass., 1975.

McFaul, John. *The Politics of Jacksonian Finance.* Ithaca, N.Y., 1972.

McKitrick, Eric L. *Andrew Johnson and Reconstruction.* Chicago, 1960.

McLoughlin, William. *Isaac Backus and the American Pietistic Tradition.* Boston, 1967.

————. *New England Dissent, 1630–1833: The Baptists and the Separation of Church and State.* Cambridge, Mass., 1971.

McPherson, James M. *The Struggle for Equality: Abolitionists and the Negro in the Civil War and Reconstruction.* Princeton, N.J., 1964.

Maddex, Jack P., Jr. *The Virginia Conservatives, 1867–1879.* Chapel Hill, N.C., 1970.

Main, Jackson Turner. *Political Parties Before the Constitution.* Chapel Hill, N.C., 1973.

Maldwyn, Allen Jones. *American Immigration.* Chicago, 1960.

Merk, Frederick. *Manifest Destiny and Mission in American History: A Reinterpretation.* New York, 1966.

Merritt, Richard L. *Symbols of American Community, 1735–1775.* New Haven, 1966.

Meyers, Marvin. *The Jacksonian Persuasion: Politics and Belief.* New York, 1969.

Miller, Douglas T. *The Birth of Modern America 1820–1850.* Indianapolis, 1970.

Miller, John C. *Origins of the American Revolution.* Boston, 1943.

————. *Alexander Hamilton and the Growth of the New Nation.* New York, 1964.

————. *The Federalist Era 1789–1801.* New York, 1960.

Mohr, James. *The Radical Republicans and Reform in New York During Reconstruction.* Ithaca, N.Y., 1973.

Morgan, Edmund S. *American Slavery American Freedom: The Ordeal of Colonial Virginia.* New York, 1975.

Morris, Richard B. (ed.). *The Basic Ideas of Alexander Hamilton.* New York, 1957.

Morrison, Chaplain W. *Democratic Politics and Sectionalism: The Wilmot Proviso Controversy.* Chapel Hill, N.C., 1967.

Nelson, William H. *The American Tory.* New York, 1961.

Neuenschwander, John A. *The Middle Colonies and the Coming of the American Revolution.* Port Washington, N.Y., 1973.

Nevins, Allan. *The War for the Union: War Becomes Revolution 1862–1863.* New York, 1960.

Nolen, Claude H. *The Negro's Image in the South: The Anatomy of White Supremacy.* Lexington, Ky., 1967.

Norton, Mary Beth. *The British-Americans: The Loyalist Exiles in England, 1774–1789.* Boston, 1972.

Nugent, Walter T. K. *Money and American Society 1865–1880.* New York, 1968.

O'Connor, Thomas H. *Lords of the Loom: The Cotton Whigs and the Coming of the Civil War.* New York, 1968.

Ogg, David. *England in the Reign of Charles II.* Oxford, 1955.

Olson, Alison Gilbert. *Anglo-American Politics, 1660–1775: The Relationship Between Parties in England and Colonial America.* New York, 1973.

Parton, James. *Life of Andrew Jackson.* New York, 1860.

Patterson, Stephen E. *Political Parties in Revolutionary Massachusetts.* Madison, Wis., 1973.

Pelling, Henry. *America and the British Left: From Bright to Bevan.* New York, 1957.

Peterson, Merrill D. *The Jefferson Image in the American Mind.* New York, 1962.

———. *Thomas Jefferson and the New Nation: A Biography*. New York, 1970.

Pilcher, George William. *Samuel Davies: Apostle of Dissent in Colonial Virginia*. Knoxville, Tenn., 1971.

Pocock, J. G. A. *The Machiavellian Moment: Florentine Political Thought and the Atlantic Republican Tradition*. Princeton, N.J., 1975.

Polakoff, Keith Ian. *The Politics of Inertia: The Election of 1876 and the End of Reconstruction*. Baton Rouge, La., 1973.

Potter, David M. *People of Plenty: Economic Abundance and American Character*. Chicago, 1954.

———. *The South and the Sectional Conflict*. Baton Rouge, La., 1968.

———. *The Impending Crisis 1848–1861*. Completed and edited by Don E. Fehrenbacher. New York, 1976.

Power, Richard Lyle. *Planting Corn Belt Culture: The Impress of the Upland Southerner and the Yankee in the Old Northwest*. Indianapolis, 1953.

Pratt, John W. *Religion, Politics and Diversity: The Church-State Theme in New York History*. Ithaca, N.Y., 1967.

Quinn, David Beers. *The Elizabethans and the Irish*. Ithaca, N.Y., 1966.

Ratner, Lorman. *Antimasonry: The Crusade and the Party*. Englewood Cliffs, N.J., 1969.

Rawley, James A. *Race and Politics: Bleeding Kansas and the Coming of the Civil War*. Philadelphia, 1969.

Rayback, Joseph G. *Free Soil: The Election of 1848*. Lexington, Ky., 1970.

Remini, Robert. *The Election of Andrew Jackson*. Philadelphia, 1963.

Richardson, James D. (comp.). *A Compilation of the Messages and Papers of the Presidents*. Washington, D.C., 1913.

Risjord, Norman K. *The Old Republicans: Southern Conservatism in the Age of Jefferson*. New York, 1965.

Robbins, Caroline. *The Eighteenth-Century Commonwealthman*. Cambridge, Mass., 1959.

Rose, Lisle A. *Prologue to Democracy: The Federalists in the South, 1789–1800*. Lexington, Ky., 1968.

Rose, Willie Lee. *Rehearsal for Reconstruction: The Port Royal Experiment.* New York, 1967.

Rostow, Walt W. *The Stages of Economic Growth: A Non-Communist Manifesto.* 2nd ed. Cambridge, Eng., 1971.

Samuels, Ernest. *The Young Henry Adams.* Cambridge, Mass., 1948.

Schlesinger, Arthur M., Jr. *The Age of Jackson.* Boston, 1945.

Schroeder, John H. *Mr. Polk's War: American Opposition and Dissent, 1846–1848.* Madison, Wis., 1973.

Sellers, Charles. *James K. Polk: Continentalist 1843–1846.* Princeton, N.J., 1966.

Sewell, Richard H. *Ballots for Freedom: Antislavery Politics in the United States 1837–1860.* New York, 1976.

Shade, William Gerald. *Banks or No Banks: The Money Question in the Western States, 1832–1865.* Detroit, 1973.

Shannon, William V. *The American Irish.* New York, 1963.

Sharkey, Robert. *Money, Class, and Party: An Economic Study of Civil War and Reconstruction.* Baltimore, 1959.

Shenton, James P. *Robert John Walker: A Politician from Jackson to Lincoln.* New York, 1969.

Shortridge, Ray Myles. "Voting Patterns in the American Midwest, 1840–1872." Ph.D. dissertation, University of Michigan, 1974.

Silbey, Joel H. *The Shrine of Party: Congressional Voting Behavior 1841–1852.* Pittsburgh, 1967.

Sisson, Daniel. *The American Revolution of 1800.* New York, 1974.

Skotheim, Robert Allen. *American Intellectual Histories and Historians.* Princeton, N.J., 1966.

Sloan, Douglas. *The Scottish Enlightenment and the American College Ideal.* New York, 1971.

Smith, Timothy L. *Revivalism and Social Reform: American Protestantism on the Eve of the Civil War.* New York, 1957.

Social Science Research Council. *The Social Sciences in Historical Study: A Report of the Committee on Historiography.* Bulletin 64. New York, 1954.

Spann, Edward K. *Ideals and Politics: New York Intellectuals and Liberal Democracy 1820–1880.* Albany, N.Y., 1975.

Sproat, John G. *"The Best Men": Liberal Reformers in the Gilded Age*. New York, 1968.

Stourzh, Gerald. *Alexander Hamilton and the Idea of Republican Government*. Stanford, Calif., 1970.

Strout, Cushing. *The New Heavens and New Earth: Political Religion in America*. New York, 1974.

Sundquist, James L. *Dynamics of the Party System: Alignment and Realignment of Political Parties in the United States*. Washington, D.C., 1973.

Sydnor, Charles S. *Gentlemen Freeholders: Political Practices in Washington's Virginia*. Chapel Hill, N.C., 1952.

Temin, Peter. *Jacksonian America: Society, Personality, and Politics*. Homewood, Ill., 1969.

———. *The Jacksonian Economy*. New York, 1969.

Thistlethwaite, Frank. *America and the Atlantic Community: Anglo-American Aspects, 1790–1850*. New York, 1964.

Thomas, Emory. *The Confederacy as a Revolutionary Experience*. Englewood Cliffs, N.J., 1971.

Thomas, P. D. G. *British Politics and the Stamp Act Crisis: The First Phase of the American Revolution, 1763–1767*. New York, 1975.

Tindall, George B. *The Ethnic Southerners*. Baton Rouge, La., 1976.

Tinkcom, Harry Marlin. *The Republicans and Federalists in Pennsylvania 1790–1801: A Study in National Stimulus and Local Response*. Harrisburg, Pa., 1950.

Trefousse, Hans L. *The Radical Republicans: Lincoln's Vanguard for Racial Justice*. New York, 1969.

Unger, Irwin. *The Greenback Era: A Social and Political History of American Finance, 1865–1879*. Princeton, N.J., 1964.

Van Buren, Martin. *The Autobiography of Martin Van Buren*. Edited by John C. Fitzpatrick. Annual Report of the American Historical Association for the Year 1918.

Van Deusen, Glyndon G. *The Life of Henry Clay*. Boston, 1937.

———. *The Jacksonian Era 1828–1848*. New York, 1959.

Veysey, Laurence R. *The Emergence of the American University*. Chicago, 1965.

Voegeli, V. Jacque. *Free but Not Equal: The Midwest and the Negro During the Civil War.* Chicago, 1967.

Walters, Ronald G. *The Antislavery Appeal: American Abolitionism after 1830.* Baltimore, 1976.

Ward, John William. *Andrew Jackson: Symbol for an Age.* New York, 1962.

Weiner, Myron (ed.). *Modernization: The Dynamics of Growth.* New York, 1966.

Wood, Gordon S. *The Creation of the American Republic.* Chapel Hill, N.C., 1969.

Woodward, C. Vann. *Reunion and Reaction.* New York, 1956.

————. *American Counterpoint: Slavery and Racism in the North-South Dialogue.* Boston, 1971.

Wyatt-Brown, Bertram. *Lewis Tappan and the Evangelical War Against Slavery.* Cleveland, 1969.

Young, Alfred F. *The Democratic Republicans of New York: The Origins, 1763–1797.* Chapel Hill, N.C., 1967.

———— (ed.). *The American Revolution: Explorations in the History of American Radicalism.* DeKalb, Ill., 1976.

Young, James Sterling. *The Washington Community, 1800–1828.* New York, 1966.

Zemsky, Robert. *Merchants, Farmers, and River Gods: An Essay on Eighteenth-Century American Politics.* Boston, 1971.

Zilversmit, Arthur (ed.). *Lincoln on Black and White: A Documentary History.* Belmont, Calif., 1971.

Zuckerman, Michael. *Peaceable Kingdoms: Massachusetts Towns in the Eighteenth Century.* New York, 1970.

ARTICLES CITED
The following journals will be abbreviated as follows:

The American Historical Review: AHR
Civil War History: CWH
The Journal of American History: JAH
The Journal of Southern History: JSH
Political Science Quarterly: PSQ
William and Mary Quarterly: WMQ

Adair, Douglas. " 'That Politics May Be Reduced to a Science': David Hume, James Madison, and the *Tenth Federalist.*" *Huntington Library Quarterly,* 20 (1957), 343–360.

Alexander, Thomas B. "Persistent Whiggery in the Confederate South, 1860–1877." *JSH,* 27 (1961), 205–229.

Ammon, Harry. "James Monroe and the Era of Good Feelings." *Virginia Magazine of History and Biography,* 66 (1958), 387–398.

Appleby, Joyce. "Ideology and Theory: The Tension between Political and Economic Liberalism." *AHR,* 81 (1976), 499–515.

———. "Liberalism and the American Revolution," *The New England Quarterly,* 49 (1976), 7–9.

———. "The Social Origins of American Revolutionary Ideology." *JAH,* 64 (1978), 935–958.

Banner, Lois W. "Religious Benevolence as Social Control: A Critique of an Interpretation." *JAH,* 60 (1973), 23–41.

Banning, Lance. "Republican Ideology and the Triumph of the Constitution, 1789 to 1793." *WMQ,* 31 (1974), 167–188.

Berkhofer, Robert F., Jr. "Clio and the Culture Concept: Some Impressions of a Changing Relationship in American Historiography." *Social Science Quarterly,* 53 (1972), 297–320.

Berthoff, Rowland, and John M. Murrin. "Feudalism, Communalism, and the Yeoman Freeholder: The American Revolution Considered as a Social Accident," in Stephen Kurtz and James Hutson (eds.), *Essays on the American Revolution.* Chapel Hill, N.C., 1973, pp. 256–288.

Bockelman, Wayne L., and Owen S. Ireland. "The Internal Revolution in Pennsylvania: An Ethnic-Religious Interpretation." *Pennsylvania History,* 41 (1974), 125–159.

Bogue, Allen G. "United States: The 'New Political History.' " *Journal of Contemporary History,* 3 (1968), 22–24.

Bonwick, C. C. "English Dissenters and the American Revolution," in H. C. Allen and Roger Thompson (eds.), *Contrast and Connection: Bicentennial Essays in Anglo-American History.* Athens, Ohio, 1976, pp. 89–112.

Broussard, James H. "Regional Pride and Republican Politics: The Fatal Weakness of Southern Federalism, 1800–1815." *South Atlantic Quarterly,* 73 (1974), 23–33.

Brown, Richard H. "The Missouri Crisis, Slavery and the Politics of Jacksonianism." *South Atlantic Quarterly,* 65 (1966), 55–72.

Brown, Richard Maxwell. "The Anglo-American Political System, 1675–1775: A Behaviorial Analysis," in Alison Gilbert Olson and Richard Maxwell Brown (eds.), *Anglo-American Political Relations, 1675–1775.* New Brunswick, N.J., 1970, pp. 2–28.

Burrows, Edwin G. "Military Experience and the Origins of Federalism and Antifederalism," in Jacob Judd and Irwin H. Polishook (eds.), *Aspects of Early New York Society and Politics.* Tarrytown, N.Y., 1974, pp. 83–92.

Bushman, Richard L. "Massachusetts Farmers and the Revolution," in Jack P. Greene, Richard L. Bushman, and Michael Kammen (eds.), *Society, Freedom, and Conscience: The American Revolution in Virginia, Massachusetts, and New York.* New York, 1976, pp. 77–124.

Curry, Richard O. "The Civil War and Reconstruction, 1861–1877: A Critical Overview of Recent Trends and Interpretations." *CWH,* 20 (1974), 215–238.

Danbom, David B. "The Young America Movement." *Illinois State Historical Society Journal,* 67 (1974), 294–306.

Doherty, Robert W. "Social Bases for the Presbyterian Schism of 1837–1838, The Philadelphia Case." *Journal of Social History,* 2 (1968), 69–79.

Donald, David Herbert. "The Republican Party 1864–1876," in Arthur M. Schlesinger, Jr. (ed.), *History of U.S. Political Parties.* New York, 1973, II, pp. 1281–1289.

Downey, Matthew T. "Horace Greeley and the Politicians: The Liberal Republican Convention in 1872." *JAH,* 53 (1967), 727–750.

Egnal, Marc, and Joseph A. Ernst. "An Economic Interpretation of the American Revolution." *WMQ,* 29 (1972), 15–24.

Elkins, Stanley, and Eric McKitrick (eds.), "Richard Hofstadter: A Progress," in *The Hofstadter Aegis: A Memorial.* New York, 1974, pp. 300–367.

Ernst, Joseph. " 'Ideology' and an Economic Interpretation of the Revolution," in Alfred F. Young (ed.), *The American Revolution: Explorations in the History of American Radicalism.* De Kalb, Ill., 1976.

Ershkowitz, Herbert, and William G. Shade. "Consensus or Conflict? Political Behavior in the State Legislatures During the Jacksonian Era." *JAH,* 58 (1971), 591–621.

Evans, E. Estyn. "The Scotch-Irish: Their Cultural Adaptation and Heritage in the American Old West," in E. R. R. Green (ed.), *Essays in Scotch-Irish History.* London, 1969.

Fellman, Michael. "Theodore Parker and the Abolitionist Role in the 1850s." *JAH,* 61 (1974–5), 666–684.

Folsom, Burton W., II. "The Politics of Elites: Prominence and Party in Davidson County, Tennessee, 1835–1861." *JSH,* 39 (1973), 359–378.

Foner, Eric. "The Causes of the American Civil War: Recent Interpretations and New Directions." *CWH,* 20 (1974), 197–214. Recently republished in Robert P. Swierenga (ed.), *Beyond the Civil War Synthesis: Political Essays of the Civil War Era.* Westport, Conn., 1975.

———. "Tom Paine's Republic, Radical Ideology and Social Change," in Alfred Young (ed.), *The American Revolution: Explorations in the History of American Radicalism.* De Kalb, Ill., 1976, pp. 187–232.

Formisano, Ronald P. "Deferential-Participant Politics: The Early Republic's Political Culture, 1789–1840." *American Political Science Review,* 68 (1974), 473–487.

Fredrickson, George M. "A Man but Not a Brother: Abraham Lincoln and Racial Equality." *JSH,* 41 (1975), 39–58.

Freehling, William W. "The Founding Fathers and Slavery." *AHR,* 77 (1972), 81–93.

Gatell, Frank Otto. "Sober Second Thoughts on Van Buren, the Albany Regency, and the Wall Street Conspiracy." *JAH,* 53 (1966), 19–40.

———. "Money and Party in Jacksonian America: A Quantitative Look at New York City's Men of Quality." *PSQ,* 82 (1967), 235–252.

Geertz, Clifford. "The Impact of the Concept of Culture on the Concept of Man," in Yehudi A. Cohen (ed.), *Man in Adaptation: The Cultural Present.* Chicago, 1974, pp. 19–32.

Gerber, Richard Allen. "The Liberal Republicans of 1872 in Historiographical Perspective." *JAH,* 62 (1975), 41–73.

Goldman, Perry M. "Political Virtue in the Age of Jackson." *PSQ,* 87 (1972), 46–62.

Goodman, Paul. "The First American Party System," in William Nisbet Chambers and Walter Dean Burnham (eds.), *The American Party Systems: Stages of Political Development.* 2nd ed. New York, 1975, pp. 56–89.

Green, James R. "Behavioralism and Class Analysis: A Review Essay on Methodology and Ideology." *Labor History,* 13 (1972), 89–106.

Greene, Jack P. "The Role of the Lower Houses of Assembly in Eighteenth-Century Politics." *JSH,* 27 (1961), 451–474.

———. "An Uneasy Connection: An Analysis of the Preconditions of the American Revolution," in Stephen Kurtz and James Hutson (eds.), *Essays on the American Revolution.* Chapel Hill, N.C., 1973, pp. 47–53.

———. "The Social Origins of the American Revolution: An Evaluation and Interpretation." *PSQ,* 88 (1973), 1–22.

———. "Society, Ideology, and Politics: An Analysis of the Political Culture of Mid-Eighteenth-Century Virginia," in Jack P. Greene, Richard L. Bushman, and Michael Kammen (eds.), *Society, Freedom and Conscience: The American Revolution in Virginia, Massachusetts, and New York.* New York, 1976, pp. 14–76.

Gribbin, William. "Antimasonry, Religious Radicalism, and the Paranoid Style of the 1820s." *The History Teacher,* 7 (1974), 239–254.

Grimstead, David. "Rioting in Its Jacksonian Setting." *AHR,* 77 (1972), 361–397.

Harris, Carl V. "Right Fork or Left Fork? The Section-Party Alignments of Southern Democrats in Congress, 1873–1897." *JSH,* 42 (1976), 471–506.

Henderson, H. James. "The Structure of Politics in the Continental Congress," in Stephen Kurtz and James Hutson (eds.), *Essays on the American Revolution.* Chapel Hill, N.C., 1973, pp. 157–95.

Hoerder, Dirk. "Boston Leaders and Boston Crowds, 1765–1776," in Alfred F. Young (ed.), *The American Revolution: Explorations in the History of American Radicalism.* De Kalb, Ill., 1976, pp. 233–272.

Hoffman, Ronald. "The 'Disaffected' in the Revolutionary South," in Alfred F. Young (ed.), *The American Revolution: Explorations in the History of American Radicalism.* De Kalb, Ill., 1976, pp. 273–316.

Holt, Michael F. "The Antimasonic and Know Nothing Parties," in Arthur M. Schlesinger, Jr. (ed.), *History of U.S. Political Parties.* New York, 1973, II, pp. 575–740.

———. "The Politics of Impatience." *JAH,* 60 (1973), 309–331

Howe, John R., Jr. "Republican Thought and the Political Violence of the 1790s." *American Quarterly,* 19 (1967), 150–163.

Huntington, Samuel. "Paradigms of American Politics: Beyond the One, the Two, and the Many." *PSQ,* 89 (1974), 1–26.

Ireland, Owen S. "The Ethnic-Religious Dimension of Pennsylvania Politics, 1778–1779." *WMQ,* 30 (1973), 423–448.

Isaac, Rhys. "Religion and Authority: Problems of the Anglican Establishment in Virginia in the Era of the Great Awakening and the Parson's Cause." *WMQ,* 30 (1973), 3–36.

———. "Evangelical Revolt: The Nature of the Baptists' Challenge to the Traditional Order in Virginia, 1765 to 1775." *WMQ,* 31 (1974), 345–368.

———. "Preachers and Patriots: Popular Culture and the Revolution in Virginia," in Alfred F. Young (ed.), *The American Revolution: Explorations in the History of American Radicalism.* De Kalb, Ill., 1976, pp. 125–156.

Kammen, Michael. "The American Revolution as a Crise de Conscience: The Case of New York," in Jack P. Greene, Richard L. Bushman, and Michael Kammen (eds.), *Society, Freedom and Conscience: The American Revolution in Virginia, Massachusetts, and New York.* New York, 1976, pp. 126–131.

Keller, Morton. Introduction to the John Harvard Library edition of *Problems of Modern Democracy: Political and Economic Essays,* by E. L. Godkin. Cambridge, Mass., 1966.

Kelley, Robert. "Taming the Sacramento: Hamiltonianism in Action." *Pacific Historical Review,* 34 (1965), 21–49.

———. "Ideology and Political Culture from Jefferson to Nixon." *AHR,* 82 (1977), 531–562.

Kerber, Linda K. "The Federalist Party," in Arthur M. Schlesinger, Jr. (ed.), *History of U.S. Political Parties.* New York, 1973, I, pp. 3–33.

Key, V. O., Jr. "A Theory of Critical Elections." *Journal of Politics,* 17 (1955), 3–18.

Kirby, John B. "Early American Politics—The Search for Ideology: An Historiographical Analysis and Critique of the Concept of 'Deference.'" *Journal of Politics,* 32 (1970), 808–838.

Kleppner, Paul. "Beyond the 'New Political History': A Review Essay." *Historical Methods Newsletter,* 6 (1972), 17–26.

Kousser, J. Morgan. "The 'New Political History': A Methodological Critique." *Reviews in American History,* 4 (1976), 1–14.

Lannie, Vincent P. "Alienation in America: The Immigrant Catholic and Public Education in Pre-Civil War America." *Review of Politics,* 32 (1970), 503–521.

Lemisch, Jesse. "Jack Tar in the Streets: Merchant Seamen in the Politics of Revolutionary America." *WMQ,* 25 (1968), 371–407.

———. "The American Revolution Seen from the Bottom Up," in Barton J.

Bernstein (ed.), *Towards a New Past: Dissenting Essays in American History*. New York, 1968, pp. 3–45.

Lockridge, Kenneth A. "Social Change and the Meaning of the American Revolution." *Journal of Social History,* 6 (1973), 403–439.

Lofton, Williston H. "Abolition and Labor." *Journal of Negro History,* 33 (1948), 249–283.

McCormick, Richard L. "Ethno-cultural Interpretations of Nineteenth-Century American Voting Behavior." *PSQ,* 89 (1974), 351–377.

McLoughlin, William G. "The Role of Religion in the Revolution: Liberty of Conscience and Cultural Cohesion in the New Nation," in Stephen Kurtz and James Hutson (eds.), *Essays on the American Revolution.* Chapel Hill, N.C., 1973, pp. 206–208.

McSeveney, Samuel T. "Ethnic Groups, Ethnic Conflicts, and Recent Quantitative Research in American Political History." *International Migration Review,* 7 (1973), 14–33.

Marshall, Lynn L. "The Strange Stillbirth of the Whig Party." *AHR,* 72 (1967), 445–468.

Mathews, Donald G. "The Second Great Awakening as an Organizing Process, 1780–1830: An Hypothesis." *American Quarterly,* 21 (1969), 23–43.

Nash, Gary B. "The Transformation of Urban Politics 1700–1765." *JAH,* 60 (1973), 609–611.

———. "Social Change and the Growth of Prerevolutionary Urban Radicalism," in Alfred F. Young (ed.), *The American Revolution: Explorations in the History of American Radicalism.* De Kalb, Ill., 1976, pp. 6–36.

Olsen, Otto H. "Reconsidering the Scalawags." *CWH,* 12 (1966), 304–320.

Olson, James S. "The New York Assembly, the Politics of Religion, and the Origins of the American Revolution, 1768–1771." *Historical Magazine of the Protestant Episcopal Church,* 43 (1974), 21–28.

Osofsky, Gilbert. "Abolitionists, Irish Immigrants, and the Dilemmas of Romantic Nationalism." *AHR,* 80 (1975), 889–912.

Paludan, Philip S. "The American Civil War Considered as a Crisis in Law and Order." *AHR,* 77 (1972), 1013–1034.

Patterson, Stephen E. "A New Look at the American Revolution: An Environmental Theory." Paper delivered at the Ninth Annual Conference of the Canadian Association for American Studies, October 14, 1973.

Pernick, Martin S. "Politics, Parties and Pestilence: Epidemic Yellow Fever in Philadelphia and the Rise of the First Party System." *WMQ*, 29 (1972), 559–586.

Peskin, Allan. "Was There a Compromise of 1877?" *JAH*, 60 (1973), 63–75.

Pessen, Edward. "The Wealthiest New Yorkers of the Jacksonian Era: A New List." *New York Historical Society Quarterly*, 54 (1970), 145–172.

———. "The Egalitarian Myth and the American Social Reality: Wealth, Mobility, and Equality in the 'Era of the Common Man.' " *AHR*, 76 (1971), 989–1034.

———. "Did Fortunes Rise and Fall Mercurially in Antebellum America?" *Journal of Social History*, 4 (1971), 339–354.

———. "Moses Beach Revisited: A Critical Examination of His Wealthy Citizens Pamphlets." *JAH*, 58 (1971), 415–426.

———. "Who Governed the Nation's Cities in the 'Era of the Common Man'?" *PSQ*, 87 (1972), 591–614.

Rayback, Joseph G. "The American Workingman and the Antislavery Crusade." *Journal of Economic History*, 3 (1943), 152–164.

Remini, Robert. "Election of 1828," in Arthur M. Schlesinger, Jr., and Fred Israel (eds.), *History of American Presidential Elections 1789–1968*. New York, 1971, I, pp. 413–436.

Rich, Robert. " 'A Wilderness of Whigs': The Wealthy Men of Boston." *Journal of Social History*, 4 (1971), 263–276.

Rietveld, Ronald D. "Lincoln and the Politics of Morality." *Illinois State Historical Society Journal*, 68 (1975), 27–43.

Risjord, Norman K. "The Virginia Federalists." *JSH*, 33 (1967), 486–517.

Ryan, Mary P. "Party Formation in the United States Congress, 1789–1796: A Quantitative Analysis." *WMQ*, 38 (1971), 523–542.

Schermerhorn, R. A. "Minorities: European and American," in Milton L. Barron (ed.), *Minorities in a Changing World*. New York, 1967, pp. 5–14.

Schlesinger, Arthur M., Jr. "America: Experiment or Destiny?" *AHR*, 82 (1977), 505–522.

Schnaiberg, Allan. "Measuring Modernism: Theoretical and Empirical Explorations." *American Journal of Sociology*, 76 (1970), 399–425.

Seller, Charles G., Jr. "Who Were the Southern Whigs?" *AHR*, 59 (1954), 335–346.

Shade, William G. "Pennsylvania Politics in the Jacksonian Period: A Case

Study, Northhampton County, 1824–1844." *Pennsylvania History,* 39 (1972), 313–333.

Shalhope, Robert E. "Toward a Republican Synthesis: The Emergence of an Understanding of Republicanism in American Historiography." *WMQ,* 29 (1972), 49–80.

Shy, John. "The American Revolution: The Military Conflict Considered as a Revolutionary War," in Stephen Kurtz and James Hutson (eds.), *Essays on the American Revolution.* Chapel Hill, N.C., 1973, pp. 121–156.

Silbey, Joel. "Election of 1836," in Arthur M. Schlesinger, Jr., and Fred L. Israel (eds.), *History of American Presidential Elections 1789–1968.* New York, 1971, I, pp. 598–599.

Smith, Elwyn A. "The Role of the South in the Presbyterian Schism of 1837–38." *Church History,* 29 (1960), 44–63.

Staiger, C. Bruce. "Abolitionism and the Presbyterian Schism of 1837–38." *Mississippi Valley Historical Review,* 26 (1949), 391–414.

Swierenga, Robert P. "Ethnocultural Political Analysis: A New Approach to American Ethnic Studies." *Journal of American Studies,* 5 (1971), 59–79.

Temin, Peter. "The Anglo-American Business Cycle, 1820–60." *Economic History Review,* 27 (1974), 85–99.

Thomas, John L. "Romantic Reform in America, 1815–1865." *American Quarterly,* 17 (1965), 656–681.

Tindall, George B. "Beyond the Mainstream: The Ethnic Southerners." *JSH,* 40 (1974), 3–18.

Tipps, Dean C. ' Modernization Theory and the Comparative Study of Societies: A Critical Perspective." *Comparative Studies in Society and History: An International Quarterly,* 15 (1973), 199–226.

Van Deusen, Glyndon G. "Some Aspects of Whig Thought and Theory in the Jacksonian Period." *AHR,* 58 (1958), 315–322.

———. "The Whig Party," in Arthur M. Schlesinger, Jr. (ed.), *History of U.S. Political Parties.* New York, 1973, I, pp. 333–363.

Vecoli, Rudolph J. "European Americans: From Immigrants to Ethnics," in William H. Cartwright and Richard L. Watson, Jr. (eds.), *The Reinterpretation of American History and Culture.* Washington, D.C., 1973, pp. 81–112.

Wallace, Michael. "Changing Concepts of Party in the United States: New York, 1815–1828." *AHR,* 74 (1968), 453–491.

Wright, Esmond. "Education in the American Colonies: The Impact of Scotland," in E. R. R. Green (ed.), *Essays in Scotch-Irish History.* London, 1969.

———. "The Loyalists," in H. C. Allen and Roger Thompson (eds.), *Contrast and Connection.* Athens, Ohio, 1976, pp. 113–148.

Wright, James E. "The Ethnocultural Model of Voting." *American Behavioral Scientist,* 16 (1973), 653–674.

Wyatt-Brown, Bertram. "Prelude to Abolitionism: Sabbatarian Politics and the Rise of the Second Party System." *JAH,* 58 (1971), 316–341.

Young, Alfred F. "The Mechanics and the Jeffersonians: New York 1789–1801." *Labor History,* 5 (1964), 247–276.

———. "George Clinton: Democratic, Middle-Class Prototype of the Revolution." Paper presented at "New York in the New Nation," a conference at State University College at Oneonta, April 26–27, 1974.

———. "Afterword," in Alfred F. Young (ed.), *The American Revolution: Explorations in the History of American Radicalism.* De Kalb, Ill., 1976, pp. 447–462.

Index

About The Author

Robert Kelley was born in Santa Barbara, California, in 1925. He received his B.A. from the University of California, Santa Barbara, and his M.A. and Ph.D. from Stanford University. He served in the Second World War as an Air Force officer, and was recalled for more active duty during the Korean War. Since 1955 he has taught American intellectual and political history at the University of California, Santa Barbara. Mr. Kelley has been a Fellow of the National Endowment for the Humanities (1975–76) and continues to serve the Endowment as a consultant/panelist and seminar director. He gave a bicentennial address in 1976 at the annual meeting of the American Historical Association on the general theme of this book. He is serving as sixth Fulbright/Hays Professor of American History at Moscow State University in 1979.

His previous works include *Gold vs. Grain* (1959) and *The Transatlantic Persuasion: The Liberal–Democratic Mind in the Age of Gladstone* (1969), and *The Shaping of the American Past* (2d Edition, 1978). He is a contributor to many journals, including *The American Historical Review,* and is co-founder and chairman of the Graduate Program in Public Historical Studies at UCSB. Mr. Kelley is a consultant to the Governor's Office and other California agencies, and he is an expert witness on the state's water resource history, to which he has made award-winning scholarly contributions. He is married to Madge Kelley, a writer and for many years an operating room nurse. They live in Santa Barbara and preside over a family of six children.

A Note on the Type

The text of this book is set in Gael, a CRT/Videocomp version of Caledonia, a linotype face designed by W. A. Dwiggins. It belongs to the family of printing types called "modern face" by printers—a term used to mark the change in style of type-letters that occurred about 1800. Caledonia borders on the general design of Scotch Modern, but is more freely drawn than that letter.